BLACK LEGACY PRESS

Ropes of Sand

(Studies in Igbo History and Culture)

By A. E. Afigbo

Professor of History
University of Nigeria, Nsukka

Ropes of Sand
by A. E. Afigbo

First Published 1981 by:
University Press Limited

Copyright © 2017
BLACKLEGACYPRESS.ORG
ALL RIGHTS RESERVED.

ISBN: 978-1-63652-149-7

Dedicated to

Ezihe

'Nevertheless, every now and again, one has a sense of an older culture lying behind what one sees, long forgotten by the people themselves, grown so faint that it is only in certain lights that one catches a glimpse of it, but the glimpse is of something so rich, so vital, that the present sinks into insignificance beside it. I heard it twice in a woman's song, saw it once in a woman's dance, once in a ritual gesture of embrace, once in the shape and decoration of a water-pot, once in the mural decoration of a *mbari* house' (Mrs. Sylvia Leith-Ross on Igbo culture in *African Women*, London, 1939, p. 55).

Contents

PREFACE

1. Speculations on Igbo Origins, Dispersal and Culture History ... 1
2. The Holy City of Nri ... 31
3. Nsukka before 1916: The Making of a Frontier Igbo Society ... 69
4. Economic Foundations of Pre-Colonial Igbo Society ... 123
5. Through A Glass Darkly ... 145
6. Aro Origin Legends: An Analysis ... 187
7. The Eclipse of the Aro Slaving Oligarchy 1807-1927 ... 239
8. Igbo Land Under Colonial Rule ... 283
9. The Impact of Colonialism on the Igbo Language: The Origins of a Dilemma ... 355

MAPS

1. Facing Chapter 3: The Old Nsukka Division showing Local Groupings
2. Bound at the end of the Book
   Igbo Land showing sub-cultural Areas and the groups studied in this book.

CHART

At the end of Chapter 2: Nri Genealogical Chart

Preface

My people of Ihube in the Ǫtanchara clan of the Northern Igbo have a saying that:

*Ofe di ǫkụ
A na-ara ya
Mgbere Mgbere*

which rendered into English means

The hot soup
Is licked
Gradually from the periphery.

Igbo history is comparable to the hot soup in the proverb. Few historians, aware of the present state of Igbo studies, would yet undertake to write a comprehensive history of the Igbo-speaking peoples. The best one can hope for now is a cautious and episodic approach leading to a collection of studies which will at once help to show how far we have advanced and how much we have lagged behind in the attempt to extend to the Igbo field[1] the revolution in African studies. Four of the nine studies in this collection deal with more or less peripheral or borderland Igbo communities—the Umunri of the Anambra valley to the northwest, the Nsukka group on the northern border, and the Arochukwu of the Cross River region to the east. To some extent I have merely started attempting to lick the hot soup of Igbo history gradually from the periphery. If therefore I have not got to the bottom of the pot, my plea is that the soup is still hot, in fact very hot. And in any case that is not my immediate

---

1. I am aware of Dr. (Mrs.) Elizabeth Isichei's recent book: *A History of the Igbo-speaking People* (Macmillan 1976). There is probably no doubt that many scholars will admire her courage and optimism that led to the writing of the book now. What is less certain, however, is that many more will follow her example at this stage in the development of Igbo studies. Only as we tackle and solve many of the basic problems of Igbo historical studies will it be possible to undertake a meaningful assessment of that work.

ambition. Only a well-planned, adequately financed and energetically executed inter-disciplinary scheme could hope to attain such a goal.

That this book has been written is a recognition of the fact that we do not have to fold our hands until some fairy-godmother floats such a scheme of research in Igbo studies. My mother tells me that her father used to say

> *Metuwe emetuwe*
> *Jiri okpoto tigbu atụ*

This untranslatable witticism could be rendered as 'The man who believes in getting on with the job somehow, killed a buffalo by striking at it with the stalk of grass, while others, presumably, were searching for the sovereign weapon.' My adopting this philosophy in this instance derives from two closely related beliefs. The first is that the problem with the study of Igbo history is not so much the scarcity of materials or the lack of heroic movements to excite the imagination, delight the heart and reward research, as the extreme timidity, and the rather withering scepticism, with which the subject has so far been approached. The second is that no matter what contributions outsiders might make, recent events teach that Igbo history has to be written by the Igbo themselves. What people think of one is important and must not be ignored. But few opinions can take precedence over what one thinks of, or believes about, oneself. Just as every age writes its own history, so every people must write their own history. Only the Igbo can build for themselves the ideology and image which will keep them afloat in the rough and turbulent sea of the contemporary world. Such ideology and image must be made of the sterner stuff of an authentic and meaningfully interpreted past.

Incidentally, even though the study of Igbo history has hardly begun, the Igbo are among the few African peoples who probably require little introduction to the outside world. In every generation of which we have any information they would appear to have carved out a niche for themselves. Their achievements in art and agriculture in early African history are more and more coming to excite scholarly interest. In the period of unrestricted slave trade they attracted attention not only because they constituted a not-insignificant proportion of the Blacks who helped to develop the Americas, but also because they were at once noted for making efficient and loyal household servants as for detesting plantation slavery to such an extent that they would commit suicide to assert their freedom. So often was this hatred of plantation slavery demonstrated that planters hesitated to buy them for plantation work. Till today there is in Haiti the saying *Ibos pend' cor'a yo—The Ibo hang themselves.* In the nineteenth century, three of their members in exile— Olaudah Equiano in Britain, Dr. James Africanus Beale Horton in Sierra Leone and the Gold Coast and Jaja of Amaigbo and Opobo—distinguished themselves as tireless defenders of the rights of the Black Man. Carrying this passionate commitment to the welfare of the Black Man into this century, they found themselves in a head-on collision with British imperialism—the most efficient, if also the most ruthless imperialism, in all history—and have paid dearly for it. However, in this century those who do not remember them for the Women's Riot of 1929/30 during which they shook British administration in Nigeria to its foundations, or for the flamboyant nationalism and Pan-Africanism of Azikiwe, may remember them as the Biafran Rebels of 1967/70.

In spite of all these the Igbo are probably the least studied of any African people of their size. The result is that they have remained the object of deep suspicion and wild speculation. Some say the Igbo are an enigma. Others say the Igbo have made themselves into an enigma. The two points of view, however, come to the same thing—that the Igbo are not understood by their neighbours. Here the educated Igbo elite have a responsibility to unveil their society to the uncomprehending world. The present writer is putting out this collection as part of his contribution towards the realization of that goal.

I wish to thank my friend Chivuzo Ude for encouraging me both to write these essays and to bring them together within two covers. Much of the oral material which went into the writing of these pieces were collected before 1967 from Igbo elders who are too many to be enumerated here, but to all of whom I am deeply indebted. My former student, J. O. Ijoma, taught me a few things about the Aro which I could not have learned from the records. To him as to Messrs. Christian Onyechere, Ambrose Duru, Simon Ugwu, E. B. Ekwueme and Ifeanyichukwu Okoli who did the typing, I extend my gratitude.

Many Igbo scholars are likely to find the present collection unsatisfactory in many respects. I would, however, wish them to see it as the progress report on an on-going research into these and related issues. I sincerely hope that its shortcomings will challenge them to publish their own progress reports for then I would have achieved one of my purposes—to prove that Mrs. Sylvia Leith-Ross was wrong when in 1939 she said Igbo 'youngmen are content to have no past so long as they have a future'.

A. E. Afigbo,
309 Marguerite Cartwright Avenue,
University of Nigeria,
NSUKKA.

1. Speculations on Igbo Origins, Dispersal and Culture History

The Igbo-speaking peoples of Southern Nigeria have, in recent times, excited the interest of many inquiring minds. To the merchant captains of the dark and bleak age of the slave trade it was mostly the Igbo who occupied the hinterland of the Bight of Biafra. In this belief they indiscriminately labelled as 'Eboe' most of the slaves exported from the ports in this region. Even the Ibibio were considered a branch of the 'great Eboe tribe', a misconception which helps to explain the fact that they were in time called *Kwa Iboe*,[1] that is the 'Ibo' whose territory is drained by the Kwa river. The later-day missionary visitors of the nineteenth century considered many of the peoples and languages of the lower Cross River as off-shoots of the Igbo people and their language.[2] Thus among the first things about the Igbo that impressed early European visitors were their great numerical strength and their impact on their less populous neighbours.

In this century, the fact that the Igbo are among the most numerous ethnic nationalities in Negro Africa (with a population estimated at between five and six million in 1906 and at between twelve and fourteen million today) has continued to draw attention and comment generally. But scholars and administrators have tended to be impressed more by the fact that the Igbo did not come under the umbrella of a single state or evolve state systems of any great size; that in spite of this Igbo society and culture enjoyed a basic uniformity of pattern and of cosmological and social ideas; that the Igbo proved difficult to govern under colonial rule even though they were very receptive to Western education. Consequently works on Igbo society and culture have often been pre-occupied with attempts to explain, first, the fact of 'statelessness' amongst so dynamic a people who had attained advanced forms in agriculture, iron technology and the organization of long-range commerce; second, the basic uniformity of Igbo culture in spite of certain differences in social institutions and dialects; and third the difficulty of governing the Igbo in spite of their easy adaptability to and avidity for Western values.[3]

Surprisingly, in spite of this early and continuing interest in the Igbo, scholarly research into their culture history has lagged far behind research into Yoruba or Edo culture history. And it can be claimed with much cogency, that of all African ethnic nationalities of about their numerical size and general dynamism, the Igbo are the least studied, the people we know the least about the main landmarks in their cultural evolution. Some reasons can briefly be offered for this.[4] Among the most important of these is the well-known fact that not only did the Igbo not know a literate culture until the imposition of European rule, but in addition their land lay outside the areas traversed by early travellers, Arab or European, until a little over a century ago. The result was that the development of Igbo culture, throughout the millennia before 1900, went undocumented. Secondly, the fact that the Igbo did not evolve centralized state systems comparable to either Benin or Oyo, which had well-developed institutions for the preservation and transmission of oral traditions, has meant that information which survives about the Igbo past is scanty and scrappy indeed.

Thirdly, and largely as a result of the above two factors, scholars have not yet made a determined effort to tackle the problem of reconstructing the Igbo past. Historians are only beginning to exploit what little information exists on pre-colonial Igbo society. The European missionaries, administrators and scholars of the early decades of this century showed only a superficial interest, and in any case they were hampered by their pre-occupation with a sweeping and simplistic hypothesis which they waved like a magic wand in explanation of the cultural situation that faced them in these parts. They assumed that Igbo society was static down the centuries except where it was impinged upon by the Bini, Igala and Jukun empires which in turn were regarded as owing their achievements to Hamitic influence from the north and north-east. It has also been suggested that these Europeans had a basic dislike for the Igbo whom they found ungovernable and, what was worse, irreverent in their attitude to members of the 'master race'. The result, says one Igbo scholar, was that some of these European scholars came out to Africa apparently determined to work on Igbo society, but before they completed the first round of their field work would 'hop' across the border to more 'respectful' peoples like the Igala and Kalabari.[5] Igbo historians on their part have until recently done little to make good this lapse either because their scheme of priorities was a little distorted or, as Mrs. Sylvia Leith-Ross and Professor Simon Ottenberg have claimed, owing to a basic lack of interest in grand history among the Igbo as a people.[6]

But it would appear we are now in a position to take the first hesitant steps towards the desired but still distant goal of building up some coherent perspective of Igbo culture history. This is so firstly because the British colonial administrators and missionaries, in spite of their basic indifference to Igbo history, went a long way towards collecting some materials relating to Igbo society and its past, even though for the most part they did not come round to analyzing the material and using it to construct a coherent explanation of our culture history. The fact was that the very difficulty they experienced in governing the Igbo forced the colonial officers to conduct some research into Igbo institutions and world view in the hope of finding the key to the Igbo situation. Secondly, the revolution which has taken place in African studies since the 1950s has providentially freed us from the shackles of the Hamitic hypothesis. We are thus in a position to take leave of Dr. M. D. W. Jeffreys and his like with their easy explanation of Igbo culture history in terms of Egyptian impact and look at the old material in a new light. This means, *inter alia*, that we can treat the Nri and the Aro as Igbo clans rather than as colonies of conquering Hamites and use their rich oral traditions to gain some insight into the Igbo past.[7]

Thirdly, this same revolution in African studies has laid the ghost of the old theory of static 'tribal' societies which were incapable of under-going internally generated changes, and could experience change only if brought under the impact of some external stimuli. It is now an accepted fact that human societies are basically dynamic, and that even 'stateless' societies are capable of undergoing internally induced changes. Professor Robin Horton has recently shown that there are in fact three possible stages of 'statelessness' through which a stateless society could pass, and that the conquest theory is not really necessary for explaining how states arose in Negro Africa. Stateless societies, he has also contended, were capable of transforming themselves into state systems depending on what challenges their environment posed.[8]

It is my contention that we should now start applying these new trends in African historiography to the re-interpretation of whatever material we have on the past of the Igbo people. In this way we shall be doing for their history what has been done for the histories of many other ethnic nationalities in Africa. We shall also be able to identify, analyze and assess the relative importance of internally and externally induced changes.

In what follows I have attempted to put forward a hypothesis of Igbo cultural development. The grounds for this hypothesis cannot all be stated in full here. But it may well be said that some of the grounds derive from what we know for certain about the Igbo past, and some from what we know about the evolution of West African societies in general. The aim is to build up some tentative framework of Igbo history which other scholars could put to test as they uncover more materials relating to the Igbo past. I have not here concerned myself with producing a detailed account of how the Igbo evolved from isolated groups of hunter-gatherers to the sedentary village-group communities with fairly advanced economies revealed in the reports of the early colonial officials and missionaries. I am concerned with a less back-breaking job—to delimit the main phases of Igbo cultural evolution, to isolate the factors responsible for the emergence of each phase and to delineate the characteristics of each stage of development.

It is now accepted by many scholars that West African societies are more ancient than was once thought and that the general location and alignment of the major linguistic and cultural groups of the region had assumed, for millenia, the form or pattern in which they were found by the early European visitors. A preliminary excursion into the glottochronology of the Kwa language sub-family, of which Igbo is a member, has yielded the suggestion that most of the member-languages of this sub-family (for instance Igbo, Ijo, Edo and Idoma) started diverging from their ancestral root between 5,000 and 6,000 years ago.[9]

For the Igbo there are other reasons which suggest that the above view is probably not as wild an estimate as Professor Richard Henderson's scepticism would suggest.[10] Among these is the fact that the Igbo have lost all memory of their migration into the area they now occupy. This cannot easily be explained away in terms only of the absence of specialized institutions for transmitting traditions. The Nri of the Northern Igbo evolved an elaborate and highly ritualized priest-kingship around which rich traditions have survived. But even they no longer have a tradition of migration from outside Igbo land. So completely has this category of traditions been lost that the Nri have substituted for it a myth of having been created where they are now found.

Another consideration which makes it quite likely that the Igbo have been where they now are for as long as the above estimate would suggest, or even for longer, is the extent to which they have altered their physical environment. All who have considered the matter agree that Igbo land lies in what must once have been tropical rain forest vegetation. The density and character of the residual vegetations surviving along the river valleys and around sacred groves and shrines support this contention. And many have expressed the view that the derived savanna of most of modern Igbo land would revert to this primeval climax of tropical rain forest if left long enough untampered with. Now only occupation and intensive use over a very long period could have brought about such a far-reaching and uniform change in the environment. One would be all the more inclined to this view when one considers the relatively low level of technology with which the Igbo had to fight such an environment in the millenia before European advent. Furthermore, a preliminary archaeological survey of Igbo land has uncovered evidence which suggests that it was already under occupation, at least the plateau and upland section of it, by the third millenium B.C. And the artifacts left behind by the occupants of those days which were recovered, would seem to lie in the same line of ethnographic development as the cultural artifacts of the present day Igbo occupants of the region.[11] The historian of Igbo culture, therefore, must have to reckon with the likelihood that the Igbo were established in their present habitat about two or three millennia before the Christian era.

Even more fundamental than the issue of the antiquity of Igbo settlement where they are now found is the question of their original homeland, the cradle land from which their ancestors migrated to what is now southeastern Nigeria. This problem has excited many minds. Until recently most of those who tackled the issue fell easy victims to what has been described as the 'oriental mirage'—that is the tendency in West Africa for most

5

ethnic nationalities to trace their origins to the East, especially to either Egypt, Yemen or the Holy Land.

The Rev. Mr. G. T. Basden, for instance, early in this century advanced the view that the Igbo were a branch of the Hebrew nation, or at least that their culture history could satisfactorily be explained in terms of Jewish impact. In his view the fact that the Igbo are deeply religious, practise circumcision and mummification and have sentence structures commonly found in Hebrew constructions was such that 'the investigator cannot help being struck with the similitude between them and some of the ideas and practices of the Levitical Code.'[12] Even long before Basden, the Igbo ex-slave, Olaudah Equiano, had on similar ethnographic and cultural grounds advanced the thesis of Jewish origin for the Igbo.[13] Later still in this century Igbo scholars have argued that their ancestors were Jews and that the words *Uburu* (the name of a number of Igbo towns) and *Igbo* are corruptions of the word *Hebrew*.

On his side Dr. M. D. W. Jeffreys who wrote extensively on the ethnography and ethno-history of the Igbo, especially of the Igbo of the Nri-Awka area, was of the view that ancient Egypt held the key to Igbo origin and history. He was particularly impressed by the feature of dual division in Igbo social structure, a phenomenon which he said corresponded to the division of ancient Egypt into Upper and Lower moieties and therefore must have been brought or learnt from there. The *ichi* facial marks of the Northern Igbo, as well as many features of Igbo traditional religion, he attributed to Egyptian origin or impact.[14] A local historian of the Aro also traced Aro origin to Egypt. The ideological and other significance of these claims to oriental origin belongs to the wider framework of West African history and ethnology as the claims are widely distributed there.[15] Here it suffices to say that they cannot be taken seriously as historical accounts of Igbo origin by the careful student of our history.

The Igbo are a branch of the Negro race. This is important to the question of their origin. Available archaeological evidence suggests that this race may have originated in the area along the latitude of Asselar and Khartoum, that is more or less on the northern fringe of the savanna. One possible meaning of this is that the homeland of the Igbo cannot possibly lie north of this latitude, that is as far north as Egypt, the Holy Land or Yemen. For their cradle land we have to focus our attention on the area south of this latitude. Now linguists are of the view that bearing in mind the distribution and alignment of the languages in the Kwa sub-group of the Niger-Congo family, it is most likely that the members of this sub-group separated in the region of the Niger-Benue confluence. Art historians are also beginning to draw attention to this same general area, especially to the region between Bida and Kotonkarifi as one of central importance in the cultural history of the Middle Belt and Southern Nigeria. Until positively contradictory evidence comes to light, it does appear that the historian will continue to look for the cradle land of the Igbo and of their Kwa brothers in this general area.[16]

Assuming therefore that the ancestors of the Igbo came down from the region of the Niger-Benue confluence, the next important question is that of their first settlement here in Igbo land, and the pattern of their subsequent dispersal. In this regard a likely hypothesis deserving very serious consideration is that, of all Igbo land, the first portion to come under effective Igbo occupation was the plateau region known to students of physical geography as the Nsukka-Okigwe cuesta. As the name indicates, this plateau runs in a more or less north-south direction from Nsukka in the north to Okigwe in the heart of Igbo land, with a south-easterly ridge stretching to Arochukwu. For our purpose we may consider what is also described as the Awka-Orlu uplands as forming part of this north-south highland area first settled by the Igbo.

The arguments for this view are easily stated, though they cannot yet be considered conclusive. In any case only exhaustive archaeological work in Igbo land can establish or overthrow this view finally. Until that happens, however, it is relevant to consider the fact that the Igbo communities here seem to have the most attenuated traditions of migration from any point more than a few miles from their present occupation sites. Most in fact claim that their ancestors either came out of the ground (*si n'ala pute*) or fell down from heaven. In most of the rest of Igbo land the situation is different in this regard. In the second place the vegetation here is much more drastically reduced than elsewhere in Igbo land and the soil much more exhausted in most parts except along the river valleys; so exhausted in fact that the inhabitants have in the course of centuries turned from dependence on agriculture to other professions which they have developed to a high degree. They are for the most part specialist traders, medicine men, smiths, potters and weavers.[17]

Thirdly, and this is probably speculative though not entirely baseless, there is reason to believe that the plains which surround this plateau region would have been much wetter in those far off days than they are now. Even today some portions of these plains are so wet that the sparseness of their human population can be attributed to the difficulty they present to human settlement. On logical grounds they would have been even more forbidding as settlement sites in the last few millennia before Christ than they are today. In this situation it is pardonable to assume that the early Igbo immigrants into this general area would have preferred the plateau region which was most likely drier than the plains and whose vegetation cover would by the same token be lighter and therefore easier to cope with than that of the plains. The occupants of this plateau region are now known to ethnographers as the Northern Igbo.

On similar grounds one can also postulate that this early population, moving south along the plateau, 'overflowed' into the plains immediately to the south of it, to multiply there and grow into the Uratta, Ikwerre, Etche, Asa and Ndoki Igbo of today. These form the main bulk of what ethnographers today know as the Southern Igbo. The main argument for this postulate is that these Igbo (the Uratta, Ikwerre, Etche, Asa and Ndoki) have, like the Northern Igbo, completely lost all memory of earlier migrations from anywhere outside the general area in which they now live. One can therefore assume that their migration into the southern plain came next in time to the Igbo settlement of the plateau. This general north–south settlement stretching from Nsukka into Ikwerre established what may be called the 'demographic spine' of Igbo land and may be said to constitute the first phase in the Igbo occupation of the area in which they now live. Subsequently from two points on this north–south 'population ridge' people set out to occupy the region west and east.

It is most likely that these early Igbo occupants came in as hunter-gatherers. The tradition of the Nri would suggest as much. The same traditions suggest that agriculture and iron technology penetrated the plateau region before any other part of Igbo land.[18] One would expect this to be so on the basis of the generally held view that these two revolutions penetrated the forest of West Africa from the Sudan. Only more intensive archaeological exploration of this plateau will enable us to establish the dates for the dawn of these two great changes as well as fill in the details of their impact on Igbo society. But judging from Nri traditions and what we know of the impact of these events on other sub-Saharan societies, there is no doubt that they wrought tremendous changes on the plateau or Northern Igbo.

Among the changes these revolutions introduced were the more effective mastery of the land, the growth of population, the elaboration of the archetypal Igbo social institutions and the evolution of a cosmological system in which the Earth (*Ala or Ani*), now deified, occupied the central place as the ordainer and guardian of morality, the source of law and custom etc. Echoes of some of these changes can be heard in the Nri corpus of myth, legends and traditions regarding the origin of the Igbo world which will be dealt with in greater detail later. But the broad outlines can be indicated here. The growing sophistication of society and the elaboration of social institutions survive in the reference to the *Eze Nri* who had control over food, as in the reference to the taking of titles and the institution of *Ichi* facial marks. The rise of local and long range commerce is also referred to in the institution of the market days through the visit of four heavenly fishmongers whose names were later adopted as the names of Igbo market days, as in the story of Nri's neighbours approaching the *Eze Nri* with their local products in exchange for yams, cocoyams, and palm trees.

With regard to the growth of the characteristic Igbo cosmology the Nri corpus of myth makes mention of *Chukwu* (*Chiukwu*) who after creating men, sending smiths to dry the land, making the land bring forth food and instituting the market days and marketing was never mentioned again as playing any part in the daily life of the people. On the other hand it was *Ani or Ala* that now became so important to the Igbo that it became one of the most vital functions of the *Eze Nri* to preside over its worship. This development is in accord with the otiose character of *Chukwu* (the High or Supreme God) In Igbo cosmology, and the domination of the Igbo world by the Earth goddess. This cosmology and the Nri corpus of traditions may well contain another dimension of historical truth which has not hitherto been recognized—the evolution of Igbo traditional religion. In the hunting and gathering stage of existence the Igbo were unlikely to have come to a full appreciation of the value and importance of land. The earlier period was probably the dynamic age of *Chukwu*, when he created and dominated the Igbo world. But with the coming of agriculture Igbo gaze would appear to have been switched from the skies above to the earth below, with *Ala* displacing *Chukwu* into remote inactivity. This would explain why in time, according to the Nri corpus, it became the chief function of the *Eze Nri* to preside over the worship, veneration and purification of the *Earth*. The place occupied by the worship of *Ala* in Igbo cosmology, as well as its rather capricious character, may also be explained by the increasingly intensive exploitation of the land and the consequent impoverishment of the soil especially on the Igbo plateau. In the absence of the deliberate use of artificial manure as a means of maintaining the fertility of the soil, the people resorted more and more to the religious worship, veneration and ritual purification of the *Earth*.

The north–south highland would thus appear to have been the heartland of Igbo culture. This culture in time penetrated to the Uratta, Ikwerre, Etche, Asa and Ndoki areas along with the practise of agriculture and the use of iron. It would also appear that the greatest impact, on the population, of these two revolutions among the Igbo of the plateau region manifested itself first in the area of present day Nri-Awka. This would help to explain the rise of the institution of *Eze Nri*, a development probably made necessary by the increased problem of maintaining law and order, especially with regard to the control of the land. The demographic impact of these revolutions would also help to explain why the next phase of Igbo dispersal started off from here according to the traditions. It was from the Nri-Awka area that the Niger-Anambara plain and the Asaba uplands to the west of the Niger were peopled. This much is clear from the traditions of the Ika Igbo. It is difficult to date this migration without the aid of archaeological evidence. But one thing seems quite clear and that is that it must have taken place long before the rise of the Bini kingdom. This was a period in south-central Nigeria (the former Biafra and the present Bendel State) when the Igbo must have enjoyed an overwhelming advantage over their neighbours by the sheer force of their numerical superiority.

If one must hazard a guess, however, one would place this westward 'overflow' of population from the Awka upland in the millenium that lies athwart the birth of Christ. The argument for this estimate may well be summarized here. Professor

Thurstan Shaw suggests that Igbo Ukwu culture (dated to the ninth century A.D.) may well have been connected with the institution of *Eze Nri* but does not definitely make the connection.[19] Mr. M. A. Onwuejeogwu's anthropological researches at Nri have however thrown up a great deal of ethnographic evidence which makes it reasonable to make such a connection.[20] Now the richness and artistic sophistication of the Igbo Ukwu bronzes suggest a culture that had already attained maturity rather than one that was still in the process of developing. And that level of culture would require about a millenium or more to evolve in an agricultural community where institutions and ideas tend to change rather slowly.

From our argument it must have been the same population expansion which made the rise of such an institution as *Eze Nri* necessary that led to the migration of land hungry Igbo peasants to the region lying west. It is unlikely that the migrants left in one massive wave. Bearing in mind the fragmented character of Igbo political systems and the fact that the pressure could not have built up overnight, we have to postulate that the settlers left in little groups of closely related kin, with the region adjoining already existing settlements being occupied before the one just beyond it. This process would take a very long time to carry Igbo population as far west as it had got before it was checked by the rise and expansion of the Bini empire. These colonists carried with them the basic culture already elaborated on the northern Igbo plateau. This also meant that even though they had gone far west, they continued under the ritual hegemony of the *Eze Nri* and his priestly aristocracy. It has in fact been argued elsewhere that it is possible that before the rise of Benin and even after, the influence of Nri went farther west than the area effectively settled by the Igbo.[21] In any case the core of Nri ritual hegemony comprised the northern Igbo plateau (the Northern Igbo) and then the Igbo who had gone west from this cultural home land.

From the traditions, it would also appear that it was the Northern Ika Igbo area that these colonists first occupied, at least effectively and that it was largely the counter pressure from Benin which in time blunted the tip of the Igbo drive to the west. The first and probably most important impact on the Igbo of the rise of the Bini empire and its subsequent expansion eastwards was to stop Igbo migration westwards. One result was that some of this population curved southwards to settle the region now known as Southern Ika and the riverine area south of Asaba—that is the region subsequently dominated by the kingdom of Aboh. On the other hand some of the population, probably those who had attempted to go, or had in fact gone farthest west, came under the direct pressure of Benin and fled eastwards. Fragments of them fled so far east that they recrossed the Niger and formed the community now known as Onitsha. In this latter group were the *Ųmų Eze Chima* group of villages. It is this general recoil of the Igbo who had gone west that has survived in the traditions of certain Ika, Riverain and Onitsha Igbo communities in the form of origins or migrations or flights from Benin—the *Obodo Idu-na-Oba* or *Ado-na-Idu* of Igbo traditions.

In some of these same traditions we encounter claims of origin, migration or flight from Idah. It is reasonable to suggest that these Idah traditions were later developments and should be associated with the period of Igala imperial domination of parts of the Niger below the confluence. Igala is not a land of high population density. Two factors alone would have caused Igala elements to abandon their more fertile and more attractive homeland for the less clement riverine lowlands. The first of these would be struggles connected with the rise of the Igala monarchy which would have forced defeated elements to flee to areas beyond the reach of the Attah. The other was the rise of the Igala kingdom as a dominant commercial and political force in parts of the Niger valley which also would give venturesome Igala elements the encouragement to settle at different points on the lower Niger, secure in the belief that they would be well received wherever they went. Neither of these two factors would have made any great difference to the demographic picture of the lower Niger valley before the seventeenth century.

Meanwhile the same factors—agriculture and the use of iron—had similarly led to a great population growth in the Orlu section of the *Awka-Orlu* uplands. It would appear that much of the surplus population from here went east instead of west. For one thing the Niger flood plain to the west of the Orlu area is a large expanse of territory and probably was not very attractive to settlers except to those who had no other choice. This will help to explain its low population density even today. In any case the traditions of the *Isu-Ama* Igbo (meaning the Isu who had gone abroad—made up of Mbama, Mbieri, Ikeduru, Osu, Ehime, Ugboma, Mbaise), of the Ọhụhụ, Ngwa and of many Cross River Igbo groups indicate that they migrated eastwards from the general area of Orlu. To many communities in this group of Igbo-speaking peoples Ama-Igbo in Orlu is a sacred and revered spot. The name itself means the *street, meeting place or headquarters* of the Igbo. These traditions claim that it was there that the Isuama, Cross River and Ọhụhụ-Ngwa Igbo originally settled before dispersing to their present locations. It is for this reason, they say, that when members of the group meet, it is the Orlu man, if one is present, who has the right to break the kola nut and to take first share whenever anything is divided—food or an assignment.

Again it is impossible to date this movement precisely until archaeology probably comes to our aid. It can be assumed, however, that it did not predate the developments in the Awka section of the uplands. The two movements may well have taken place about the same period as among these Igbo who went east we also come across, especially in the Ọhụhụ-Ngwa complex, fragments of claim to Nri or in any case Awka origin. Though this may well have sprung from a much later desire to be associated with the famed spiritual centre of Nri. But Orlu and Awka are not two far apart for the agricultural and technological revolutions which instigated these dispersals to have affected the two areas at the same time, and to have led to the growth of their populations about the same period. But it is also significant that we encounter in some of these communities fragments of tradition referring to origin or migration or flight from Benin. This could be taken to mean that this movement to the east came to be speeded up with the sealing off of the western frontier by Benin pressure which forced not only the Igbo to recoil eastwards, but also some Ijo to move further east. That this contention is likely seems to be borne out by the result of a preliminary archaeological work in Bende, of the Eastern Igbo area. Here a site which an Igbo family said it had occupied continuously for about twelve generations and then abandoned about 1904 was excavated and found to yield artifacts carbon-dated to A.D. 850 ± 95. When the character of this migration and the time it would take to carry the Igbo as far east as Bende are taken into account, it becomes clear that it is reasonable to posit that it was more or less contemporary with the dispersal that took the Igbo out of the same plateau to the Asaba uplands.

The movement from Orlu in a general eastward direction soon encountered opposition in the form of the westward expansion of the Benue-Congo speaking peoples. This had important consequences for the Igbo. For one thing the Igbo expansion was 'deflected' northwards leading to the foundation of the *Ada Group* of the Cross River Igbo (Aka-eze, Edda, Nkporo, Afikpo, Amasiri, etc.) and of the large northeastern group also known as *Ogo-Ukwu*. The traditions of these peoples indicate a general northward movement of population. The Edda and the Afikpo, for instance, point to the Okigwi-Arochukwu ridge as the home land from which they migrated. It would also appear that some of the Igbo who encountered these Benue-Congo peoples were made to move westwards. There is a tradition encountered by the present writer that the Uturu clan in Okigwi (Northern Igbo) came from Enna on the Cross River.

The traditions of the Ohuhu, Ngwa, Eastern and North-Eastern Igbo also are rich in accounts of fierce encounters with various sections of the Benue-Congo-speaking peoples who appear in their traditions as the *Ego, Nkalu* and *Igbo*.[22] This conflict reported in the Cross River Igbo area may have been a continuation of clashes which characterized the meeting of the Igbo and Benue-Congo peoples further south. We hear of it again in the Eastern Ngwa traditions. Similarly Arochukwu is said to have been founded after one such war in which the Igbo drove out the Ibibio. In the North-Eastern Igbo area this conflict continued unabated until the imposition of European rule, with the Igbo sweeping all before them. The reports of the early British administrators who served in this area are full of references to these later encounters. It has also been investigated in some detail by Rosemary Harris in her study of the Mbembe people of Ogoja.[23] In the North-Eastern Igbo area this northward flow of population would appear to have taken some of the non-Igbo peoples from the rear. There are even today in this area small islands of them, such as the Orri, Mtezi and Effium. These are probably no more than surviving remainders of non-Igbo populations which were at one time more numerous than they are today but who were outflanked, encircled and then either systematically killed off or absorbed in a ruthless struggle for 'living space'.

The above, in brief, is the pattern of early Igbo dispersal suggested by the evidence presently available. This broad outline of population distribution was to be modified in many places and to varying degrees by the movement hither and thither of small groups of peoples who migrated either out of choice or in response to some disaster or pressure. One example of such movements is that connected with the disturbance of the middle Cross River region by invaders (Ukwa Onyeocha) armed with firearms, stories about which are encountered among the Edda and the Aro for instance. These later movements though small in scale compared to those sketched above were nonetheless important. At least they helped to fill some of the empty spaces between major groups. They also served as a means of carrying cultural traits from one region to another. It would also appear that by the time of European advent in the sixteenth century, the major movements were more or less completed and that the basic character of Igbo culture and society had emerged, with the differences between the various Igbo sub-cultural groups becoming increasingly noticeable in consequence of the cultural impact of non-Igbo neighbours to be discussed below.

For purposes of periodization the era of dispersal from the Awka-Orlu upland dealt with above may be designated the *Eri Period* after the mythical personage to whom Nri traditions attribute the origin of their highly ritualized culture and kingship institutions. The main features of this period included:

(i) the introduction of agriculture and iron technology into Igbo land,
(ii) the rise of mounting population pressure on the Awka-Orlu uplands and the dispersal of the surplus population west and east,
(iii) the rise of the divine kingship institution of the Nri and the emergence of the basic features of Igbo society and culture,
(iv) the predominance of agriculture over commerce, though increasingly the latter became important as revealed by Shaw's excavations,
(v) the encounter in the west between the Igbo and the Edo, and in the east between them and the Benue-Congo-speaking peoples with consequences some of which have been discussed and the remainder of which will be dealt with below.

This was the period when the Nri probably enjoyed unchallenged ascendancy on the Nsukka-Okigwi cuesta, the Awka-Orlu uplands, the Anambara-Niger flood plains and the west Niger Igbo area, with some echoes of this influence being heard by the Igbo who settled on the undulating lands of the south and the

Cross River plains. The *Eri* period was thus a momentous one in the history of the Igbo-speaking peoples. But so also was the period soon to follow and which we shall here designate the Era of Aro Ascendancy.

But before we go on to examine the main features of this period, it may be necessary to comment briefly on the differences between the picture of Igbo dispersal presented above, and that hitherto advanced by Major A. G. Leonard, Dr. P. A. Talbot and Mr. G. I. Jones.[24] These scholars have argued that the Awka-Orlu upland was the 'centre or core' from which waves of Igbo migrants settled the rest of Igbo land. The main objection of the present writer to their approach is that it makes no effort to say how the Igbo came to find themselves in the Awka-Orlu area. Or do these authors suggest that they fell from heaven as is maintained by Nri creation legends? If we take this latter problem into account and also concede that it is most likely that the Igbo, like their immediately neighbouring Kwa-speaking groups, probably started off from around the region of the Niger-Benue confluence then we are likely to see, on the basis of the arguments already advanced, that the Nsukka-Okigwi cuesta and the Akwa-Orlu uplands may have been settled during the period of primary migration. The present writer recognizes the importance of the Awka-Orlu uplands in the early history of the Igbo, but only as a centre from which the second stage of Igbo dispersal took place.

And now for the Era of Aro Ascendancy. The designation of this period is one which many historians of Igbo culture may question for this was a period when so many currents of history crossed one another in Igbo land. It was, for instance, when the alien and imperialistic states of Benin and Idah exerted their greatest influence on the Igbo. Consequently the historians of the 'conquest theory' are likely to suggest that it be called the Era of Bini-Igala hegemony. But this designation is unacceptable on two grounds. Firstly only the West Niger Igbo and the northern fringes of the Nsukka plateau came under Benin and Idah influence respectively. Furthermore, the exact character of this influence in either region is still a matter for argument and has yet to be studied in detail. Over four-fifths of Igbo land did not feel the direct impact of Benin and Idah and hardly heard of them except as the romantic and legendary lands, lying in the zone between the world of men, the world of spirits and the world of animals where men, the tortoise, the other animals and the spirits enacted some of those episodes always being retold in Igbo folklore. Many folk tales among the Northern Igbo begin with the following statement: *otu ubochi na obodo Idu-na-Oba Mbe na Agu zoro iwu*—'one day in the land of Idu and Oba the tortoise and the leopard had a bet etc.'. There is also the objection to using an external scheme of reference for the periodization of a people's history where more relevant indigenous referents could be found.

Similarly it could be argued that from the sixteenth century an important factor in Igbo history was the slave trade, that inhuman process by which the 'surplus' populations of Igbo land were moved across the Atlantic to the New World, as well as northwards to the Central Sudan and beyond. Thus those scholars who consider the slave trade as a main watershed in African history are likely to suggest that the period of Igbo history about to be dealt with be designated the era of the slave trade. But there are many objections to this proposition, the most important of which is that the place of the slave trade in Igbo history has been unduly exaggerated and we should not perpetuate this error by erecting that theme into a referent for the periodization of Igbo history. Also the slave trade was largely external to Igbo society and, as already mentioned, it is unnecessary to use an external scheme of reference where a more relevant indigenous one could be found.

Finally it could be contended that even if we should decide to use an indigenous scheme of reference, we should not single out the Aro as there were many other Igbo institutions or groups at this time whose activities and influence also embraced wide tracts of Igbo land. Among these other Igbo groups were the Awka, Nkwerre, Abiriba, Umunneoha and of course the Nri, who continued to be a force to be reckoned with in a large part of Igbo land until the advent of colonial rule. This is probably the most telling objection to the designation used here. But problems arise when we try to find a simple and all-embracing phrase which would satisfactorily cover the activities of these various groups. The Awka were smiths and oracular agents, the Aro were traders and oracular agents, the Nkwerre were smiths and professional spies, the Abiriba were plain smiths, the Umunneoha were plain oracular agents, while the Nri remained ritual specialists. A designation like the era of oracular hegemonies would not cover the activities of the Nkwerre, Abiriba and Nri, just as the era of commercial oligarchies would not cover those of the Nri, Abiriba and Nkwerre.

There are good reasons for the choice of the designation: the Era of Aro Ascendancy. Of all the specialist groups mentioned above the Aro were the most important, their influence the most widespread. In fact if ever during this period there was an institution which enjoyed pan-Igbo influence, it was the *Ibini Ukpabi*. Aro commercial activities penetrated most parts of Igbo land in varying degrees. In some parts it was the dominant factor in the exchange economy, in others it played a subsidiary but important role in the assemblage and distribution of goods. Thus the Aro combined the two dominant professions of the period—trade and the manipulation of oracles. There is yet another consideration which makes it reasonable to regard the Aro as constituting the single most important group in Igbo history in this period. True, the activities of each of the specialist groups went beyond the borders of Igbo land, but in this regard no other Igbo group made a greater impact on a larger number of non-Igbo peoples than the Aro did. Their commercial and ritual influence penetrated Ijo, Edo, Idoma, Ogoja, Ekoid and Efik-Ibibio societies. It is thus not entirely without foundation to say that the Aro came first among the groups of Igbo specialists who helped to make this period the age of Igbo dominance in much of south-eastern Nigeria. They epitomized the spirit of Igbo culture during this period, and thus deserve the prominence which the designation adopted here gives them.

As we contended above, Igbo society entered this period more or less as a mature society—in the sense that its basic institutions had already emerged. Also the highest level of social integration (the clan stage) attained by the Igbo and which proved adequate for their needs and environment had already been reached. Most likely what took place in Igbo society in the era of Aro ascendancy was the modification in detail of different aspects of Igbo culture in response partly to pressure from non-Igbo neighbours and partly to the activities of the different oligarchical Igbo interest-groups mentioned above. Here we have space enough to discuss only the main lines of change and not the details. We shall deal firstly with the changes induced by outsiders before going on to developments which could be said to be due largely, if not solely, to the internal dynamism of Igbo society.

Of all the non-Igbo who exerted influence on Igbo land, the Edo Kingdom of Benin was probably the most important. We have already seen how the encounter with the expanding Bini empire altered the course of Igbo immigration and dispersal west of the Niger and probably added to those other impulses which were already compelling the Isu of Orlu to move eastwards.

The other great impact of Benin on the Igbo who had gone west was political and cultural. This has been emphasized by all who have had cause to express an opinion on the history of Benin and of the western Igbo. This impact is seen most in the rise of village chieftaincies and monarchies all over the western Igbo area. It is seen in the regalia of these chiefs, in their court ceremonials, in some features of their title system as in the claims that many of these institutions came from Benin. How these cultural transformations came about is a matter that is still to be investigated in detail. Some would say they were imposed by the Oba who on conquering these lands appointed over them provincial governors who were schooled in Benin court ritual and ceremonial and who strained to imitate their master the Oba. Some Ika Igbo historians would suggest successful resistance to Benin political conquest, but at the same time the borrowing of social institutions and practices from Benin as part of the process of reorganizing their society to be better able to counter the onslaught of the enemy. Whichever was the case, however, the story of the development of west Niger Igbo institutions is not a simple matter. In telling it the culture historian must bear in mind the highly ritualized cultural traditions and practices which the original settlers probably carried with them from the Nri-Awka area, the impact and pressure of Benin and the impact of the Niger commercial highway.

After Benin probably the next most important external factor to make an appreciable impact on the Igbo was the Igala Kingdom of Idah. It is the view of the present writer that the extent and nature of Igala impact on Igbo society is still to be satisfactorily researched and objectively assessed. So far the issue has provided a very tempting ground for easy assumptions to which many have fallen victims. The matter is investigated at some length in a subsequent essay in this collection. Only the main arguments will be summarized here to maintain the broad perspective of the present essay. The north-western fringe of the Nsukka plateau was an area of intensive Igala activity. A critical analysis of Nsukka traditions, social institutions and level of social integration would seem to reveal that these activities at some period took the form of devastating slave raids which broke up certain communities and left an indelible impression on the minds of the people as seen in the traditions woven around the legendary character called Ọnọjọ Ogboni (or Oboni). But even before and after these raids the northern portions of the Nsukka plateau had been in economic and other contacts with Igala land. This multi-dimensional contact between the two peoples left its mark on the culture of the northern fringe of Nsukka—on their material culture, and on their dialect which incorporates Igala words used at times to describe familiar Igbo institutions. Whether the Nsukka actually borrowed any institutions from the Igala, is still to be firmly established.

Then we come to the cultural impact of the Benue-Congo-speaking peoples of the Cross River plain and valley. Again, as in the case of Benin, apart from changing the direction of Igbo population flow as already shown, the contact with the Benue-Congo peoples left an important mark on the culture of the 'Isu who had gone abroad' (Isuama). Since the Benue-Congo peoples were as politically weak as their Igbo neighbours, it can only be assumed that this cultural impact took place through the usual informal processes of culture borrowing—marriage, the absorption of minorities and immigrants, commercial contacts, etc. If we should assume that the culture of these eastern Igbo at the time of the initial contact was basically the same as that of their Orlu homeland, it becomes fairly easy to pinpoint some of the modifications which the Benue-Congo-speaking peoples induced in the pre-contact culture of these Igbo.

Among the most important of the institutions and practices borrowed by the eastern Igbo from their Benue-Congo neighbours was the highly developed secret society as a vital instrument of social control. This is not to say that secret societies are entirely alien to indigenous Igbo society. It is found in the form of *Mmọ* or *Mmanwụ* or *ọmaba* or *Odo* in many other parts of Igbo land. By impersonating ancestral spirits they had a role to play in social control, as in promoting relaxation and conviviality. But the political role of these indigenous Igbo secret societies was not as articulated as was that of secret societies among the Benue-Congo peoples of the Cross River plain and valley. And we find among the eastern Igbo, the Ngwa, the Ọhụhụ and the Cross River Igbo secret societies, whose names, rituals, and functions denote something of their origin, playing a very prominent role in political and social matters. These societies included the *Akang, Ekpe, Ọkọnkọ* and *Ọbọng.* Secret societies bearing these or similar names, observing similar rituals and fulfilling similar functions are found among the Efik-Ibibio as among the Ekoi and other peoples of the Cross River zone. Here they were even better organized as well as politically and socially more powerful. This would be sufficient evidence to lead one to suspect that it was from there that these institutions filtered into the general eastern Igbo area. But even beyond that, traditions associated with these societies in Igbo land emphatically state that they were borrowed from the non-Igbo peoples of the Cross River area.

Another important institution borrowed by these Igbo from the Benue-Congo peoples of the Cross River was the fully articulated age-set and age-grade system with formal rites of passages. To be sure in all Igbo land there is a general recognition of, and respect for, the distinction between children, youths and elders, with each having its own functions and privileges. But not in all Igbo communities was the transition from one stage to the other marked by a formal rite. But among the Benue-Congo-speaking peoples of the Cross River plain, especially among those living in the middle and upper Cross River regions, the age-grade institution was highly developed and played a prominent role in political and social life. It was specifically an ideal system for organizing offence and defence. Again this age-set and age-grade system was better developed among the Cross River and North Eastern Igbo who were in close touch with the Benue-Congo peoples of the middle and upper Cross River, than it was in the rest of Igbo land. The eastern Igbo must have come to recognize the value of this institution in the course of the wars they fought with these their non-Igbo neighbours and latterly adopted it. Though it must be recognized that the very fact of frequent wars over land, usually prosecuted by young men, could by itself have been sufficient to induce Igbo society to improve upon the organization of its earlier loosely-integrated age-grade system. In such a state of constant war it would not take too long for it to become the tradition for each new generation of youths to announce their attainment of manhood by waging a war or accomplishing some other deed recognized by the society as demanding bravery, intelligence, cunning and so on. Nonetheless it must be conceded that it was most likely the encounter between the Igbo and the Benue-Congo peoples that one way or the other induced this development in eastern Igbo society.

Other evidences of this cultural impact are found in the dialects of these eastern Igbo which contain many words and phrases borrowed from the Benue-Congo-speaking peoples. There is also the factor of double descent found among the Cross River Igbo which scholars have similarly attributed to the impact of these non-Igbo neighbours. Dual descent is not found any where else in Igbo land. And in the view of Professor Simon Ottenberg, among the Cross River Igbo it must have been the result of the culture clash between patrilineal Igbo and matrilineal Benue-Congo peoples.[25]

Finally there is the practice of head-hunting found amongst the Cross River Igbo. This has also been attributed to the impact of the same Benue-Congo peoples, as the practice is not found elsewhere in Igbo-land, but is widespread among the non-Igbo peoples who live between the middle and upper Cross River. This practice can also be related to the long tradition of inter-group fighting which, as already mentioned, characterized the history of this zone for centuries. In the days of frequent wars, a man would have the opportunity of proving himself in his community by taking the head of an enemy in battle. But if more peaceful conditions supervened with the stabilization of frontiers, that opportunity would be closed. As society would have already institutionalized the practice of each man proving himself by taking a head, it was only to be expected that those who reached manhood in peace time would have to take to head-hunting. After a few generations of this, head-hunting would become the established method for a man to win acceptance in his community as was the case in these eastern Igbo communities by the nineteenth century or even earlier.

But as already pointed out above it was the activities of the different Igbo specialist groups—of the smiths, traders, and of the ritual and oracular agents—that dictated the tone and determined the character of most of Igbo society in this period. It is impossible yet to date the rise of these specialist groups with any precision. But one thing appears certain: their origin goes back to developments which took place in remote antiquity. There are a number of arguments to support this view. The activities in which the different groups specialized—the manipulation of spiritual forces for material ends, the working of iron and the exploitation of long-range commerce—were such as could be associated with the earliest phases of Igbo social evolution. Of these three activities, only the working of iron can be dated if eventually the study of the archaeology of Igbo land is taken up seriously. Nri traditions associate it with the earliest phase of the making of Igbo society. Long distance trading in Igbo land must have emerged in consequence of the increasing contrast between the ecology of the Nsukka-Okigwi cuesta and that of the low lands around it. This was made necessary not only by the need to exchange the products of one zone for those of the other, but also by the fact that as the soil of the cuesta deteriorated badly the occupants were forced to turn from wholesale dependence on agriculture to other professions. In this regard it is instructive that all the specialists groups were from this cuesta. Again this differentiation between the ecology of the cuesta and of the lowlands must have been ancient indeed.

With regard to the manipulation of spiritual forces, a similar argument pointing to its antiquity could be advanced. The Nri associate their emergence as ritual specialists with the coming of the agricultural revolution. The Aro say they became the agents of *Ibini Ukpabi* from the foundation of their community. The problem connected with this are discussed in another essay in this collection. The Bonny, however, affirm that the Aro oracle was being widely consulted before their ancestors migrated to where they now live. The European records, as well as the traditions of many other communities, make it clear that by the time the Portuguese got to the Bight of Biafra in the fifthteenth century the coast was already settled. There is thus sufficient reason to reject the earlier views put forward by European writers that the rise of these oligarchies was a direct consequence of the impact of trans-Atlantic trade on Igbo society. No doubt the inauguration of the European trade expanded the activities and widened the horizons of these groups. It would not, however, have been responsible for the decision by our people to adopt these different professions as part of the process of adjusting to their increasingly hostile environment.

It is thus quite likely that by the opening of what Europeans call their modern times, the Aro, the Awka, the Nri, the Abiriba and the Nkwerre were already famed in many parts of Igbo land for the professions which subsequently the Europeans saw them pursuing. Though their areas of influence were probably not as mutually exclusive as the European administrators would have one believe, each had some part of Igbo land where it had the upper hand over other rivals. For the Nri ritualists this was the Northern, Western and Riverain Igbo areas, for the Awka smiths it was the same, for the Aro traders and oracle specialists it was the Northern, Southern, Eastern and North-Eastern Igbo regions, for the Nkwerre smiths it was the Southern Igbo area while for the Abiriba smiths it was the Cross River plain and valley. But even beyond that, the activities of these groups went beyond Igbo land. The Nri are mentioned in Igala and Edo traditions. The Aro were very influential in Ibibio land, as well as among the Ijọ, the Bantoid peoples of the Cross River and in Idoma land. The Abiriba dominated smithing in much of Ibibio land and the Cross River valley where they so exploited the people that they came to be known as rogues. The Awka penetrated parts of the Delta as smiths and oracular agents and in these spheres of activity constituted an influence to reckon with as far west as Isoko. Nkwerre smiths penetrated the Eastern Delta and were particularly active in Ogoni.

These specialist groups organized their business in two main ways. All, but the Aro, relied on periodic occupational wanderings known variously as *iga uzọ ije* or *iga mbia* or *iga n'ụzụ* for the prosecution of their business. Under this arrangement the specialists travelled in small bands of close friends or kinsmen, each band choosing a strategic village, usually located near an important market, where they resided for a period or from time to time to ply their business in the case of smiths; or from where they scoured the neighbouring region performing ritual services or administering cures in the case of ritual, religious and medical specialists. In the case of those who combined these activities with serving as oracular agents, they took their clients with them as they visited home from time to time.

The Aro organized their business differently and probably better. In Central, Southern and Eastern Igbo areas as in Ibibio land, where they were most active, they established permanent settlements at strategic points to serve as collecting and distributing centres for the wares in which they traded. Furthermore they established enduring links with various well-organized local groups and where necessary operated through these. Among such groups were the Nkwerre of Orlu, Nike of Nkanu, the Abam, Abiriba, Edda and Ohafia of the Cross River Igbo.

Of these alliances one of the most important, if also one of the most misunderstood, was that with the warlike clans of the Cross River Igbo. The early Europeans described the Abam,

Ohafia, Edda, etc., as Aro mercenaries. But closer study would show that the relationship was a symbiotic one. These clans had developed a tradition of head-hunting as already shown and would, with or without Aro encouragement, hunt for heads each time an age-group attained manhood or a great man died. The Aro themselves were widely travelled and knew most of Igbo land. They were thus in a position to serve the head-hunters as guides. The result was that when the Aro had a quarrel with some other communities they would call on one or other of these Cross River Igbo groups whose young men would seize the opportunity to obtain the heads that would establish them in their society. As time went on other groups, not just the Aro, also came to exploit the passion of these Cross River clans for human heads by inviting them to fight their own wars. Even on such occasions the Aro served as guides. The relationship between the Aro and these head-hunters was thus much more complex than the simple arrangement by which one group were the mercenaries of the other.

It was on a society more or less at this level of social development that European impact, mainly in the form of the slave trade, came to be increasingly felt from the sixteenth century onwards. The impact of the slave trade on Igbo society has usually been exaggerated if not entirely misunderstood. Some have said it depopulated Igbo land while to others it coincided with an unprecedented expansion of Igbo population as a result of which the Igbo came to occupy the area known today as North-Eastern Igbo. Similarly some have blamed the slave trade for the disintegration of Igbo society and institutions thus hampering the formation of an Igbo state, while others have claimed that it inspired the emergence of the various professional groups discussed above, and thus brought the Igbo very close to forming a state or states.[26] To the present writer the impact of the slave trade and European activity on Igbo society in the period under consideration, has to be discussed in less extravagant terms; and in any case is still waiting for its historian.

Meanwhile, one can on the basis of the available evidence argue that European activity on the coast, especially in the form of the slave trade, widened the range of activity of the Igbo specialist groups mentioned above. The Igbo were, as has been suggested by Professor Shaw, by the ninth century A.D. probably already participating indirectly in the traffic that went across the Sahara. But latterly the presence of the Europeans just a few miles to the south must have increased Igbo chances of benefiting from international commerce, as well as of suffering from its then peculiar afflictions. On logical grounds, therefore, the business of some of these men expanded, especially of those of them like the Aro who were mainly traders. Even the business of the Nri as ritualists and peace-makers must have expanded too. The selling of near-kinsmen was as much an abomination as murder, and required the ritual purification of the land and of the culprits and there can be little doubt that the onset of the slave trade increased the incidence of this crime, thus offering the Nri more opportunities for business.

Secondly, it provided an extra, and in fact a more important, outlet for surplus Igbo population. Some moved down the delta as free men to participate in the new openings for business, while many more left as slaves who were either retained in and integrated into coastal society or shipped across the Atlantic. One would therefore say that it eased the population congestion which could have otherwise increased the pressure on the land, intensified the struggle for that commodity and probably either led to state formation or to further Igbo expansion at the expense of their neighbours. But this is not to say that it ensured an era of peace. One is merely arguing that if all the Igbo sent abroad had remained at home the resulting pressure of population would have produced other consequences for the Igbo and their neighbours.

The argument of those who blame the slave trade for the failure of the Igbo to evolve a state is that it instigated wars which broke up existing unities and engendered deep animosities amongst neighbouring groups. On the contrary the evidence would tend to show that it is incorrect to say the slave trade engendered an era of chaos in Igbo land. The researches of Talbot and Jones have shown that wars played only a very small part in the process by which slaves were recruited in Igbo land.[27] The Fulani and Ijo raids so loudly advertized in the colonial period as the cause of devastation and disintegration of Igbo land have been shown not to have affected the area directly. The fact is that, as argued above, by the time the European era dawned along the coast, Igbo society would appear to have already attained a sophisticated level of development. With the groups of specialist traders, diviners and oracle agents and with codes of moral and legal rights and wrongs already well established, Igbo society was in a position to meet the demands of the new commercial world to the south through the use of these institutions and groups. Thus, for instance, those who formerly distributed only salt, beads and the like, now assembled and distributed slaves also. In the same way criminals who would have had other types of punishment meted out to them, were now condemned to be sold. While oracles and institutions which hitherto were used to tell fortunes and sort out tangled property claims, were now used also in detecting serious criminals who were then sentenced to 'transportation' across the seas.

The Era of Aro Ascendancy thus witnessed the further maturation of Igbo culture and society. In the West Niger and Riverine area it was a period during which village and village-group heads under the impact of Benin and of expanded trade on the Niger built up their positions into village monarchies, and as part of this process constructed elaborate ideological charters linking them in differing degrees with Benin, Idah and Nri. For the rest the coming and going of ritual and business specialists effectively served to integrate the impoverished plateau region with the more fertile plains around it, to carry Igbo institutions, ideas and customs to and from different parts of Igbo land thus helping to maintain basic cultural uniformity over a wide area. In addition their activities integrated Igbo land with other societies around, thus ensuring that Igbo culture did not develop in isolation. In this regard just as the Aro carried the *Ekpe* and *Akang* to many parts of Eastern and Southern Igbo area, they carried the worship or veneration of *Ibini Ukpabi* to many communities in the Cross River valley, to the Mbembe for instance. Part of the process by which this era was undermined and brought to an end is the subject of the chapter entitled 'The Eclipse of the Aro Slaving Oligarchy'.

The student of pre-colonial Igbo culture history thus has to recognize three main epochs. The first is the era of primary migration leading to the settlement of the Nsukka-Okigwi cuesta and the Awka-Orlu uplands, and the region immediately south of this north–south ridge. We know next to nothing about this period as hardly any reference to it survives in the traditions of the people. But we have to postulate its historicity on the basis of linguistic and other cultural data which seem to indicate that the Igbo did not originate where we now find them and must have moved in from some point further north—probably from the area of the Niger-Benue confluence.

The second period deals with the evolution of the basic

organism we know as Igbo society, which event took place with the expansion of Igbo population thanks to the coming of agriculture and iron technology or the increased mastery of these techniques. This led to the dispersal of the Igbo from this hill region to the lowlands west and east. Events relating to this epoch survive in the traditions, especially in those of the Nri who associate the emergence of their society with a mythical figure *Eri* and his equally mythical descendants. This period we designate the *Eri Period* and the era before it the *Pre-Eri Period*. The third period deals with the further maturation of Igbo culture and society from about the fifteenth century until the overthrow of Igbo independence by the British. This maturation took place under the impact of Benin, Igala and the Bantoid peoples from nearby, of the various specialist oligarchies from within and of the European slave trade from without. We have, for convenience, designated this period the <u>Era of Aro Ascendancy</u>.

NOTES

1. D. Forde and G. I. Jones, *The Ibo and Ibibio-speaking Peoples of South-eastern Nigeria* (London, 1950), p. 9.
2. A. G. Leonard, *The Lower Niger and Its Tribes* (London, 1960), see p. 4, where he says:

   'It has been suggested by missionaries and travellers that the languages spoken by the Ibibio, Efik, Andoni, and others have all been derived from Ibo at some ancient period; also that there is a distinct dialectal affinity between the Ijo dialects of Oru, Brass, Ibani, and New Calabar, and the Isuama dialect of Ibo.'

3. See for example J. E. Flint, *Nigeria and Ghana* (New Jersey, 1966), p. 63; Simon Ottenberg, 'Ibo Oracles and inter-group relations', *Southwestern Journal of Anthropology*, Vol. 14, pp. 294–317; J. C. Anene, *Southern Nigeria in Transition* (Oxford, 1966), pp. 1–25; J. S. Coleman, *Nigeria, A Background to Nationalism* (California, 1958), pp. 40–1. For a criticism of some of the explanations offered by these and other scholars, see A. E. Afigbo, *The Warrant Chiefs* (London, 1972), pp. 10–14.
4. For more detailed statements of these and related problems of writing the history of preliterate acephalous communities, see A. G. Leonard, *op. cit.*, pp. 20–56; R. Horton, 'Stateless Societies in the history of West Africa', in Ajayi and Crowder (eds), *History of West Africa*, Vol. I (Longman, 1971); S. N. Nwabara, 'Ibo Land: A Study in Administration' (Ph.D. Northwestern, 1965), pp. 1–26; S. Ottenberg, *Leadership and Authority in an African Society* (University of Washington Press, 1971), p. 40.
5. See the *Introduction* to *Conch*, Vol. III, No. 2, pp. 1–15.
6. S. Ottenberg, *Leadership and Authority etc.*, p. 40; S. Leith-Ross, *African Women* (London, 1939), p. 54.

7. The earlier attitude to these materials propagated by Jeffreys, Palmer, Meek and their other colleagues of the diffusionist school is examined in chapters 2 and 6 of this collection.
8. R. Hotton, 'Stateless Societies etc.', in Ajayi and Crowder (eds), *op cit.*, pp. 78–119.
9. R. G. Armstrong:
    (i) *The Study of West African Languages* (Ibadan, 1964), p. 26.
    (ii) 'Glottochronology and West African Linguistics', *Journal of African History*, Vol. 3, No. 2, 1962.
    C. C. Wrigley, 'Linguistic Clues to African History', *Journal of African History*, Vol. 3, No. 2, 1962.
    R. S. Smith, *Kingdoms of the Yoruba* (Great Britain, 1969), p. 13.
10. R. N. Henderson, *The King in Every Man* (Yale, 1972), p. 39.
11. D. D. Hartle, 'Archaeology in Eastern Nigeria', *Nigeria Magazine*, No. 93, June 1967.
12. G. T. Basden, 'Notes on the Ibo Country', *The Geographical Journal*, Vol. 39, January–June 1912, pp. 246–7.
13. Olaudah Equiano, *The Interesting Narrative* (Norwich, 1794), p. 25.
14. M. D. W. Jeffreys, 'Dual Organisation in Africa', *African Studies*, Vol. 5, No. 2, June 1946, and Vol. 5, No. 3, September 1946. See also Jeffreys, 'The Winged Solar Disk', *Africa*, Vol. xxi, No. 2, April 1951.
15. Enugu Archives, see the file A.D. 635; Aro Sub-Tribes; Second Report on the Aro by H. F. Mathews.
16. R. N. Henderson, *op. cit.*, p. 39.
    Professor Arnold Rubin, see his review of Philip Allison's *African Stone Sculpture* and Frank Willett's *Ife in the History of West African Sculpture*, in *African Notes*. Bulletin of the Institute of African Studies, University of Ibadan, Vol. 6, No. 2, 1971, pp. 113–23.
17. On this matter R. N. Henderson writes: 'The upland Igbo traditionally raised a variety of root crops and livestock, but those occupying the leached white lands of the Awka-Orlu area have long suffered chronic food shortages. The soil has in many places undergone such extensive deterioration that it cannot support the dense population, and in these areas textile weaving, oil palm tending and processing of palm produce, blacksmithing, and other specialized economic activities such as slave trading traditionally supplemented farming', *op. cit.*, pp. 36–7. As I have argued in the main text this development was not limited to the Awka-Orlu upland only. It was characteristic of the entire Nsukka-Okigwi plateau.
18. For a more detailed analysis of these traditions, see chapter 2 in this collection.
19. T. Shaw (ed.), *Nigerian Prehistory and Archaeology* (I.U.P., 1969), pp. 37–46.
20. Mr. Onwuejeogwu's views are summarized in his two articles in *Odinani*, The Journal of the Odinani Museum, Nri, Vol. 1, No. 1, March 1972.
21. See Chapter 2 in this collection.
22. S. Ottenberg, *Leadership and Authority*, etc., p. 47.
23. Rosemary Harris, *The Political Organisation of Mbembe of Nigeria* (H.M.S.O. 1966), pp. 83–90.
24. For the clearest statement of this hypothesis, see G. I. Jones, *The Trading States of the Oil Rivers* (Oxford, 1963), p. 30.
25. K. O. K. Onyioha, 'Biafra in Four Centuries of History, 1500–1900', unpublished manuscript. This work, written between 1967 and 1970, is based to a large extent on oral sources many of which come from West Niger Igbo area.
26. S. Ottenberg, *Leadership and Authority*, etc., pp. 3–8.

27. For various aspects of the question of the impact of the European slave trade on Igbo society, see:
   - (i) G. I. Jones and H. Mulhall, 'An examination of the physical type of certain peoples of South-eastern Nigeria', *Journal of Royal Anthropoligical Institute*, Vol. 79, 1949, pp. 11–18.
   - (ii) W. R. G. Horton, 'The Ohu System of slavery in a Northern Ibo village-group', *Africa*, Vol. 24, No. 4, 1954, pp. 311–35.
   - (iii) J. S. Harris, 'Some Aspects of Slavery in Southeastern Nigeria,' *Journal of Negro History*, Vol. 27, No. 1, January 1942, pp. 37–54.
   - (iv) S. Ottenberg, 'Ibo Oracles, etc.', *loc. cit.*, pp. 295–317.
   - (v) S. Leith-Ross, 'Notes on the *Osu* system among the Ibo of Owerri Province, Nigeria', *Africa*, Vol. 10, 1937, pp. 206–20.
   - (vi) J. C. Anene, *Southern Nigeria, etc.*, pp. 1–25.
   - (vii) R. N. Henderson, *The King In Every Man*, pp. 23–75.
   - (viii) K. O. Dike, *Trade and Politics in the Niger Delta* (Oxford, 1956).

28. G. I. Jones and H. Mulhall, 'An examination of the physical type, etc.', *loc. cit.*, p. 11.
P. A. Talbot and H. Mulhall, *The Physical Anthropology of Southern Nigeria*, p. 4.

2. The Holy City of Nri

The publication in 1970 of Professor Thurstan Shaw's monumental two volume work entitled *Igbo-Ukwu: An account of archaeological discoveries in eastern Nigeria* was an event of great significance for the study of the history and culture not only of Igbo land but also of Southern Nigeria and in fact of West Africa as a whole. Here, however, it is sufficient to observe that one of its main achievements was to decisively draw the attention of scholars of Igbo history to the important place which Nri civilization, of which the Igbo-Ukwu bronzes probably constitute the earliest concrete evidence so far known, occupies in the culture history of the Igbo-speaking peoples. Yet it would be a serious historical error to fail to recognize that Shaw's book is one, although however the most successful and the most dramatic so far, of many attempts to focus attention on this fact.

The truth is that quite early in the period of British penetration of Igbo land it would appear to have been recognized by the more anthropologically minded among the white missionaries and administrators, that Nri was a place of some importance among the Igbo. As early as 1857 the Reverend Mr. J. C. Taylor of the Church Missionary Society, then stationed at Onitsha, came into contact with Nri priests and agents, and it is probably a measure of his recognition of the importance of that city that he recorded meticulously the visits which 'Itshi men from Inzi' (Nri) paid him. He probably also knew that they travelled widely in Igbo land hence he seized every opportunity of meeting with them to improve his knowledge of the interior, and particularly to gather information on the distance between Onitsha and various important centres in the Igbo interior. But no matter how important Taylor thought Nri was, he would appear to have considered Bende even more important, at least he regarded it as 'the capital of Igbo'.[1] The Roman Catholic Missionaries on their side must also have recognized the importance of Nri early as this would help to explain the fact that it was one of the first centres they visited beyond the immediate environs of Onitsha, their operational base in what later became Eastern Nigeria.²

But it would appear that it was only with the dawn of this century that a proper estimate was come to of the importance of Nri in the social, religious and cosmological systems of the Igbo people. Perhaps the first person to come to this accurate estimate and to draw attention to it in writing was Major A. G. Leonard who in 1902 was Divisional Officer in charge of the Central Division of the then Southern Nigeria. The Central Division embraced, among other places, what later became the Awka Division in which Nri is located, and much of unspecified territory beyond. Leonard evinced early interest in the culture and traditions of the Igbo, Ijo and Ibibio as well as in their women. He had many of the latter as mistresses. And one suspects that it was probably more for this 'indiscretion unbecoming of a representative of His Majesty's Government in barbarous parts of the world' than for his alleged brutality to those under his charge that he was soon after dismissed from the service. One wonders how if the latter charge were true he would have commanded the confidence of the people to the extent he would appear to have done. Only in a situation in which he enjoyed such confidence could he have been able to gain access to the religious ideas, lore and traditions of the people to the extent he did. His researches, published as *The Lower Niger and its Tribes*, holds pride of place amongst early colonial writings on the Igbo, Ijo and Ibibio for understanding, sympathy and penetration.

Writing as early as 1906 on the importance of Nri in the life of the Igbo Major Leonard said:

> It is in a certain measure evident that somewhere in this locality of Isuama, in which the purest Ibo is said to be spoken, is to be found the heart of the Ibo nationality; consequently it is quite reasonable to look among its people for the original fountain-head from which all the other clans have sprung. This inference too is supported not only by the purity of the language but by this right of dispensing or rather conferring royalty which is undoubtedly the prerogative of the Nri or N'shi people ... the highest representatives of sacerdotalism in the Ibo race ...³

This early and penetrating comment was later confirmed by the researches and writings of many after him. Mr. Northcote Thomas, the first anthropologist engaged by the Government of the Colony and Protectorate of Southern Nigeria to help unravel the customs and traditions of the people, equally reported that Nri occupied a place of eminence in Igbo land. He described the Eze Nri as 'a somewhat striking figure' who inspired so much awe that 'when probably for the first time in history an Eze Nri entered the Native Court at Akwa while a sitting was going on, the whole assembly rose and prepared to flee.'[4]

Equally emphatic was the testimony of Archdeacon G. T. Basden who lived for many years in and around Awka where he was able to study Nri culture and influence at close range. In his *Among the Ibos of Nigeria* published in 1920 he said the name 'Nri was so well known over much of Igbo land and Nri priests so ubiquitous and influential that the name "Nri" had come to be given early in the century "in mistake, to the whole country lying east of Onitsha"'.[5] Much more importantly a little latter he saw the area around Nri as offering the best opportunity for a study of unadulterated indigenous Igbo culture. 'Where then,' he asked,

> can ancient Ibo law and custom, religion and language be best studied? In my opinion the conditions are most favourable at Nri, the home of the priestly cult, and in that immediate neighbourhood. There and at Awka, the people were left free and undisturbed from generation to generation.[6]

Dr. P. A. Talbot merely elaborated on these earlier testimonies in his momumental four volume survey of the peoples and culture of Southern Nigeria.[7] But Mr. M. D. W. Jeffreys in a staggering report which he wrote for the colonial administration in the 1930s added significantly to these testimonies by posing and seeking to provide answers to such questions as who were the Nri, what was the nature of their culture and its provenance, how old was it and what was its impact on the Igbo peoples. Mr. Jeffreys unearthed much valuable information which however was ruined in presentation by his concern to fit all the vital facts of Igbo culture history into his pet hypothesis of Heliolithic culture missionaries who left Egypt sometime in the remote past to spread light and civilization to most parts of the earth.[8] This report by its sheer volume and doctrinaire generalizations understandably strained the patience of an already harrassed Administration that merely wanted a report 'devoted to questions of native "law", the personnel of Native Courts and the establishment of councils.'[9] Even today it still taxes the patience of even the most dedicated and patient scholar.

Yet in spite of these and other equally eloquent testimonies to the important place which Nri occupies in Igbo history, scholars failed until lately to recognize that it was for the Igbo what Ile-Ife was for the Yoruba peoples—the centre around which their world was believed to have been created, their cultural homeland and that probably its history holds some of the answers to the many complex questions posed by early Igbo history. Why this was so belongs to the issue of the shortcomings of colonial historiography and its implications for the study of Igbo history, a subject that will be taken up elsewhere. Here we are concerned to emphasize for scholars interested in Igbo history the important place of Nri in Igbo culture history by briefly discussing such questions as who the Nri are, the probable origin and character of the civilization of which they are regarded as the highest representative, the nature and extent of their influence in Igbo land, their relationship with their non-Igbo neighbours (Igala and Edo) and the decline of their hegemony.

The question who are the Nri is a complex one especially in view of the confusion which seems to reign supreme at present in the use of the term 'Nri' by historians and ethnographers working in the Igbo field. Mr. Onwuejeogwu, anthropologist and ethnographer presently actively engaged in the reconstruction and reinterpretation of Nri history and culture as a follow-up to the archaeological work of Professor Shaw at Igbo-Ukwu, has tried to explore the various meanings of the word. He has distinguished its use as an ethnological concept, as a cultural concept, as a term referring to the highest title attainable within the Nri culture system and as a geographical concept. The question posed in this paragraph limits us to an investigation of the meaning of the word as an ethnological concept, that is in so far as it is used to describe a specific ethnic group among the Igbo-speaking peoples, and to an investigation of the origin of that group.

In this regard the use of the term would appear to have become a controversial matter, or in any case it would appear that no effort has so far been made at standardization. Most of the early writers, for instance Mr. Northcote Thomas, Archdeacon G. T. Basden, Dr. P. A. Talbot, Dr. M. D. W. Jeffreys and Mr. G. I. Jones used 'Nri' as another name for Aguku, a village which lies about 29 kilometres east of Onitsha.[10] The people of the Agukwu themselves would now appear to prefer the more famed and revered name 'Nri' to Agukwu which is a mere geographical term devoid of deeper ethnological or cultural associations.[11] It is not clear whether at the time of British conquest Agukwu had already appropriated this name 'Nri' in which case they passed it on to men like Northcote Thomas and Basden as their alternative name; or whether these early European writers were the first to assign the name, probably by mistake, to Agukwu. The latter was probably the case for reasons which will be adduced below.

There is a second usage of the term in its ethnological context. Mr. M. A. Onwuejeogwu applies the word Nri to a federation of three villages of which Agukwu is one, though no doubt the pre-eminent. The others are Diodo and Akamkpisi. 'The present town of Nri', he has recently written, 'comprises three major villages that amalgamated into one—viz. Agukwu, Diodo and Akamkpisi' with an estimated population of about 12,000 persons.[12] It must be said, though, that Mr. Onwuejeogwu is by no means rigidly consistent in his application of this term to ethnic groups. Thus in the same paper he uses 'Nri' to describe any 'peoples who claim to have some kind of relationship with Nri people'. Under this rather amorphous group he lists some sixteen village-groups and talks of an unspecified number of what he terms 'Nri lineages' in towns which make no claims to Nri origin or connection.[13] Mr. G. J. Lawton, one time Divisional Officer in charge of Awka, used the term in a similar manner, applying it to a 'tribe' which he said comprised the village-groups of Nteje, Umuleri, Aguleri, Igbariam, Amanuke, Urenebo, Enugu and Oreri.[14]

There is yet another usage in which Nri is the name of a clan (Jones's 'tribe'). In 1950 Mr. Jones used Umunri and Nri as synonyms for an ethnological group which he described as a 'sub-tribe' and which he said comprised Agukwu, Enugu, Osunagidi and Nawfia. According to him this group formerly formed what he described as a 'tribe' with Aguleri, Igbariam, Nteje, Nsugbe, Nando, Umunya and Amanuke.[15] This usage has recently been urged by Chief S. O. N. Okafor, *The Obidigbo II, The Okpalariam* of Enugi-Agidi. 'It is important', he has written,

> to mention for the Historians to note, that Nri is NOT a name of a particular town within the Umunri clan. I consider it in this wise, that Enugu-Agidi, Enugu-Ukwu, Nawfia and Agukwu could, if (it be) decided, be called Enugu-Agidi Nri, Enugu-Ukwu Nri, Nawfia Nri

and Agukwu Nri, as Agukwu town has abandoned her name, Agukwu, and registered Nri. May be this is just a way of changing the history of Umunri or there is a political motive behind this change.[16]

Judging by traditional Igbo practice the objective student can only say that history appears to be on the side of Chief S. O. N. Okafor of Enugu-Agidi. It is unusual among the Igbo for a segment of a clan (Jones's tribe) to be named after the mythical founder of the clan. Thus it is very unlikely that a village-group which is a mere segment of a clan, much less a village which is further down in the lineage hierarchy, could have been christened after the founder of the clan. Where the group in question is considered a recent and artificial federation of hitherto autonomous units, the situation would not arise either as there would have been no mythical ancestor. On the other hand jealousy and rivalry amongst the member villages or village groups would ensure that no member unit, no matter how dominant or important in the new community, gave its name to the federation. Usually either a purely geographical name would be chosen like *Ofemili* (in full *Ndi Ofemili:* those who inhabit the other side of the River) or they would add their number as a suffix to the Igbo word *Mba* (town). Thus we have such groups as *Mbanese* (the five towns), *Mbanasato* (the eight towns), *Mbanasa* (the seven towns).

The confusion in the use of the name Nri was most likely the creation of impatient and uncomprehending political officers and was later carried into serious ethnographic and historical work by scholars who were none too familiar with the Igbo system of naming social segments which claim a common descent or ancestor. According to the genealogical charter of what may more appropriately be called the *Umueri Tribe* (see the accompanying chart), Eri the founder and his first wife had four male children called Nri, Aguleri, Igbariam and Amanuke in that order of seniority. These sons founded what may be called the *primary tribal segments*. Nri the eldest son had five boys and a girl. Only four of these sons were able to found communities which have survived till date, namely Agukwu, Enugu-Ukwu, Nawfia, and Enugu-Agidi. These four communities may be called the *secondary tribal segments*. The only daughter of Nri then got married and produced four sons each of which was able to found a viable community, namely Awkuzu, Umuleri, Nando and Ogbunike. These may be called the *tertiary tribal segments*. Three other communities—Nteje, Nsugbe and Umunya—are mentioned as belonging to this same 'tribal' fraternity but would appear not to have been properly fitted into the genealogical charter. Members of the *tertiary tribal segments* are known within the group as *Umuiguedo* and have been described as such by ethnographers. The *secondary tribal segments* are known as *Umunri* while the three members of the *primary tribal segments* which did not expand and multiply as successfully as did Nri, the first born, have been described by ethnographers as *Umueri*. How far this name was indigenous to the group in the period before the British advent it is now impossible to determine. But in strict Igbo usage all the members of the three main segments should be embraced by the term *Umueri*, as they all lay claim ultimately to Eri descent. However what is important is that neither in the *primary* nor in the *tertiary* segments do we find any member-unit bearing the name of the founder of either group. By the same token there is no reason why one of the member-units of the *secondary tribal segments* should bear the name of the founder of the group.

This is as far as nomenclature goes. But at a deeper level, that is in the cultural and spiritual sense, there can be no doubt that *Agukwu*, as the *Okpala* or the descendant of the first son of *Nri* who was also the first son of *Eri*, and therefore the community which houses the 'big' *ọfọ* not only of the Umunri clan but also of what has been described here as the *Umueri tribe*, harbours the 'soul' of the entire group, and in that sense may be regarded as 'the heart of Igbo nationality' which Major Leonard spoke of. It is for this reason that it can be called *The Holy City of the Igbo-speaking peoples*.

Another relevant aspect of the question: who are the Nri? concerns the issue of their origin. The Nri simply say that their founding father, *Eri*, and his wife *Namaku* were sent down from Heaven by *Chukwu*, the Igbo Supreme God, and that they landed at Aguleri, an Igbo village-group in the Anambara valley. There, they claim, all the important features of Igbo culture were evolved or rather received as gifts from *Chukwu*. In the absence of any more helpful information on this matter, the most reasonable thing would be to assume that the Nri are just another branch of the people whose language they speak, whose social, cultural and religious systems they share, especially since many other branches of this people trace their origin from them (the Nri). But the matter is no longer as simple as that, thanks largely to Jeffreys and those other white ethno-historians of a bad colonial past who appear to have uncritically lapped up even the wildest of his ideas. Interpreting the above Nri creation legend and certain features of Igbo society and culture out of their contexts and in the distorting light of the pet hypothesis mentioned above, Jeffreys came to the conclusion that the Nri were not originally Igbo even though they have been bred out by the latter.

He started off from the assumption that Igbo culture, with its characteristic features of *Dual Division* in social organization, and the *ọfọ* and *aro* (*alo*) as ritualized symbols of office and status, is reminiscent of a cultural archetype which he described as *Heliolithic*. He said for instance:

> The peculiarity of dividing towns into two parts is found distributed throughout the world and is always associated with a suncult known as the Heliolithic culture ... In other words the presence of a dual organisation indicated that the present Igbo culture is an acquired one and not an evolved one.[17]

This culture he said originated in the east[18] and must have been imposed on the Igbo by a small conquering military aristocracy. He went on:

> This culture had its origin between 4,500 and 4,000 years ago, and the evidence suggests that a small colony of a military aristocracy settled among the indigenous Ibo and imposed on the Ibo this high culture but were bred out by the Ibo.[19]

Like others before him Jeffreys found the highest development of this borrowed Igbo culture within the Umunri area. Thus in one of his writings he described Nri as 'the centre of Ibo culture as it were'[20] and in another he said:

> Within this (Umunri) group is the fount and source of all the present Igbo culture ... All Igbo culture came from this group.[21]

To him, therefore, the Umunri must have been the original carriers of this culture. They were therefore the intrusive group of conquering military aristocracy he referred to earlier. To clinch the argument he said:

> As history it (the Umunri tradition) would also fit in with the fact that the Umundri are not Igbo. In a prayer heard at Aguku, occurred the sentence, '*ofo ainyi ji eli Igbo*' (*ofo* sacred emblem) with which we eat

the Igbo. These words indicate that the Igbo were in existence when the Umundri invaders arrived who subdued or 'ate' them through the power of the *ofo*.[22]

In his view rather than being Igbo, the Umunri, were either of direct Igala descent or at least of the same stock with the Igala.[23] And since to Jeffreys the Igala were a branch of the Jukun and 'the Jukun arrived at their present site from the east'[24] the ultimate origin of the Umunri must also lie in the east.

For now it is only necessary to say that Jeffreys's arguments are not valid and that until valid arguments are adduced in support of the view that the Nri are not Igbo, the objective scholar must continue to regard them as Igbo and to study them as such. On the other hand it must be quite obvious to every student of African history and anthropology that Jeffreys's theory of Nri origin is merely an extension to the Igbo field of the Hamitic hypothesis which was once believed to provide the key to the culture history of most Negro peoples but which has since been exposed as sophisticated racial rubbish. More than that of any other Nigerian people, the study of Igbo history suffered immeasurably through the application of the above hypothesis. For most colonial officials and writers, like the sceptics of biblical fame who doubted that anything good could come out of Jerusalem, believed that nothing that was culturally important could come out of Igbo land. Thus any Igbo-speaking group, be it the Aro or the Nri, which would appear to have achieved anything historically significant, was severed from the Igbo stock with one savage blow of the Hamitic axe.

On the other hand the argument based on the fact that the Nri refer to their Igbo-speaking neighbours as *Igbo* but would not apply the name to themselves has also been used to 'prove' that the Onitsha, the Oguta and the Aro are not Igbo. But this reasoning would seem to be based on a serious misunderstanding of the usage of that word amongst the Igbo peoples. The fact is that no group of Igbo-speaking people refer to themselves as Igbo. Reporting on this fact as far back as the 1850s Dr. W. B. Baikie wrote as follows:

> In Igbo each person hails, as a sailor would say, from the particular district where he was born, but when away from home all are Igbo.[25]

Much more recently Mr. Onweujeogwu has written:

> Igbo is used to refer to other Igbo-speaking groups other than one's

own. Thus the West Niger Igbo refer to all East Niger Igbo as IGBO. The Onitsha refer to all living east of them as Igbo, the Nri refer to others including Onitsha as Igbo, the Aro refer to others including Nri and Onitsha as Igbo.[26]

The original meaning of the word 'Igbo' is still in dispute. Some have suggested that at first it meant 'the people of the bush', and later 'slaves' or people of 'servile status'. Mr. Ọnwụejeọgwụ has suggested that it meant 'the community of people'.[27] The matter probably requires further investigation. But on the available evidence one can only regard the Umueri tribe, as defined here, as part and parcel of the Igbo people amongst whom they have lived and had their being. The significance for our purpose of their creation legend mentioned above will be discussed in the section immediately following which treats the origin and character of the civilization of which they became the high priests, interpreters and preachers.

The main material available to us for dealing with this question comes from oral traditions collected at Nri in the first decade of this century by Mr. Northcote W. Thomas, between 1930 and 1931 by M. D. W. Jeffreys, since 1966 by Mr. M. A. Ọnwụegeọgwụ. The Nri traditions probably constitute the richest single corpus in Igbo land. Even for this alone Nri would occupy a place of eminence in Igbo history. Jeffreys was certainly impressed by this fact in his time. Thus talking of the Nri traditions he said:

> not all Ibos are aware of these facts or of this ritual. It must be expected that the farther away from the centre investigations are made, the fewer will be the facts obtained and that those that are obtained will be liable to distortion.[28]

And because the Nri traditions are said not to be known to other Igbo groups, Mr. Jeffreys thought it had nothing to do with the history of the Igbo-speaking peoples. In his view the traditions told about the ritual basis of the ascendancy of his presumed conquering group of culture carriers from the east. Said he:

> But the Igbo do not tell this story. It is told only by the royal Umundri families in Aguku and not elsewhere. This fact, that the story, the myth, the word is the sole property of a number of royal families in one town points to the conclusion that it is not Igbo history ... the statement is an oral dramatization of a ritual step and as such is Umundri ritual history.[29]

But this is not an unanswerable argument for concluding that the Nri traditions are not about the past of the Igbo-speaking peoples. Recent researches into the character of oral traditions and how they are preserved have brought to light the key part which institutions of kingship (secular or divine) play in the formulation and preservation of oral history. Not only are such kingships able to evolve specific institutions for recording and reciting the lore and history of the group but they incorporate such lore and history into their ceremonial and ritual and in both cases contribute to the preservation of tradition. The Nri are pre-eminent amongst the few Igbo groups who evolved a divine kingship institution to any significant extent. Their ability therefore to retain and retail these traditions while the other Igbo groups have forgotten them cannot be regarded as proof of their 'non-Igboness'. In any case fragments of these traditions are extant in various Igbo communities, even in those communities which could not be regarded as having come under the sway of Nri.

And now for those aspects of these traditions from which we hope to draw some conclusions on the rise of the culture in question. These assert that when *Eri* came down from the sky he sat on an ant-hill as the land was a morass or waterlogged or to use the Igbo phrase *ala di deke deke* (or *neka neka*). When *Eri* complained, *Chukwu* sent an Awka blacksmith with his bellows, fire and charcoal to dry up the land. After the Awka blacksmith had finished his assignment *Eri* rewarded him with an *ofo* which conferred on him special claims to the smithing profession. While *Eri* lived *Chukwu* fed him and his people on *azu igwe* (substance from the back, i.e. the interior part of the sky). Throughout the period when men lived on this substance they did not sleep.[30] But this special food from heaven ceased after the death of *Eri* whereon *Nri* his first son complained to *Chukwu* who ordered him to kill and bury in separate graves, his first son and first daugher. After trying in vain to evade this command, *Nri* complied with it, in consequence of which after three Igbo weeks (*izu ato*) yam grew from the grave of the son and coco yam from that of the daughter. When *Nri* and his people ate these, they slept for the first time. Later still Nri killed a male and a female slave, burying them separately. Again after *izu ato*, an oil palm sprang from the grave of the male slave and a bread fruit tree from that of the female slave.

With all this new food supply *Nri* and his people prospered but here came the rub. *Chukwu* asked him to distribute the new food items to all people but *Nri* refused because he had bought them so dearly with the life of his own children and slaves. Eventually *Nri* and *Chukwu* made a bargain. For agreeing to distribute to all people the food he obtained by sacrificing his children, *Nri* got a number of rights over the surrounding people conceded to him. Says one version of the tradition:

> As a reward for distributing food to the other towns Ndri would have the right of cleansing every town of an abomination (*nso*) or breach, of crowning the *eze* at Aguleri, and of tying the *ngulu* (ankle cords) when a man took the title of *ozo*. Also he and his successors would have the privilege of making the *Oguji*, or yam medicine, each year for ensuring a plentiful supply of yams in all surrounding towns, or in all towns that subjected themselves to the *eze Ndri*. For this medicine all the surrounding towns would come in and pay tribute and Umundri people then could travel unarmed through the world and no one would attack or harm them.[31]

However, according to another version the bargain was between Nri and the neighbouring peoples who came to him to ask for yams. He told them he would not sell and that they should produce seven fowls, chalk, a pot and goats. With this he made medicine, *Ifejioku*, the *yam spirit*, which he handed over to the applicants. They took this home, apparently with the new crops and sacrificed to it. In return they were required to entertain Nri priests and agents free of charge whenever these passed through their lands. Should they fail to do so, the Nri man would simply plant his *Otonsi* (ritual staff) in their soil and pull it up again, in which case the yams would follow him. To obtain yams again the people would have to strike the bargain afresh with the *eze* Nri.[32]

This tradition tells, in a highly ritualized form, a story which should be familiar to scholars of early African history. This is that the coming of the knowledge of iron was a major breakthrough in Igbo culture history just as it was with other societies. Before that event the Igbo, who dwelt in a thickly forested area, could not effectively exploit the land. Hence the tradition tells us that *Eri* sat on an ant-hill rather than that he stood with his two feet firmly on the ground. Then the Awka blacksmith came, which is a symbolic reference to the introduction of the knowledge of iron, and *Eri* climbed down from his ant-hill to take effective possession of the land. It is still hotly debated by anthropologists and archaeologists whether iron was necessary before the forest dweller could gain effective control of his environment since some maintain that lithic tools were probably sufficient for the purpose. The Nri tradition would appear to say that for the Igbo the knowledge of iron was necessary. In any case there can be no doubt that the advent of iron conferred increased efficiency on the methods of fighting the forest and tilling the ground.

There are other aspects of this first section of the legend which have not been understood because they are wrapped up in highly symbolic language. One of these is the claim that when *Eri* came down *ala dị deke deke* (the land was still soft, or a morass or waterlogged). This is the usual Igbo motif for antiquity. Thus to 'prove' their claim that the bird *okpoko* (hornbill) is one of the most ancient of animals they say that when it came into the world (i.e. was created) all the land was covered with water. Consequently when its parents died, it had to bury them on its head which is considered an explanation for the type of head it has. Another animal which the Igbo consider ancient is the chameleon, *ogwumagala*. Thus they say when this reptile came into the world the land was very soft and so it had to walk carefully in order not to pierce it with its feet, which is the explanation for the way the cameleon walks. Thus the tradition that *ala dị deke deke* when Eri came down is an assertion of the antiquity of the Nri, and through them of the rest of the Igbo where we now find them. When it is remembered that test excavations in the Nsukka Igbo area have yielded evidence of occupation by advanced Neolithic communities whose pottery are said to resemble those of the Nsukka Igbo of today, the basic truth of this claim begins to unfold.[33]

The other aspect is in the claim that *Eri* came down from heaven, on the order of *Chukwu* to take possession of the land. This is an assertion of title to land rather than an account of creation. In an agricultural community especially that in which, as in the case of the Igbo, the density is relatively high, rival claims to land are an ever present reality. In a highly militarized community such claims could be based on the fact of conquest. But among the Igbo where wars of conquest and occupation were rather the exception than the rule, these claims have to be based on other 'facts' or grounds. Two such grounds have been found. One is that the community in question sprang from the soil. This appears to be more widespread. The other is that put forward by the Nri that they fell from Heaven. Of the two, the former would appear to be more convincing, for as the matter usually in dispute is the land, the man *in* the ground, even if he came out late could always show that he was there before the man who fell down from heaven. This fact may well explain why amongst the matter-of-fact Igbo the claim of springing from the ground is more widespread. At times it exists side by side with traditions of migration from elsewhere ready to be played up in the event of a land dispute. Jeffrey's informant told him, along with this tradition that

> These other towns that came and settled around us are not colonies of Ndri but subjects of Ndri. They were not in the beginning of Umundri stock. However part of Enugu (Awka) and Akampesi say all this great field is theirs.[34]

Unfortunately Jeffreys thought this was an irrelevant digression and decided 'it was necessary to head off my informant from this topic'[35] thus missing what much of the tradition was about.

Then the other great break-through in early Igbo history was the coming of agriculture. According to this same corpus of traditions, in the period before *Chukwu* gave yam, coco-yam and the other food crops to Nri, men 'walked in the bush like animals', *na awaghari n'ọfia (ọhia) dika ụmụ anụmanụ*. The English translation of this Igbo statement given by Mr. Northcote Thomas is not an accurate or idiomatic rendering of what the Igbo mean. *Iwaghari* is not just 'walking about' but also implies 'a ceaseless search'. Thus the statement refers to a period when the Igbo lived by hunting and gathering which necessarily implied moving about ceaselessly in search of food. *Dika ụmụ anụmanụ* implies the lack of a permanent home, of any traces of advanced culture and the insecurity this way of life carried with it. This very picturesque description of the pre-agricultural phase of Igbo history helps to emphasize the revolutionary changes which the introduction of agriculture brought to Igbo society. So far-reaching and beneficent were the changes that the Igbo could only regard this improved technique of earning a livelihood as the gift of *Chukwu*. It was the same for the coming of iron. Hence these traditions talk of Chukwu sending first an Awka blacksmith and then food crops from his heavenly abode.

This statement is not an Igbo account of the origin of food crops. Its meaning can be appreciated only through an understanding of certain aspects of Igbo philosophy of life. The Igbo are a deeply religious people, with a highly developed and intricate conception of an all-powerful God, *Chukwu*. But even though they believe *Chukwu* is all powerful they are not fatalistic. They believe in the necessity to make sustained effort. *Onye mebe ma chi ya tinyere ya aka* (let everyone struggle so that their *chi* will help them) is basic to Igbo philosophy of life. Hence before the introduction of iron, i.e. the coming of the Awka blacksmith, *Eri* had to initiate action by complaining bitterly to *Chukwu* about the land being *deke deke*. Similarly with regard to the introduction of food crops *Nri* had to make the first move and was lucky when *Chukwu* 'lent him a hand' (*nyere ya aka*). The Igbo know that not all efforts bear the desired fruit. Only efforts blessed by *Chukwu* or *Chi* produce such results. Thus when an Igbo makes substantial progress in his profession even after a tiresome struggle, he calls it *onyinye Chukwu* (the gift of God). Thus when they say *Chukwu* gave food crops and taught them how to grow these and weave a picturesque legend around these events they are not attempting to tell the story of how they acquired the knowledge of agriculture, but dramatizing in those symbolic phrases, with which their language is richly endowed, how great and beneficial the event was—so great and beneficial that it can only be explained in terms of *Chukwu* having blessed their efforts to achieve a surer livelihood.

Some of the changes which agriculture brought to Igbo society are preserved in the legend, especially in that section of it which talks of the concessions which Nri extracted from *Chukwu* in return for making food available to all peoples. Thus the right of cleansing every *town* of abomination (*nso*) implies the rise of villages and village-groups (towns). It also implies that with the coming of agriculture, as a result of which the Igbo became directly dependent on land, they had to evolve a whole system of rules, laws and rituals to control land use. Because the land fed human beings with food just as a woman feeds her children, it came to be conceived as a *woman, a mother*. And because of the way it transformed crops when sown, godlike powers came to be attributed to it, leading to the deification of *Ala* known in parts of Igbo land as *Ajala* (*Aja Ala*—the Sand of the Earth). When *Ala* came to be deified the rules and laws guiding its use acquired religious sanctions. The deification of *Ala* in turn required working out a system of relationships between it and the ancestors and the other gods recognized by the community. This meant the evolution of a whole cosmological system by the Igbo people.

The other remarkable change, also mentioned in the legends was the evolution of an elaborate social organization. Thus the legends talk of *Nri* being given the right to crown the *eze* of neighbouring towns and to officiate at the taking of the *ọzọ* title. As one would expect, the dawn of a sedentary way of life and the growth in population brought about by the agricultural revolution meant the rise of new types of social problems which the earlier forms of social organization, no matter what they were, could hardly cope with. This led to the rise of leaders who assumed different forms in different communities. In the first place this probably meant that lineage heads who were hitherto not highly differentiated came to be so. Not only did they acquire distinct names—*ọkpara* or *eze*—but they also acquired ritual symbols of office, for instance the *ọfọ*. They also came to be ranked in some order of seniority. Furthermore accession to this office of lineage head came to be marked by a distinct ceremony—the handing over of the *ọfọ* which is probably what the Igbo phrase *ichi eze* originally meant rather than *crowning* as the translation into English in the colonial records erroneously implies. Furthermore the authority of lineage heads had to be supplemented with the authority of other men in the community who had marked ability and had attained a status of public importance. The attainment of this status also had to be marked by a public ceremony—*ichi echichi* taking title, which among the Nri and their neighbours came to be called *ichi ọzọ*, *ọzọ* being the name of the title most popular in this area.

In the early stages of this revolution, or in fact for a long time, commerce was probably of little consequence and the Nri legends say very little about this. In fact when *Nri's* neighbours came pressing him for his food crops, he told them he would not sell. Thus in one version, as shown above, the contract for making food available to all peoples was between *Chukwu* and *Nri*, the people playing no part in it. In the other version, also mentioned, it is said the people offered cocks, pots, goats and so on in return for the food crops. This may well be a reference to the eventual development of an exchange economy based at first on barter. But we hear little about this in the legends since Nri hegemony had very little to do with commerce and trade but was founded mainly on the control of the *Yam Force* (*Ifejiọku*) and Earth Force (*Ala, Ani, Ajala*) which were the key factors in the agricultural phase of Igbo history during which the *Nri* came into prominence.

From the above analysis, therefore, it would appear quite evident that the emergence of a distinct Igbo culture and the rise of the Nri as a dominant group was directly related to the coming of iron technology and agriculture into Igbo society. But a question which arises from this is what part did the present inhabitants of the Nri-Awka area play in this revolution. Were they the first group of Igbo-speaking peoples to acquire these revolutionary techniques and therefore the first people who introduced them into Igbo land? Or was it that they simply exploited ideas and techniques which were already well-established in the community in which they lived? There is no easy answer to these questions but a few comments may be made here.

As already shown above, Mr. Jeffreys is of the view that the Nri were a branch of a group of military adventurers and culture carriers from the east and that they introduced these new techniques amongst the Igbo who, before this providential conquest, 'walked about in the bush like animals'. But as also already shown his hypothesis has weaknesses so serious as to make it untenable. Still it is possible that the Nri introduced these techniques into Igbo land without necessarily being a branch of Jeffreys's Heliolithic peoples from the east. If the Upper Niger Valley was as important a centre in the evolution of Negro African civilization as modern research would appear to make it, then it is quite possible that these ideas in moving down the river would penetrate the Nri-Aguleri zone in the Anambara basin first and from there spread to other parts of Igbo land. Here it may be necessary to point out that Mr. Onwụejeọgụ has come to emphasize the probable primacy of the upper Anambra valley as a centre of civilization ancestral to Igbo and Igala cultures. 'Nri oral tradition', he argues,

> indicates that an early civilization was nurtured on the valleys of the upper Anambra and in due course a part moved westward to the northern part of the lower Niger Basin to develop the proto-dynastic cultures of the Igala as fossilized in the Onoja-Oboni clan in Idah. A part moved southwards to Aguleri and then to Nri and Oreri.[36]

But there are certain facts which would appear to make it unlikely that the *Nri* were the first to introduce these techniques into Igbo land. The first is that the Nri are not in fact among the great farming communities of Igbo land. The land on which they live is not fertile. On this Mr.Ọnwụejeọgwụ has written:

> Around Awka, Nri, Nanka, Nnewi and Igbo-Ukwu, farming is not very productive, because the soil has been subjected to centuries of surface erosion and leaching. This disaster which might have begun dozens of centuries ago might have set in a serious famine still remembered in oral tradition.[37]

Could this have been caused by excessive cultivation in which case the Nri may well once have been great farmers? But this is unlikely for Aguleri which, according to the same Nri legends, was one of the earliest sites of Igbo settlement is still very fertile and a key zone for Igbo agriculture. According to the same legends, when the Nri settled where we now find them it was already an *agụ*, and because it was so extensive and unoccupied they put the suffix—*ukwu* to it to get the name of their capital city *Agukwu*. The word *agụ* which Jeffreys probably accurately renders as *prairie* has an undertone of *poor* and *porous soil* and would indicate that the area in question was probably never important for agriculture.

But since the coming of agriculture into Igbo land was said to have taken place at Aguleri where the *Nri* first lived, it could be argued that they first acquired and practised it at Aguleri or even further north before moving south. And that it was the poverty of the latter place that left them clinging on to life by manipulating the rituals of a technique of which they were the first practitioners in Igbo land. But this raises the question why a community of great farmers would abandon a fertile area like Aguleri for their present habitat. It could not have been as a result of war for there is no trace of this in the traditions of either the Nri or Aguleri. And in any case these same traditions indicate that the Umunri were the senior partner of the two, not only in ritual status, but also in population.

This leaves one with the second alternative that the Nri came to attain dominance in a predominantly agricultural community, not because they were the first to introduce the technique but by systematically building up for themselves the position of a privileged group specially vouchsafed access to and control of those *vital forces* that rule the life of every farming Igbo community. In that case, in the legends discussed above we see the deliberately and carefully formulated ideology with which the Nri buttressed their claims and functions. And Mr. Ọnwụejeọgwụ has pointed out that the geographical location of

Nri headquarters aided their assumption of this status. On this matter he has written

> The topographic location of Nri in a depression, thickly forested and almost encircled by high ridges might have contributed to almost near complete isolation of Nri from other Igbo settlements. It is not therefore surprising that in the past Nri men were seen performing politico-ritual and ritual-political services without anyone knowing definitely where they came from.
>
> The mysterious and awe-inspiring attributes associated with Nri is (thus) partly derived from the physical isolation of Nri....[38]

Mr.Ọnwụejeọgwụ's work is still in progress and he has not finally formulated his views on these matters. But he appears to subscribe to the view that Nri ascendency was probably based on the emergence of a new cosmological system which they claimed to have special powers of controlling. Whether this means that he does not subscribe to Dr. Jeffreys hypothesis that it was based on the introduction of iron and agriculture is not certain as he is yet silent on that. 'It seems', he argues

> that a basic autochthonous culture had long been established probably before A.D. 900 in the upper Anambra. Around A.D. 900 one of these autochthonous cultures of the Anambra Valley developed new ideas, giving rise to a new culture—the Nri culture.... It is very probable that the autochthonous Igbo culture of the Pre-Nri period had not developed the concept of 'Chukwu'. Nri people developed the concept of 'Chukwu' and a theocratic monarch that controlled the 'earth force' by the use of ọfọ.[39]

This calls for a few comments. Whether it was the Nri who originated this new body of ideas, this new cosmology or not, is still to be established. For now the present writer is only prepared to subscribe to the view that they attained eminence by manipulating that cosmology. That much is certain from a study of the nature of their hegemony which will be given below. Also it is necessary to point out that if the Nri 'developed the concept of Chukwu' it is strange that they did not base their influence to any significant extent on the control of that power. It was the Aro who achieved a more of less unparalleled hegemony by claiming the power to manipulate that force, and they were so successful that they soon came to be known as the 'sons of Chukwu'. The Nri on their side were satisfied to base their claims on the manipulation of *Chukwu's* feminine counterpart—*Ala*.

This question of whether the Nri originated and spread this

new cosmology or merely exploited what already existed is no idle academic matter. It is fundamental to the question of the extent of their hegemony in its heyday. If they originated such basic Igbo cosmological ideas and institutions as *Chukwu*, *Ala* (the Earth force), *Ifejioku* (the *yam force*), *ofo*, (the all-important Igbo ritual staff for controlling virtually every known spirit force), then one must conclude that at one time or the other they controlled the entire Igbo land for these are the basic ingredients of the culture of any community that claims or is claimed to be Igbo. And in that case the *Nri* must be considered one of the most successful missionary groups of all time. There would appear to be a contradiction between the view that the Nri originated these ideas and the view that their area of influence was limited largely to the section of Igbo land delimited as Northern and Western Igbo by Forde and Jones in their ethnographic survey of the Igbo and Ibibio peoples. On this question of the extent of *Nri* hegemony Mr. Onwuejeogwu has written:

> Sufficient facts have been collected, which indicate that in the past Eze Nri at Nri, at different periods controlled certain aspects of ritual, political and economic activities of the older Igbo settlements lying between Agbo in the West and Nsukka in the East and between the upper part of Anambra to the North and Okigwe in the South.[40]

Dr. Talbot on his side thought Nri influence was limited to the 'western Igbo' by which, judging from his other discussions of this matter, he probably meant Igbo land west of Okigwe. The area in the centre, to the east and south he said was under the control of the Aro.[41] These efforts at delimitation are necessarily approximate. The present writer has discovered that the further east the Nri priest, the Awka smiths and the Umudioka carvers and surgeons went the more indistinguishable one from the other they became. Thus in some of the villages east of the Okigwi escarpment, that is in the Cross River Plain, these peoples were undifferentiatedly referred to as *Ojenamuo* or *Ojenammam* (those who walk the land of the dead). Thus it may well be that the influence of these men went further than has so far been considered likely or possible. It is quite possible that a more comprehensive research than has so far been done may reveal many more different names by which the Nri and their associates were known in parts of Igbo land distant from their home land, and thus establish that their influence was more widespread than has hitherto been suggested.

But this notwithstanding, it is also possible to show that there were parts of Igbo land, especially the southern and the eastern fringes of Igbo land where Nri influence hardly got to, or in any case was at best mimimal. Yet in some of these areas we have many of the above concepts and institutions usually attributed to Nri origin being more highly developed than in other parts of the Igbo culture area. Thus the *Chukwu* concept achieved its maximum development and manipulation among the Aro, a small Igbo community on the border with the Ibibio. Furthermore the concept of *Ala, Earth Force*, attained its finest development among the Ngwa, another group of the Igbo probably beyond the territorial limits of Nri hegemony.

What, one may ask, was the exact nature of the hegemony which the Nri exercised over those parts of Igbo land which came under their effective influence? Many writers have made general statements on this matter, but as far as the present writer is aware no really satisfactory analysis of it exists. Nor can we expect a comprehensive assessment probably until the Nri research project currently going on has been completed and the report made public. But a beginning could be made here and now by taking a fresh look at the available evidence.

The first, and perhaps the most important point to note, is that the character of this hegemony was determined by the fact that it rose in a predominantly rural and agricultural community and probably long before the commercial aspect of the life of that community had been fully developed. By the time the latter development took place, Nri hegemony had not only matured but ossified and so could not successfully adjust to it. Thus Nri dominance was founded on the control and manipulation of the Igbo agricultural world. On the one hand this meant the control of the agricultural cycle and calendar. The Igbo year was a rather complicated one since it was not only divided into days (each of which was divided into *ụtụtụ*—morning, *ehihe*—afternoon, *mgbede* or *ururuchi*—evening, *anyasi*—night), weeks (*izu*—with *izu nta*, four days and *izu ukwu*, eight days) moons (*onwa*—thirteen in the year); but also into ritual and farming cycles. This created the need for specialists who, from observing the heavenly bodies and the seasons, would declare the beginning and the end of each moon or cycle or year. This, in Igbo, was known as *Ịgụ Afọ* (counting the year) and was very important since to it was tied the very survival of the community. A miscalculation could mean starting to plant in the wrong month which in turn would mean a bad harvest and then famine and disaster.

In Igbo land this was and still is in many parts a very formal ceremony requiring public announcement, acclamation and at times celebration. Writing on eighteenth century Igbo land Olaudah Equiano said:

> We had priests and magicians, or wise men... They calculated our time, and foretold events, as their name imported, for we called them Ah-affoe-way-cah, which signifies calculators or yearly men, our year being called Ah-affoe.[43]

And on the ceremony of calculating the year he said:

> We compute the year from the day on which the sun crosses the line; and on its setting that evening, there is a general shout throughout the land; at least I can speak from my own knowledge, throughout our vicinity. The people at the time make a great noise with rattles... and hold up their hands to heaven for a blessing. It is then the greatest offerings are made; and those children whom our wise men foretell will be fortunate are then presented to different people.[44]

This keeping of the calendar and the proclamation of the different ritual and economic cycles was only one aspect of the business of ensuring rich harvests. There were more direct steps which the Nri had to take in this regard. They had to prepare the yam medicine, *ọgwụ ji*, at the right season for 'ensuring a plentiful supply of yams in all surrounding towns or in towns that subjected themselves to the eze Nri'.[45] Closely related to this was the business of removing *nsọ* or *arụ* (abomination) on which most scholars of Nri civilization have generally laid emphasis. The philosophy behind this was effectively summarized as long ago as 1906 by Major Leonard and should be quoted here if only to show again the extent to which Leonard's researches successfully recaptured many aspects of Igbo life and culture. 'Again', he wrote,

> there are certain actions which, as being, in the native opinion inconsistent with the requirements of the earth, are regarded as serious offences. Whenever, therefore, anyone belonging to a community commits an offence of this nature, the rest of the people take alarm because it is generally regarded as an upsetting of the order and harmony of things, both in their spiritual and temporal affairs. At this juncture the Nri step into the breach, as peacemakers, to effect a reconciliation between the offenders and the gods, for misconduct of this nature is always considered to be a crime against the land, or a general pollution of the material earth.[46]

The point is that such abominations, if not *removed* would anger the *Earth Force* and precipitate a number of disasters. One of these usually was that the *Earth* would refuse to reward the peoples' labour, that is to produce, and this would lead to bad harvests and famine. The other is that the *Earth would grow hot* (known in Igbo as *Ala iku oku*) leading to premature deaths and so on.

Another function of the Nri was to officiate in the ceremony of *title taking* (*ichi echichi*), an aspect which again Leonard, Thomas, Talbot, Basden, Jeffreys and Ọnwụejeọgwụ have emphasized in their writings—some calling it the 'crowning of kings' others the 'conferment of titles of nobility'.[47] But we still need to fit this into its proper context. In the early phases of Igbo culture history, agriculture was the main source of wealth and it remained so for centuries. In such a society title-taking was a form of public declaration that *mother-earth*, the *Earth Force*, had blessed a man's efforts, that he had achieved success. It was also in a sense a celebration of the fact that the Nri had been successful in keeping the *Earth Force* happy. The latter therefore had to be present at this celebration of their effective performance of the two major functions mentioned above—keeping the calendar and placating a fairly capricious deity. And they registered their presence by tying the *ngwulu* (ankle cord) round the legs of the titled man, and giving him an *ọfọ*. For these services the Nri had to be paid. But as time went on and trade became a major source of wealth, successful traders also sought for and obtained titles. In doing so they went through a ceremony which had long become standardized. But this fact should not prevent us from seeing that Nri participation in the title-taking ceremony over such a wide area probably originally derived from their established position as the chief manipulations of the *Earth Force* and agriculture on which the life of the community so heavily depended.

The Nri were also celebrated as peace-makers. Nót only were their persons sacred and therefore immune from violence, but they were particularly effective in settling disputes and separating combatants (*igbo ọgụ*) in those villages which came within the sphere of their influence. But although this function had political implications, it was not primarily a political one. It was another aspect of the control of the agricultural life of the people. Bloodshed generally was considered a serious offence, a crime against the *Earth Force* especially if it took place amongst peoples who could claim ritual or actual kinship. Such a serious crime against *Ala* was likely to interfere with rich harvests and had to be prevented. Should it occur at all, then the pollution had to be removed. There is evidence in the traditions that the Nri tried to go into some alliance with the Aro in order to control the ravages of the Abam which were believed to be *spoiling the land through bloodshed.*

From these four main functions there derived a fifth, the making of different types of medicines (*ọgwụ*) and divining (*ịgba afa*). With their reputation as controllers of the all important *Earth Force*, of *Ifejioku* and a number of other *spirit forces* that inhabit or haunt the world of rural agricultural communities, the Nri came to be seen as a people with a peculiarly effective access to the entire spirit world and therefore able to cure illnesses, tell fortunes and manipulate the ancestors and the spirits. The people of this general area, especially those from Nando, were widely famed as native doctors. In parts of the Okigwi and Bende Divisions, and perhaps in many other places, they were known either as *Ojenamọ* or *Ojenammam* (those who walk the land of the dead).

In sum therefore, the nature of Nri hegemony was largely ritual, religious and psychological, but because of the holism of the Igbo world—the fact that there were no clear distinctions between the religious, the political and the economic—this meant that it was also economic and political. A refusal on the part of the Nri to remove pollution from a community would threaten such a community with economic disaster. It would also undermine the authority of anybody or group whose actions were deemed responsible for alienating the Nri. By the control of the yearly cycles, they also controlled the economic life of the people and to some extent even the movement or utilization of labour. In the same manner their role in *ichi echichi* had economic and political implications. By helping people to attain this status which was vested with so much prestige and ceremony they helped to stimulate the productive energies of the community as most people would struggle to earn the wealth that would qualify them to take titles. On the other hand titled men played a leading role in the social and political life of most Igbo communities. The role of the Nri in *ichi echichi* thus helped in the selection of the leadership elite of those communities which came under their influence. Through *ịtụ nsọ ana* (revealing those things the *Earth Force* abhored) they played a part of fundamental importance in legislation and the interpretation of existing laws, customs and traditions.

The result of all these was that in some Igbo communities the Nri exercised an influence almost amounting to rulership. On this Mr. Ọnwụejeọgwụ has written:

> The power and authority of Eze Nri were based on the belief and recognition of many Igbo settlements that Eze Nri had spiritual authority over them. In Igbo traditional concept, spiritual and temporal authority cannot easily be isolated, one implies the other. Thus a ritual taboo placed on a settlement paralysed the physical movement of the people to and from the settlement. Similarly a ritual curse imposed on a settlement by Eze Nri was believed to cause an epidemic of small pox and paralyse economic activities of the settlement... Nri men would withdraw from the settlement leaving it in a state of ritual blockade and siege. It would in addition be in a state of economic blockade as its markets would be closed....[48]

Mr. Ọnwụejeọgwụ has collected his information mainly from Nri, and it would be understandable if the picture is a little overdrawn. The political fragmentation of the Igbo, the fact that each village-group cherished its autonomy imposed a serious limitation to the use of this influence and power. Thus each village-group in Igbo land usually had its own families reputed as ritual specialists, diviners, doctors and even artists and surgeons who could be called upon to play these roles when the situation in question was not considered very grave or the Nri and their associates were not easily available. As a result, in some settlements, the use of Nri men became the momentous exception rather than the routine practice. But there is no doubt that in most of those communities under effective Nri hegemony, the use of Nri priests and diviners was usually considered desirable for as Major Leonard correctly pointed out

> it is... believed that no religious rite is so striking or so effectual as that which is performed by these (Nri) priests, who hold their office merely as a divine and sacred right; for by virtue of this sacred priority they are said to be in possession of numerous attributes that have been imparted to them by their ancestors.... Moreover, they have a special and peculiar method of utilizing or expressing these attributes. Indeed their manner of conducting religious ceremonies, more especially with regard to touch, and to the way in which they handle the various emblems of worship, is considered to be particularly practical and effective.[49]

But this is not to say that they had attained indispensability, a state which even some Igbo gods could not attain. There are many instances, recounted in tradition, in which Igbo communities took particularly implaccable gods beyond the village frontiers and consigned them to flames.

Another question of interest is the age of this culture in which the Nri achieved their dominance, that is at what point in time it probably came into existence. This, it must be confessed, is a tricky question, a dangerous bait for the romanticist and the sceptic alike. But again with the aid of what solid evidence we have of the probable antiquity of the institution of *Eze Nri*, it should be possible to arrive at some cautious estimate until more archaeological work has been done in the area as in other parts of Igbo land. The evidence just referred to is Professor Shaw's archaeological find at Igbo-Ukwu close to Oreri, the latter village being, according to tradition, a splinter-group of Agukwu—the Nri of most writers on this matter. It is probably no longer in doubt that the artistically highly impressive and ritually very symbolic bronze finds made by Shaw are to be regarded as associated with the divine kingship of Nri. Writing rather cautiously, probably owing to lack of adequate and up-to-date ethnographic support, Professor Shaw said:

> It is inviting to associate the finds at Igbo-Ukwu with the institution of the Eze Nri, the priest King of the Umeri clan of the Ibos ... The material remains found appear to have certain things in common with what is known about the practices associated with the institution of *Eze Nri*, but there are also certain noticeable differences—which are perhaps to be accounted for as changes which have come about in the institution during the passage of many centuries.[50]

Following up Professor Shaw's work and with an enormous amount of ethnographic evidence at his disposal Mr. Ọnwụejeọgwụ has little doubt that Shaw's Igbo-Ukwu finds belong to the institution of Eze Nri. The results of his researches, he argues, indicate that these Igbo-Ukwu finds 'belong to a highly symbolic and ritualized culture parallel to the highly symbolic and ritualized cultures' existing in that area and its environs today. A brief comparative list, he goes on,

> will illustrate this point. The coiled python snake in the Igbo-Ukwu finds parallel in the occurrence all over the area of the taboo against killing and eating the python snake (*Eke*). The bronze pendant with the facial marks (*Itchi*) is similar to the facial marks still to be found all over the area and more identical to the type that spreads down the neck and cheeks still to be found on living human faces at Umana and Ebenebe north east of Awka etc.[51]

Now the Igbo-Ukwu finds have been radiocarbon-dated to about the middle of the ninth century A.D. Professor Shaw's reconstruction of the culture and the institution with which these finds were associated show that by the date recorded, the communities around Igbo-Ukwu had attained a high degree of social sophistication and evolved an economy based on the cultivation of yams and long ranging trade.[52] The close similarity which scholars have noticed between the culture depicted by the Igbo Ukwu finds and the culture of the Northern Igbo in the present century attests to something like the rate at which these societies changed over the centuries. Using this criterion as some sort of guide one can say the culture with which the Igbo-Ukwu bronzes were associated must have taken at least a millenium and a half to attain that degree of sophistication and social wealth. That takes us back to about 600 B.C. Now Mr. Onwuejeogwu in his paper 'An Outline Account of the Dawn of Igbo Civilization' says it was probably around A.D. 900 that one of the earlier autochthonous cultures of the Anambra basin underwent drastic changes 'giving rise to a new culture—the Nri culture'.[53] This however is strange in the light of the date established for Shaw's finds and in the light of the argument adduced above. The ultimate solution to the question as already pointed out lies in more archaeological work in the Igbo area which may help to establish the earliest dates for the iron and agricultural revolutions in Igbo land.

However, scientific method requires not that we impose a moratorium until such counsels of perfection are attained but that we draw tentative conclusions on the basis of the available evidence. Among such evidence, apart from that already mentioned, is Professor Hartle's archaeological work in Nsukka which returned results showing that by about 2555 B.C. Neolithic communities using more or less the same type of pottery as the Nsukka peoples of today were already occupying those highlands. This could be regarded as an upper limit for the origin of the culture in question. The other point that ought to be taken into account is Professor Rubin's very remarkable argument that it may well be wrong to regard Nok as the ancestral centre from which iron technology, bronze casting and other aspects of culture diffused south. The Nok area, he points out, is probably one of the least habitable areas of the Nigerian savanna-forest interface and therefore the least likely centre at which civilization could have originated in these regions.[54]

The contest for that envied position is thus still open. Unless we are to rule out from the contest on *a priori* grounds certain sections of this savanna-forest interface, it may well prove rewarding to consider the claims of the Anambra basin. By about the ninth century we had here communities capable of producing artifacts of such rich artistic beauty used for purposes suggestive of highly developed social and cosmological values and ideas.

The relationship between the Igbo culture area and other important cultural centres like Idah and Benin has engaged the attention of a number of scholars. But in this, as in the treatment of many other aspects of their history, the Igbo have received less than their due. This is in spite of what the available traditions claim. On relationship between Nri and Idah, for instance, the tendency has been to say the Nri are Igala. Writing in the 1930s for instance, Mr. G. J. Lawton said that Nri deserved close study but 'must carefully be distinguished from the Ibo tribe. The Nris are of Igarra stock who spread southwards from Idah.'[55]

What, one may ask, was his evidence for this opinion? Mr. Lawton interviewed a number of people at Nri and none at Idah and recorded the testimony of two of his Nri informants. One of these, Chief Henry Umeadi, whom he described as 'one of the most intelligent chiefs' in the Division told him 'there were five brothers, Igarra, Igbariam, Amanuke, Agoleri and Nri, and that Igbariam was originally Igarras'.[56] The other informant Obalike of Nri, disagreed with Chief Umeadi, insisting the Nri came from Aguleri, though related to 'Igbariam and to Igarra'.[57] These statements could mean one of three things: (1) that the Igala came from Umunri, (2) that the Igala and the Umunri originated from a third stock, (3) that the Nri came from Igala. For reasons which are not quite clear to the present writer, Mr. Lawton preferred the third interpretation. In fact in the context of the rather vague and all embracing Igbo kinship terminology, *nwa nne* (child of the same mother, which is what Lawton translated as 'related') could mean no more than just ritual kinship based on blood-oath or blood covenant (*Igbandu*).

On the same matter Dr. M. D. W. Jeffreys wrote in 1956: 'If the Umundri are not of actual Igala extraction, then the Umundri and Igala have a common origin'.[58] However the whole tone of his writings on this matter shows that he was inclined to the first alternative. Again it can be shown here, as was done in the case of Mr. Lawton that Jeffreys tended to give more weight to the scantier Igala claims than to the fuller Igbo accounts of relations between the two on which Jeffreys in fact had more information than Lawton had and should have been able to revise the latter's earlier conclusions. For instance the Nri were able to furnish Jeffreys with a rich tradition accounting for the origin of Idah, and 'showing' that the Igala descended from a younger son of Eri their founder. On this they said:

> Eri had another wife (apart from Namaku), and from her came Idah. He was the only child of his mother, and when Eri died she fearing lest his four half-brothers by the Namaku, would destroy him, advised him to separate from them and make a place for himself. She made magic with a round stone which she placed on Idah's head, and sent him across the Niger and told him to walk with the stone on his head and not to touch it with his hands. He was to settle where the stone fell. He did so and that is how the town of Idah started.[59]

Jeffreys informants again told him that the Nri enjoyed the right of crowning the Attah of Idah and mentioned the names of three people then still alive, who had officiated at the coronation of an Attah of Idah. Jeffreys was unable to cross-check this information with the men in question. One may now ask what evidence Jeffreys had to suggest to him that the Nri were probably of direct Igala extraction. This would appear to be no more than the vague claim in Idah 'that the Attah bestows titles on the neighbouring Igbo'.[60]

The treatment of oral tradition has undergone far-reaching revolutions since the days Jeffreys grappled with these intractable problems. It would no doubt be absurd to regard these traditions as embodying the factual report of the origins of the two peoples. If the Igbo and the Igala were of the same stock, from what we now know of the distance between their languages, it is unlikely that this fact would still survive in oral tradition today in such picturesque details. We have to deal with the entire corpus as one would deal with a coded message. To the present writer the import of the claim that Idah was the son of a younger wife of *Eri* would appear to be that the Idah monarchy was younger than the priest-kingship of Nri, a claim that now appears most likely from what we know of the probable age of the Nri culture and the rise of Idah during the first half of the second millenium A.D. Also the claim that Idah was founded from Nri could be seen as that the stimulus behind the rise of the

Igala kingdom with capital at Idah came from Nri. This again was a likely thing judging from the long-ranging activities of Nri priests and diviners, and the Igala tradition that their first Asadu was an Igbo.[61] If all these were the case, then the Nri claim of officiating at the coronation of an Attah would fall in place. In any case the very fact that Nri traditions about Idah are richer and more comprehensive than Idah traditions about Nri probably reflects the fact that in the relations between the two, Nri remained the senior partner, ritually at least and on grounds of chronological seniority.

A similar tendency to suppress Igbo claims to primacy or even parity and to play up the claims of their neighbours has characterized the treatment of Igbo-Benin relations in the pre-colonial era. This has also happened in the case of Nri relations with Benin. Thus in his account of the Igbo-Ukwu discoveries, the only significant reference by Shaw to Nri-Benin relations was his suggestion that probably after some disaster, the casters that made the Igbo-Ukwu bronzes ceased to exist. Thus it became necessary to send to Benin which had meanwhile become an important centre for bronze casting, for the brass pectoral mask which formed part of the ritual regalia of the Eze Nri.[62] Even assuming that his was so, would it not imply earlier contact between Benin and Nri when the latter was in the ascendancy and that even after Nri's supposed decline that her priests and diviners continued to scour Edo lands which would explain how they came to know of Benin as an important centre for bronze casting?

Yet Nri has never made any secret of its primacy over Benin. In the first decade of this century, the Eze Nri told Northcote Thomas that among the areas subject to him was Idu, the common Igbo name for Benin.[63] On the same matter Mr. Lawton wrote:

> A marked feature of this (Nri) tribe is its hostility to the European natural enough when it is remembered that prior to the arrival of the British *the Obalike was Eze Nri and crowned the Kings of Benin and generally presided over all the religious observances of surrounding peoples.*[64]

The fact is that Igbo-Edo relations require closer and more objective study especially in the era of Nri ascendancy preceding the rise of the Edo monarchy. Jeffreys himself reported hearing stories that 'when a new king of Benin is enthroned an Umundri man must attend: no message is sent, merely a travelling Umundri is roped in.'⁶⁵ One may ask in what capacity the Nri man was present, and if at the time of the report he was 'merely roped in' had this always been the case? And in any case would that not imply that the Benin Empire came, at one time or the other, within the *ala mbia*⁶⁶ of the Nri? It is also noteworthy that the Aro claim to have been active in Benin during the early phase of the rise of that monarchy and that *Chima* the founder of Onitsha, supposed to be a Benin refugee, was in fact an Aro agent operating in Benin city. Finally it is noteworthy that Edo historians have sought to grapple with the rather inconvenient facts of the relationship between their people and their Igbo neighbours. In doing this they have placed the emphasis on the period after 1500 when their empire was in the ascendant as a military power. But one would ask what the relationship was like before that date, or did the Edo and the Igbo suddenly become aware of each other in the sixteenth century. Would Benin's campaigns towards the Niger not suggest that before that kingdom achieved stability and regular existence that the Igbo and the Edo were in meaningful contact and that probably the Igbo occupied an important place in their calculations, whether economic or ritual? Jacob Egharevba, the renowned Bini traditional historian and chronicler, mentions Aro Chukwu, on the Eastern boundary of Igbo land as a Bini outpost, in fact a provincial capital.⁶⁷ Taken literally this would make no meaning. But we can see the claim as suggestive of the fact that the Aro featured sufficiently prominently on the Bini horizon as to be fitted into the Bini world in some manner. And for an expansionist and imperialistic state this meant fitting it in as a province of the glorious Empire.

There certainly was more to Bini-Igbo relations than military 'conquests' and 'subjugations' in the 400 years before British conquest. Probably the more enduring contacts and inter-reactions between the two predated the rise of Bini to imperial greatness, going back to those quieter days when Nri priests moved from 'one corner of the globe to the other' (*eluwa dum*) spreading the gospel that they came down from the sky and that *Chukwu* had empowered them to crown kings, make yam medicine, remove *nso*, control the agricultural calendar and make peace in return for giving yam and other food crops to all peoples.

Writing on Edo market days, Egharevba says:

There are four days in the week representing the four quarters of the earth, namely *Eken* (the East) *Orie* (the West) *Okuo* (the North) and *Aho* (the South). *Eken* is a day of rest. People do not go to the farm on that day but may do any work in the home.[68]

Egharevba does not tell us how the names came about. The Nri say the days of the Igbo week—*Eke, Orie, Afọ (Ahọ)* and *Nkwọ*—were revealed to them in the beginning by *Chukwu*, and that these were the names of sky-beings or spirits. *Eke* is the first day of the Igbo four-day week. It is their sabbath on which farm work may not be done. It was the day *Chukwu* created man. Furthermore, just as the Edo week days are pairs of opposite: East-West, North-South, so are the days of the Igbo week. *Eke* and *Afo* are men, and being men are the husbands of *Orie* and *Nkwo* in that order. These close similarities are striking. They cannot be explained by military imperialism originating in the sixteenth century. They may be explained by ritual and religious hegemony going back to the first millenium A.D. or earlier. The Aro explain them by saying they taught the Edo these mysteries of life and of the universe.[69] But it is more likely that if the Edo got their cosmological education from an Igbo group, it was more likely to have been from the missionaries of Nri, the Holy City of the Igbo-speaking peoples.

I mention these traditions because they deserve to be investigated further rather than suppressed as inconvenient 'facts'. It would in fact be no surprise if the Nri ritually and spiritually dominated much of south-central Nigeria (the present Bendel) and South-eastern Nigeria (Nigeria south of the Benue) in the centuries before the rise to eminence of Benin and Idah. After all, as has been pointed out by Mr. M. A. Ọnwụejeọgwụ, in Nri we probably have the most highly developed priest-kingship in West Africa.[69] It was the view of Jeffreys, when he was investigating Nri culture in the 1930s, that he was 'witnessing the last stages of the decay and breakup of what must have been at one time a large empire'.[70] No doubt Nri influence must have paled with the rise of the two militaristic states of Benin and Idah on its frontiers. Nri's influence was, as already emphasized ritual and cultural. And the historian would be unrealistic to expect to hear much of the still small voice of culture and ritual in an era filled with the intoxicating din of war drum and armed clashes of the two rival militaristic states of Benin and Idah, unless he keeps his ears very close to the ground.

Surely, it was not just the rise of Benin and Idah that was solely responsible for the gradual recession which probably set in for the Nri from about the time of those events. There was a more fundamental flaw in the culture which Nri manipulated to attain eminence. This was that it was based on a set and rigid cosmological concept which did not easily adjust to change. Religion and ritual are probably in the most conservative spheres of man's life. Nri rose on the manipulation of *spirit forces* and to the end sought to subject every thing to such manipulation. They rose to eminence in a predominantly agricultural age. Later, trade came to be a fairly important economic activity. But the Nri never became great traders. They were satisfied to make medicine and manipulate the *spirit forces—Eke, Orie, Afọ* and *Nkwọ*—each of which ruled its own Igbo market day. It was the Aro who had the ruthlessness to convert their own shrine into a commercial institution.

This will help us to appreciate to the full a point made by Mr. Ọnwụejeọgwụ. He explained Nri's stagnation and decline in terms of a 'ritual philosophy' that 'was constant' and which because it saw homicide as a 'sin against the Earthforce' hindered the growth of militarism. Consequently, he says,

> Blacksmiths around made spears and cutlasses and in later dates dane guns. But these primitive instruments of naked force were transformed into ritual objects. Thus spears were used as the staff of peace (*Ọtọnsi*), and as the staff of political office (Alo). The club was used as the staff of ritual-political authority (ofo), and cutlasses as objects of yam cult (Ifejioku).

This remained so with the Nri to the end. When the nineteenth century European missionaries started penetrating the African interior, various African rulers and interest groups sought to secure military equipments and the arts of carpentry, tailoring, book learning and so on from them. Some failed, some succeeded. When some Nri agents got in touch with the C.M.S. missionaries at Onitsha they asked for items to augment their ritual symbols. One of them had on the first visit obtained a small looking glass from Rev. J. C. Taylor and his group. He soon came back, and what happened on this occasion has been preserved for us in Taylor's journal which is quoted below:

> About noon, the former Itshi man, to whom Mr. Jonas gave a small mirror came to pay us another visit. He told us that the looking glass we gave him broke. We told him that we were sorry about it, but how

did he manage to get it broken. He frankly told us without concealment that as he was a great doctor, pretending to drive out *moa* (spirits) the people paid him so much respect ... One day he wanted to exhibit wonders to them, by saying he had been to see Beke or Oibo, his *moa* companions, they had given him a wonderful reflector. He then placed it upon his ofos and unfortunately smashed it to pieces. He came to ask us to spare him another or anything else.[72]

1905 was the year of the famed Onitsha Hinterland Expedition led by Colonel Moorhouse. With this the British gained effective control of the Awka area. Missionaries, traders and administrators followed suit into the interior. Soon there were complaints of all kinds of obstruction placed in the way of civilization, christianity and trade by the influence of the Eze Nri over a wide area. Apparently the British wanted to detach various villages and settlements from the Eze Nri but failed because the people warned that they would be committing *Nsọ* if they obeyed the British. The latter then decided to put an end to 'this barbarous nonsense' once and for all. And this was done at an impressive ceremony at Awka at which the Eze Nri himself officiated. *"All the tabus mentioned above in connection with human beings"*, wrote Dr. P. A. Talbot in 1926, *"were revoked at Awka in 1911 by the Ezana in the presence of Eze-Nri and other chiefs who at the end of each chant, during which they danced, and at the breaking of each Nsaw, touched the ground with their right fingers"*.[72]

In retrospect one cannot but see this as a dramatic and moving example of ritualized poetic justice in keeping with the ritual character of Nri hegemony. The Nri rose to eminence by manipulating the unseen forces that ruled their cosmos. They marked the formal end of this ascendancy by ceremonially 'terminating' those links that bound them to these forces. At least so the British thought. In reality, however, the Nri continued to pursue their ancient profession and to perform their traditional functions for over fifty years after. The famed *ojenamụọ* medicine men can still be seen, from time to time, 'walking the streets of the living' in villages as far away from Nri as those on the eastern side of the Okigwi highlands.

NOTES

1. Entries for 8, 27 and 29 August, 8 September 1857 and 18 January 1958 in the *Journal of the Rev. J. C. Taylor at Onitsha*, in S. Crowther and J. C. Taylor, *Niger Expedition 1857–59*, Frank Cass Reprint (London, 1968).

2. Holy Ghost Fathers, Onitsha Diocese: *Short Life of Bishop Shanahan*.
3. A. G. Leonard, *The Lower Niger and its Tribes* (London, 1906), pp. 34–6.
4. N. W. Thomas, *Anthropological Report on Ibo-speaking Peoples of Nigeria*, Part I (London, 1913), p. 48.
5. G. T. Basden, *Among the Ibos of Nigeria* (London, 1920).
6. G. T. Basden, *Niger Ibos* (London, 1938), p. xx.
7. P. A. Talbot, *Peoples of Southern Nigeria*, 4 Vols. (Oxford, 1926).
8. E.P. 8766, Awka Division, Intelligence Report by M. D. W. Jeffreys.
9. Memo. No. 90 of 23.3.31 from C. K. Meek, Anthropological Officer in AW. 444 Jeffreys M. D. W., D.O. Papers concerning.
10. N. W. Thomas, for instance, wrote 'The Ezenri or King of Nri, *a town otherwise known as Aguku*', *op. cit.*, p. 48.
    Dr. Talbot also wrote 'The right of conferring the title of Eze, or king, was conferred to the inhabitants of *the sacred town of Nri or Aguku*, sometimes called Nsi by distant Ibo, near Awka', *Peoples of Southern Nigeria*, Vol. 3, p. 395.
11. Chief S. O. N. Okafor, *The History of Umunri Clan* (Yaba, n.d.) p. 2.
12. M. A. Qnwuejeogwu, 'An Outline Account of the Dawn of Igbo Civilization in the Culture Area', *Odinani*, The Journal of the Odinani Museum, Nri, Vol. I, No. 1, March 1972, pp. 42, 44.
13. *Ibid.*, p. 45.
14. E.P. 6810, Intelligence Report on N.A. in Awka Division.
15. D. Forde and G. I. Jones, *The Ibo and Ibibio-speaking Peoples of Southeastern Nigeria* (London, 1950), pp. 30, 31.
16. Chief S. O. N. Okafor, *op. cit.*, p. 2.
17. E.P. 8766, Awka Division, Intelligence Report by M. D. W. Jeffreys.
18. M. D. W. Jeffreys, 'The Umundri Tradition of Origin,' *African Studies*, Vol. 15, No. 3, 1956, p. 131.
19. AW. 252, Anthropological Research, see Report by Jeffreys entitled 'Concise Report on the Ritual for acquiring the *ezeship* of Aguku (Nri) and of Qzq title in the Awka Division'.
20. *Ibid*.
21. E.P. 8766, Awka Division, Intelligence Report by M. D. W. Jeffreys.
22. M. D. W. Jeffreys, 'The Umundri Tradition of Origin', *loc. cit.*, p. 127.
23. *Ibid.*, p. 126.
24. *Ibid.*, p. 131.
25. W. B. Baikie, *Narrative of an Exploring Voyage up the Rivers Kwara and Benue in 1854*, Frank Cass Reprint (London, 1966), p. 307.
26. M. A. Qnwuejeogwu, 'An Outline Account of the Dawn of Igbo Civilization . . .', *Odinani*, Vol. I, No. 1, p. 40.
27. S. R. Smith, 'The Ibo People', 2 Vols (unpublished manuscript, 1929).
    M. D. W. Jeffreys, 'The Umundri Tradition of Origin', *loc. cit.*, p. 127.
    M. A. Qnwuejeogwu, 'An Outline Account of the Dawn of Igbo Civilization, etc.', *Odinani*, Vol. I, No. 1, pp. 40–1.
28. A.W. 252, Anthropological Research, see Report on Aguku by Jeffreys.
29. M. D. W. Jeffreys, 'The Umundri Tradition of Origin', *loc. cit.*, pp. 127–8.
30. According to traditions collected by the author from villages in the Otanchara clan of the Northern Igbo, there was another danger in feeding on this material. If one cut too much of it, it shrank in cooking and he would run the risk of not having enough to eat. If on the other hand one cut too little, it swole in cooking and if the one did not finish it at a sitting, the punishment was instant death. It was also said that when cooked, this material looked and tasted like the 'inside' (yolk) of an egg. The point of this description would appear to be to reinforce the point that one could easily have more of the *azu igwe* than he could finish; for among this people the egg yolk has a reputation

for *iju ọnụ* (filling the mouth) and *itụ mkpụ* or *igbụ agbụ* (getting one easily fed up [with eating it]).
31. M. D. W. Jeffreys, 'The Umundri Tradition of Origin', *loc. cit.*, p. 123.
32. N. W. Thomas, *op. cit.*, p. 138.
33. D. D. Hartle, 'Archaeology in Eastern Nigeria', *Nigeria Magazine*, No. 93, June 1967.
34. M. D. W. Jeffreys, 'The Umundri Tradition of Origin', *loc. cit.*, p. 121-2.
35. *Ibid.*, footnote 2 on p. 122.
36. M. A. Ọnwụejeọgwụ, 'An Outline Account of the Igbo Civilization, etc.', *Ọdịnanị*, Vol. I, No. 1. In fact Mr. Ọnwụejeọgwụ entitled an earlier version of this paper 'An Ethno-Historical Survey of an Anambra Civilization in the Lower-Niger Basin'.
37. *Ibid.*, p. 25-6.
38. *Ibid.*, p. 42.
39. *Ibid.*, p. 44.
40. *Ibid.*, p. 7.
41. P. A. Talbot, *Peoples of Southern Nigeria*, Vol. III, pp. 592, 596.
42. Entry of 18 January 1858 in the *Journal of Rev. J. C. Taylor at Onitsha*, in Crowther and Taylor, *op. cit.*, pp. 331-2.
43. Olaudah Equiano, *The Interesting Narrative of the Life of Olaudah Equiano or Gustavus Vassa the Africa.* Eighth Edition Enlarged (Norwich, 1794).
45. *Ibid.*, pp. 19-20.
46. A. G. Leonard, *op. cit.*, pp. 37-8.
47. *Ibid.*, pp. 34, 37-8.
    P. A. Talbot, *Peoples of Southern Nigeria*, Vol. III, pp. 595-6.
    G. T. Basden, *Among the Ibos of Nigeria*, pp. 78-9.
    N. W. Thomas, *op. cit.*, p. 51.
    M. A. Ọnwụejeọgwụ, 'A Short History of the *Ọdịnanị* Museum Nri', in *Ọdịnanị*, Vol. I, No. 1, p. 7.
48. M. A. Ọnwụejeọgwụ, 'An Outline Account, etc.', *Ọdịnanị*, Vol. I, No. 1, pp. 47-8.
49. A. G. Leonard, *op. cit.*, p. 30.
50. Thurstan Shaw, 'Igbo-Ukwu, Eastern Nigeria', in T. Shaw (ed.), *Nigerian Prehistory and Archaeology* (Ibadan University Press, 1969), p. 45.
    See also T. Shaw, *Igbo-Ukwu: An Account of Archaeological Discoveries, etc.*, p. 270.
51. M. A. Ọnwụejeọgwụ, 'A Short History of the Ọdịnanị Museum, Nri', in *Ọdịnanị*, Vol. I, No. 1, p. 6.
52. T. Shaw, *Igbo-Ukwu, An Account of Archaeological Discoveries, etc.*, pp. 268-85.
53. M. A. Ọnwụejeọgwụ, 'An Outline Account of the Dawn of Igbo Civilization, etc.', *Ọdịnanị*, Vol. I, No. 1, pp. 44-5.
54. Arnold Rubin, 'Review of (I) Philip Allison *African Stone Sculpture*, (II) Frank Willet *Ife in the History of West African Sculpture* in *African Notes*, Bulletin of the Institute of African Studies, University of Ibadan, Vol. 6, No. 2, 1971.
55. E.P. 6810, Intelligence Report on N. A. Awka Division.
56. *Ibid.*
57. *Ibid.*
58. M. D. W. Jeffreys, 'Umundri Traditions of Origin', *loc. cit.*, p. 126.
59. *Ibid.*, p. 121.
60. *Ibid.*, p. 125.
61. S. J. Boston, 'The Hunter in Igala Legends of Origin', *Africa*, Vol. 34, No. 2, 1964, p. 118.
62. T. Shaw, *Igbo-Ukwu, An Account, etc.*, p. 285.

63. N. W. Thomas, *op. cit.*, p. 51.
64. E.P. 6810, Intelligence Report on N. A. Awka.
65. M. D. W. Jeffreys, 'The Oreri Mask', in *The Nigerian Field*, Vol. 10, 1941, p. 142.
66. This is a technical Igbo term meaning a territory within the area of operation of ritual specialists or oracle agents.
67. Jacob Egharevba, *A Short History of Benin* (Ibadan University Press, Fourth Edition, 1968), p. 80.
68. *Ibid.*, p. 82.
69. I owe this information to Mr. K. O. K. Onyioha who has done a tremendous amount of work on Igbo traditions and cosmological ideas.
70. AW. 252, Anthropological Research. See the 'Concise Report on the Ritual for acquiring the ezeship of Agukwu (Nri) etc.', by Jeffreys.
71. M. A. Qṅwụejeọgwụ, 'An Outline Account of the Dawn of Igbo Civilization, etc.', *Ọdịnanị*, Vol. I, p. 50.
72. S. Crowther and J. C. Taylor, *op. cit.*, p. 261.
73. P. A. Talbot, *The Peoples of Southern Nigeria*, Vol. III, p. 725.

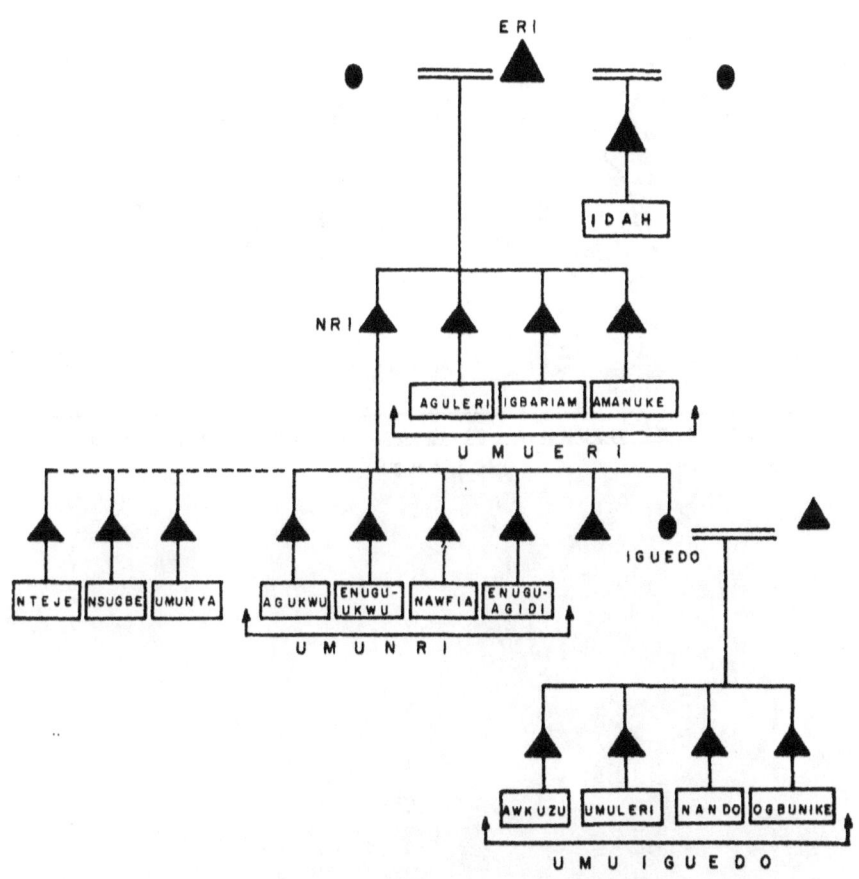

NRI GENEALOGICAL CHART

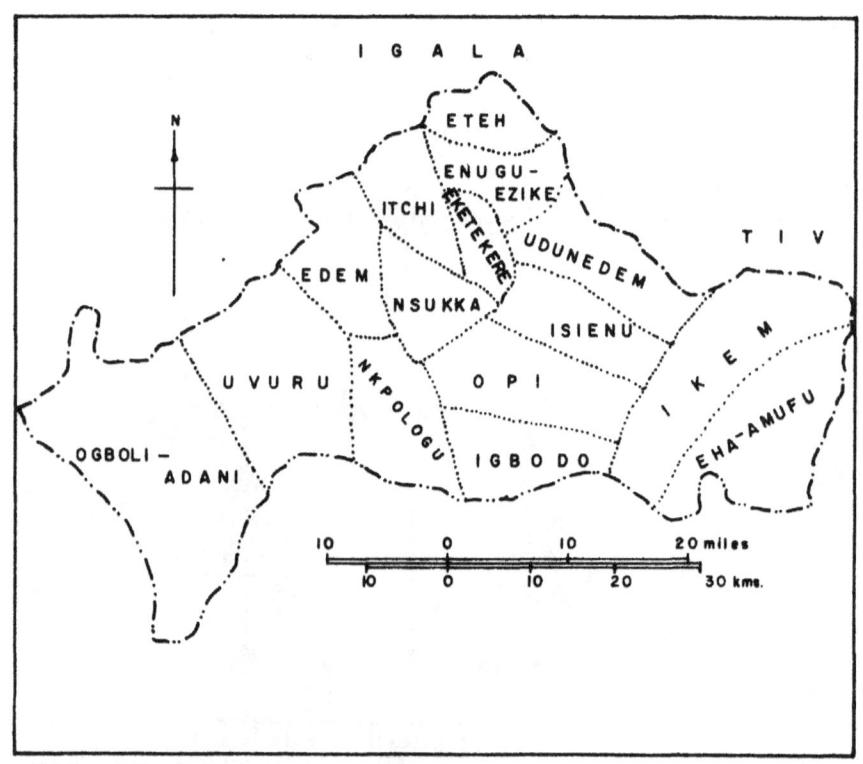

MAP OF <u>OLD NSUKKA DIVISION</u> SHOWING LOCAL GROUPINGS (CLANS)

3. Nsukka before 1916: The making of a Frontier Igbo Society

The communities dealt with in this paper occupy the northernmost portion of that section of Igbo land which ethnographers have traditionally described as Elugu (Elugwu) sub-cultural group of the Northern Igbo. They may be regarded as forming the arrow head of the Igbo drive, under the pressure of population in the palm belt to the south, northwards into the wooded savanna of the Middle Belt. To the north-east they are bordered by the Idoma (Àkpọ̀tọ̀—the Okpoto of colonial records) and to the north and north-west by the Igala. This group of Northern Igbo communities has two main distinguishing characteristics. The first is that unlike many other Igbo groups to the south, south-east and south-west of them, they did not attain the clan stage of social integration. In the Nsukka area the village-group, generally small in territorial and population size, was not only the largest unit of political integration as in other portions of Igbo land, but it rarely, if ever, had any strong or well-articulated traditions of common descent with neighbouring groups. Using the criterion of functional co-operation, especially alliances for offence and defence usually traced back to the nineteenth century or so (see below), ethnographers have grouped them into fourteen associations of villages. These are Ogboli-Adani, Itchi, Enugu-Ezike, Edem, Nsukka, Eketekere, Udunedem, Uvuru, Nkpologu, Opi, Igbodo, Isienu, Ikem and Eha Amufu.[1] Their second common characteristic, 'which they share with the communities of the Nri-Awka sub-cultural group of the Northern Igbo, is the strong evidence of Igala cultural impact. The extent and character of this and how it came about is one of the controversial aspects of these communities' history. This will be dealt with in some detail below.

These communities of the Nsukka area came to acquire a measure of political consciousness as a group under colonial rule, though not immediately with the onset of that era. First between 1906 and 1908 they were tagged on precariously to the administrative sub-district of distant Awka to the south-west. Then between 1908 and 1919 they were attached to the administrative division of Okpoga (the Okwoga of colonial records) in Idoma land. With the dawn of the third decade of this century, they were detached from Okpoga and constituted into, first the Obolo, and then the Nsukka Division. It was as Nsukka Division that this amorphous group of villages came to achieve a distinct identity in recent Nigerian history and politics. And in spite of the vagaries of administrative policies since 1967,[2] they have continued to regard themselves as one people with a unique interest in the context of local and national politics and development.

With regard to the reconstruction of their past, the peoples of Nsukka would appear to have been luckier than many other Igbo groups. The attempt to build a coherent perspective of their history could be said to go back to about 1930 when Dr. Charles Kingsley Meek wrote his fairly detailed *Ethnographic Report On the Peoples of the Nsukka Division, Onitsha Province*. Unlike many other ethnographical works of those and later days, Dr. Meek's *Report* combined to some extent the structural-functional with the historical approach. However, the trail which he blazed was only belatedly followed by others, in fact not until after at least a quarter of a century had passed by unutilized. But since the middle fifties Nsukka history has come to interest a number of people.

Among these is Mr. D. C. Ugwu, one of the prominent sons of Nsukka who in 1959 put out a booklet entitled *This is Nsukka* which could be described as a work of social and political history—particularly the latter. Exploiting oral traditions and archival materials, Mr. Ugwu traced the development of Nsukka over the centuries in a bid to get to the root of her contemporary problems and find solutions to them. In 1960, Nigeria's year of independence, Mr. J. S. Boston, then a Research Fellow in the Nigerian Institute of Social and Economic Research, published in the *Journal of the Historical Society of Nigeria* a very informative and learned paper entitled 'Notes on Contact Between Igala and the Ibo' in which he devoted some appreciable space to interaction between the Igala and the peoples of Nsukka over the centuries, mainly since the sixteenth century or so. Relying mainly on archival material and Igala oral sources he came to the conclusion that contact with the Igala was a major factor in the socio-political evolution of the Nsukka peoples. Then in 1966 the Department of Geography, University of Nigeria, Nsukka, produced a geographical appraisal of the Nsukka area. This offered Mr. S. C. Ukpabi of the Department of History of the same University the opportunity to attempt a summary of the existing evidence on the pre-colonial history of the area. Another contributor, Mr. J. E. Wilmer, discussed the political and administrative developments in the area under British rule. Finally since 1968 Mr. A. J. Shelton, who was formerly of the University of Nigeria, has been producing a number of studies of the Nsukka-Igala area as a culture contact zone. He has attempted, in an article, a critical analysis of the legend of Ọnọjọ Ogboni, one of the most widely distributed legends in the entire region. Also Professor Shelton has attempted an exhaustive ethnohistorical study of this zone in his book *The Igbo-Igala Borderland* which he sub-titled 'Religion and Social Control in Indigenous African Colonialism'.

It is probably accidental that so many people have come to be interested in the history of Nsukka. But the reason for their interest could be related to the fact that Nsukka is a frontier community, and that such communities often pose historical and other problems which scholars find both interesting and challenging. In this regard one advantage of being situated in a zone of intensive culture contact is that even scholars who may not ordinarily be interested in the history of the community as such, may be compelled to study it all the same in consequence of their interest in the past of the people just across the frontier. This has happened in the case of Nsukka. J. S. Boston's main interest is in the Igala kingdom. But in his pursuit of the development and structure of that kingdom he became involved in the study of aspects of Nsukka history. Also Professor Shelton's main interest would appear to be the entire Igala-Nsukka-Idoma culture contact zone. But as already mentioned this has drawn him into the early history of the Nsukka area.

A close study of the works of the scholars mentioned above will show that they have been pre-occupied with three main problems: the peopling of Nsukka, the nature of the impact of the Nri and Igala on Nsukka culture and society, and finally developments in Nsukka society in the course of the nineteenth century. The present writer strongly feels that the treatment of these problems has suffered seriously from a certain lack of critical awareness of the shortcomings of the sources used, especially of the colonial records. A failure to appreciate the theoretical assumptions behind the historical and ethnographical reconstructions attempted by the colonial researchers and administrators as well as the purposes these reconstructions were designed to serve is bound to lead to serious errors of interpretation.

The question of the peopling of the Nsukka area belongs to the larger problem of the origin of the Igbo-speaking peoples and how they came to occupy that portion of Southern Nigeria where we now find them, an issue in which we cannot hope to reach definite conclusions until more evidence is thrown up by linguistic and archaeological research. Those who have attempted to deal with this problem in its relation to the Nsukka area would appear to have been misled by certain traditions found in this region which should be better seen as concerned with an attempt to explain the derivation of the cultural influences which helped to determine the cultural landscape of the people. The groups of traditions referred to here look upon Nri and Idah as the homelands of certain communities in the area.

In the Eketekere group, for instance, the village-group of Ihọhọrọ claims that it was founded by a man called Owere Eze who 'came' from Idah.[3] The fact that all the names of this mythical founder are Igbo, and therefore that he could not have been an Igala and could not have come from Idah has not been sufficient to warn scholars against thinking that this story is a historical account of origins and migrations. In the same Eketekere group is the village-group of Ihaka which according to its own legendary history was founded by Oshi Amoke who was in turn said to have been the son of a man called Ọka Nandichie (Ọka in the olden days). The British officer who unearthed this story saw it as evidence of migration from Awka. He came to the same conclusion with regard to the village-group of Ihakpu which is said to have been founded by one Ọkara Ogbara.[4] With some village-groups, different sections have been derived some from Idah and some from Nri. Thus in the village-group of Nibo, one section claims descent from a man called Igbota who is said to have come from the north. In the context of the cultural idiom of this area this could be read as Idah since for these peoples the component elements of their society and culture are derived from two polar locations—Nri to the south and Idah to the north. The other half of the village-group, known as Ukpabi, is said to have been founded by a man called Dimaneke who is said to have come from Nri. According to the story this man left Nri in order to avoid *igbu ichi* (having his face marked with *ichi*).[5]

Reviewing these stories and others like them, Mr. S. C. Ukpabi came to the conclusion that many of these communities were founded by populations which moved into the area from Nri and Igala. With regard to the group from Nri he argues:

> The next influx of people came from the Nri group in Awka division. Moving north from the Awka-Orlu centre of settlement the migrants traversed the southern plains of the Anambra until they reached Nibo. From here the main arm struck eastwards through Nkpologu to engulf the villages south of Opi where Nri tradition is still very strong, whilst another arm curved north-eastwards through Ugbene, Nsukka and Eha Alumona.[6]

According to him these events took place in the seventeenth century in consequence of the expansion of Benin towards the Niger which he said forced many peoples to move eastwards.[7] The non-Igbo populations of the Nsukka area he regards as remnants of Igala invading armies who settled in the eighteenth century and were later augmented by refugees fleeing south in the wake of the Fulani wars of the nineteenth century.[8]

This hypothesis calls for a few observations here. Mr. Ukpabi's hypothesis of a wave of settlers from Nri agrees with the more generally held view that the Nri Awka, Orlu-Okigwi region is perhaps the earliest centre of Igbo settlement, and that from there two early waves of migrants left, one northwards to the Udi-Nsukka highlands and the other southwards to form the Southern Igbo.[9] One new element is Mr. Ukpabi's dating of this event. Those who subscribe to this view, men like Mr. G. I. Jones and Talbot, are inclined to believe that this migration took place so early in the history of the Igbo that it no longer survives in the traditions of the people. The new tendency to date this event to the seventeenth century and to link it with the expansion of Benin reminds one of a certain attitude which was quite common amongst the colonial administrators, that is the tendency to think that nothing important happened in Igbo land until the rise and expansion of Benin and Igala power and the onset of the transatlantic slave trade. This view we now know to be wrong. The peopling of Nsukka which we are talking of took place in remote antiquity and cannot be accounted for by events which occurred in the seventeenth century let alone in the eighteenth and nineteenth centuries. There is evidence which makes it reasonable to assume that by the fifteenth century the population map of Southern Nigeria had come to assume more or less the form it wears today. Mr. Ukpabi would also appear to concede that by the time his 'seventeenth century waves' arrived, the Nsukka area was already peopled. Thus he talks of these immigrants 'engulfing the villages to the south of Opi'. Another new element in his account is the precision with which he has traced the route followed by his would-be first settlers of Nsukka. The evidence for this, however, is nowhere hinted at let alone discussed in full. It is probably based on the assumption that his immigrants would necessarily prefer travelling along a plain to following the Udi-Nsukka highlands. Yet it is these highlands which appear to have the earliest evidence of human occupation and are more heavily settled today.

What, therefore, does one make of those traditions summarized above which apparently claim that the Nsukka area was settled in the probably not distant past, by immigrants from Nri and Idah? The key to the meaning of these legends perhaps lies in the fact that Nri and Idah were two important centres from which various items of culture diffused to the communities of the Anambra basin and the northern portions of the Udi-Nsukka highlands. It is, however, chastening to consider that many more communities in this area and beyond make similar claims to Nri and Idah origin, but on logical and commonsense grounds it is unlikely, if not impossible, that all these communities could have originated from these two centres. It appears reasonable to assume that these traditions merely indicate sources of cultural influence, and that the so-called ancestors refer to innovators who first imbibed and introduced into these communities specific aspects of these cultures, that they are best regarded as culture heroes rather than as genealogical fathers.

Criticizing the view which seeks to derive the different clans of the Igbo from the Nri, Mr. D. M. W. Jeffreys wrote early in the 1930s as follows:

> In the past it had been advanced that all the Igbo were descended from this group (the Nri). This statement confuses the origin of a culture with the origin of a people.

In his view what happened was that the Nri spread their culture to the rest of Igbo land rather than founded all Igbo communities.[10] This observation is also applicable to the Nsukka area. Writing in a similar vein Dr. J. S. Boston observed:

> Another difficulty about the origins of these migrants is that the general background evidence often suggests that the place of origin may be attributed on contemporary political rather than on strictly historical grounds. There seems a tendency for a group that is now connected politically with an area to be described as coming from that region.[11]

The type of attraction which Boston talks of here could also be exerted by a centre of undoubted ritual and religious eminence such as Nri and Idah were. It would thus be misleading to seek to account for the peopling of the Nsukka area in terms of these legends, including the legends of descent from Idah. The claim that the Nsukka Igbo area attracted Igala migrants in the eighteenth and nineteenth centuries will be dealt with when we come to consider Igala impact on this region.

One other area which has attracted attention in the attempt to account for the peopling of the Nsukka area is Enugu-Ezike, the northernmost Igbo community, and one of the fourteen groups into which the Nsukka communities have been divided. Enugu-Ezike is very densely populated, in 1953 its population was put at 61,000, with an average density of more than 800 persons per square mile. It is considered the most densely populated rural village-group in West Africa. For this reason ethnographers have been inclined to regard it as an area of 'early and probably independent... settlement',[12] a centre from which migrants went to settle the plains to the east of the Udi-Nsukka highlands. It is not quite clear what is meant here by an 'independent' centre of settlement—independent of what? This is of course an attempt to rationalize the high concentration of population in the Enugu-Ezike area, But it would appear to me that there are other more convincing explanations for this.

One is the physiography of the area—the fact that it is on a hill and appears to have a richer soil than many other portions of the Udi-Nsukka escarpment. It could also be accounted for in terms of that area having formed a population 'trap' as a result of the Igbo and their northern neighbours having achieved a 'balance of power' which made it difficult, if not impossible, for the Igbo to continue to expand northwards. The result would be that many more Igbo from the south, not knowing that the era of territorial expansion in this region was over, would for some time continue to pour into Enugu-Ezike only to find themselves 'trapped' and unable to gain more land to the north. It would require detailed investigation of Igbo-Igala relations in the past two centuries or so to confirm this. But even a mere look at the map which shows how this portion of Igbo land juts out into Igala land like an arrow-head would tend to suggest such an explanation. There is yet another likely explanation, and this is connected with the disturbed state of the central Nsukka escarpment in the nineteenth century which will be dealt with below. The insecurity which this caused, probably led to the movement of population northwards to Enugu-Ezike and southwards to the region lying between Opi and Ukehe which is another important area of population concentration. In contrast the central Nsukka area where most of these wars were fought in the last century is thinly populated. The coming of British rule helped to freeze this demographic accident.

A consideration of other available evidence of Nsukka's past and comparison with what is known about other parts of Igbo land and in fact of West Africa, would appear to indicate that the Nsukka area was settled very early in the history of the Igbo-speaking peoples. From linguistic evidence, the Igbo language would appear to be about 6,000 years old, or at least that estimate would give some idea of when it started emerging as a distinct form of speech. On the basis of similar evidence it is estimated that the peoples of southern Nigeria, and in fact of West Africa, would appear to have occupied the areas they now inhabit for thousands of years. Assessing the few facts we have about Nsukka in the light of these generally accepted deductions we begin to gain some idea of the antiquity of the Igbo communities of the Udi-Nsukka highlands and elsewhere.

One evidence is the absence of any clear traditions of migrations from elsewhere; all we appear to have is the kind of migration stories centred around culture heroes which we dealt with above. From this negative evidence one could argue that migrations into this region took place so long ago that they have been completely forgotten. When pressed for their original homeland, many communities in this area have returned the answer that they sprang from the soil. Eke Nweze of Ibagwa Nkwo claimed that God created Ibagwa-Nkwo where it is now found.[13] Reporting on the villages which make up the Igbodo group, a British officer wrote in the early 1930s

> With the exception of Umuna and Ohebe, no two villages claim a common ancestor, and in all cases the founder is assumed, for want of more accurate information to have arisen from the earth.[14]

During a recent seminar on the Nsukka peoples, Chief Peter Omeje, an elder of the Nsukka village-group, ridiculed all efforts to derive these communities from either Idah or Nri, asserting that their people have been here from the beginning of time!

These claims of springing from the ground have been explained in Chapter 1 as denoting antiquity as well as assertions of right to land. It could be argued that stories of earlier migrations may have been lost not so much because the events took place so long ago, as because the Nsukka communities, like other Igbo communities, being acephalous did not evolve institutions specialized in the preservation of oral tradition. This may well be so, but it may be relevant to bear in mind that what little archaeological evidence there is about the early history of these parts, would seem to point in the same direction as the above negative evidence. Thus a site at the University of Nigeria (Nsukka) Agricultural Farm which was test-excavated by Professor D. D. Hartle of the Department of History and Archaeology of the same University, yielded evidence of human presence in the nature of potsherds. Carbon-dated, this site returned a date of 2555 B.C. ± 130.[15]

To this, one may pose the question that if Nsukka was already occupied by human groups as early as the third millenium B.C., what evidence is there that these early occupants were the direct ancestors of the Igbo inhabitants of today? There is no direct evidence to that effect, but from indirect evidence one can make some tentative deductions. An analysis of the pottery sherds associated with the above site showed that these were unfired clay vessels 'much like the unfired clay vessels used in the area today'.[16] This conclusion suggests such a degree of enthnographic continuity as would tempt one to suggest that there has been continuous occupation by the same cultural group ever since. It is yet not known where the Igbo language started separating from its Kwa sister-languages, but should it be assumed to be around where the Igbo now live, which would help to explain the absence of Igbo linguistic enclaves or islands in any of the neighbouring areas, this would take Igbo occupation of these parts back to the fourth millenium B.C., a date which would make the occupants of the Nsukka area around the third millenium B.C. most likely Igbo. What ever happens, bearing in mind the probable region of origin of the Negro race, the Igbo must have come into Southern Nigeria from the Northern direction. Unless we make the unlikely assumption that they came in a single file, we have to assume that they came over a broad front in little groups over a long period of time. In any case they would settle the Nsukka area before going down to the area of modern Bende Division. Yet in the latter place the excavation of a site said to have been under continuous occupation until about 50 years ago yielded remains which have been carbon-dated to A.D. 805.[17] All these are highly significant and tend to suggest the antiquity of Igbo occupation as postulated above.

It is also significant that these Nsukka communities of about the third millenium B.C. are said to have attained the stage of 'well-developed Neolithic.'[18] From this evidence it is possible to postulate that they had attained such a level of social and economic stability as would enable them to perpetuate their kind over the area and around unless brought under overwhelming pressure and either driven out or exterminated. Some idea could be gained of the character of the Nsukka communities of those far-off days by comparison with other neighbouring West African groups of about the same date about whose society some definite characteristics have been postulated. Two such examples are the Yoruba-speaking peoples to the West of the Igbo and the Idoma-speaking peoples to the north-east just across the Nsukka border. Yoruba and Idoma are genetically related, and are said to have separated about 6,000 years ago. A study of the cognates still found in the two languages has shown that the original stock from which each language had hived off, already

> had pottery, at least in the form of large, open-mouthed *pots* that may hold beer. They had *rope*, *bags* and *boxes* and had some idea of *time*. They could count at least as far as *twenty*. They *hunted*, and they *worshipped* local gods or spirits, including *ancestral spirits*. They dug *graves* which were in some sense *taboo*. The men had *wives*. They lived in *houses* which they *built*. They had fire and canoes. . . . They kept *goats*. They grew several crops, including *beans*, *cotton* and *yams*. They had *markets* and *money* and bought (and sold) for *profit*. They had some form of legal procedure under which cases could be tried,

witnesses heard and people found *guilty*. . . . They drank *palm-wine* . . . They *cooked* their food etc.[19]

A comparison of the cognates from which these conclusions are drawn with their counterparts in the Igbo language are very illuminating. If these deductions are reasonable ones to make, we must agree with Professor Armstrong that West African Societies are very ancient indeed. And if the people who left the artifacts excavated by Professor Hartle at the University farm site were Igbo-speaking we would have to conclude that their societies were not very far from the stage of development which characterized the Igbo for the greater part of the second millinium A.D.

Judging by the traditions of the Nsukka communities, the next important landmark in their history was the extension of Nri influence to their area, an event which has survived in the form of migration stories of a few individuals each of whom was believed to have founded a village or village-group. No tradition has yet been unearthed about the coming of metallurgy or agriculture. The problem of the rise of the Nri to a position of eminence in Igbo land has already been discussed. The relative cultural sophistication of West African societies at about 4000 B.C. or so would seem to reinforce the argument advanced in Chapter 2, that the Nri achieved prominence probably not through the introduction of iron metallurgy and agriculture into these parts as postulated by Jeffreys, or by formulating a new cosmology as postulated by Mr. Onwuejeogwu, but by setting themselves up as manipulators of the *spirit-forces* underpinning an already existing culture. This would mean that the Nri made their influence felt as ritual agents who worked in close co-operation with Awka iron smiths and Umudioka artists and surgeons. Today Nri influence is most remembered in the sphere of religion and the institution of title societies.

The religious and ritual influence of the Nri all over this northern section of the Udi-Nsukka highlands survives most vividly in the form of legends deriving the principal deities of various village-groups in the area from Nri. According to Dr. C. K. Meek, in many of these Nsukka villages

> the principal cult of the town is one which is said to have been introduced by immigrants from Nshi (Nri). Thus at Eha Alumona it was stated that the cult of Ezogwele was introduced by one Ezeokpaka who came from Nshi; at Nsukka the principal cult in the town (known

as Ezoguda) is associated with ancestor who is said to have been a son of the priest chief of Nshi; at Nibo the cult of Ogbala, with which the life of the people is intimately bound up, is believed to have been brought to Nibo by a person of high rank at Nri

driven out of the 'Holy City' by fear of undergoing *igbu ichi*.[20] A look at the map shows that Eha Alumona and Nsukka situate in the heart of the Nsukka group of communities, while Nibo lies further to the south-west. It is likely that inquiries in many other communities will yield similar responses. In any case to the south of the Nsukka and Eha Alumona group of villages, as to the east of them, there are other evidences of Nri influence. This would tend to indicate that the Nsukka highlands and the plains to the east and west were at some point in the past within the area effectively controlled by the Nri (Chapter 2).

Another matter deserving comment in the tradition quoted above is that neither of the deities mentioned in the passage exists at Nri. This would warn us against taking the story literally. It is unlikely that the legend could be used to establish more than that, as already mentioned above, the Nri operated as ritual and religious agents in the Nsukka area just as they did in other parts of Igbo land. The point of the claim that these deities were actually brought in from Nri by the Nri would appear to lie in the further claim that these Nri culture bearers also founded the institution of *Eze* in those same communities. 'It is noteworthy', writes Dr. Meek,

> that in most towns owning a cult of Nri origin the priest who introduced the cult became the Eze or ruler of the town. Thus at Niibo the first Eze was the person who brought the Agbala cult from Nri and at Nsukka the first Eze (and the only real Eze Nsukka ever had) was the person who brought from Nri the iron staff which is the symbol of the Ezoguda cult. At Eha Alumona it is said that Ezokpaka, who introduced the cult of Ezogwele from Nri . . . was Eze of half of the town of Eha Alumona, and that on his death all his sons assumed the title of Eze.[21]

Bearing in mind the point made above that the cults mentioned do not have their Nri counterparts, it is justifiable to believe that the main function of these stories is to legitimize the claims of the families concerned at Eha Alumona, Nsukka and Nibo to the positions of high priest and chief political leaders in their village-groups. Nri was a distant, mysterious, if also romantic, city with a reputation that reverberated far and wide. It had a highly developed institution of divine kingship and was a centre that radiated cultural influences to most communit.:s around. What would be more natural than to claim that one's authority came from there? Later in this essay we shall see that when Idah rose as a centre of political power, and maybe of culture, the elite of many of these Northern Igbo communities shifted their gaze from the south-west to the north-west, from Nri to Idah and not only forged legendary kinship links with the place as already shown, but also made social and political pilgrimages to the courts of the Attah of Igala and his chief official, the Achadu. From this fully authenticated response to the rise of Idah, response which probably goes back to the eighteenth century, and which survived in varying degrees of attenuation till the coming of the British, it would not be out of place to postulate that earlier on, in those days of yore, when Nri's was the unchallenged influence in the Anambra basin, such similar ritual, social and quasi-political pilgrimages were undertaken to Agukwu, the cultural metropolis of the Igbo and some of their neighbours.

In fact there is some fragment of direct evidence that such pilgrimages were made and continued to be made until the coming of the British, that is in spite of the subsequent rise and rivalry of Idah as a socio-cultural metropolis. Thus Meek was told that during the annual sacrifice at Nsukka which usually takes place in January, the people of Eha Alumona would contribute the dried livers of all antelopes, hares, bush cows and other wild animals killed by them during the previous year. Parts of these offerings would be ritually consumed during the sacrifice while the remainder would be 'sent back to Nri through the Eze of Obimo, the Onyishi of Nkpologu and the Onyishi of Ugbeke.' It is also instructive that the ritual symbols for the worship of Ezoguda, which included an iron staff, brass bells and a sacrificial knife, were said to have been obtained from Nri, which again would suggest such a pilgrimage.[22]

As mentioned above, another aspect of Nsukka culture which came under the influence of Nri was the taking and giving of titles—the process by which men who had achieved success in agriculture and/or trade got themselves admitted into the class of social elite in their communities. The origin and character of the title system in the Nsukka area have been widely misunderstood largely because of the tendency for most people who have studied this matter to look up to Igala as providing most, if not all, the answers to any questions asked on the matter. This aspect of the issue will be dealt with in full when we come to reassess the role of Idah in the culture history of the Nsukka communities. But it is the view of the present writer that the Nsukka title system, contrary to the impression which at present prevails, must be seen as deriving from Igbo land, probably from the Nri-Awka area. In spite of over a century or so of Igala influence and an understandable encrustment of Igala culture, it still retains its basic Nri-Awka features. The Nsukka title system has been held to be of Igala origin largely because it is believed that the term *ama* applied to it is not Igbo, that the names of some of the grades are not Igbo and because when the British came in this century they saw aspirants to the highest grades in the title hierarchy making the pilgrimage to Idah as part of the initiation rites. Finally it has been assumed that the Igala conquered the Nsukka area (or most of it) and incorporated it into their empire ruled from Idah, and therefore must have introduced this title system as an institution of imperial control. These arguments will be dealt with in detail in the section which will discuss the impact of the Igala. Here the present writer wishes to show that a structural comparison of the Nsukka and Nri-Awka title systems would tend to indicate that the former derived from the latter, differences in nomenclature notwithstanding. As far as the writer knows this structural approach has not hitherto been adopted by any other person.

First the Nri-Awka system as exemplified in the system which obtained at Agukwu, the heart of the Nri-Awka culture area. The title system here had eight grades or stages each of which was obtained only after the appropriate fees had been paid and the prescribed ritual acts performed. But on closer analysis these eight stages fell into two main categories. The first or lower category was made up of the first four stages—*Agwu, Ifejioku, Amanwulu* and *Amanchi*—which were taken by 'most men of any consequence in the village'. These were among some of the minimum requirements which any man had to fulfil to assert his *manhood* amongst members of his age-grade and in the village at large. They gave one social standing in the village and reinforced integration into the community. They reaffirmed that a man was a free born (*amadi*)—not a slave.[23]

But for all its social value and importance this group of titles did not give a man any special or privileged status outside his village. Only the four higher titles in the second category— *Nliwamadu, Ekwu, Agu Oji* and *Ofo Mmuo*—conferred such rights. Appropriately they were much more costly than the titles of the first category. They gave one status and a measure of political authority outside ones immediate kin groups (village), or as the Igbo would put it *na ama* (literally *in the street, in the meeting grounds of the village-group*). Rightly, therefore, they could be described as *Ama* or *Isiama* titles. But it is necessary to emphasize here that whereas the titles of the first category gave only social status and prestige, those in the second or higher category gave political power and influence within the largest unit of political authority evolved by the Igbo. This was not despotic authority, but authority enjoyed and exercised in conclave with others who had attained the same or similar grade. On this matter Mr. G. I. Jones has written:

> In the past the council consisted of the Ndinze—the Ozo titled men. The head of each village section was its senior Nze (titled man), this seniority being based not on age but on the order of completion of the title. These section heads supported by other Nze titled men in the section formed the village-group council.[24]

Within the Nri-Awka culture area this title system was called *ọzọ*. There was no attempt to find one name for the lower category of titles, and another for the higher category as came to be the case in the Nsukka area to the confusion of the British and many of those who have uncritically used the wealth of ethnographic information they left behind on this matter.

In those Nsukka communities north of the Igbodo, the title system was similarly structured. These communities have gone down in the works of ethnographers as *Ndiama* communities because they call those titles which are recognized throughout the village group *Ama or Isiama* titles, as distinct from the junior titles which gave status only within the village and which they called either *ọzọ* or *amaulo* titles. 'The Ndiama titles', Mr. G. I. Jones has written, 'are graded into greater and lesser titles, the lesser titles are recognized within the village but not outside it, only the senior or greater title-holders being recognized throughout the community and in neighbouring village-groups as well.'[25] Investigation of this matter has concentrated on the higher titles—the *Isiama* grades with the result that no one now knows for certain what are the grades in the junior or *amaulo* group. But the *isiama* titles are generally, in ascending order of importance *Asadu, Iwu* (Ishiwu), *Ozioko, Asogwa* and *Eze*. The order varies slightly in a few places. So important were these *isiama* titles that generally in these communities, a village or village section would recognize the *Onyishi* (*the Ǫkpara* or eldest lineage head) as its head and leader in its internal affairs, but would regard its senior titled man 'as its head and representative in its external relations with other sections, for instance at the village or village-group council meeting.' Mr. Jones reports that 'in many village-groups the council was said to have consisted of a limited number of the senior titled men only'.[26]

Apart from the above close structural similarity, there was also the fact that the method of obtaining the various grades in the two cultural areas were similar. In both places, if a man wanted to purchase a junior title, he paid fees only to those members of his village-section or village who had attained the particular grade. It was the same for obtaining the higher grades. Here again a man paid only to those throughout the village-group who had already bought the same grade.

It has often been pointed out that the Nsukka communities to the south of Opi had only ǫzǫ title systems and not the *ama* titles. The present writer feels that two much emphasis should not be placed on these minor differences in terminology. The people themselves were not so rigid in their use of these terms. In some communities the junior titles were called *ǫzǫ* while the senior titles were called *ama*. Thus Mr. D. C. Ugwu of Obukpa says *ama* referred to titles which gave not only social status but also political power, while *ǫzǫ* referred to titles which gave only social recognition. 'While the political titles were always referred to as "Ama",' he writes, 'the social titles were named ozor'.[27] At the same time there were people who regarded *ama* and *ozo* as synonymous hence such people would use *isiama* for the higher, and *amaulo* for the lower grade titles, and would also call the entire system *ǫzǫ*. In a report on the social and political system of the Eketekere group in 1934 a British political officer noted:

> The people describe their titles as *Ama* but on being asked why, they could give no reply at first. They were then asked the difference between *Ama* title and ozo title, they said our titles are ozo but we call them *Ama*.[28]

We shall hear more of this *ama* system later. But from what has been said so far it is not unreasonable to suggest that the Nri certainly had something to do with the introduction, elaboration and the determination of the character and structure of the title system of the Nsukka communities. Thus they exercised a measure of influence in selecting the social and political elite of these communities. From oral tradition it is likely that in the early days, the taking of titles had something to do with the killing of *atụ* (buffaloes) which probably constituted a menace to the people and their farms. In the Anambra valley *atụ* and *enyi ọhịa* (elephants) constituted such nuisances until lately. In any case it is known that among the Nsukka communities, a titled man was expected to carry, in addition to brass bells, *Okike* (elephant tusk) and *ọfọ*, some other status symbol known as *ọdụ atụ* (the tail of a buffalo). This was usually reinforced with a metal rod or stick, impregnated with *ọgwụ* (magical preparation) and used as a whisk which came ready to hand for driving off flies and evil spirits. These insignia point to the essentially Igbo character of the institution and to its antiquity. It was only later on that *ọdu anyinya* (horse tail) came to be used in place of *odu atu* even though the insignia continued to be called *odu atu*.

This would tend to show that all the insignia of the institution were at first obtained locally, and that it was only later that the horse, an animal which came into these parts from the north, came to be substituted for *atụ*. We shall discuss the significance of this later. When this change took place, we do not know. One of the artifacts recovered from Igbo Ukwu is a bronze pendant which shows a man with *ichi* marks riding what looks very much like a horse.[29] This would tend to show that by about the ninth century A.D. some Igbo were familiar with the horse and with the fact that it could be ridden. This find along with some other artifacts establish the existence of an important trade between the Northern Igbo and the Sudan at least, and that one of the items of exchange was the horse. But whether as early as the ninth century the horse had come to be used for taking titles no one can say. Probably the animal was yet too scarce for that and in any case it is unlikely that by that date *atụ* had become so scarce in these parts that the apparently gentler process of buying a horse could be regarded as equivalent to the very hazardous business of killing *atụ*. Thus most likely, it was in later centuries that the horse came to take the place of the *atụ* in initiation ceremonies connected with *ọzọ*.

Another sphere of life in which Nri-Awka influence would appear to have been marked was that of *ichi* facial marks. In the villages south of Opi, just as in the communities of the adjoining

Agbaja sub-cultural group, *igbu ichi* was very widespread and remained popular until not long ago. Dr. Jeffreys in his study of these marks came to identify two main patterns—an *Agbaja pattern* and an *Nri pattern*.[20] There is reason to believe that *ichi* marks were more widespread in the Nsukka area some time in the past, than they were at the time of British advent. As already mentioned above some of these communities say they were founded by Nri dignitaries who fled Nri because they wanted to avoid marking their faces with *ichi*. This beautifully constructed story may well not mean that from the beginning the societies in question rejected this particular cultural trait. It may well be that at some stage in their history these communities gave up the practice of *Igbu ichi*, probably in consequence of increased Igala influence, but were still anxious to retain their other cultural links with the Nri-Awka area. And to explain this decision evolved the legend summarized above.

It is not yet possible to be certain about the date of the rise of Nri civilization and when it started establishing a hegemony over the neighbouring communities. One hypothesis is that it rose around the period 320 B.C. to 30 B.C. and started expanding and imposing its sway on neighbouring peoples from about the period 30 B.C. to 550 and probably got into the Nsukka area between 1130 and 1710. The chronological problem of this early part of Igbo culture history has been briefly dealt with in Chapter 1. It still awaits full-scale investigation. But what probably requires emphasis here is that during this period of Nri hegemony the Agbaja cultural base of the Nsukka communities was drastically modified either under Nri tutelage or as a result of local initiative in absorbing and transforming outside influence. A critical study of Nsukka social system at the beginning of this century tells us something of the character of the transformations which that organism underwent under Nri influence.

There is for instance the virtual 'dichotomy' between *lineage* or *ascribed* authority and *title* or *achieved* authority. At the level of the village and the village section the dominant authority was that of lineage heads. This would tend to suggest what the structure of society and politics in the remote eras of these communities history was like, before the growth of prosperity making possible the accumulation of reserve wealth and capital and the investment of this in titles. Before this revolution, the village was probably the highest unit of social and political integration and was firmly in the control of the lineage heads. Then came the transformations in the economy of the people and the penetration into the region of Nri-Awka influence. This stimulated a whole series of changes—the coalition of villages into village-groups and the rise of a group of new men who had wealth, had made the pilgrimage to Nri or paid prescribed fees to Nri men for the conferment of certain ritual status which in time came to be known as *ọzọ*. These new men seized power at the level of the village-group, restricting the lineage heads and their now slightly outdated systems to the village and its sections.

But the relationship between the two groups must be clearly understood. It must not be thought that those who purchased status entitling them to some authority in the village-group assembly (*ama ala*) necessarily reduced the *Onyishi* or *Okpara* (lineage head) to subordinate status. On the contrary it would appear that the titled men held more or less the position of *messengers* of the *onyishi*. They went to the *ama ala* to represent the village—to be the eyes and mouths of their villages. They reported proceedings and decisions to the *Onyishi* who then communicated these to the village assembly. And since the village-group council had no law enforcement agencies of its own, and had to depend on each village agreeing to and enforcing decisions agreed upon at that level, this meant that the position of *onyishi* remained largely unimpaired. This arrangement continued under British rule. In fact by tradition any one who wanted to purchase an *Isiama* title had to obtain the consent of his *onyishi* whose duty it was to present him to the group concerned as the candidate for the title. Reporting on how this system worked within the Ori-Ada lineage in Nsukka village-group, Dr. Meek said:

> Any of the family who wishes to acquire a public title must first obtain the sanction of Oyeze (the *onyisi*) and present him with gifts. Oyeze holds himself responsible and would be held responsible by the Government for the tax due from each member of the family ... his brother bears the title of Asogwa and as such is the representative of the Ori-Ada family in all its external relations. He represents the head of the family at public meetings, and reports to him all public matters. ... If any stranger has a complaint against an Ori-Ada man he will take his complaint to the Asogwa in the first instance, the Asogwa will then report the matter to Oyeze.[31]

Here the *Asogwa* looks like the 'foreign minister' of his

village. Further it was the duty of the *Isiama* titled men to enforce decisions imposed by the village. This division of functions could be seen as deriving also from the traditional conception of the office of the lineage head. More often than not he earned his position by age. Also because his functions were largely ritual and religious he had to observe certain taboos relating to food, and travel. All these meant that an *Onyishi* was not the ideal person for representing his unit in the village-group. The more highly ritualized office of *onyishi* would indicate that it is of a very ancient origin. The title system would be of later origin and would have been evolved to meet the new contingencies created by the amalgamation of villages and to carry those social and political burdens which the *onyishi* was ill-qualified to carry.[32]

Another important development which probably took place in the Nsukka communities during the period of unchallenged Nri ascendancy in the Anambra basin was increased contact with the north in general and with the Igala in particular. Nri traditions of contact between the Igbo and the Igala have so far not been fully exploited. But even a scholar afflicted with the most withering scepticism, after examining some of the tantalizing hints on this matter contained in Nri and Igala traditions, cannot fail to concede that the Nri culture probably had an important part to play in the rise of the Idah monarchy. Some reference to this has already been made in Chapter 2. What appears to be certain, however, is that under Nri hegemony there was increased trade with the Middle Belt, the Sudan and beyond. Professor Shaw has expressed the view that the culture with which the artifacts he exavated at Igbo Ukwu were associated must have been to some extent dependent on a far-flung commerce which brought in the beads and the material for the bronzes while taking away slaves and ivory.[33] We have also mentioned the likelihood of trade in horses. It is not unlikely that the Igala played some part in this trade as middlemen between the Sudan and the South and that the wealth derived from this trade contributed in time to the rise of Idah. It would therefore be reasonable to surmise that it was during this period that the Igala made their first significant contact with the Northern Igbo, especially with the Nsukka peoples and the Igbo of Nri-Awka—thus initiating those centuries of mutually beneficial contact which was to influence the cultural evolution of both groups so powerfully.

Thus contact between the Nsukka Igbo and the Igala, as well as cultural borrowings between the two, must be seen as going back to a period earlier than the rise of the Igala as an imperial power. This must be kept steadily in view in any attempt to study relations between the two, especially as it has not always been emphasized by scholars of the subject. Gradually this earlier relationship in which, thanks to Nri influence, the Igbo were more or less the senior partners was upset in favour of the Igala with the rise of the Idah kingdom. We do not know for certain at what date the Igala monarchy came into existence. But it is known that by the early sixteenth century that kingdom and the Edo kingdom were becoming involved in border conflicts. In one of such engagements (in 1515) Idah was defeated by Benin with the aid of the Portuguese who carried fire-arms. It would appear, however, that it was not until the later part of the seventeenth century, but certainly during the eighteenth century, that Idah became an imperial power of note on the left bank of the Niger with influence extending to the lower valley of the Anambra. The Igala state was, apparently, a highly militarized state; at least Igala influence had a more militaristic base than that of the Nri based on quiet ritual and religious influence. Naturally this meant a period of recession for the Nri in the upper and middle Anambra valley and in the communities on the northern portions of the Nsukka highlands. This fact focused the gaze of the Nsukka communities north-westwards to Idah which now became the most important political and cultural centre of the world of the Anambra valley. The increased prestige which this brought to the Igala placed a higher premium on their culture than had hitherto been the case and thus led to increased borrowing from Idah on the part of the Igbo communities of the lower Anambra and Nsukka highlands.

To the colonial officers and scholars, Igala military and political ascendancy was the most important single explanation for the character and structure of Nsukka communities at the beginning of this century. They propagated the view that the Nsukka area, at least Nsukka north of the Igbodo, was militarily conquered by the Ata who administered it through a chain of bureaucratic titled officials who maintained an Igala *pax* throughout the area, collected and forward tribute in the due season. It was during this period of conquest and rule, it was argued, that the Igala imposed on these Nsukka communities the *ama* title system and, says Professor Shelton, appointed priests (the *atama*) to control the 'dangerous alusi' of these Northern Igbo as a means of effective imperial control.[34] On this matter one officer wrote:

> There is no doubt that the Ata of Idah did exercise authority over those parts (Nsukka) and Igala influence remains in varying degree to this day.[35]

In much more detail another said

> The origin of the Eze title... is a matter of pure conjecture. In the writer's opinion there was at one time an Igala invasion and the area covered by the Enugu-Ezike towns was governed by a lieutenant of the Atta of Idah and a hierarchy of officials and presumably troops. This invasion receded and after some time the Enugu-Ezike people began to make the Eze title which represented in a distorted way the representative of the Atta. Similarly the other towns made the titles of the officials who had previously been stationed in their towns. These new titles were but vaguely interconnected and the real authority of the Igala organization vanished and each town governed its own affairs.[36]

But what, one may ask, were the grounds on which these men believed that northern Nsukka communities were *conquered* and *administratively integrated* into the Igala empire. First the grounds for the conquest theory. There were two, the first and the most oft repeated being that centred around the career of the legendary character variously known as Onoja Oboni, Onu Oja Obeni, Onoja Ogbonyi, etc. who is believed to have been a giant with six toes on each foot and six fingers on each hand. According to some accounts, he was a scion of the Idah royal house whose claim to the throne was through a female and was therefore unenforceable. According to some other accounts he was the bastard son of a temporary union between an Igbo hunter (*Abatamu:* I have come in) who later founded Ogurugu and an Igala woman Aboli. According to an Nri account he was the eldest son of *Idah* who on his part was the son of *Nri* by a second wife. There are so many versions, some of them highly attenuated and virtually uninformative, of this legendary character's career. The fullest versions which the present writer has seen are included as appendices to the present chapter and were collected around 1926 from the Nsukka Division and Kabba Province respectively.

All the versions attribute to him super-human and super-foolish deeds. Among his super-human achievements were uprooting an iroko tree with one hand and replanting it upside down, falling down from heaven on to a hill with such a bang that left the imprints of his palms on the rocks, and ravaging most of Igala, Akpụtụ and Nsukka north of Opi single-handed and peopling Ogurugu with the captives of the raids. Among his foolish deeds was deciding to fight those dwelling in the heavens. To this end he decided to build a tower to take him to heaven, but before the right height could be attained, the foundation gave way as a result of which the walls crushed all those working for him. Disappointed and infuriated but by no means wiser, he decided to fight those dwelling in the ground and got his workers to dig a mighty tunnel into the bowels of the earth. When this had attained a depth of eight miles he sent in 500 of his wives, 500 boys, 500 men armed with guns, 500 people bearing boulders and 1,000 drummers before jumping in himself and asking his nobles to follow him. But the latter not only refused to follow but sealed the mouth of the tunnel. 'To this day no one will follow the road leading to this hole. The place is said to be haunted and at night the sound of drums and kakakiya can be heard there.'[37]

Dr. Meek in 1930 considered this character a historical personage and said he led Igala armies in conquest of Nsukka north of Opi. Meek's example has been followed by Mr. S. C. Ukpabi and Professor Shelton. The latter scholar recognizes the difficulty of handling this tradition, thinks there are so many Onojo Ogbonis involved in all these traditions but that one of them was a historical figure, an Igala war lord who conquered Nsukka for the Attah of Idah. 'Despite numerous embellishments and mythification' he writes,

> Onojo Ogboni appears to have been a real war leader, an Igala probably related by uterine ties to the ruling family at Idah yet either not able or not willing to reside there.... From Ogrugu he led his armies eastward in wars of conquest continuing Igala imperial expansion which probably intended to secure trade routes at the expense of Aro traders rather than to colonize the area with actual Igala settlers.[38]

Shelton even claims that Onojo Ogboni led Igala armies that conquered the Urhobo of the Western Delta and that this would account for the fact that the title *Anaja* is found there, at least according to a report by Allen and Thomson in 1848.[39]

It is the view of the present writer that it is most unlikely that there was a historical Onojo Ogboni who was an Igala war leader and that such a character conquered Nsukka. In any case if there were such a personage, his historicity has so far been assumed by Meek, Ukpabi and Shelton rather than established. The super-human dimensions and character of the deeds attributed to him should warn us against taking any of the stories associated with his name literally. It is also noteworthy that stories about this legendary character are not limited to the Igala-Igbo and Idoma borderland, but would appear to have spread into Urhobo and Yoruba land. Mr. Richard Burton in his *Abeokuta and the Cameroon Mountains* (London, 1963) recorded the story of a six-fingered giant who dwelt in an Egba town in the days of yore.[40] Yoruba and Igala languages are said to have separated only about 2,000 years ago and the political systems of the two peoples have been shown to be very similar in structure and in the matter of succession to political office. It is therefore most likely that this legend of the six-fingered, six-toed giant can be regarded as characterizing the two cultures. In this regard if the *Anaja* of Urhobo land mentioned by Shelton can be related to the legendary giant, it is most likely the tradition got into Urhobo land via Yoruba land and that careful research into this amongst the Itsekiri may prove rewarding. To the present writer the legend of Onojo Ogboni is best regarded as a *cultural indicator*, something that could be used in detecting how widespread the influence of Igala culture and its allied branches went, not necessarily by conquest, but more likely by informal diffusion.

It is noteworthy that the martial side of these legends is not emphasized in the Igala versions. For the Igala the importance of Onojo Ogboni would seem to lie in another direction. There is a *spirit-force* at Ogurugu at times known as *Akwata*, at other times as *Onojo Ogboni*. This spirit is said to inhabit a sort of wooden chest. Each Attah on accession would send a slave to Ogurugu. Then the *Akwata* would be sent to Akwacha near Idah where the Attah goes to consult it as a means of acquiring the power of upright judgement. Without going through this ritual, it is maintained, an Attah's rule would not be a successful or happy one. Now this cult is said to have been founded by the legendary Onojo Ogboni. According to the story he was sitting by the river one day when he heard something groaning in the water. When he managed to drag this thing out he found it to be a wooden seat with two lids. When he opened the lids and looked in, 'his eyes turned' and it was said after that he could no longer recognize anybody, that is, he became so impartial in pronouncing judgement that 'even if his own son were charged with some crime he would sentence him as if he did not know him'. A British officer at Kabba said the Attah's of Idah continued to consult this cult under British rule.[41] In this case the legend provides the explanation for this ancient belief and practice without necessarily saying how it came into existence. It remains to mention that among the Igbo having six fingers and six toes would make Onojo Ogboni a monstrous abomination. The attempt by him to stop the flow of the Niger with his bare hands, to build a tower to reach the heavens and to conquer the underworld are standard literary motifs for stupidity and overweening pride. The legend of Onojo Ogboni is a riddle whose meaning is still to be unravelled by research.

There is a second ground on which it has been popularly believed that the Igala conquered all Nsukka north of the Igbodo. There are a number of structures each made up of a ditch and an encircling wall which has been found distributed on the Nsukka highlands from Unadu to Ogurugu. Eleven of these have been found at varying stages of disintegration. The proponents of the 'conquest' theory say these structures were military forts of the Nsukka province of the Igala empire. Mr. Ukpabi talks of Igala 'military control, reinforced by a chain of fortifications.'[42] But the two main questions which arise in connection with these structures have not yet been satisfactorily answered.

The first is who built these structures? Some traditions, especially Igala traditions, attribute them to the Igbo who are said to have used them in defence of their local chiefs. Thus the elders of Ejigbo village near Ankpa told Shelton 'that fort at Nsukka was built by Igbo as a place for them to protect their chiefs from enemies'.[43] Nsukka traditions are even vaguer in this respect, evading the whole question of who built the walls. One such tradition said

> A long time ago the people from Idah lived in this place. There had been some war with men from the north, the Igala. They were not all from Idah for some came from Ogurugu, under the one called *Onoja*. The Igbo had only cutlasses to fight with, so the Igala conquered them. But when they (Igala) left this place, long ago, the walls remained.[44]

Apart from the above the Nsukka call these structures 'Okpe Igala' which is said to mean 'Igala Wall'. Well this is a very vague phrase as Igala wall could mean a wall built by the Igala or structures the construction of which was learnt from the Igala by the Igbo who came home and built some themselves, just as today the people in this zone make and use Igala type baskets. This may well be the case for these structures are found not only in Igbo and Idoma land which could be called 'the frontiers of the Igala empire' and where it could be said they were built as frontier defences. They are also found in many parts of Igala. Shelton's informants in Ankpa told him these structures 'used to be all over Igala'.[45]

This raises the second question: What were the structures used for? Mr. Ukpabi and Professor Shelton are definitely sure they were fortifications and describe them as such. But if they were found all over Igala this would make this interpretation untenable. Unless it be argued that the Igala were in such a permanent state of revolt that the Attahs found it necessary to hold them down militarily and to this end built forts all over the land. But this would make the Igala state so unstable that expansion into the Igbo and Idoma areas, and Shelton would say into Urhobo land, would be out of the question. In an attempt to solve this problem Professor Hartle says he excavated the Okpe Igara found on the grounds of the University of Nigeria but found nothing. No effort has been made to restore any of these utterly dilapidated structures so that from a detailed study of the construction more definite conclusions could be arrived at regarding the functions they performed. But one may observe that if these structures were fortifications, and Igala power were firmly established on the western plains and the Nsukka highlands as postulated by some scholars, one would expect to find such forts placed to guard the approach from the eastern plains and from the south. In view of their 'deployment' on the western half of Nsukka one feels attracted to Professor Hartle's suggestion that they were 'temporary stopping places for slaves being shipped down the river to Onitsha'.[46] Also from considerations of their distribution one could conclude that if they were forts, they were built by the communities in which they are found for defence against Igala raiders. In this sense the structures would be 'Okpe Igara' because they were used against the Igala. What emerges from the above analysis, therefore, is that there is not enough evidence for a categorical assertion to the effect that these structures were fortifications, that they were built by the Igala and that they attest to Igala conquest and occupation of the Nsukka zone in the eighteenth century.

Now we come to examine the grounds on which the same set of scholars have come to believe that Nsukka north of the Igbodo was administered by the Attah through a chain of officials running from the provincial to the village level. Unfortunately these grounds have never been stated in detail or proved, but have been assumed and described. But generally those who hold this view have deduced the 'historicity' of Igala rule in Nsukka from what they assumed were its effects. Thus Mr. Ukpabi talks of the Igala having imposed on the Nsukka their 'political system (of Ezeship and rule by state officials).' He says it was this rule that 'modified the names of Nsukka, Eha Alumona, Okpuje and Obukpa' by the addition of 'Asadu-Attah', which he believes signifies that 'they were under the domination of the Attah'. Finally he uses a more general point advanced by the colonial administrators that the *ama* title system came from Igala as shown by the fact that 'the Ezes of Enugu-Ezike, Akpugo, Nkpologu, Ibagwa Ani and Opi continued to receive their titles from Idah and did not consider themselves properly installed until their position had been confirmed by the Attah,'[47] Professor Shelton not only subscribes to these points but has added another. He believes that the fact that in Nsukka priests bear the Igala title *Atama* proves that they were Igala men whom the Attah appointed to control the dangerous 'alusi' of the conquered peoples. 'The Igala', he said,

> wished to control the Igbo so that tribute might flow from the people through Igala-appointed chiefs in major population areas, but even more important they wanted to prevent the people from combining effectively (possibly with Aro mercenaries) to wage war against the Igala side of the frontier which would interfere with Igala trade. Accordingly, they installed in the subjugated villages shrine priests with the Igala title, *attama*. . . . These *attama became* the major agents of Igala social control.[48]

We shall now re-examine these grounds in some detail to find out to what extent they justify the view that the Igala administered the northern communities of Nsukka. First we consider Ukpabi's general claim that the Igala imposed their political system on the Nsukka peoples. This view was expressed in 1966 at a time when no detailed study of the political system of the Igala kingdom existed. But since then Dr. J. S. Boston has brought out the first ever scholarly investigation of this matter and his views are significant from our point of view. This is important because, of all the criteria adduced by Ukpabi, Shelton and Meek, the political system is probably the only one that could have been imposed by colonial conquest and rule alone. The other Igala traits could easily have been acquired by means of trade, marriage and other social contacts. According to Boston the Igala socio-political system is very close to that of the Yoruba in which 'succession to office is controlled by a rotating system . . . in which the major branches of a descent group hold office in turn'. Contrasting this with the Igbo system Boston wrote:

> (Igala) lineages are the structural divisions of a clan, and each clan divides into a group of lineages that takes it in turn to hold political offices and other rights that belong to the whole clan. The way in which Igala clans divide is quite different from the way in which descent groups subdivide within segmentary system of descent. The Ibo, for example, have a system of lineages in which each lineage subdivides into a number of equal parts that are defined by the principle of contraposition. In the Ibo system the parts are not significant on their own but act in opposition to one another, like two teams on a football field. In the Igala system, on the other hand, the segments of the descent group are not constantly in interraction with one another. The authority of the clan is not fragmented amongst the different branches but held indivisibly by them in rotation. An Igala lineage is either in office or out of office, and when it is out of office it has no right to interfere in the running of the clan's affairs. This is characteristic also of the Yoruba system.[49]

Those who have any acquaintance with any Igbo community know that the Igbo political system with its characteristic wide diffusion of political authority and rights throughout the component segments is as unlike the Igala and Yoruba systems as anything could be. And one characteristic of the Igbo is the general similarity of their political organization in this respect. The authorities who have studied the problem agree that the government of any local Igbo community, including those of the Nsukka area 'consisted of a federation of equivalent segments whose leading men met together in a council which was said to consist of the senior age-grade in the community and was referred to collectively as elders'.[50] Earlier on in this chapter we demonstrated how, in an Nsukka village-group affairs were conducted through the accredited representatives of the component segments. Thus the Nsukka political system was not the Igala system and could not have been imposed by Igala rule.

The next ground is the belief that the *ama* title system is of Igala origin and must have been imposed by Igala rule. We have already shown, in this study, that structurally the Nsukka title system fitted into the Nri-Awka system and must have derived from it. Those who attribute it to Igala origin have never bothered to demonstrate by such structural analysis that such a concurrence exists between the Igala and the Nsukka systems. In fact a study of the Igala title systems discussed by Dr. Boston in his book *The Igala Kingdom* brings out clearly how different the Igala and Nsukka systems were. One reason for believing that the Nsukka title system is Igala-imposed is the mistaken linguistic conclusion that *ama* is an Igala not an Igbo word. This has not been demonstrated but assumed. So far the present writer is not aware of any use by the Igala of the word *ama* in connection with titles. This error was stated by people who understood neither Igala nor Igbo, and has been continued by those who at least understand Igbo. This word has brought so much confusion to students of Nsukka society that it ought to be explained in some detail.

Ama is an Igbo word which basically means the village square, the ritual and spiritual centre of any group in question being the meeting ground not only of the elders, but also of the venerated ancestors and the titulary deities of the community. Thus the village-group assembly which meets here to take far reaching decisions is called *Ama Ala* (*literally the meeting place of the Earth Goddess*) while the members of the assembly were known as *Ndị Ama Ala* (*those who meet in the meeting place of the Earth Goddess*). But just as the village-group has its own *Ama*, each village has an *Ama*. To distinguish between the two, the *Ama* of the village-group is either *Ama Ukwu* (Big Ama) or *Isi Ama* (Head Ama), while the others are regarded as junior to it. It is this which explains why in these Nsukka communities those who had bought titles which qualified them to participate in discussion in the village-group *Ama* were known as holding Isiama (or Amaukwu) titles, while those whose titles only qualified them to operate within the village were known as holding *Amaulo* titles.[51] Where this distinction is not plainly stated, the former are known as *Ama* title-holders while the latter were referred to as *ọzọ* title holders, but as already shown the use of these terms was very fluid, though on each occasion it was understood what was meant by interpreting the word in its context.[52] The word *Ama* is met with in many other contexts, but always carrying this basic meaning. Thus we have *Amadi* or *free born* or *son of the soil*; *Ama* or *Ọnụama* as street. In the latter sense it means the world outside the group in question. Thus if a man took a dispute which should be settled within the sub-lineage to the lineage council, he is accused of *ịchịpụ nwanna ya ụkwụ na ama* (literally carrying his brothers legs outside). It is thus clear that neither the structure nor the name of the system is Igala.

There is still a third ground on which the Nsukka title system is believed to have been introduced or imposed by the Igala; this is the fact that by the time the British came those who took the higher titles in Nsukka communities made the pilgrimage to Idah to receive the blessing of the Attah or of the Achadu. It is perhaps impossible to be definite as to how this practice came about and what it signified. But one thing appears certain and that is, if the other grounds on which Igala conquest and rule have been assumed are untenable, this single 'fact' cannot prove that the Attah was once the military and political overlord of the Nsukka. More supporting evidence is needed. For there are in fact other more likely explanations of this fact. One is that it came into existence through the usual practice by which peoples and communities tend to detach themselves from a falling power and attach themselves to a rising power. As already said the rise of Idah meant the eclipse of Nri in Anambra valley and this change in the balance of power (or rather of influence) could have induced such a reaction. We are now witnesses to the process by which the Ikwerre Igbo are detaching themselves from the Igbo of the interior whose fortunes they now consider to be on the wane. We suggested earlier that from the evidence available, it would appear titled men and priests maintained close touch with Nri in the days of its ascendancy as a way of advertising their legitimacy. The rise of Idah may have led to this class 'refurbishing' their legitimacy by building up links with Idah. Or Igala raids for slaves into Nsukka, for such raids there were as will be shown, probably led to the rise of a new class of leaders who sought to secure immunity from such raids for themselves and their communities through cultivating links with the Attah and Achadu.

There is also another likely explanation and this had already been hinted at above. Initially, as I suggest, title-taking had something to do either with the killing of a buffalo (*atu*) or an aspirant to a title had to obtain the tail of *atu* as part of the symbol of his new status. In time, because *atu* became scarce or horses more popular, the horse became one of the ingredients for the initiation process. In addition, as the trade with the north expanded certain types of rare cloth and beads penetrated the Nsukka and Nri-Awka area from the north and also came to be valued as forming parts of the habiliments of a titled man. All these came from the north, and as already suggested the Igala played an important part in this trade, with Idah as a most likely important market centre. With the rise of the Idah state, partly through the exploitation of this trade, an attempt would be made by the monarchy to control the flow of these highly valued articles out of Igala land, and those who wanted them had to make the perilous journey to Idah to procure them. In this way the Attah could maintain adequate control of the revenue from this business as well as make his capital the commercial metropolis of much of the region east of the Niger and south of the Benue. No doubt for an imperially-minded state an attempt would be made to exploit this relationship politically. It can therefore be understood if the simple process of purchasing the goods and receiving the good wishes of the Attah or his representative for a safe journey home were soon made to look like a system of paying homage and receiving investiture. This was what the practice looked like to the early Europeans who saw it as a perfect reenactment on the African soil of the fuedal state system. Professor Shelton has in fact used the term *enfeoffment* in describing the system of relationship in the Igala state.[53]

In this matter it may well be rewarding to consider the results of the more detailed investigation of the meaning and implications of similar contacts in other parts of pre-colonial Nigeria. In the Western Delta, for instance, many Ijo communities claim Benin origin. Also many of their ruling families tell stories of how they made the 'long and hazardous' journey to Benin to obtain various ritual objects which had come to constitute the emblems of their office and to take titles. Some of them also appealed to Benin on occasions to help settle their internal succession disputes. The question then arises whether these links necessarily meant that the communities concerned were under the rule of Benin. After an analysis of these traditions Professor E. J. Alagoa concluded that whereas they constitute evidence of early contact between Benin and these communities of the Western Delta, they do not prove that the latter were provinces of the Benin empire. 'That these acts did not mean direct subjection of the Isoko to Benin', he has written,

> is shown by the fact that other groups such as the Abraka sent their kings to the Ibo ruler of Aboh to seek the external recognition thought necessary to their internal prestige. In fact, this type of informal relationship was practised in other parts of Nigeria. Even in quite recent times, the Tiv are reported to have sent their chiefs (*Tor*) to serve a period of apprenticeship, to learn the ceremonial and obtain insignia at the Jukun courts at Wukari and Katsina Ala. For this the Tivs paid fees to their Jukun hosts and did not consider themselves subject.[53a]

The argument based on the fact that certain communities modified their names by suffixing Igala terms (Nsukka became Nsukka-Achadu-Atta), and that the priests of local gods came to answer *atama* is probably as convincing as that the British ruled the states in the Bight of Biafra in the eighteenth century because some of the ruling families adopted English royal and aristocratic titles then. This view derives from the mistaken assumption that cultural borrowing can take place only in a situation of imperial rule and colonial subordination. Modern research has shown that imperialism is not the only method for spreading 'light and civilization' and diffusing culture especially where peoples are in direct contact. For this purpose trade, inter-marriage and so on may prove even more effective. Shelton's hypothesis about the *atama* having been instruments of Igala rule is interesting but unconvincing. For one thing there is no proof that it was not just the old Igbo priests of the local shrines who through increased contact with the Igala appropriated the term *atama* for themselves. The Igbo language does not appear to have any single word for priest. Secondly it has not been shown that the system of rule through priests postulated here is characteristic of Igala imperialism. Did the Igala use priests as political agents within the Igala state? Or is the system postulated here, like indirect rule, specially designed for the administration of subject peoples? These are questions which Shelton did not ask, let alone answer.

To round off this question of whether the Igala conquered and administered Nsukka, it is necessary to observe in a general sort of way that it was propagated by British colonial administrators. For one thing these people would appear to have believed at the time that their history taught them that cultural impact could only be the result of conquest—at least that was the way they spread pax Britannica, Westminister democracy and the English tongue to America, Africa and Asia. This inculcated in them that peculiar philosophy of history in which conquest, subjugation and rule loom very large. In the second place the colonial administrators in their search for native rulers of status through whom to keep the masses under control, had no patience with the so-called barbarous and atomistic societies like those of the Igbo and the Tivi. The result was that rather than study these societies by themselves, they tended to study them in terms of neighbouring groups who had evolved large scale political systems. The Western Igbo were seen through Bini-tinted spectacles, while the Nri-Awka and Nsukka Igbo were seen through Igala-coloured lenses with the consequences we have been trying to deal with. This issue will be taken up in greater detail elsewhere.

This Anglo-Saxon historical prejudice has been perpetuated because of a certain regrettable tendency amongst African historians to assume that large empires reflect favourably on *African Personality* while small state systems probably do not. The result has been a readiness to assume that wherever any trace of the culture of a neighbouring centralized state is found, then that area must have been systematically conquered, 'pacified' and incorporated into the state through the establishment of provincial governorships, district and village headships as well as through the imposition and collection of tributes. Because of this easy assumption scholars have not yet faced up to the problem of evolving definite criteria for delimiting the frontiers of African states and empires. Also there has been a certain reluctance to distinguish between 'areas of rule' and 'areas of informal or indirect influence'. Even now we do not know the boundaries of the Igala kingdom. It would appear African historical study has produced more than its fair share of academic statesmen—that class of historians who by the simple use of broken lines blithely build states and empires on paper.

If contact between the Igala and Igbo communities of Nsukka did not take the form of conquest and subordination, what form did it take? We mentioned above that in the days before the rise of the Igala kingdom relationship between the Igala and the Igbo was dominated by trade, the Igala playing a key part as middlemen in the process by which wares from the north—beads, horses, textiles, iron, bronze and the like—got into Igbo land and slaves, ivory and the like moved nórth. Those Igbo and Igala who lived close enough probably also inter-married. One would also suspect that the widely famed Nri priests and diviners penetrated into Igala land. The Igala claim that their first Achadu was a successful Igbo hunter. It is also said by some versions of the legend that Onojo Ogboni was the bastard son of a famous Igbo hunter who penetrated into Igala land and did not return to found Ogurugu before he had given his Igala concubine a son. These stories establish not only early contact between the two peoples at the border, but that both groups probably penetrated each other's territory in pursuit of their business. The Igbo are not famed as hunters. When one considers the intimate association between hunting and magic—a great hunter had also to be a great magician—the writer is inclined to suggest that the early Igbo people who penetrated Igala land were not hunters but reputed native doctors, priests and diviners from the Nri-Awka area.

The tempo and character of the relationship between the two peoples started changing from the sixteenth century or so. The city states of the Central Sudan were at this time beginning to flourish and expand, thanks to the increased flow of commerce with North Africa. This commerce not only brought in more goods for export to the south, but demanded more of the goods—slaves and ivory from the south also. In the same century the European slaving business was established at the coast. This coastal trade spread up the Niger gradually, probably making its impact on the Igala by the late seventeenth century. In response to all these pressures the Igala not only organized themselves better politically speaking, but also resorted to raiding for slaves instead of merely waiting to buy them from their agents and brokers across the frontier. The earlier peaceful phase of this relationship still survives in oral tradition in an attenuated form. Thus the same elders of Ejiogbo village near Ankpa told Shelton that:

> At first, in the olden times, Igala would take horses down to Nsukka and sell them to the Igbo for slaves, and then our fathers would sell the slaves to river people at Idah who would take them down the river to Beke (i.e. White Man).[54]

It is probably noteworthy that no mention of the earlier overland trade was made, yet it was probably on the profits of this trade that the Igala kingdom was built. The important point, however, is that it talks of a period when the trade was based on peaceful exchange. Probably from the tail end of the seventeenth century the emphasis came to be laid on raiding as a means of recruiting to meet the increased demands of the northern and Atlantic slave traffic in which Idah, by its strategic location was involved. It is significant that the legends do not talk of Onojo Ogboni conquering and ruling any village, but capturing slaves from the Igbo and Idoma areas and carrying these away 'to settle at Ogurugu'. As will be shown later Ogurugu was on an important trade route leading to Idah and was later frequented by the Aro.

This is another ground on which the present writer thinks that it was unlikely the Igala incorporated the Northern Nsukka area into their kingdom and administered it as usually alleged. The question is: what would be their interest in so doing? It could not be quest for territory for the Igala have plenty of rich fertile land and their population is thin on the land. It could not have been the disinterested desire to civilize the savage. One could argue that it was motivated by lust for dominion but this is hardly convincing. The Nsukka area is not rich in food products nor in livestock so that it could not have been in quest of tribute. From the point of view of the present writer the one interest the Igala state could have had in the Nsukka area is in its population—the fact that here was a fairly densely populated area from which slaves could be recruited to satisfy the demands from the north and from the coast. This purpose would be defeated if the area were conquered and regularly administered as a province of the Igala state for the Attah could not then turn round to deplete his dominions. Though it could be argued cynically, but unconvincingly, that the Attah could conquer and make the place a 'slave reserve' just as today states establish game reserves. It is perhaps these rather uncoordinated raids for slaves which survive in the Onojo Ogboni legends as wars of conquest. Meek would appear to have recognized this when he wrote 'it cannot be said that the wars of Onu Ojo Ogbonyi led to a definite conquest of the Ibo by the Igala'. Dr. Boston agreed with him.[55]

It is in the light of this predatory character of Igala ascendancy in the Anambra basin and Nsukka highlands that an effort should be made to determine Igala impact on the Igbo of Nsukka and how far it went. The matter is still to be fully investigated but a few remarks will be made here based on a reassessment of the existing evidence and the authors own preliminary field inquiries. It must be re-emphasized that Igala impact on the Nsukka Igbo culture must not be discussed only in terms of the rise of the Igala state and its warlike excursions across the border. Before the Igala kingdom was founded the Igbo and the Igala had been living side by side. In that earlier era the Igbo had the advantage. To start with they were more in population. Later still rose the Nri theocratic hegemony. The present writer posits that except probably in the short period of Igala ascendance (c. 1650–c. 1830) the Igbo population was pushing northwards and seizing territory at the expense of the Igala and the Idoma by the sheer weight of their population. This movement was not dramatic nor accompanied by alarums and the rolling of war drums. It must have gone on rather imperceptibly but none the less steadily. The result of this would be the outflanking of isolated Igala settlements and their absorption into the Igbo population. When to this is added the usual acculturation that goes along with trade, inter-marriage and so on, we find ourselves in a better position to explain the amount of elements of Igala culture we find in Nsukka society, than if we depended on the attractive but superficial explanation of military conquest and rule.

Just as in an industrial community migration is towards the centre of great economic advantage, that is to commercial and industrial centres; so in a predominantly rural and agricultural community migration is in the direction of lower densities which offers the advantage of more land for cultivation. This is in obedience to the same principle that men tend to move from areas of reduced economic advantage to areas which offer enhanced economic benefits. Thus it is unlikely that the elements of Igala and Idoma in the Nsukka population were settlers who came in the wake of Igala conquest and rule as suggested by Mr. Ukpabi. No doubt some of them came as horse and slave traders. But the majority must be accounted for in terms of people outflanked and engulfed by the Igbo. In the same way too, some of the border elements indiscriminantly labelled Igala may well have been Igbo migrants who moved too far ahead of the advancing population and got absorbed.

This population movement was no doubt halted or checked by the rise of the Igala state largely because the Igala raids would deplete Igbo populations across the frontier either by carrying them into slavery or by forcing those who escaped capture to move back. But as will be shown below, Igala power started declining during the nineteenth century. This would enable the northward advance to be resumed only to be drastically reduced again by the coming of the British who virtually 'froze up' the frontiers. Early in the establishment of European rule, some of the officers who had the ears and the eyes for it noted that whereas the Igala language was hardly spoken across the border in Igbo land, in Igala land the Igbo language penetrated some appreciable distance across the border. 'East of the Niger', wrote Mr. Northcote Thomas, Government Anthropologist, in 1914,

> I found a knowledge of Ibo extending fully one day's march into the Igara country, but no corresponding knowledge of Igara on the Ibo side of the frontier.[56]

This suggests that if only scholars would look at the Igala side of the coin, they would discover Igala peoples and families bearing Igbo names as well as aspects of Igala society showing unmistakable signs of Igbo impact. Some work among the Idoma has revealed that the names of the four days in Idoma week 'are derived from Ibo'.[57]

Though the acculturation process must be seen as having gone on for centuries and as still going on, the period covered by the rise of the Igala monarchy must have contributed immensely to the spread of Igala culture across the border. Just as Nri ascendancy probably would explain the construction of putative kinship links between certain Igala clans (like the *Igala Mela*) and Igbo land, the rise of the monarchy at Idah led to similar developments across the border. The most important example here is the way certain ancient institutions started looking for a new legitimacy by building links with the Attah. This point has already been discussed in general above. Here a specific example will be given.

Among those aspects of Nsukka society which most attracted the attention of the British administration was the institution of *Eze* since they were interested in discovering whether it could be built up into a powerful agency of imperial rule at the local level. They, therefore, investigated it, especially that of Enugu-Ezike, in some detail. The official charter of the *Eze* of Enugu-Ezike helps to illustrate how these institutions sought a new legitimacy. The first *Eze* of Enugu-Ezike, it is said, was a son of Ezeke himself the son of the *atama* of Amube. Ezeke was captured in an Igala slave raid and taken to Idah where he stayed for some time before he managed to escape and go home. When he reached Enugu-Ezike he was first discovered by the *Eze* of Akoye village who wanted him to come and live in his village—apparently he came back with something new which made him highly sought after. But the *atama* of Amube soon discovered that his son had returned and wanted him back to Amube. After some dispute the two villages came to an agreement. Ezeke would marry the daughter of the *Eze* of Akoye and settle at a point half-way between the two villages. Ezeke had four sons the eldest of whom, called Ezodo, 'was a very vigorous man'. He soon established his influence over all the neighbouring villages, and 'after giving gifts to the principal persons in each village (i.e. taking an *ama* title) he was given authority over the whole group under the title of Eze of Enugu-Ezike'. Having established himself Ezodo made the 'pilgrimage' to Idah to procure those symbols of his new status which came from the Northern direction. There, in the local idiom of the people, the Attah 'presented him with a horse, a red fez and red gown'.[58] When he came back he handed these things over to his grandfather, the *atama* of Amube who took some chalk mixed with oil and annointed the Eze on the forehead and shoulders saying, 'Eze, what you say will stand. If your brothers refuse to obey you, you must come to me.'[59]

Maybe in this legend we are witnessing the effort of the people to adjust to the new circumstances sketched above through attempting to present a traditional Igbo title as a gift from Idah. One point of the story is that until Ezeke's political apprenticeship at Idah no Enugu-Ezike leader had thought of such an institution with powers extending over all Enugu-Ezike villagegroups. Then Ezeke got the idea from Idah and through his own exertions and his sons got this chiefly institution transplanted to Enugu-Ezike soil. More detailed investigation revealed that in spite of his claims and pretensions, the Eze of Enugu-Ezike had no real powers, and in fact by the time the British came no one had bothered to occupy that position for decades. The above elaborate legend of origin could thus be seen as part of the process of arrogating to the *Eze* powers similar to those enjoyed by the Attah of Idah. Such legends as that just discussed have baffled scholars to no end and created immense problems with regard to tracing the outlines of Nsukka's cultural history.

Meek was looking for a solution to the problem when he argued that

> The probable course of events was that the Ezeship was originally introduced from Nri in close association with a cult, and that as a result of intercourse with the Igala it became gradually secularized.[60]

Mr. D. C. Ugwu on his side anxious to reconcile the conflicting traditions and interpretations said 'The Eze title ... reached us from Igala. ... The same can be said of Nri of Awka Division who introduced Eze title in many places (in Nsukka Division).'[61] We can thus assert with some measure of certainty that one consequence of subsequent Igala ascendancy was that the earlier culture of Nsukka area, derived from Nri, Agbaja and Nkanu Igbo to the south, was encrusted with Igala elements. This was particularly so in the area dealing with legends of origin of institutions or even of ethnic fragments, and more generally in the area of folk history. In those areas, at least, the earlier links with Nri and the Igbo homeland to the south came to be considerably weakened.

It is also tempting to say that the two centuries or so of Igala slave raids into the northern Nsukka area not only slowed up the migration of the Igbo from the central highlands to the western plains which were both fertile and thinly peopled; but that also it hindered the socio-political evolution of the Nsukka communities. As pointed out in the introduction, the Nsukka communities did not attain the clan stage of socio-political development but stopped at the level of the village group. The unity found existing today between these village-groups was at times, unlike in many other parts of Igbo land, the result of recent coalitions[62] rather than of ancient sense of community generating a belief in common descent. But to the east of the Nsukka Division live the Ezza, Izzi, Ikwo, and Ngbo whose socio-political development is said to have attained the 'tribal' stage. Yet they inhabit a similar ecological zone characterized by derived and open savanna. Also to the south of the Nsukka are the Agbaja and Nkanu who at least attained the clan stage and live in similar ecological zones. The question then is why did the socio-political evolution of the Nsukka communities stop at the village-group level where, according to our hypothesis, it was at the time of the introduction of the title system under Nri hegemony long before the rise of Idah?

A tempting explanation is that this was owed to the devastation and insecurity caused by Igala slave raids. These raids led to the break up of many communities in the western plains and the central highlands and probably affected, indirectly, even the communities south of Opi said not to have experienced this scourge first hand. It has also been postulated by Dr. Barry Floyd that this same fact would help to explain why much of the Nsukka population is concentrated on the highlands, leaving the richer western and eastern plains poorly peopled. This, again, is linked up with the question of the nature of Igala activities in the Nsukka area. If this had taken the form of orderly administration, the natural course of events would have been for these communities, especially those placed under one Igala provincial chief, to continue coming closer together. In the event two centuries of Igala political tutelage would have led to the emergence of larger agglomerations than eventually was the case.

It was not the Nri and the Igala alone that helped to determine the circumstances in which the Nsukka communities hammered their own way of life out of the basic autochthonous culture which they would appear to have shared in common with their Agbaja and Nkanu neighbours to the south. Another Igbo group apart from the Nri, this time the Nike and the Aro were to take a hand in it. There is evidence to suggest that by about 1750 the Aro Chukwu sphere of influence had penetrated far into the Northern Igbo from the south—getting probably as far north as the Agbaja-Nkanu area.[63] By the end of the century Aro commercial tentacles were spreading into the Nsukka area, at first indirectly through Agbaja-Nkanu agents, especially through members of the Nike confederation who were well placed and equipped to act as middlemen in this trade between the Aro and the fragmented communities of the Nsukka highlands.[64] According to tradition Nike and the Aro went into a blood pact (Igbandu) which covered co-operation in commercial, military and cultural matters. With this Nike, or rather the Nike-Aro League, became a force to be reckoned with in the life and politics of the Nsukka communities.

It is the view of the present writer that the intrusion of this new combine into the Nsukka highlands contributed something to the decline of Igala power. At least it set up a powerful rival demand for slaves which helped to reduce the number of Igbo slaves who passed through the hands of Igala traders. This situation became worse in the nineteenth century as the Nike-

Aro axis came to dominate the important slave fairs of Ibagwa Nkwo and Nkalagu and as the Fulani wars in the Central Sudan set up hostile waves that spread as far south as Idah. These caused a substantial recession in Igala power. Allen and Thomson in 1841 described the Igala kingdom as no longer in a position to undertake aggressive campaigns, but pre-occupied with its own defence.[65] In spite of this, however, the Igala were still in a position to participate effectively in the slave trade of the Nsukka area. And it would appear they abandoned their eighteenth century method of slave recruitment by raids for the earlier method of peaceful commerce. They were still the purveyors of goods—horses and exotic textiles—for which the Nsukka elite had developed appetite. The Aro and Nike also started buying horses and these rare textiles and beads for export further south. In this century a major trade route ran from Idah to Ogurugu, through Ibagwa and Nkalagu to Uburu, an important salt-producing centre. Other routes linked Ibagwa, Opi, Egede and Abo and from there ran further south.

Thus the nineteenth century, or at least most of it, was for Nsukka a period of trade expansion and some prosperity. The area started recovering from the Igala ravages of the past century both in terms of population and material wealth. Some of this population which had been expelled from the western plain, started moving back. But the Enugu Ezike area would appear to have attracted most of the population. Not only had it a fairly more fertile land than the central Nsukku plateau, but it had an advantage which the western plains had not. Being on a hill it was more easily defended. Another important development which the traditions would attribute to this period is the evolution of loose confederations of village-groups all over this area. Neighbouring villages went into alliances not only to facilitate the movement of trade, but also to reduce the ravages of the slave trade as kidnapping was rampant. Suitable legends were built up to support these confederal structures. An example could be given of how this operated. One such group was centred around Edem and included such other village-groups as Okpuje, Orobo and Ede. According to the official charter Edem, Orobo and Ede were founded by three brothers—Orogu, Eke and Nome—who are said to have been the children of Ugwuanyi. At the same time Edem says though Okpuje is not a blood relation, they have been friends for 'ages', this friendship starting with an indissoluble union which their two rulers contracted in the remote past. 'These two men' it is maintained,

> decided to symbolise their friendship by joining their ancestral iron staffs. They therefore called in a black-smith who welded the two together. At an appropriate ceremony the single staff was cut into two, Ugwu (the ruler of Okpuje) taking one half and Alazi (the ruler of Edem) the other.[66]

But towards the end of the nineteenth century, the peace and trade boom of the earlier part were shattered in consequence of a series of wars which rocked the central Nsukka plateau. Traditions about three such wars have survived most vividly in folk memory. Among the most serious was probably the protracted and devastating engagement between Obukpa and Itchi on one side and Ibagwa Ani, Ibagwa Nkwọ, Iheakpụ, Ovoko and Ihọhọrọ on the other. The trouble started as a land dispute between Itchi and Ibagwa Ani. Then Obukpa which suffers from shortage of fertile land and has no direct access to the Adada River seeing this as an opportunity to improve her lot, enthusiastically accepted an invitation for help from Itchi. The other towns are said to have intervened to prevent the extermination of Ibagwa Ani as that would only make the 'headstrong and unruly' Obukpa more insufferable. The second important engagement was between the Opi of Nsukka and Nike to the south-east. The trouble started as a result of break-down in commercial relations between the two groups, in particular between Opi and the Idi-Nike village-group. In this conflict the Aro came to the aid of their Nike allies by bringing the Abam-Ohafia warriors against Opi. The third major disturbance of the peace in the Nsukka area in the later part of the century arose from the activities of the populous Aku village-group who are said to have harrassed their neighbours incessantly for slaves and land. In all these wars the Aro have been mentioned as playing the role of instigators. The wars not only yielded a large crop of slaves, but converted the Nsukka area into one large market for dane guns, gunpowder and matchets.

To some extent these wars, which were probably not as devastating as the eighteenth century Igala raids, would appear to have encouraged the two major developments mentioned above. Firstly, the earlier inter-village alliances for fostering trade and reducing the incidence of kidnapping were converted into defensive and offensive alliances, thus bringing the villages in each group closer together. In the Igbodo group in particular, it is said that it was the menace of Aku that forced the other members of the group to attach themselves to Ukehe which had the population to check the bully. In the 1930s when the British wanted to reorganize local governments in these parts on the basis of traditional kinship or other ties, they found these groupings still fairly strong in spite of the disintegration caused by over thirty years of their earlier wrong policy. Secondly, the incessant disturbances in the central plateau would also appear to have speeded up the movement of population northwards and southwards to account for the present distribution of the Nsukka population in which the centre has low density and is flanked to the north and south by areas of high density. Some people also moved into the western plains. One effect of these wars on the population could be seen in the fact that Erọ was said to have been broken up during this period by a surprise raid of Abam warriors acting on the side of Nike. The survivors fled in different directions. Later, elements of them came back to the original site to constitute the little community now known as Ero Ulo. Another group constituted themselves into Erọ Agụ. Other elements got integrated with the populations of the villages where they had taken shelter.

The nineteenth century in Nsukka did not end at midnight on 31 December 1899 as the events and developments sketched above continued until the establishment of British rule and this latter was not effectively achieved until 1916, though a beginning had been made in 1903. It was in the latter year that the first group of officials of the Southern Nigeria Protectorate set foot on Nsukka soil. They were the commanders of the Igala Expedition of 1903–4 who got to Nsukka and found, as they put it, Obukpa at war with all her neighbours. The Expedition made a half-hearted attempt to settle the dispute but failed and so continued on its way to Idah, its destination. In 1906 Nsukka was declared part of the Awka sub-district. But not until after two years did that proclamation have any practical meaning for the Nsukka communities. In 1908 the Niger-Cross River Expedition was mounted to bring much of the area between these two rivers under control. In its promenade through these lands one of the columns got to Nsukka and found the people in no mood to receive the white man. The political officer attached to the column, Major Heron, asked the troops to teach the people a lesson as a result of which many villages were burnt and looted.

This earned Major Heron the name *Otikpo Obodo* (the destroyer of villages) and the commanding officer the name *Akpoko* (pepper). Reporting this encounter about thirty years later, a British officer said:

> The first taste of discipline was given by Major Heron known locally as *Otikpo* (the Destroyer). He seems to have done his work thoroughly, but the people bear him no ill-will and speak of him with reminiscent smile and a shake of the head.[67]

This was not to be the end of the matter even though the following year Nsukka was detached from Awka and placed under almost equally distant Ọkpọga (Okwoga) in Idoma land. The area continued largely as before to be agitated by ancient conflicts. Thus again in 1911 a military patrol had to visit the combatant villages and impose heavy fines on them. Then in 1914 the Obollo Native Court was established, the first colonial institution on Nsukka soil. But neither Obukpa nor those with whom she was lately in conflict would allow the officials of this court to operate in their area. This again led to these villages being visited and terrorized in 1916 after which the Nsukka communities could be said to have come under effective British rule. This brought to an end the long era which is the subject of this essay.

NOTES

1. D. Forde and G. I. Jones, *The Ibo and Ibibio-Speaking Peoples of South-eastern Nigeria* (London, 1950), pp. 33–4.
2. In 1967 the Government of the Republic of Biafra constituted this group into the Nsukka Province sub-divided into three administrative divisions—Igbo-Eze, Igbo-Etiti and Isuizo. On the demise of Biafra, the Government of the East Central State either ignored or abolished the Provincial system, but retained the divisions. As a result the Old Nsukka Division is now administered as three units, each named as it was in Biafra. But so strong is the sense of unity inculated into these peoples during the colonial era, that it is within the framework of the Old Nsukka Division, that it is likely to survive this administrative fragmentation for some time. *Vis-à-vis* peoples from the former Udi, or Awgu or Abakaliki Divisions, peoples from here still refer to themselves as plain Nsukka.
3. O.P. 899, Intelligence Report on the Eketekere Group, Nsukka Division, para. 17.
4. *Ibid.*, para. 19 and 21.
5. O.P. 977, Intelligence Report on Uvuru, Nibo, Ugbene and Abi towns in Nsukka, para. 15.
6. S. C. Ukpabi, 'Nsukka before the Establishment of British Administration', *Odu* New Series, No. 6, October 1971.
7. *Ibid.*

8. *Ibid.*
9. G. I. Jones, *The Trading States of the Oil Rivers* (Oxford, 1963), p. 30.
10. E.P. 8766, Awka Division, Intelligence Report by M. D. W. Jeffreys, para. 7.
11. J. S. Boston, 'The Hunter in Igala Legends of Origin', *Africa*, Vol. xxxiv, No. 2, 1964, p. 118.
12. D. Forde and G. I. Jones, *op. cit.*, p. 28.
13. Oral information collected in September 1971.
14. O.P. 1020, Intelligence Report on Ukehe, etc. (1934), para. 10.
15. D. D. Hartle, 'Archaeology in Eastern Nigeria', *Nigeria Magazine*, No. 93, June 1967, pp. 136-7.
16. *Ibid.*, pp. 136-7.
17. *Ibid.*, p. 138.
18. *Ibid.*, p. 143.
19. R. G. Armstrong, 'The Use of Linguistic and Ethnographic Data in the Study of Idoma and Yoruba History', in Vansina, Mauny and Thomas (eds), *The Historian in Tropical Africa* (Oxford, 1964), pp. 127-38.
20. C. K. Meek, *Ethnographical Report on the Peoples of Nsukka Division, Onitsha Province* (1930), para. 13.
21. *Ibid.*, para. 14.
22. *Ibid.*, para. 97.
23. G. I. Jones, *Report on the Position, Status and Influence of Chiefs and Natural Rulers in the Eastern Region of Nigeria* (Enugu, n.d.), para. 87.
24. *Ibid.*, same para.
25. *Ibid.*, para. 81.
26. *Ibid.*, same para.
27. D. C. Ugwu, *This Is Nsukka* (Apapa, 1964), pp. 15, 29.
28. O.P. 899, Intelligence Report on Eketekele Group, 1934.
29. T. Shaw, *Igbo-Ukwu: An account of archaeological discoveries in Eastern Nigeria*, Vol. I, pp. 193-5, Vol. II, p. 262, Plates 365-7.
30. C. K. Meek, *Ethnographical Report on the Peoples of Nsukka Division* (1930), para. 13.

    M. D. W. Jeffreys, 'The Winged Solar Disk or Ibo Itchi Facial Scarification', *Africa*, Vol. XXI, No. 2, April 1951.
31. C. K. Meek, *Ethnographical Report, etc.*, para. 19.
32. I have been encouraged to draw these far-reaching conclusions by Professor Murdock's insistence that the social scientist should be prepared to 'infer anterior forms of social organization from the internal structural inconsistencies which reflect the conservatism of certain features from the past'. Quoted in Vansina, Mauny and Thomas (eds), *The Historian in Tropical Africa* (Oxford, 1964), p. 69, footnote 27.
33. T. Shaw, *Igbo Ukwu etc.*, pp. 284-5.
34. A. J. Shelton, *The Igbo-Igala Borderland* (N.Y., 1971). This is the thesis of this book. In an article published in 1968 he wrote:

    'There is abundant evidence, of course, that the Igala conquered Nsukka and installed in the subjugated villages a shrine priest called Attama (Lord of the Spirits) who was the major intermediary between the Igbo villagers of their *alusi*', see 'Onojo Ogboni' in *Journal of American Folklore*, Vol. 81, No. 321, 1968, p. 248.

35. O.P. 213/1931, Annual Report Onitsha Province, 1931, para. 28.
36. O.P. 899, Intelligence Report on Eketekere Group, 14.2.34, para. 16.
37. O.P. 398/26, Legend of Onojo Oboni of Ogurugu: Extracts from Notes on Kabba Province On.

    O.P. 398/26, Notes on the History of Ogurugu by the Ag. D.O. Nuskka enclosed in No. Conf. 262/24 of 24.10.26.

C. K. Meek, *Ethnographical Report on The Peoples of Nsukka Division*, para. 9.

A. J. Shelton:

   (i) *The Igbo-Igala Borderland*, Chap. 2.
   (ii) 'Onojo Ogboni, etc.', *Journal of American Folklore*, Vol. 81, No. 321, 1968.

M. D. W. Jeffreys, 'The Umundri Tradition of Origin', *African Studies*, Vol. 15, No. 3, 1956.

38. A. J. Shelton, *op. cit.*, p. 20.
S. C. Ukpabi, 'Nsukka before the Establishment of British Administration', *loc. cit.*
C. K. Meek, *op. cit.*, para. 9.
39. A. J. Shelton, 'Onojo Ogboni', *loc. cit.*, p. 243.
40. M. D. W. Jeffreys, 'The Umundri Tradition of Origin', *African Studies*, Vol. 15, No. 3, 1956, see footnote 2 on page 121.
41. O.P. 398/26, Legends of Onojo Oboni of Ogurugu: Extracts from Notes on Kabba Province On.
42. S. C. Ukpabi, 'Nsukka before the Establishment of British Administration', *loc. cit.*
43. A. J. Shelton, *The Igbo-Igala Borderland, etc.*, quoted on p. 22.
44. Quoted *ibid.*, p. 23.
45. Ibid., p. 22.
46. D. D. Hartle, 'Archaelogy in Eastern Nigeria', *Nigeria Magazine*, No. 93, June 1967, p. 136.
47. S. C. Ukpabi, 'Nsukka Before the Establishment of British Administration', *loc. cit.*
48. A. J. Shelton, *The Igbo-Igala Borderland* etc., p. 23.
49. J. S. Boston, 'Igala Political Organisation' in *African Notes*, Vol., 4, No. 2, Jan. 1967, pp. 18, 19.
50. G. I. Jones, *Report of Commission into the Position, Status, Influence, etc.*, p. 6.
51. *Ibid.*, para. 87.
52. This matter confused Meek and the political officers in the Nsukka Division to no end. Thus Meek said *ama* applied only to the higher titles while this was contradicted by the officer who wrote the intelligence report on the Eketekere Group. He said it applied to the higher and lower grades alike. What we can make out of this is that Meek got his information from an elder who referred to the higher grades as *ama* and to the lower grades as *ozo*; while the investigator after him talked to an elder who referred to the higher grade titles as *Isiama* and the lower grade as *Amaulo* titles.
53. A. J. Shelton, 'Onojo Ogboni', *loc. cit.*, p. 247.
53a. J. F. Ade Ajayi and Michael Crowder (eds), *History of West Africa*, Vol. I (Longman, 1971), pp. 273–4.
54. A. J. Shelton, *The Igbo-Igala Borderland*, p. 21.
55. C. K. Meek, *Ethnographical Report on the Peoples of the Nsukka Division*, para. 8.
J. S. Boston, 'Notes on contact between the Igala and the Ibo', *Journal of Historical Society of Nigeria*, Vol. II, No. 1, 1960, p. 56.
56. N. W. Thomas, *Anthropological Report on Ibo-speaking Peoples of Nigeria*, Part IV (London, 1914), pp. 5–6.
57. R. G. Armstrong, *The Idoma-Speaking Peoples* in D. Forde (ed.), *Peoples of the Niger-Benue Confluence* (London, 1955), p. 93.
58. In the light of the argument advanced above on the title system, this should be read to mean he went to Idah to purchase a horse, a red fez and a red

gown as symbols of his new status.
59. C. J. Meek, *Ethnological Report on the Peoples of the Nsukka Division*, para. 133.
60. *Ibid.*, para. 14.
61. D. C. Ugwu, *op. cit.*, p. 29.
62. This matter is adequately dealt with in the fourteen Intelligence Reports written on the Nsukka communities and now housed in the Enugu and Ibadan branches of the Nigerian National Archives.
63. Unless where otherwise stated the material used in reconstructing history of Nsukka in the nineteenth century is based on traditions collected from elders in the old Nsukka Division and in Nike. These investigations are still continuing. It is therefore quite likely that the reconstruction put forward here will be substantially revised at the conclusion of the research in the light of new evidence.
64. W. R. G. Horton, 'The Ohu System of Slavery in a Northern Igbo Village-Group', *Africa*, Vol. 24, No. 4, 1954.
65. W. Allen and T. R. H. Thomson, *A Narrative of the Expedition sent by Her Majesty's Government to the River Niger in 1841*, 2 Vols. (London, 1968, Frank Cass Reprint), Vol. 1, p. 326.
66. O.P. 1083, Intelligence Report on Edem, Orobo and Okpuje (1934). The iron staff is part of the regalia of a titled man. And there is a traditional practice in the Nsukka area by which two friends could combine to take one title. When anything was shared among titled men they would take one share. We see this being reflected in this legend.
67. E.P. 1175, Intelligence Report on the Villages of Nsukka, Ibagwani, Ero, etc. See also E.P. 1171/9A; O.P. 1067; O.P. 899, O.P. 1470, etc.
Professor Shelton's account of the coming of British rule into Nsukka is confused, being based on oral evidence uncrosschecked with the abundant official records. His dates are wrong and Major Heron appears in his account as Mr. Aaron. See his *Igbo-Igala Borderland*, pp. 26–7. Any familiarity with these parts teaches how European names easily get distorted in indigenous mouths. Dr. O. Ikime, a colleague of mine working in the Western Delta, has told the story of how some elders assured him there was once amongst them a European officer called Mr. Tiger. He later found that the man's name was McTaggart.

Legends of Onojo Oboni in O.P. 398/26 at Enugu Archives

1. Extracts from Notes on Kabba Province, Enclosed in O.P. 398/1926 of 25.9.1926.

Onojo Oboni was the son of one Abatamu of Ogurugu, who married Obudali, the sister of Ebele Jawne and, therefore, the grandson of Agenapeje. The latter was according to general belief the first Attah, although a woman. Onojo Oboni was derisively called 'The son of a woman' (Oben—the female genital organ) because he could only claim relationship to the Attahs through his mother. He is said to have been a giant in height, and to have had six fingers and toes. His personal prowess were such that a whole village would flee on seeing him approach alone.

He made war on every one he could find till all were beaten or had fled. He then settled in Alo, near Itebe, for a long time saying he was going to fight the people in the heavens above. For this reason he set thousands of people to work to build an immense tower on Ojuo Ubakeji (Ojuo = hill, Uba = visible from afar, Keji = close to the sky). As was inevitable, the building collapsed when it had reached a height beyond the sustaining strength of its walls and vast numbers of people were killed in its downfall.

Leaving Alo in disgust he went to Ogurugu. This place he peopled with slaves taken from many different places, and the different parts of the town are still distinguished by the name of the tribe or place whence he brought them.

Here he said he was determined to fight the people underground, and set an army of men to work to dig a long deep hole, sloping into the earth. It is supposed to reach a length of eight miles. Into this he first sent 500 of his wives, then 500 boys, 500 men armed with guns, 500 Okute bearers, 1,000 drummers.

After which he himself rode in on horseback and bade his nobles follow him. Their leader Chimebogbo, addressed them as follows: 'He wishes us all to die with him. We will not follow him. Let us fill in the hole before he can get out.' This they did with rocks, tree trunks, stones and earth. To this day no one will follow the road leading to this hole. The place is said to be haunted and at night the sound of drums and kakakiya can be heard there.

Another version of the story of his death is that he was afflicted with syphilis and his life became a burden to him. He therefore had an immense hole dug and entered it with all his people, then called on those left above to fill it in.

Before his death Onojo Oboni was sitting by the river one day when he heard something groaning in the water. He entered the water and saw something but could not make out what it was. He caused 1,000 jars of palm oil to be poured into the River, whether as an oblation, or to have an effect on the mysterious something, is not clear. He was then able to seize something solid which he dragged to the bank and found to be a chair or seat made from a hollow tree trunk. It has two lids or coverings. He opened them and after looking in 'his eyes turned'. After that he was unable to recognize people. The idea being, so far as I can gather, that he who looked inside thereafter became so righteous in his judgements that if his son were charged with some crime he would sentence him as if he did not know him.

After his accession each Attah send to Ogurugu a slave, and the Akwata (this juju) is sent to Akwacha (near Idah) where the Attah goes and takes the covers off, thereby acquiring the power of upright judgement.

A eunuch called Adachi used to be in charge of this at Ogurugu, but he was driven out by the Ogurugu people. The late Attah wanted to send for the Akwata but quarrelled with the Ogrugru people over the amount of money to be sent in lieu of the slave, so that Akwata was never sent.

It is said that Oboni when at Alo, despairing of the efforts of various witchdoctors to prophesy truly—or to help him obtain the title of Attah—it is not clear which—killed his son on the top of Ubakeji Hill and cut off his head. With this he tried to practise divination saying that a son would not deceive his own father. This is now a common saying among Igalas 'Omaw Kionebi yia dawla gwogwon'. Literally 'Son born to one will not deceive one'.

2. Notes on the history of Ogurugu by the Ag. D.O. Nsukka enclosed in No. Conf. 267/24 of 24.10.26 to the Senior Resident, Onitsha.

Abatamu the founder of the town, was a hunter born at Adada in Onitsha Division. In the course of his hunting he came to where Ogurugu is now and decided to stay there (he apparently had a wife or wives but little seems to be known about them except that his progeny now form the Abatamu quarter). He continued hunting and whilst in the Idah country he met a woman Ebuli, stayed with her for a time and returned to Ogurugu. The result of this meeting was the birth of a son to Ebuli whom she named Onoja-Aboli.

The latter grew up and was scorned by his associates as being fatherless, and as he grew older he asked his mother as to the whereabouts of his father. She told him his father's name was Abatamu and she understood that he lived at Ogurugu. She gave Onoja-Aboli a ring which she said had been given her by his father, and if he, Onoja, took the ring and found Abatamu, the latter would recognize it.

Onoja then went in search of Ogurugu. Apparently by that time he had grown to be a tremendously big man physically, and on arriving at Ogrugru he met a man who, immediately on seeing him, knelt down to show him homage. Onoja found that this man was Abatamu and made himself known to him by showing him the ring. Abatamu recognized it and acclaimed him as his son, giving him a plot of land called Obia to live on. Onojo stayed there for some time, when he had a dispute with the other sons of Abatamu, fought with them and killed most of them. Abatamu was naturally annoyed at this and told Onoja that in future he would not have him living so near and made him move his house to a safe distance (now Ati-Idah). The two quarters Abatamu and Ati-Idah were formed in this way and Obia became waste and has been so ever since.

Onoja-Aboli was a warrior and a giant. He had six fingers on each hand and six toes on each foot. He was evidently of a roving nature, and after moving to Ati-Idah he went all over the country, raiding villages everywhere, bringing back captives from each one and putting them on land at Ogurugu to live. It was these captives who founded the other seven quarters of Ogurugu.

Rumour has it that Onoja made all these raids single-handed without assistance from anyone. He was feared everywhere on account of his great stature and strength. Tradition also has it that Onoja died suddenly by his own act. He contracted yaws which he was unable to cure and so grew tired of life. He had a huge pit dug, and when ready, he assembled a number of his captives and jumped with them into the pit. By his order it was filled in and all were buried alive. Onoja's sceptre was planted there and the founders juju was made, which is recognized to this day by all Ogrugru. The oldest man in Ati-Idah is Eze of the town and Atama Onoja-Aboli.

The custom has always been that an Atah of Idah, on assuming the Atirate should always consult the Onoja-Aboli juju in order to be successful and Just in his reign. The Atah would send one of his eunuchs with a messenger to the juju priest. They would take a male slave, a female slave, a dog, a ram and a fowl. The dog, ram and fowl were sacrificed to the juju and the slaves remained slaves of the juju and kept the place clean. The Atah's eunuch also remained with the juju and stayed until he died. This was the custom up to the reign of the last two Atahs who have not consulted the juju.

The history above which was given by the elders of Ogrugru, varies in parts from information gathered from Igaras I have met. They agree that Onoja was a giant and had six fingers on each hand and six toes on each foot, that he was a warrior and that he single-handedly raided towns in the Igara, Okpoto and Ibo countries and took his captives to Ogurugu where he finally died. But they state that he was an Atah of Idah or next in succession, that being a giant and of a roving nature he grew tired of the humdrum of life at Idah and went all over the country raiding and conquering towns, with such success that there was little more to conquer on this earth. So he decided to attempt the conquest of the gods above, and to that end he had a high tower erected; but before it reached the height he wanted, it fell to the earth and the project was abandoned. They say the ruins are still in existence, but it is not known exactly where they are. Onoja is said among other things to have attempted to stop the flow of Niger—with little success. Finally he determined to try his strength against the powers under the earth, and at Ogurugu, whilst his slaves were digging a pit sufficiently deep for him to come to grips, the walls fell in and his slaves were buried alive.

There is a similarity between the two tales, and the tradition of the Igaras that he was an Atah supplies a reason for succeeding Atahs consulting the Onoja-Aboli juju. There is no question that they did so. To my knowledge when the present Atah assumed the Atirate, he made overtures to Ogurugu saying that he wished to consult the juju. Nothing came of it, apparently, perhaps, because the fee of £20 asked by Ogurugu was too heavy, but it has always been a genuine belief that an Atah could not reign successfully without consulting the juju, which the people regard as the spirit of their ancestors.

Note: 'Aboli', I understand, is an Igara word with the same meaning as 'Danduru' in Hausa, which signifies, to use a more polite expression than the literal equivalent, a bastard.

4. Economic Foundations of Pre-Colonial Igbo Society

Detailed study reveals that pre-colonial Igbo society was strikingly variegated. This was so not only in the area of language where almost every autonomous village-group evolved its own dialect, but also in the sphere of political and social institutions. In the area of government, for instance, the present writer has identified at least four broad political types involving the differing articulations of the role of kinship and non-kinship institutions, as of individual and group leadership.[1] With regard to social institutions some communities evolved highly developed title systems while placing relatively litte importance on secret societies, some emphasized the role of secret societies at the expense of title systems, while others still gave both more or less equal weight with either type of association moderating the influence of the other. In the field of religion, apart from a few gods (such as *Chukwu*, *Ala*, *Ihiejiọkụ* or *Ifejiọkụ*) which were worshipped throughout Igboland, every autonomous community and, in fact at times, every segment of it, had deities exclusive to it. Again apart from the festivals associated with *Ala* and *Ihiejiọkụ* most festivals were exclusive to particular communities.

Yet at a slightly more removed level, pre-colonial Igbo society can be seen to have enjoyed a striking uniformity. Throughout Igboland political fragmentation obtained, with the village-group (what is at times called the town) being the largest unit of definite political integration. And within the village-group authority was dispersed, with lineage and non-lineage institutions, individuals and groups, hereditary and non-hereditary office-holders, men and women, the gods and the ancestors playing recognized roles in government. This was so even in those communities (like the West Niger and Riverine Igbo areas) where individual and hereditary leadership was emphasized. Land tenure, settlement pattern, religious beliefs, social stratification, attitudes to politics and government, to wealth and poverty, to life and death were basically the same. Even in the sphere of language where differences were at times most marked, there was on the whole mutual intelligibility.

In this chapter we shall view pre-colonial Igbo society from this convenient 'slightly more removed level' and discuss its economic foundations without undue preoccupation with those minor differences in economic structure and organization which most surely existed, and which must have constituted part of the explanation for the variegation and differences noted above. Also here we are going to distinguish between two sides to the issue of the economic foundations of pre-colonial Igbo society. The first deals with the economic sub-structure on which Igbo society rested, the second with the extent to which economic factors determined the character of Igbo society and culture.

Without doubt the Igbo, like their Edo, Igala, Ibibio and Yoruba neighbours, are an example of successful adaptation to the tropical rain forest environment of West Africa. Their economic system and its history can be studied under three major heads; agriculture, trade and manufacture. Each of these three main provinces of economic activity played an important part in the survival of the Igbo as a group and in determining the character and quality of their culture, even of their religion and cosmology. But they did not all receive equal attention from the Igbo and consequently did not all attain the same level of development by 1900.

1. *Agriculture:*

In pre-colonial Igbo society agriculture was the most important economic activity with regard both to the number of people engaged in it either on full or part-time basis and to the prestige attached to it. Dr. V. C. Uchendu has aptly described farming as 'the Igbo staff of life'.[2] He states:

> To remind an Igbo that he is *ori mgbe ahia loro*, 'one who eats only when the market holds' is to humiliate him. This does not imply that traders are not respected: all it means is that the Igbo see farming as their chief occupation and trading as subsidiary not a substitute for it.[3]

One result of this Igbo attitude to agriculture was that every Igbo man and woman was a farmer. Most families produced enough of such staples as yam, cocoyam, cassava and vegetables to last them all the year. But there were some communities whose soils were so fertile and who gave so much of their time to farming that by the dawn of 'modern times'[4] they had started producing for outside markets. Among the latter were the North-Eastern Igbo (Ogu-Ukwu), the Eastern Igbo, Ikwerre and riverine Igbo. These exported some of their surplus agricultural products to areas outside Igboland, and helped to supply the needs of certain Igbo groups whose soil had deteriorated so badly that they had increasingly come to pay less and less attention to farming. Of this trade in agricultural produce more will be said in the section under trade.

According to Dr. Yehuda Karmon[5] the Igbo originated farther north in the forest-savana interface which, having more food in those days than the Guinea forest, enabled the Igbo to multiply fast as a result of which they moved into the forest to overwhelm the Ijo and the Ibibio who probably preceded them there. If this was so, it would lend weight to the argument that Igbo agriculture is older than hitherto suspected for only cultivation could have had the dramatic effect on Igbo population that would give them such numerical advantage over their predecessors in the forest. In any case it is significant that Igbo agriculture had by the first millenium A.D. become so advanced that it could support the civilization with which the Igbo Ukwu finds have been associated. And it must have taken centuries of slow development for it to attain that stage. Whatever the case, the traditions of the Nri, a Northern Igbo group, make it quite clear that Igbo agriculture is ancient indeed, so ancient that they tend to associate the coming of cultivation with the emergence of Igbo society, or even with the very creation of the Igbo world.

From these and other traditions, as from ecological and other evidence, the Northern Igbo area would appear to have come under the impact of the agricultural revolution before other parts of Igboland with consequences which give it pride of place in Igbo traditions and culture history. As in the case of their neighbours in the Guinea zone, we can envisage three stages in the evolution of Igbo agriculture. The first stage was marked by the crossing of the barrier from incipient cultivation to agriculture based on experimentation with local crops, such as certain species of yam and the palm tree. This transition probably derived from local initiative which owed little or nothing to ideas and techniques from South-east Asia as formerly thought. Scholars are coming round to the view that

African agriculture is so ancient that it would not make sense to explain its origin in terms of lessons learned from outside Africa. The second stage was marked by the coming of the South-east Asian crop complex—certain species of yam, cocoyam, banana etc.—either by the northern routes via Egypt and the Sudan, or across equatorial Africa or by the sea route round the Cape of Good Hope. The main importance of this lay in the increased variety of cultivable food crops which it made available, thus making it possible for the land and social units to support larger densities of population. The third stage was reached when European enterprise linked West Africa with America and the Caribbean from where many food crops like certain species of maize, mango, breadfruit, cassava etc. were brought in.

Pre-colonial Igbo agricultural was very efficient. In this regard Professor J. E. Flint has described it as 'perhaps the most efficient in Africa' and he thinks it was largely for this reason that Igbo population 'developed a density per acre only matched in Africa by that of the Nile Valley.'[6] It was also intensive as shown by the fact that using such simple tools as the matchet and the hoe the Igbo reduced to either grass land or palm bush a vegetation which most authorities think must have been originally tropical rain forest. It is also seen in the system of land tenure under which, firstly there was no freeborn (*amadi*) who had not a piece of land over which he enjoyed usufructuary rights, and secondly there is no piece of land, not even that over which stood 'bad bush', without an 'owner'.[7] It was the role which agriculture played in the life of the pre-colonial Igbo that determined the great importance which they attached to land as well as the key place which *land* and its spirit-force (*Ajala* or *Ala*) occupied in their lives.

Agriculture in Igboland was highly ritualized. This would point both to the importance of the occupation and to its antiquity among the people. The beginning of the farming season, the date of which varied from one part of Igboland to another for ecological reasons, was a formal occasion marked by a festival and a ritual. It was the same with the beginning of the harvest season which was marked by the very important *New Yam* festival. It was not only the practice of agriculture that was ritualized. But those crops, especially yam and cocoyam, which constituted the backbone of Igbo agriculture were also ritualized, and each was believed to have a spirit-force, *arusi*, which laid down the specific code of conduct for cultivating, harvesting, cooking and eating it. The yam was the king of Igbo crops. Its spirit-force (*Njoku* or *Ihiejioku*), was very powerful, widely feared and venerated. It was reputed to strike, with either diarrhoea or swollen stomach (*afo otuto*) those who broke the rules for handling yam. Its more serious taboos forbade people fighting or defecating in a yam farm, yams being cooked in the same pot and at the same time with cassava which, being an inferior crop, would pollute *Njoku*. Also once yams had been planted, *Njoku* would forbid anybody cracking palm nuts at night. The cocoyam (*ede*) also had its own spirit-force, known as *Njoku ede*, but which had fewer rules guiding the treatment of this crop than *Ihiejioku* had for yams. But in many Igbo communities it had its own special festival, largely an affair of the women. On that day husbands, who should normally have finished planting and tending their yams, would work for their wives in the latter's cocoyam plantations and be feasted. In some communities in the Okigwi Division, this festival was known as *Nta Ede*. The other crops, different species of beans, cassava, grains and banana were not thought of as possessing any spirit-force—except in the general sense that in Igbo thought every individual thing, including stone, had its *chi*.

Igbo society is patrilineal, at least for the most part. The relevance of this to our discussion is that yam, the most valued crop in Igboland, is regarded as male, while cocoyam the next in importance, is considered to be female. This is most dramatically told in the Nri legend on the origin of food crops. According to this corpus of myth:

> When Eri died this food supply (from heaven) ceased and Ndri at Aguleri complained to Chukwu that there was not food ... and Chukwu told him he was to kill and sacrifice his eldest son and daughter ... This killing of eldest son and daughter was carried out and the bodies buried in separate graves. Three native weeks later shoots appeared out of the graves of these children. From the grave of his son Ndri dug up a yam ... The next day Ndri dug up *Koko* yam from his daughter's grave ... for this reason the yam is called the son of Ndri and *koko* yam the daughter of Ndri.[8]

Also illustrating the primacy of yam in Igbo agricultural economy, was the institutionalization of the *Eze ji* (yam king) title among the Igbo. This title society was open only to such freeborn Igbo as were successful farmers, planted the right type of yams and could boast of at least a certain quantity of yams (counted in units of *nnu*—400). Each new entrant would feed the members of the society for a fixed number of days with yams from his own barn and pay the prescribed fees. Members of this society served as experts in yam cultivation, and their opinions were generally sought in disputes over yams and farm land, and by young men new in the farming business.

The above Nri legend, coupled with another which will be quoted below, emphasizes the primacy of these two crops—yam and cocoyam—in Igbo economy. It was probably for this reason that they were called the children of Nri, that is they were as valued and cherished as children, the yam by men, the cocoyam by women. The palm tree on the other hand, though it provided food, fuel, plank, broom, rope, wine and so on, was only of subsidiary importance in Igbo economy before the rise of the oil trade in the nineteenth century. The bread fruit, *ukwa*, also, though it provided delicious food, was even of less importance than the palm tree. Thus in the legend quoted below, these two crops are said to be of servile origin—that is alien to the community. Furthermore, to emphasize the inferior position of the breadfruit *vis-à-vis* the palm tree, it is said to have derived from a female slave. The breadfruit, like the cocoyam, is a woman's crop. On this the Nri legend says:

> Ndri also had a male and female slaves killed and buried (in separate graves) and in three native weeks there sprang from the grave of the male slave an oil palm, and from the female slave, a breadfruit tree.[9]

The absence of all mention of the other crops like maize, beans and grains in these legends may well indicate something of their place in pre-colonial Igbo economy. The banana, a member of the South-east Asian crop complex, was despised and remained the poor man's food. The cassava, though in the course of this century it became the chief staple of the Igbo, was a late arrival on the scene and also for long was despised. No titled man would touch it. The Igbo did not regard maize as 'food' in the sense that it would not normally be taken as either breakfast, lunch or supper. It served more as snacks.

An important question which remains to be dealt with here is how pre-colonial Igbo society met the labour demands of agriculture. Early European visitors to Africa often gave the impression that the average African, especially the men, that is the freeborn men, despised manual labour. As far as pre-colonial Igbo society was concerned nothing could be farther from the truth. Igbo society placed a high premium on hard-work and so not only valued the hard-worker but held him up for admiration. He provided the theme for edifying songs and tales, while the lazy man was the subject of ribald songs and jokes. A common Igbo folk-tale talks about the chimpanzee which in the beginning was human, but is said to have been so frightened of handling the hoe that he ran into the bush rather than face the rigours of farm work. If a child showed early signs of laziness he was invited to consider the lot of the chimpanzee (*adaka sọrọ egu ọgụ gbaba ọhia*) and mend his ways.

Thus Igbo society was one in which every able-bodied person was actively engaged in farm work. The result was that most people, male and female, did their own farm work. In areas where the land was first tilled before yam mounds were made, that was done by both men and women. The man sowed the seed yams in the mounds, while the women planted the maize and beans in the spaces between the mounds. The man cut the sticks and tended the yam vines, while the women did the weeding and the planting of cassava. Though cocoyams could be planted at the base of the yam mounds, for the most part they were planted separately, and this was largely a woman's job. But this is not to say the men would not help their wives in this if they could find the time and the relationship was good. It was not unusual, however, for a man who helped his wives too often with the planting of cocoyams to be taunted by members of his age-grade.

It was largely because each family did its own farm work for itself, that the Igbo came to value large families. A man who wanted to prosper as a farmer had to have many wives and children. It is a common Igbo saying that *mbe nwa Okochieọha sị na aka ọtụtụ dị mma n'ọrụrụ ma ọ dịghị mma n'oriri* (Tortoise, the son of Okochieọha, said that many hands are good for doing work, but are not good for taking food). This saying clearly illustrates the dilemma of the Igbo *di ji* (a successful farmer) who would want to have many hands to do his work but would, if he could help it, prefer to feed few mouths if he must accumulate enough yams to take the yam title. But that Igbo love for large families is not entirely explained by the demands of farm work is shown by such sayings as *ririri bụ ugwu ezi* (numbers are the prestige of pigs) and *igwe bu ike* (multitude is strength). An *ogaranya* (a wealthy Igbo man) would normally want to have a large and thickly-peopled compound.

But the *di ji* could never do all his farm work depending on his wives and children alone. Most families, especially successful families, would normally have large retinues of slaves who helped with farm work. But as Olaudah Equiano pointed out in his *Narrative*, the slave probably did not do much more work than the freeborn. Only a foolish man would leave the fate of his yams, or as the Igbo would put it, 'the stomach of his family', in the hands of slaves. Slave labour merely supplemented rather than supplanted the labour of the freeborn.

Another source of labour was clientage. Clients of the *di ji* were those who had either taken yams or money on loan and could not pay back or were required to pay back in labour given on stated days of the week for a specified period or until the loan was repaid. They could also be people who enjoyed the support and protection of the rich farmer generally and in return gave their labour to him. Other sources included the trading of labour (*ohe ọrụ*) amongst the members of an age-grade or the reciprocal exchange of labour which normally took place between families linked by marriage. If a farmer was the head of an extended family, he was entitled to the labour of all the able-bodied men and women of the unit on one day in the eight-day week. In parts of central Igboland, at least, this labour was exacted on the *Orie* day following the big *Eke* market day.

2. *Trade:*

Although subsidiary to agriculture, trade was nonetheless an important aspect of Igbo economic activity. Just as *Chukwu* is believed to have instituted agriculture, so is he believed to have institutionalized trade and marketing, by creating the Igbo market days, naming them after four heavenly fishmongers each of whom went round Igboland establishing markets bearing his name. A Northern Igbo legend dealing with the origin of markets and trade deserves quoting at some length to illustrate this matter. 'In the beginning', it says,

> the days of the week had no names, for there was no way of counting the days because the sun was always shining and no one slept. Then four strangers arrived at Aguleri with four baskets. Ndri asked Chuku where they came from. Chuku refused to say, but said he would send a person who would divulge their names and tell where they came from. A wise person (Okpeta) was sent to Ndri. Okpeta brought a rat (oke) with him. At night he tied a string round the rat and told the rat to enter the first basket: the rat did so and made a noise therein. One of

the unknown visitors shook the owner of the basket and said 'Eke, Eke' and told him that something was making a noise in his basket. When Eke was about to get up to find out the cause of the noise, Okpeta pulled the rat away. So when Eke looked in he saw nothing to cause the noise. Eke went to sleep, Okpeta noted the name, Eke, and sent the rat into another basket to make a noise therein and the next man woke up and called to the owner of the basket saying 'Oye, Oye something is in your basket.' Okpeta did as before and so on for the other two baskets and secured the names Afo and Nkwo.... These four men founded four markets, and that is how the Igbo got their four-day-week. These four strangers were sent by Chukwu, and their baskets contained fish...."[10]

From this legend it is quite clear that the Igbo regard the origin of the market and trading in their society as ancient indeed, going back to those far-off days 'when the world was young' (*mgbe ụwa dị na nwata*) and when men held discussion directly with *Chukwu*.

Another interesting aspect of the legend which is worthy of emphasis, is that the four strangers traded in delicacies or luxury items.

Much more important from the point of view of this chapter is the development of long-range trade in pre-colonial Igboland. There are two aspects of this matter, viz: the development of regional trade within Igboland and the development of long range trade linking the Igbo people with their neighbours. On this we do not have much information.

But it is reasonable to suggest that the two kinds of long-range trade developed in consequence of differences, or growing differentiation in ecological conditions, leading to a situation in which one part produced more of one kind of goods that it could consume, and had to exchange the excess for those goods which it needed and could only get from its neighbours who either produced them or were in a position to procure them from their other neighbours.

In Igboland the key to the situation would appear to be the increasing ecological differentiation between Northern Igboland and the other areas surrounding it. From all currently available indications, Northern Igboland was the first part of Igboland to be effectively settled by the Igbo. It was from there that they subsequently spread to the neighbouring lowlands to the west, south and east. The result was that its vegetation was soon 'eaten' down and the soil overworked, while the neighbouring areas of relatively late Igbo settlement remained fertile and comparatively under-exploited. The Northern Igbo, in response to their worsening environmental conditions, turned increasingly to other professions, especially to trading, manufacturing, medicine, and the exploitation of occult forces as ritualists and diviners. The justly famed Aro, Awka, Nri and Nkwerre specialists are on this Northern Igbo ridge. Though they did not entirely abandon agriculture, they became increasingly dependent on their neighbours for the extra with which to supplement the meagre produce of their exhausted soil.

Furthermore there was long-range exchange of the natural resources with which the different parts of Igboland were differently endowed. The Northern Igbo plateau was and is rich in iron ore deposits and in smelters and smiths who transformed the ore into iron, tools and ritual objects. The Niger-Anambara valley produced fish, while the North-Eastern and Cross River Igbo areas were endowed with salt lakes (at Uburu), lead (at Abakaliki) and fish (from the Cross River).

With regard to the development of long-range trade linking Igboland with its neighbours, similar factors were important. The Ijọ to the south produced salt and fish which they exchanged for agricultural produce from Igboland, while the Igala to the North were in a position to bring into Igboland horses, glass beads and bronzes in exchange for ivory and slaves. The trade between the Igbo and the Ijọ and the Igala probably constituted the most important external links of the Igbo. It is doubtful whether a significant East–West trade developed, except probably the one in beads and cloth which went from Aboh through Benin and Yorubaland to Akan land.

It is as yet impossible to be precise as to when the kind of long range trade discussed above developed both within Igboland and between the Igbo and their neighbours to the north and south. Perhaps only further archaeological work will reveal such evidence as would make it even remotely possible and safe to hazard a definite guess on this matter. But what information we have tends to show that by about the ninth century, the trading system of Igboland was such that one can firmly assume that both regional trade linking different parts of Igboland and long-range trade linking Igbo land and the region further north (the Sudan and beyond) were already long established. The Igbo Ukwu finds (dated back to the ninth century) suggest that by that date Igboland was already engaged in the exchange of slaves and ivory for horses, beads and bronze coming from the north. The assembling of slaves and ivory in quantities large enough to cover the cost of the luxury, and no doubt expensive, items from the north would also suggest regional trade within Igboland. It is also likely, as suggested by Professor Shaw, that the rich regalia and artifacts discovered at Igbo Ukwu were not all made in or immediately around Igbo Ukwu, though certainly many of them were made in the area east of the Niger and south of the Benue. This again would suggest highly developed long distance trade.[11] To the south Dr. E. J. Alagoa has uncovered evidence which suggests that the trade between the Ijọ and their hinterland neighbours was already firmly established before the dawn of the era of European contact.[12]

Reinterpreting the tantalizing bits of evidence on the state of trade in the hinterland of the Bight of Biafra, David Northrup has convincingly argued that long before the Europeans showed up on the Nigerian coast in the fifteenth century, the lower Niger had become an important commercial highway in which Aboh occupied the important position of an emporium visited by Edo, Igala, Ijọ, and Northern Igbo traders.[13]

It is suggested here that this Niger waterway was the main axis of the trade of Igboland west of the Northern Igbo plateau, that its use and level of development as a trade route in those far off days would suggest the existence of a trade net-work east of the Northern Igbo plateau, at about the same level of development and serving to link the Northern Igbo area with the plains to the east of it. The items of this trade most likely were salt and lead from the North-Eastern and Eastern Igbo, and beads, iron wares and horses from the Northern Igbo plateau. The traditions of the Northern, Eastern and North-Eastern Igbo never mention obtaining salt from the South before the introduction of European salt. The fact is that from the Igbo town of Uburu northwards into Ogoja there are brine lakes from which salt was made by evaporation. It was from here that most of Igboland got its salt popularly known as *nnu Ọkpọsi* or *nnu Uburu*. It is suggested here that this salt trade was ancient indeed, at least predating the fifteenth century. It is not known if the people who left behind the Igbo Ukwu bronzes ate salt or still depended on bitter herbs, as Nsukka traditions claim the Igbo man did before the discovery of salt. But if they did, it is most likely that they obtained it from the Cross River basin rather than from the Ijọ of the Niger Delta. The Jukun, also referred to as *Akpa*, are frequently mentioned in connection with trade on the Cross River. If there is any truth in this, they may well have participated in the salt trade of the Uburu-Ogoja axis.

There was also probably another trading system linking the Northern Igbo area with the salt and lead producing regions of the North-Eastern and Eastern Igbo and through them with the Cross River waterway. Of the Southern Igbo area we have little information. But it might not be wide off the mark to assume that they traded agricultural produce for salt and fish with the Ijọ as it is unlikely that the latter would have got all the carbohydrate and vegetable foods they needed from Aboh. It can also be assumed that the Southern Igbo got their iron tools, weaponry and some ritual objects from the Northern Igbo, the only part of Igboland which was endowed with iron ore. Basically this pattern of exchange economy persisted in Igboland until the imposition of colonial rule in the first decade of this century.

The organizational structure for carrying on this long distance trade certainly improved with time. At first the most likely method is that items moved in a relay fashion from one village to the next in the direction of greatest demand. This means of distributing trade items remained very much in vogue in Igbo land into this century. Most people never travelled outside their village. And even at the time when the trading system in Igboland was most developed, it was only a small fraction of people who travelled from one region of Igboland to the other for business.

However, as conditions for agriculture on the Nsukka-Okigwe cuesta and the Awka-Orlu uplands became more difficult as a result of progressive overworking and impoverishment of the land, different communities there turned increasingly to different non-agricultural pursuits. It is perhaps here that we see the origin of the professional groups of traders with which Igboland had come to be richly endowed by the eighteenth century. We cannot easily date their origin, but must see their emergence as taking place over centuries. It has often been suggested that it was the impact of the European trade that instigated the rise of these men. The claim usually made that the Aro trading oligarchy came into existence about the eighteenth century is a case in point. It is the view of the present writer that the rise of these groups preceded the coming of the Europeans in the fifteenth century, though the impact of the European trade widened their business horizon, expanded the range of goods they handled and improved their organizational structure.

Among the famed long-range professional trading groups of Igboland were the Aro, Awka, Nri, Nkwerre, Abiriba, Ụmụnneọha and Aboh. Of these groups only the Aboh of the lower Niger, and the Ụmụnneọha are not located on the Northern Igbo plateau. Also with the single exception of Aboh, all the others combined long-distance trade with some other specialist service. The Awka, Nkwerre and Abiriba were smiths in addition; the Aro and Ụmụnneọha were oracle agents while the Nri were equally ritual and medical specialists.

There were many others, especially among the Northern Igbo who travelled widely. Among such groups were the Nike whose role as traders in Northern Igboland was first revealed by the researches of Mr. W. R. G. Horton. The Aku of the Nsukka area, and the Isuochi of Okigwe were equally dynamic in the regional trade of their respective zones. The Aku on their side even set up a system which sought to sidetrack the Aro system through establishing direct access to Uburu for salt and to Bende for imported European goods. It is thus necessary to recognize that the Aro trade system, so often discussed as if it were the only one in Igboland, was only one out of many, though no doubt it was the most successful, and the one with the longest reach. Through the reminiscences of Olaudah Equiano, we get an idea of how some of these men operated in eighteenth century Igboland. By that time slaves had become the most important export of Igboland.

In the absence of large-scale state systems in pre-colonial Igboland to ensure the safety of travellers generally and of traders in particular, people have often wondered how trade and marketing reached such a high level of development among the Igbo. The explanation lies in the fact that the Igbo evolved an intricate system for ensuring the safety of well-meaning travellers. Igbo law, custom and morality forbade the molestation, let alone the wounding, killing, kidnapping and enslavement of a fellow clansman. This meant that a trader could travel in safety within his clan. Between one clan and another a ritual brotherhood could be established by means of the *Igbandu* blood pact. Under this arrangement the leading representatives of the clans or village-groups concerned met at their common boundary and after performing the prescribed ritual, drew blood from their veins and mixed it in a container. Then they would dip pieces of kola nut in the blood and eat. This ceremony was believed to constitute the groups concerned into a blood union whose members were bound to treat each other as clansmen. Thus by this means an outward-looking community could extend the area within which its citizens could travel in safety. But with inward-looking communities where people felt self-sufficient, conflicts over land could create such a permanent state of feud as could almost completely hinder communication even for neutral travellers unless they practised crafts in such great demand as those of the Nri, Awka, Aro, Abiriba and Nkwerre.

There were other Igbo institutions which were used to encourage trade and travel. One of these was marriage. Most long distance travellers were polygamists, and usually took care to choose their wives from important and strategically placed towns along their normal route of business. By marriage such a traveller became an accepted member of his father-in-law's clan, especially where the father-in-law came from an influential family. The mere mention of the father-in-law's family could constitute a safe-conduct pass. Furthermore the father-in-law's house provided hostel and warehouse facilities which were otherwise lacking in pre-colonial Igboland. Thus the traders went so far as to leave some wives in their natal homes where they built them houses into which they themselves could turn in as the occasion demanded without unduly bothering their parents in-law.

If the trader subsequently retired, he could place the connections and links he had built up at the disposal of his townsmen and friends trading along the same route. He could do so either by introducing them personally to his parents-in-law and friends along the route or by 'arming' each troupe with a walking stick or snuff-box or some other rare item with which he was widely identified during the active period of his life. The troupe would produce one of these items if it ran into trouble along the route or wanted hostel and ware-house facilities. In either case the walking stick or snuff-box would serve as a passport. Similar links and connections were built up in other ways such as through enrolling in the leading secret and title societies in all the major towns along a trader's route. The advantages which these conveyed were also used in the same way as sketched above for the links created by marriage.

Then there were the specially privileged travellers like the Aro, and the Awka who traded in articles that were in great demand

and were believed to be specially protected by powerful spirit forces. The Agbala of Awka and the *Ibini Ukpabi* of the Aro were widely feared in Igboland. There are today many abandoned habitation sites in different parts of Igboland which are said to have belonged to communities which had 'foolishly' or 'unknowingly' killed or enslaved an agent of one of these oracles and were decimated by the oracles as a result. Similarly each market in Igboland was believed to have its own spirit-force, and the more successful the market the more powerful this spirit-force was believed to be. And it was widely 'known' that to attack or enslave anybody going to or coming from such a market was to court disaster, as such a trader was believed to be the client of the spirit-force that 'owned' the market. This belief was even more widely held in respect of people going to or coming from the shrine of any of the oracles. It was through the exploitation of these beliefs and institutions that the professional traders and other specialists whose calling required long-range travel built up their business.

Sophisticated, developed and wide-ranging as it was, the trade of pre-colonial Igboland mainly depended on the least efficient form of transportation—human head porterage. The Igbo for the most part were landlubbers, apart from the Aboh and some other riverine Igbo communities who learnt to travel and move their wares by canoe, on the Niger. Transportation by canoe was never developed to a great extent on the Imo River which passes through the heart of Igboland, probably because it is a small river whose course was often blocked by snags and fallen trees. It was only in the second part of the nineteenth century that the Opobo and Bonny men started navigating its larger lower course in search of palm produce. No other river which drained Igboland offered significant facilities for the development of canoe traffic.

The Igbo, like the other forest peoples of West Africa, did not use animal transport because, it has been argued, the tse-tse fly made it impossible for such animals to thrive in the forest zone. The horse was brought in for ritual and ceremonial purposes only. The donkey, as already mentioned, was probably not known to the Igbo before the colonial era. And even today their immense capacity for transportation has not been exploited by the Igbo. Such domestic animals as the humpless short-horned cow and goats which bred and still breed well in Igboland are not good as transport animals.

In the event Igbo traders and other travellers depended on human porters for moving their wares. It was here that slaves had a great advantage over other goods. They were not only self-transporting, but would also help to carry non-self-transporting wares. For this reason most pre-colonial Igbo long distance traders were slave dealers, in addition to dealing in other wares since they needed the slaves to carry these other wares. When the market was good both the slaves and the wares would be sold. If not, the slaves were retained to move the goods back. Thus, those traders who bought slaves primarily because of their value as a means of transportation, would not normally dispose of their slaves until they were sure their other goods were sold out. In addition to slaves, a prosperous trader could always raise young men from his own community to carry his wares to and from the market. These he paid at agreed rates. But this practice did not lead to the rise of a class of professional carriers for the term *ndi ibu* or *ndi oburu* (carriers) was one of contempt in Igbo society. And in any case the risk was immense. The whole troupe could be caught and enslaved. The bridges over the streams were not always reliable and the risk of being drowned was often real. Also there was the additional risk that an unscrupulous trader could sell his carriers as Igwegbe Odum did on one occasion.[14] Finally, traders also relied on their apprentices to carry their goods to and from the markets.

It must be borne in mind that, before the rise of the oil trade, few of the goods for long distance trade were bulky. Among these goods were salt from Uburu and then probably ivory. The smiths solved the problem of transporting their wares, which would be otherwise difficult to move, by settling in those communities where their products were in great demand and manufacturing them there. Invariably it was the practice for customers to come to the smiths' forge to buy their needs and it was not unusual for smiths to have their forges at one corner of the market and to work on their customers' orders as the market was in session. Yet the smiths had to solve the problem of transporting the unworked iron. At times, too, they worked in the homes of their hosts and had to move their wares to the market as occasion demanded. On these occasions they depended, like the trader, on the same sources for carriers.

Another aspect of pre-colonial trade in Igboland, which requires mention here, is the question of currency. It is as yet impossible to be precise as to when money transaction was introduced into Igboland. But one thing which is quite clear is that this development preceded the dawn of the European era in West African trade. It would appear that by the eighteenth century much of the commercial transactions in Igboland were done in money. Using information gathered in the nineteenth century and early in this century, one would discover that many currencies were in use in pre-colonial Igboland. These included *salt, ụmụmụ, cowries, manillas, brass rods* and *copper wires*.

The use of salt as currency is a phenomenon found in many communities the world over. And, it is quite possible that salt was the oldest currency in use in Igboland. The salt which came in earthen jars from Uburu was ground into fine powder and moulded into cones of different sizes and used in exchange transactions. Probably coming next to salt in time was the iron money, known as *ụmụmụ*, which was perhaps minted on the Northern Igbo Plateau. The *ụmụmụ*, says Archdeacon Basden, 'consisted of tiny pieces of iron resembling small squashed tin-tacks, half an inch in length, with arrow-shaped heads, and stem about the thickness of a large pin.'[15] It would appear to have been most in use throughout the Northern Igbo area and to have spread into Idoma and Tiv, at least judging from the reports of Dr. W. B. Baikie. It may well have been in use in other parts of Igboland, especially in Southern and Cross River Igbo area, before it was squeezed out by brass rods, manilla etc.[16]

There is evidence to suggest that cowries were in use in Igboland before the advent of the Portuguese. Salt, *ụmụmụ* and cowries were available in small units and were extremely useful for small purchases. The *brass rod, manilla and copper wire* came with the Europeans and were useful for large purchases, as their exchange rates were much higher than those of the pre-European currencies. An attempt has been made by Mr. G. I. Jones to demarcate Igboland into *cowrie, manilla, brass rod* and *copper wire* zones,[17] but information available to the present writer would tend to show that as much as one or two currencies might be dominant in one part, there was no area of Igboland where any of them would not have been recognized and used as money.

3. *Manufacture:*

The Igbo manufactured a wide range of items—agricultural tools, war implements, various kinds of baskets, cloths, earthen jars, household furniture and so on. Some of the crafts which produced these wares could be, and were, practised by anybody, but some were practised only by select communities, either because only they had the necessary raw materials, or because the crafts demanded more time than could be combined with full-scale farming. But by and large it could be said that no region of Igboland lacked specialists in at least one particular craft. Pottery, for instance, was carried on wherever the necessary clay could be found. Such were Inyi, Ishiagu and Ibeku. But apart from these, there were innumerable other little communities which met local needs in pottery in areas far away from the famous centres.

Smithery, salt manufacture, cloth weaving and carving were among the best developed of Igbo industries. We shall deal with each of these briefly.

Of all Igbo communities which engaged in smithery, the most famed and the best organized were the Awka, Nkwerre and Abiriba. The Awka dominated the industry in Northern and Western Igboland, and were active among the Isoko of the West Niger area, as among the Igala and Idoma of the Middle Belt zone. The Nkwerre carried on the industry among the Southern Igbo, Ogoni and Ijo; the Abiriba in the Cross River area. However, by the end of the last century the lines of demarcation were no longer that neat. The Awka and the Nkwerre, in particular, were beginning to encroach upon each other's sphere of influence, as upon that of the Abiriba. To an agricultural people like the Igbo, smithery was very important; so important in fact that a Northern Igbo legend says it was the smith who dried up the land at the beginning of the world, thus making smithery the first profession in Igboland.

The Awka and Nkwerre obtained iron from the Agbaja of Udi and the Nsukka people who smelted the ore partly to meet their own smithing needs and partly for export. The Abiriba mined and smelted their own ore. Smithing was a particularly difficult profession, requiring artistic ingenuity and physical strength. It was also believed to be a mystical profession which established special links between the smith and the spirit world. Consequently, it was hedged by many taboos and required a long period of apprenticeship. Smiths enjoyed special rights of passage wherever they went. The Awka smiths organized themselves into a guild, one half only of whose members were allowed to travel in any one year, while the other stayed back to guard the home. Among the Nkwerre and the Abiriba, there does not appear to have been any such organization and arrangement. In the Western Igbo area there were local smiths who are believed to have learned the craft from travelling Awka master smiths. But no large community of smiths developed there to rival the Awka men.

It would be futile to attempt to enumerate all the products of Igbo smiths. It suffices to say they made all the varied iron tools which the Igbo needed in the home and farm, in war and peace, for rituals and ceremonies. Very artful and adaptable, they soon learned to make dane guns and to build imitations of imported European metal wares. There is an Igbo saying that *odigh ihe asi uzu kpuo o na-akpugh*—'there is nothing a blacksmith is asked to forge that he cannot forge'—which summarizes the competence of these smiths and the faith the Igbo had in them.

The salt industry, like smithery, was one which was associated with spirit-forces. It was limited to the North-Eastern and Eastern Igbo area—Uburu, Okposi and Abakaliki—which had brine lakes. But of these Uburu and Okposi were the most famous and a large fair developed at Uburu, to which people from all parts of Igboland and beyond came to trade. The brine lakes were associated with a local god, which is believed to have laid down the rules guiding their exploitation. One of these was that only women could fetch and evaporate the brine. Another was that such women must be non-menstruous, and to ensure that this was so, women had to approach the brine lakes stark naked. Also, strangers were forbidden to participate in the business.

The industry required little training and little initial capital outlay. The women fetched the brine in pots and evaporated this over slow fire in special earthen jars known as *oku* until each *oku* was filled to the brim with solid salt. The Uburu area is grassland dotted with shrubs. This made it difficult to find enough firewood to heat the earthen jars. The women, therefore, supplemented what little firewood they had with grasses, the ashes of which easily flew back into the jars. As a result, the *nnu oku* from Uburu was always of a dirty grew colour. The grains, however, were so large that a pinch or two could easily season a whole pot of soup.

Another women's industry in pre-colonial Igboland was the weaving of cotton cloth. The Igbo Ukwu excavation has revealed that this industry is a long established one among the

Igbo, stretching back to a period beyond the ninth century A.D. Even before they learned to use cotton, the Igbo made cloth from the fibrous bark of certain trees, especially the *aji* plant. The making of this particular type of cloth was a man's affair, as it was very exerting. But with the introduction of cotton, cloth weaving became women's business. The industry was so time-consuming that it was carried on largely in fattening rooms, by old women and by young girls who would normally not be involved in farm work. Yet an energetic young woman could engage in it as a hobby, and weave as she found the time.

The weaving industry was most highly developed in Northern Igboland, especially among the Elugwu and in the West Niger Igbo area. It has, at times, been suggested that the industry was introduced into these areas by the Igala and Edo respectively, but the evidence for this opinion cannot yet be considered conclusive. Two main colours of cloth were produced—white and blue. Cloths were dyed blue by steeping either the thread or the finished woven material in liquid preparations from local berries (*uri*) and herbs (*alulu* or *alu*).

In spite of the increased quantity of cheap European cotton goods sent into Igboland from the nineteenth century, the cloth industry of the Northern and Western Igbo retained its vigour well into this century. And, even today, it is still being practised on a surprisingly significant scale. It still has its advantages over imported cloth, especially for ritual and ceremonial purposes.

Another important Igbo village craft, which also deserves mention, is carving. This was a very lucrative occupation in pre-colonial Igbo society, where it had to meet the needs of religion, of practical utility and of entertainment. Each of the myriads of gods and goddesses in Igboland had its representation in wood and owing to the ravages of white ants, these were constantly being replaced. The headpieces of the even more numerous masquerades, which performed on festive and ritual occasions, were the handiwork of Igbo carvers. The Igbo carver also made stools, doors, panels, wooden utensils and other domestic gadgets, whose production required working on wood.

Probably only in one instance, that of the Umudioka of Awka in Northern Igboland, did a whole community specialize as carvers and organize a guild. Otherwise, the craft tended to run in individual families. It was an art and the Igbo tended to believe that one was born, not made, an artist. But this is not to say that carving was not taught or learned. The point was that the natural born carver would normally show his mettle in boyhood, before being apprenticed to a master carver, who then helped him to develop, taught him the motifs, concepts and techniques of Igbo carving.

The carvers of Ụmụdiọka were specially famed for the manufacture of ritual objects and insignia. They made plenty of money from carving the ceremonial stools, doors and panels used by titled men. This was a particularly lucrative line of business, for each rank in the hierachically ordered ọzọ title society had a special design of stool appropriate to it. As a man moved from one rank to the next, he bought the stool that went with it. So also did he acquire and display the right types and number of carved wooden doors and panels attached to each rank. It is not known how much the Ụmụdiọka and other Igbo carvers pursued their profession to produce objects which were bought and cherished for purely aesthetic reasons. What does appear to be certain, however, is that their work was determined mostly by the demands of religion and utility, though in execution they did not ignore proportion, form and beauty.

Limited patronage for decorative objects must, to some extent, have circumscribed the economic horizon of Igbo carvers. But what horizon existed they exploited to the fullest. Carvers were not a despised group in Igbo society. On the contrary, they were highly respected. Not only was their inspiration admired and respected, so also was the material well-being which it brought. The word *omenka* (literally maker of art) could be applied to any highly skilled man or woman in the manufacturing professions, but it was applied more often to carvers, the word *nka* (art) being, in fact derived from *ka* (cut, carve). Thus, the praise-title *omenka* was one to which any Igbo manufacturer would normally aspire. It showed approval and acceptance and says something of the economic, aesthetic and ritual place of carvers in pre-colonial Igbo Society.

Comments and Conclusions

The economic side of pre-colonial Igbo society thus rested on three legs—agriculture, trade and manufacture. Agriculture was the main economic activity, with trade and manufacture coming as subsidiaries. Trade distributed the products of agriculture and manufacture, while the latter not only offered some relief from the other two more strenuous occupations, but also supplied the technological base of Igbo society, as well as providing some of the items made necessary by social and ritual life. There is evidence to show that trade and manufacture grew in importance as time went on, and in consequence of which, by the nineteenth century, Igbo society could be said to have reached a stage at which some people, or even some communities, were coming to live more and more by trade and manufacture.

Most of the communities which were becoming professional traders or manufacturers, professional diviners or oracle agents, were located on the Northern Igbo plateau. This was also that portion of Igboland where agriculture was beginning to fail, owing to poor soil. So the two events were probably connected. But in accounting for this development, we cannot leave out the trade with Europe, which, by offering a wider range of goods in exchange for others, contributed to the general broadening of the scope for business activities among these communities.

NOTES

1. A. E. Afigbo, 'The Indigenous Political Systems of the Igbo-speaking Peoples' in *Tarikh*, Vol. 4, No. 2, 1973.
2. V. C. Uchendu, *The Igbo of Southeast Nigeria* (Holt Rinehart and Winston, 1965), p. 30.
3. *Ibid.*, p. 27.
4. I mean here the period after 1450 or so.
5. Yehuda Karmon, *A Geography of Settlement in Eastern Nigeria* (Jerusalem, 1966), pp. 28–9.
6. J. E. Flint, *Nigeria and Ghana* (New Jersey, 1966), p. 63.
7. In traditional Igbo thought it is not usual to talk of a man owning land (*Ala*). On the contrary *Ala* was believed to own every man.
8. M. D. W. Jeffreys, 'The Umundri Tradition of Origin', *African Studies*, Vol. 15, No. 3, 1956, pp. 122–3.
9. *Ibid.*, p. 123.
10. M. D. W. Jeffreys, 'The Umundri Tradition of Origin', *loc. cit.*, pp. 124–5.
11. Thurstan Shaw, '*Igbo Ukwu, An Account of Archaeological Discoveries in Eastern Nigeria*' (London, 1970).
12. E. J. Alagoa, 'Long Distance Trade and States in the Niger Delta', *Journal of African History*, Vol. 11, No. 3, 1970, pp. 319–29.
13. David Northrup, 'The growth of trade among the Igbo before 1800', *loc. cit.*
14. A. E. Afigbo, 'Chief Igwegbe Odum: The Omenuko of History', *Nigeria Magazine*, No. 90, 1966, pp. 222–31.
15. G. T. Basden, *Among the Igbos of Nigeria* (London, 1921), p. 201.
16. S. N. Nwabara, 'Ibo Land: A study in British penetration and the problems of Administration' (Ph.D. Northwestern, 1965), pp. 195–6.
    W. I. Ofonagoro, 'The Opening-up of Southern Nigeria to British Trade, etc., 1881–1916' (Ph.D., Columbia, 1971), pp. 131–3.
    A. E. Afigbo, 'Trade and Trade Routes in Nineteenth-century Nsukka', *Journal of the Historical Society of Nigeria*, Vol. 7, No. 1, 1973, pp. 77–90.
17. G. I. Jones, 'Native and Trade Currencies in Southern Nigeria in the Eighteenth and Nineteenth Centuries', *Africa*, Vol. 23, No. 1, 1958, pp. 43–54.

5. Through a Glass Darkly

Eighteenth Century Igbo Society Through Equiano's Narrative

On 1 March 1789 a freed slave by name Olaudah Equiano, or Gustavus Vassa the African, published his autobiography. This little book by a little-known and socially handicapped 'black moor' excited a great deal of interest in certain circles in Britain and the European continent. It was in demand for about fifty years, went into several editions in English, and was even translated into German and Dutch. By the 1850s the author was long dead, and the book had been relegated to a limbo. Interest in it did not revive for over a century. Then in 1960 the celebrated Africanist, Mr. Thomas Hodgkin, dug it up and included an extract from it in his selection of documents on Nigerian history.[1]

As often happens in history, this fortuitous event inaugurated the rehabilitation of Olaudah Equiano and his autobiography. And ever since scholars have been engaged in an attempt to understand and reassess the importance of the book. In fact from about that time hardly any year has passed without something being published on Equiano. In 1962 Mr. Christopher Fyfe, in his monumental history of Sierra Leone, discussed Equiano's part in organizing the expedition for the settlement of Sierra Leone and his role in the anti-slavery movement generally. In 1963 the book *Many Thousands Gone* by C. H. Nichols which makes a study of the slave narratives was published. Equiano's autobiography was one of the works given prominence in it. In 1964 the great Igbo novelist, Mr. Chinua Achebe, published in the *Spear Magazine* an article entitled 'Handicaps of Writing in a Second Language' in which he discussed Equiano as one of the first successful pioneers of that tricky enterprise. The same year Dr. D. I. Nwoga gave extended treatment to Equiano in his doctoral thesis on *West African Literature in English*. The following year, 1965, Mr. O. R. Dathorne devoted one short article entitled 'Olaudah Equiano:

145

A Nigerian Writer of the 18th Century', which he published in the *Nigerian Magazine*, to Equiano and his book. Then in 1967 two works came out on him. On the one hand Mr. Paul Edwards, sometime Lecturer in English in the University College of Fourah Bay, brought out an abridged edition of the book with an introduction and notes under the title *Equiano's Travels*. On the other an anthology edited by Professor Phillip Curtin and entitled *Africa Remembered* carried an extract from Equiano with a brief introduction by Mr. G. I. Jones—lecturer in Social Anthropology in the University of Cambridge. In 1968 the present author gave him some prominence in dealing with the abolitionist movement while Longman inserted his photograph where that of Wilberforce or Clackson would in earlier days have appeared in such a book.[2] This work of rehabilitation and revival was to have reached its peak with a reissue of the whole book by Frank Cass and Company under their laudable scheme for reprinting vital works long since out of print. The present writer was to contribute a new introduction to the edition but the Nigerian Crisis frustrated this plan. Mr. Edwards has since brought out the unabridged edition. Equiano and his book would thus seem to have returned to the full glare of history.

In spite of this growing interest in Equiano and in spite of the volume of literature to which this reawakened interest has given rise, there is yet no full scale study of the man placing his work in its historical context and drawing out his full significance for us today. Yet such a study is necessary. It is made all the more necessary by the fact that some of the works mentioned above have given us conflicting and questionable interpretations of Equiano's book, *The Interesting Narrative*. Some writers have seen its importance as lying in the fact that it contains the earliest description of the Igbo and their society that we have. They thus see it as a source of historical and ethnographic information on pre-colonial Igbo society without making an attempt at a critical evaluation of that information. This observation applies specifically to those scholars who have taken extracts from it for inclusion in historical anthologies. Here we shall deal with this aspect of the problem by focusing our attention on Equiano and Igbo society.

To the historically minded Equiano's chief importance would seem to lie in the fact that his book, *The Interesting Narrative*, contains what has been described as 'his recollections of Ibo village life in the mid-eighteenth century'.³ In this sense it is the earliest eye-witness account of the Igbo which we have. The next was to be that of the Landers based on information which they collected during their epoch-making journey down the Niger in 1830. For the rest all we have before about the fifth decade of the nineteenth century are the bits of information, based largely on hear-say evidence, contained in the records of the slave captains who visited the coast of the Oil Rivers in the era of the slave trade. Scarcity confers value not only on consumer goods but also on historical records. In the absence of any other source of evidence on the Igbo earlier than Equiano's *Interesting Narrative* or contemporary with it, historians have tended to treat it less critically than they should. It is this fact which explains Hodgkin's enthusiastic acceptance of the account as based on Equiano's recollections. More directly Hodgkin states that it is 'especially valuable in the absence of other written records relating to the period'.⁴ But we cannot forever close our eyes to the question: How far was Equiano's description of Igbo society based on his own 'recollections'? How much of it is authentic historical record and how much was imaginative reconstruction or a hotch-potch built up from scraps of information collected from fellow slaves or ex-slaves who came from different sections of Igbo land or even of Africa? We would be abandoning our responsibilities as critical historians should we subscribe unreservedly to the slogan 'better a bad document than no document at all'.

According to Equiano's own testimony, he was born about the year 1745 and was kidnapped and sold into slavery in the year 1756, that is at the age of eleven.⁵ This fact of his having been sold into slavery at such a tender age must be kept steadily in view in any attempt to estimate what amount of historical and ethnographic authority to attach to his *Narrative*. Between his being kidnapped from his village and his being taken into a slave ship for transportation to the West Indies was a period of about seven months by his reckoning. 'Thus I continued to travel', he said,

> sometimes by land, sometimes by water, through different countries, and various nations, till, at the end of six or seven months after I had been kidnapped, I arrived at the sea coast.⁶

He was thus less than twelve years old when he left the Bight of Biafra. The question is how much of his people's customs, institutions and culture would a child of that age know, and how much would he remember after over thirty years of brutalization, humiliation and despair in a slave colony?

This is a crucial question in view of the relatively humble position which women and children occupied in traditional Igbo and similar African societies. Though both were valued rather than despised, their place in society was determined by custom. Putting it crudely, but nonetheless accurately, they were for the most part to be seen rather than heard. Women and children were not generally admitted into the secrets of the tribe. Unless specifically requested to do so, they would not present themselves before the council of the village elders where issues of great moment to the group would normally be dealt with. Though, as Equiano correctly pointed out[7] a rich man could buy titles for his son or initiate him into secret societies, this did not entitle the boy to know the secrets of these societies as it was feared that 'children, like women, could not keep their mouths shut'. Such initiation of little boys into these privileged and restricted organizations was largely a matter of financial investment, as it entitled a man who had so initiated his sons to take many shares when the entrance fees of new members were being shared.

Equiano would be specially subject to these handicaps since he was a last son—last sons being usually more closely attached to their mothers than to their fathers. This was one of those aspects of Igbo society which Equiano recaptured with precision. As a last son he was his mother's, not his father's favourite and special responsibility. 'I was', he said, 'very fond of my mother, and almost constantly with her'.[8] He was so fond of her that he followed her to the local markets, to her mother's grave when she went there to make sacrifices,[9] and could not keep away from her during her menstruous periods when, by Igbo custom, women should stay away from men, especially titled men in order to avoid the ritual contamination of those personages. On this Equiano says:

> I was so fond of my mother I could not keep from her, or avoid touching her at some of those periods in consequence of which I was obliged to be kept out with her, in a little house made for that purpose, till offering was made, and then we were purified.[10]

On another occasion he wrote: 'As I was the youngest of the sons, I became, of course, the greatest favourite with my mother, and was always with her, and she used to take particular pains to form my mind'.[11] Being thus educated by his mother he would be vast in domestic crafts and folklore. Had he been a first son, the one to succeed to his father's *Obi* and *Ọfọ*, he would have been attached to his father who would take responsibility for 'forming his mind', for introducing him to the secrets and structure of the group as he grew up. He would be entitled to accompany his father to the meetings of the village elders (*ama ala*) and of the titled but not secret societies as he had to carry his father's stool and skin (or raffia) bag. If intelligent, he would then have an early chance of understanding his society.

Equiano was thus not only too young to have known much about his people's way of life because his was a society in which education was slow and informal, but in addition he was a stay at home child attached to his mother. Consequently, in writing his book he probably had to depend to a substantial extent on information collected from fellow slaves and ex-slaves, and on the travellers accounts of Guinea which were popular in his time.

There is, scattered throughout the book, evidence that Equiano maintained contact with fellow Igbo slaves. When he landed at Barbados, for instance, he fell in with some other members of the unfortunate gang that had just done the Middle Passage with him who were also Igbo. While he was in a state of astonishment over seeing horses and their riders for the first time, he said,

> one of my fellow prisoners spoke to a countryman of his about the horses, who said they were the same kind they had in their country. I understood them though they were from a distant part of Africa, and I thought it odd I had not seen any horses there; but afterwards when I came to converse with different Africans, I found they had many horses amongst them.[12]

It is most likely that the first group in the above passage who talked about the horses with Equiano were Igbo. Since these unfortunate men had just landed in the West Indies, they could not have acquired even a smattering of the bastardized English which was the language of communication amongst the slaves and between them and their masters. They must, therefore, have spoken in their native tongue which most likely was one of the many dialects of Igbo—what Equiano in another passage described as different languages. According to him, from the time he was kidnapped he always found somebody that understood him until he came to the sea coast. To explain this he wrote:

> The languages of different nations (in his part of the world) did not totally differ, nor were they so copious as those of the Europeans, particularly the English. They were therefore easily learned; and while I was journeying thus through Africa, I acquired two or three different tongues.[13]

Sense of 'country' was very narrow in pre-colonial Igbo land, so narrow that it could at times be limited to the village-group. With a young boy who had never travelled out of his village before and had not attended any of the large inter-group markets or fairs where speakers of many different Igbo dialects met, this narrowness of outlook would be even more pronounced. This would then explain why what must have been dialects of the same language were described by him as different tongues and how the young Equiano who was being hustled down the coast to be sold, could learn 'two or three different tongues' within a space of about seven months even though no special efforts could have been made by his masters to teach him these tongues. The Ijọ of the coast occupy only a narrow belt of territory. Thus it can be understood if in moving south he travelled for the most part in Igbo land.

Coming back to the question of the first Igbo people who talked to him at Barbados, they probably came from the Northern Igbo area into which horses had penetrated quite early in history in the course of the north-south and south-north trade that brought the Igbo and the Igala into close contact. The second set of Africans who discussed horses with Equiano could have come from any part of the northern fringes of the West African forest zone. By the time this discussion was held, Equiano described it as 'afterwards', he and his friends had probably acquired some knowledge of the *lingua franca* of the slave plantations. It is also likely that during this and other discussions, they talked of other aspects of their life in Africa. This and such other discussions, probably provided one likely source from which some of the non-Igbo elements entered into Equiano's description of Igbo society.

Even after leaving the West Indies, Equiano continued to maintain contact with his fellow Africans, especially with other

Igbo slaves and ex-slaves. 'Deformity', he argued at one point, 'is indeed unknown amongst us, I mean that of shape. Numbers of the nation Eboe (Igbo) now in London, might be brought in support of this assertion...'.[14] And there were likely to be many such Igbo in London and elsewhere in Britain as the planter class were in the habit of travelling back home with their loyal and serviceable slaves. And Igbo slaves were considered particularly loyal and hardworking as household servants. Testifying to this quality of the Igbo, Captain Hugh Crow wrote in 1830:

> This race (Eboes) is, as has already been remarked, of a more mild and engaging disposition than the other tribes, particularly the Quaws (Annang Ibibio) and though less suited for severe mannual labour of the field, they are preferred in the West Indian colonies for their fidelity and utility, as domestic servants.[15]

Another source of information on Africa generally which Equiano would appear to have exploited, was the series of travel narratives written by the slave captains who travelled to West Africa. Equiano referred specifically only to one of these, A. Benezet's *Some Historical Accounts of Guinea*, published in Philadelphia in 1772.[16] It is not unlikely that he depended on a number of other such sources. In appraising Equiano's description of Igbo society in mid-eighteenth century, therefore, it is necessary to take into account these facts of his limited knowledge and the erosion which that little knowledge was bound to suffer under years of slavery in the West Indies, his dependence on information gathered from other slaves, and from the impressionistic accounts of Guinea produced at the time by European visitors to West Africa. Thus equipped we shall now go on with an examination of aspects of Equiano's description of Igbo society.

After reading *The Interesting Narrative*, one of the first things that strikes the critical scholar is how scanty and muddled Equiano's 'recollection' of Igbo society is. Mr. G. I. Jones describes it as 'disappointingly brief and confused'.[17] Thus such key Igbo institutions as *ọfọ, ọzọ, mmọ* or *mmanwu* (masquerade) etc. escaped his notice. This was either because being a stay-at-home child attached to his mother he knew nothing about these particularly male concerns, or because his knowledge had been seriously eroded by the passage of time and by brutality. The only institution of note which he described is *itchi* which appears in his *Narrative* as *Embrenche*. And in his description of this institution, at least two institutions would appear to have been confused. These are *Igbu ichi* (facial scarification) and *Ndichie* which in parts of Igbo land means elders, and in others ancestors. He said,

> My father was one of those elders or chiefs I have spoken of, and was styled Embrenche, a term as I remember, importing the highest distinction, and signifying in our language a mark of grandeur. This mark is conferred on the person entitled to it, by cutting the skin across at the forehead, and drawing it down to the eyebrows etc.[18]

The closest Igbo term to Equiano's *Embrenche* is *Mgburuichi* or *Mgbirichi* which in parts of Igbo land is a titulary deity, and was never used in addressing a person. *Igbu ichi*, the art of facial scarification, was not used as title or style before a man's name, but Equiano talked of the men being styled *Embrenche*. Furthermore a man with an *ichi* mark did not necessarily or automatically become a member of the village council, *ama ala*. It was usual for a wealthy man to make his beloved son undergo *igbu ichi* early in life and at his expense. But this did not necessarily mean that the young man had achieved renown or acquired the right to sit with the elders in council. Yet Equiano says 'Those Embrenche, ..., decided disputes and punished crimes...'[19] It was more likely that highly distinguished elders could be saluted or styled *Ndichie* or *Ichie*, the two terms meaning elder. Thus Equiano's conception of *Embrenche* combines the two ideas of *igbu ichi*, facial decoration by scarification, and *Ndichie*, the status of an elder, also a form of title and salutation whose bearers were invariably members of the village council or *ama ala*.

Among the more astounding omissions by Equiano is his failure to mention his father's, or mother's or even sister's name. We do not in fact know whether Equiano was the family name or his father's name. But even particularly more disturbing was his failure to call his mother and sister by name, yet he was fond of them. He apostrophizes his sister in a number of moving passages, but not once in the whole narrative did he give us her name. It can only be assumed that he had forgotten it. And if it was possible for him to forget such intimate things, his childhood comrades and so on, how much of his people's institutions and customs in which he could not have been so intelligently interested and so widely versed so early in life would he remember?

This question is very pertinent as an answer to it should enable us to settle a number of problems which the book presents. The first of these is the question of from what part of Igbo land he derived. Many scholars have tried to answer this question through the use of internal evidence from *The Interesting Narrative*. On the basis of this Mr. Chinua Achebe, probably impressed by the close similarity in sound between 'Essaka' and 'Iseke', thinks he came from Iseke in Orlu.[20] Dr. D. I. Nwoga probably also impressed by the similarity in sound between Essaka and Nsukka, and placing a great deal of weight on Equiano's description of the route by which he was moved out of Igbo land, derived him from Nsukka,[21] a Northern Igbo border community, now the seat of the University of Nigeria. Equiano, by his own account, said he travelled in the south-westward direction and that he travelled most of the time without leaving Igbo land. Those who place emphasis on this description say it rules out the possibility of his having come from the West Niger Igbo area or from among the Southern Igbo. The present writer would personally rule out the idea of the young Equiano having had sufficient peace and presence of mind to note so accurately, as he claimed, the direction in which the sun set and rose, while he was being hurried out of his familiar environment through the bush. 'I was now carried to the west of the sun's rising', said Equiano at one point, 'through many dreadry wastes and dismal woods, amidst the hideous roaring of wild beasts'.[22] 'We should not', argues Mr. Edwards, 'expect a precise record of a journey made in childhood under such terrifying conditions . . .'.[23] Furthermore, the fixing of terrestrial positions by reference to the motion of the heavenly bodies I would consider a science too sophisticated for a boy of eleven years in mid-eighteenth century Igbo society.

Another scholar, Mr. G. I. Jones, is definite that Olaudah Equiano came from the West Niger Igbo area. 'We can locate his home with some certainty', he writes, 'in the Northern Ika Ibo region; which is the eastern part of the present Benin Province'.[24] His reasons include the assumption that *Equiano* is *Ekwuno* which he describes as 'a common Ika and riverain Ibo name', Equiano's description of the dress of his people, and claim to have come from Benin. On the question of what were precise Igbo versions of Olaudah Equiano's names, there can be no certainty or agreement, especially if an attempt is made to correlate meanings attached to his names with internal evidence from the book. Equiano says he was named *Olaudah* 'which in our language, signifies vicissitude or good fortune also, one favoured, and having a loud voice, and well spoken'.[25] Unless we are to assume that between the middle of the eighteenth and the beginning of the twentieth century the Igbo language had undergone radical transformations, it is impossible to think of any reading of Olaudah which would give it such meaning as 'vicissitude or good fortune' 'one favoured' by God. On the other hand if his first name meant 'loud voiced' then it should be something like Olu-ụda (contracted, *Oluda*) or *Olu-ude* (contracted *Olude*) and not *Ọla-ụdah* which would mean literally 'the resonant ring' or probably more figuratively *Ogene* (gong). If we took his second name, Equiano, we run into similar problems. There are many personal names in the Igbo language which an ex-slave who had lost a fine control of the language could have rendered as *Equiano*. These include *Ekwuno* as suggested by Jones, or *Ekweanọ* as suggested by Mr. Achebe or *Ekwoanya* as suggested by the present writer elsewhere.[26] There is thus no particular reason for Jones's choice of *Ekwuno* which, in any case, is not peculiar to the Ika Igbo.

Then there is the argument based on Equiano's description of his peoples attire. 'The dresses of both sexes', says Equiano, 'are nearly the same. It generally consists of a long piece of calico, or muslin, wrapped loosely round the body. . . . This is usually dyed blue, which is our favourable colour.'[27] Jones thinks this could not apply to the Eastern Igbo. Cotton he says, 'except in a few areas where it has been introduced from Igala, is not grown by Ibo east of the Niger. . . . Similarly indigo dyeing is confined to the Western side of the Niger and to Igala. . . .'[28] The least one can say of this opinion here is, first, to observe that it is the old theory of all civilized elements amongst the Igbo coming from the ruling aristocracies of Idah and Benin to whom Palmer attributed a Hamitic ancestry.[29] Secondly, it should be pointed out that there are villages in the Nsukka area which traditionally manufactured cloth dyed blue which they exported to Uburu, in Ohozara, in exchange for salt. This cloth penetrated the rest of Igbo land as *Akwa Uburu*. In Nsukka this industry is still a going concern and much of the mop cloth used in the University of Nigeria comes from it. Even if Jones established that this industry derived from Igala, unless he also established that its introduction did not predate the eighteenth century, there would be no ground for assuming that

Equiano could not have been describing the dress and industry of a Northern Igbo people. Thirdly, cotton spinning and the use of indigo as dye was more widespread in Igbo land than Jones recognized.

And then there is the point of Equiano's claim that his part of Igbo land was under the distant and vague suzerainty of Benin. 'This kingdom (Benin)', he says, 'is divided into many provinces or districts: in one of the most remote and fertile of which I was born in the year 1745 ... our subjection to Benin was little more than nominal ...'[30] On the basis of this claim Mr. Jones produced an ethnographic description of the Ika Igbo area, with the influences from Benin emphasized, as a description of Equiano's part of Igbo land. But this would appear to me like making too much of this more or less casual reference to Benin, and as a misunderstanding of the significance of that passage.

In order to grasp clearly the significance of the passage we have to pin down briefly but precisely the message of Equiano's *Narrative*. Most scholars have seen it primarily as Equiano's autobiography or as a travel narrative. But it would appear that this book is not so much about a slave, as about the slave trade, especially about its evil side. To drive this home Equiano had to tell the story of an idyllic life in a rich and beautiful vale suddenly disrupted by the iniquitous slave raider, a disruption which even emancipation could not restore. To do so with good effect and verisimilitude he had to place his early life in a political context which his readers would understand. This matter cannot be fully dealt with here, but it must be observed that Olaudah Equiano was a skilful propagandist. At least in this regard he has held his readers spell-bound for nearly two centuries. To find the familiar context against which to tell the story of his early life, he most likely depended on the travel literature of the age which never tired of talking of Benin. His description of the extent and power of this empire could have been taken from any of the standard eighteenth-century studies or rather speculations on the political geography of that part of Guinea. Thus he talks of the empire of Benin being bordered on one side by the empire of Abyssinia.[31]

Partly because of his upbringing under the influence of his mother, Equiano did not have a wide knowledge of his environment, he did not know the names of the villages and towns bordering his own. How easy it would have been to locate the community in which he was born if only he had mentioned the names of one or two more villages apart from his own. Had he been a first son who had had the opportunity of following his father to the assemblies of his people, he would have had a more intimate knowledge of the political geography of his area. He would also have known a few more proverbs than the one about the bitter herb (*utazi* or *onugbu*) which he probably picked up from his mother's fireside. I would therefore discount the idea of Equiano who did not know the names of their neighbouring villages knowing of the distant and vague political overlordship of Benin. I would also discount the possibility of locating Equiano's home village on the basis of the evidence contained in his *Interesting Narrative*. What appears to be possible and probable is that most of the ethnographic information supplied by Equiano put together would tend to point to his having derived from a Northern Igbo community.

Another important issue raised by *The Interesting Narrative* is contained in Equiano's account of war in Igbo society. According to his story Igbo society was fairly highly militarized, while wars and rumours of wars were a common occurence. On this matter Equiano writes:

> Our tillage is exercised in a large plain or common, some four hours walk from our dwellings. . . . This common is *often*[32] the theatre of war; and therefore when our people go out to till their land, they not only go in body, but generally take their arms with them for fear of surprise; and when they apprehend an invasion, they guard the avenues of their dwellings, by driving sticks into the ground which are so sharp at one end as to pierce the foot and are generally dipt in poison.[33]

Also the militarization of society had gone so far that even the women had become lusty warriors wielding broad swords and javelins where the battle was thickest. He says:

> Even our women are warriors, and march out boldly to fight along with the men. Our whole district is a kind of militia. On a given signal, such as the firing of a gun at night, they all rise in arms and rush upon the enemy . . . I was once a witness to a battle in our common. We had all been at work in it one day as usual, when our people were suddenly attacked. I climbed a tree at a distance, from which I beheld the fight. There were many women as well as men on both sides; among others my mother was there and armed with a broad sword.[34]

One of the casualties on this occasion, he says, was a young virgin. In another passage Equiano claims: 'I was trained up from my earliest years in the art of agriculture and war *my daily exercise was shooting and the throwing of javelins; and my mother adorned me with emblems, after the manner of our greatest warrior.*'[35]

Mr. G. I. Jones found the reference to Igbo women taking an active part in war 'surprising' but then added that 'there are recorded cases, however, of Isuama Ibo villages which were smaller than their neighbours and which made up for their deficient manpower by encouraging their womenfolk to fight alongside their husbands in defence of their farmlands. This may have been more general in the eighteenth century and in Olaudah's area'.[36] Much as one would not wish to postulate that Igbo society was static throughout the eighteenth and nineteenth centuries, it must be observed that such a drastic change almost amounting to a revolution, as would have obliterated such a long standing social practice as postulated by Jones must be ruled out. What was the change in inter-group relations in Igbo land between 1745 and 1900 that would bring about a decline in militarism, if it had been a feature of Igbo life? Also the kind of militarization of Igbo society which Equiano and Jones suggest would have, if it existed, left behind other noticeable social effects, like increased political integration. What evidence exists tends to show that the nineteenth century was probably no less turbulent in Igbo land than the preceding centuries in which case such militarization of society should have survived into this century. There are many aspects of Igbo society vividly recaptured by *The Interesting Narrative* which remained recognizable in Igbo land till the early 1940s at least. There are enough documentary and oral records on Igbo warfare in the nineteenth century and early part of this century, but in neither has any reference to women taking an active part in bloody wars occurred, except probably the one referred to but not discussed in detail by Jones. Surely Mr. Jones's rationalization will not serve.

One key to the problem may well lie in the fact that the Igbo word *ogu*, usually translated *war*, is a vague term indeed covering many shades of hostile encounters. There is for instance what the Igbo know as *ogu okpiri* which refers to a war fought with sticks only. This type usually obtained amongst people who were related in one way or the other and between whom the drawing of blood, let alone the taking of life, was prohibited. In such ọgụ women and children freely took part. But beyond that was ọgụ egbe na mma (literally, the war of knives and guns). This shade of war was usually less frequent than the first and could only obtain amongst enemies who were not related by blood. In this second category of war, women and children had no direct part.

Traditionally there were two main roles which women played in such wars. The first, and closest to direct participation, was for them to offer supporting services to the young men who did the fighting. In the event of a pitched battle, they would remain at a safe distance behind the men to ensure that the latter had plentiful supplies of stones and short sticks for use as missiles. They would also help in evacuating the dead and wounded after these had been dragged out from the scene of action by the men. Recording an instance of this in the nineteenth century Rev. S. Crowther of the C.M.S. said about the two inveterate enemies, Onitsha and Ogidi, as follows:

> When they do come to an open fight in the plain, it is said they are fierce. They do not capture to make slaves, but they kill everyone they lay hold of, and take their heads as trophies to their homes. To prevent their own dead bodies being taken away by their enemies, women follow them in their battles, and are employed in removing the dead and wounded out of the way so that the men do not lose time in doing this, but continue to face their enemies.[36a]

The second main role of the women in ọgụ egbu ebi ishi was to initiate and effect early and speedy settlement of the matter at issue between the warring villages. Here the institution of inter-village marriage in Igbo society came ready to hand. Neighbouring Igbo villages were, except in cases of extreme estrangement, usually linked by marriage, trade and other cultural ties. Thus if village *A* fell out with village *B*, women born in the latter village but married in the former would meet women born in village *A* but married in *B* and decide to impose peace. The group, known as ụmụ ada or ụmụ ọkpụ would approach the battle field carrying green leaves and twigs, especially folded palm fronds (ọmụ), with appropriate songs on the evils of war and the benefits of peace. This move invariably forced the combatants to separate and initiate peace discussions. Should they not disengage, which was unheard of, they would run the grave risk of injuring their own daughters in anger and this would be an abomination against the Earth Goddess, *Ala*. Apart from the above there is no evidence available to the present writer of women engaging directly in *ogu egbu ebi ishi*. For the rest women traders going to distant markets would travel in large caravans and carry studded cudgels for defence against raiders, robbers and head-hunters. In traditional Igbo society the sword was not a woman's weapon.[37] Because of Equiano's acquaintance with descriptions of other parts of Guinea, already established above, it is likely that here he was using material more relevant to Dahomey where the *ahosi* or the Amazons played a major part in warfare.

What is surprising in Equiano's account of warfare in eighteenth century Igbo land is not only the role he assigned to the women. There is also the question of its endemic character. Thus he argues it was because of the almost eternal imminence of war that the entire village had to have their farms in one zone any one year, and the men carried their swords and guns when going to the farm. One would not deny the menace of slave raiders and head-hunters in eighteenth century Igbo land or even later and these to the young Equiano would all pass for war. Nor would one minimize the incidence of inter-village fracas over farm land. In fact the battle which Equiano says he watched in their common was more likely to have been a straight land dispute. Equiano's village had probably gone there with the specific purpose of asserting effective ownership when the news reached the opposing village whose young men then went there to contest the claim. If it had been a slave raid, as Equiano implied, it would have aimed at surprise and been executed either at night or early in the morning.

There were reasons other than consideration for security why an Igbo village would go to the farm in a body and cultivate a contiguous area each year. The habit of everybody farming in the same area at the same time had something to do with the traditional system of bush-fallowing and the fact that in those years it was the village head, *okpara*, and the other elders who every year decided which portion of the village land had 'matured' for planting. The people went in a body partly because being all agriculturalists and observing the same calendar and week days with detailed rules and regulations on farming time etc., the pressure 'to get done with it' was more or less equally on all concerned at the same time. Also anybody who was in the habit of going to the farm lands alone, was usually suspected to be a thief. Of the arms the men carried, only the gun was not needed in the farm. But then all grown up Igbo were also hunters of sorts and experience showed that one could encounter some game any time.

Why, one would then ask, did Equiano give such a prominent place to war and warfare in eighteenth century Igbo land? Was it again a case of eroded memory or outright ignorance? I think it was probably neither. The emphasis on war and warfare was related to his larger purpose—to show in lurid colours the harm which the slave trade was doing to Africa. Thus he says most of these wars were waged for purposes of catching slaves, and in fact were instigated by slave dealers. 'From what I can recollect of these battles', he writes,

> they appear to have been irruptions of one little state or district on the other, to obtain prisoners or booty. Perhaps they were incited to this by those traders who brought the European goods I mentioned amongst us. Such a mode of obtaining slaves in Africa is common; and I believe more are procured this way, and by kidnapping, than any other.[38]

Other evidence on this matter, is not in support of Equiano. The 1841 Niger Expedition asked the Obi of Abo specifically whether he usually made war in order to catch slaves. The Obi denied this, pointing out, however, that when people made war on him, he took prisoners and sold these as slaves.[39] On the same matter P. A. Talbot had the following to say:

> Although large numbers of Ibo were exported as slaves from Bonny, Old Calabar, and other Oil Rivers ports, these were not obtained in slave raiding expeditions or wars, but were mostly debtors, criminals, those who had committed abominations in their villages and other people whom their communities wished to be rid of.[40]

Talbot came to Southern Nigeria early in this century and saw traditional Igbo society in action. He also engaged in extensive ethnographic inquiries into indigenous society. His testimony can thus be regarded as reflecting the view of his Igbo informants. His conclusions in this regard have also been upheld by the results of inquiries made by the present writer.

But in spite of all the questions raised above, it cannot be denied that Equiano's account, no matter how he came by his materials, gives some idea of the character of traditional Igbo society, especially with reference to Igbo village government, some of the methods of procurring slaves, economic and social life, religion and medical science. In many cases, his description of these aspects of Igbo society could be corroborated by evidence collected from Igbo elders today. Today any Igbo man of forty years and above who observed his village environment closely even as late as the early forties of this century would, on reading Equiano, be reminded of his childhood days. The cultural continuity which this would imply would also seem to rule out the view that the discrepancies noted above between Equiano's descriptions and Igbo society of the early years of this century can all be accounted for by the normal processes of social change.

Let us first examine the general pattern of an Igbo family compound which Equiano described for eighteenth century Igbo land. This continued to obtain with little or no modification until very recent times.[40a] One feature which still obtains is that of the family compound being walled round, with the wall having at least three gates. The main gate led to the village square and market. The second in importance led to the farm lands and the stream. The third, usually small and concealed, was an emergency escape gate. Equiano omitted these gates from his description or probably assumed them. The reason for the wall was partly for defence, to prevent surprise attack. But probably even more important was the need to demarcate the 'habitable' from the 'unhabitable' bits of land. The Igbo did not believe that all bits of land were suitable for habitation. Some bits, either because of past and 'unremoved' abominations committed by the ancestors there or because they were haunted by malevolent spirits, could prove 'too hot' for human habitation and bring on any family living there incessant tribulations and disasters. In fact so much was this kind of situation feared that before a family chose a living land, it would invite a native doctor to determine and demarcate the habitable portion. The compound wall would follow this demarcation line, for if even a square foot of the 'bad' land were included in the family compound it could cause untold hardship until walled off. The third reason was that the wall made the keeping of livestock like goats easier as they were then let loose and allowed to roam within the compound. It is most likely that Equiano saw the point of the wall as mainly defensive—hence he said where there was no wall, there was a moat. The practice of walling compounds has persisted, and in the villages native doctors still help in the selection of habitation sites.

Another striking point mentioned by Equiano in this connection is what he calls 'the principal building appropriated to the sole use of the master (family head) and consisting of two apartments, in one of which he sits in the day with his family, the other is left free for the reception of his friends'. The building thus described was most likely what the Igbo call *obi* and which in general terms could be described as the family temple. In it the venerated ancestral symbols like *ọfọ* and *ndichie*, or family gods like *erim* and *ọmụmụ* were housed. It was also there that the family head prayed for the entire family every morning. In the day it served, as Equiano said, as a reception room. If the family head was a craftsman, like a carver or basket-maker, there too he would betake himself to pursue these occupations. The *obi* has continued to be an important building in an Igbo compound, though owing to the inroads of christianity it may no longer serve as the store for ancestral symbols and the like.

About the houses themselves Equiano says 'they are always built of wood, or stakes driven into the ground, crossed with wattles, and plastered neatly within and without'. This type of house is still found in many parts of Igbo land, especially in present Bende, Umuahia and Nsukka divisions. In some other places, especially where white ants prevail, they have disappeared fast in the last forty years or so. Probably westernization more than white ants has been largely responsible for their disappearance. With regard to the labour for building these houses Equiano says: 'The whole neighbourhood afford their unanimous assistance in building them, and in return receive and expect no other recompense than a feast.' This use of communal labour in the building of houses has continued amongst the poorer classes in Igbo land. The elite would now hire contractors who have the know-how to erect the type of modern structures they want. But at the end of the Nigerian civil war when most families came back to find their houses demolished and had to hastily put up some shelter to live in, this ancient tradition of communal aid came ready to hand. There was hardly any case in which anybody remained unhoused after a month or so of returning home. It is still considered a serious crime in many parts of Igbo land for a man to refuse his brother's call for help in building or repairing his house.

On Igbo village government Equiano was brief, but nonetheless recaptured the essential spirit of it—democratic representation. In his village, he said, it was the '*Embrenche*, or chief men' who 'decided disputes and punished crimes for which purpose they always assembled together'.⁴¹ This was a case of representative democracy as each segment of the village would be represented by at least each of these 'chief men'. Since in no part of Igbo land did *ichi* marks alone confer a right to membership of the *ama ala*, in the context of Equiano's description of Igbo village government, his *Embrenche* should be read as *Ndichie*. As already pointed out Equiano's use of this term combined the two institutions. What is important for our purpose, however, is that Equiano, in spite of the obvious romance and attractions of the Benin monarchy and empire, did not describe Igbo village government in terms of monarchy, but talked of a general assembly in which all men of weight participated. How one wishes that he had said something about what obtained below and above the village level, though it must be conceded that Equiano's terminology in this matter is by no means precise for he talks of the 'family or village'. But it may be assumed that he was not describing the governmental system of the village wards or section where direct rather than representative democracy obtained. There is a sense in which Equiano's use of the word 'family' as a synonym for 'village' is meaningful. In Igbo social and political ideology all members of the same socio-political unit are officially represented as descendants of the same founding father and thus as forming a family.

Related to the above was Equiano's brief, but vital statement on Igbo law on adultery. 'Adultery', he said, 'was *sometimes* punished with slavery or death'.⁴² The young Equiano, ignorant of the fact that Igbo customary law distinguished between various shades of adultery, talked of the crime being *sometimes* punished with slavery or death. This would make the application of the Igbo law on the matter rather erratic. The fact was, and is, that the Igbo distinguished between adultery as private wrong, and adultery as a criminal offence. If a woman committed adultery outside her husband's compound, this was a private injury to the husband and could be settled through the imposition of a fine. But if she brought her lover to her husband's house or compound, or had an affair in the farm or with a relation of her husband's, this was a serious crime involving an offence against the Earth Goddess. In pre-colonial times, the woman would be dealt with as indicated by Equiano, as she had polluted the land. The British were later to run into immense difficulty for failing to grasp the principle of representative democracy in Igbo government above the level of the village section, as for treating all classes of adultery as private wrong.[43]

But even more vividly accurate was Equiano's other description of the other method by which slave dealers procured their wares in eighteenth century Igbo land—kidnapping, and the measures which families took to counter it. Generally, writes Equiano,

> when the grown up people in the neighbourhood were gone far in the fields to labour, the children assembled together in some of the neighbour's premises to play; and commonly some of us used to get up a tree to look out for any assailant, or kidnapper that might come upon us for they sometimes took these opportunities of our parents' absence, to attack and carry off as many as they could seize.[44]

According to Equiano's own story, he was kidnapped and sold into slavery during one of such surprise attacks by slave dealers. 'One day', he says, 'when all our people were gone to their works as usual, and only I and my dear sister were left to mind the house, two men and a woman got over our walls and in a moment seized us both; and, without giving us time to cry out, or make a resistance, they stopped our mouths, tied our hands, and ran off with us into the nearest wood'.[45]

This story is fully corroborated by the accounts left behind by some of the more perceptive of the early British political officers who served in Igbo land, and by the traditions of our elders today. From all these sources one can fairly confidently assert that kidnapping probably was more important than organized wars as a means of recruiting slaves in Igbo society. One striking point in Equiano's story quoted above was that women should be taken along by the slave dealers, when engaged in the risky enterprise of kidnapping. The uninformed would be inclined to dismiss this detail as unlikely on logical grounds especially on the basis of our argument above that Igbo women were probably not as martial as Equiano sought to make them in his *Narrative*. Mr. Frank Hives, an Australian who served as a political officer in Igbo land from the early days of British rule not only confirmed this but explained it. The crafty Aro, he said,

> had many methods of stealing children at small risk to himself. A favourite dodge was for three or four Aros, usually armed, to work along a path accompanied by one of their womenfolk, whose own infant had been left with a confederate in a town some miles away.

The little band would choose paths which went through yam farms, not too near a town, until they saw a woman with an infant in arms. The natives had to take their babies when they worked in their farms. Having selected their victim one of the Aros went up to her at the first favourable opportunity ... and asked directions for reaching some town or other, then while talking he hit her on the head with a heavy stick or a matchet, it was all very simple. The Aro did not care whether he killed her on the spot or only laid her unconscious for a time. What he wanted was the baby. *Having seized it, he handed it to his female confederate and the gang moved off. The Aro woman suckled the child and treated it as her own. To any passer-by on the road they would appear to be a peaceful family party—father, mother, the child and a few male relatives.*[46]

On the more general question of kidnapping there is great concurrence between the accounts of Equiano and Mr. Frank Hives. According to Equiano after he and his sister had been bound hands and feet they were then carried off by the kidnappers who:

> continued to carry us as far as they could, till night came on, when we reached a small house, where the robbers halted for refreshment, and spent the night. We were then unbound ... The next morning we left the house and continued travelling all day. For a long time we kept to the woods, but at last we came into a road which I believed I knew. I had now some hopes of being delivered; for we had advanced but a little way before I discovered some people at a distance, on which I began to cry for their assistance; but my cries had no other effect than to make them tie me faster, and stop my mouth, and then put me into a large sack.[47]

On the basis of information which he collected from Igbo elders early in this century on kidnapping, Mr. Hives made the following reconstruction of the tactics of the trade:

> A favourite trick among the Aro dealers was to wait concealed near the watering place where the villagers draw their supplies. The late evening was the customary time for boys and girls of all ages to come for water. This made an ideal opportunity for the traders, giving them the whole night for travel and diminishing their risk of meeting anybody who might ask awkward questions. When they had selected from their post of observation the children who would fetch the highest prices, they rushed out and seized them. ... The selected children were gagged and bound with tie-tie. ... Then each child was put into a long narrow basket and carried away at the double on the head of an Aro. The child lay in the basket at full length and was covered up probably with banana leaves, so that if the marauders encountered other people on the way, they would appear to be going to market with farm produce—for these were the usual market baskets. ...'[48]

In the course of his service at Bende Mr. Hives managed to rescue one boy of about thirteen years of age who had been kidnapped along with his sister and cousins in this manner by a group of Aro slave dealers.[49]

It was the rampancy of this mode of procuring slaves, that forced Igbo parents to adopt the practice, which Equiano accurately describes, of herding their children into one compound under the care of some elder before they left for the market or farm. Usually each child took along his or her lunch so that there would no be necessity to go outside the watchful eyes of the elder, as this could be dangerous. This practice survived until the early forties at least in the Okigwi and Orlu Districts where the Aro have their largest settlement or colony outside Aro Chukwu. The present writer remembers very vividly how before he started schooling, he used to be herded together with other children in this manner and severely warned not to attempt to go back to the house before his parents returned from wherever they went. In our ward this practice had come to be more rigorously observed because about 1939 or 1940 an older cousin of mine, was nearly kidnapped by a group of Aro people because he had stupidly left the company of his fellow children to 'see if a thief came to their house'. There he saw two men and a woman who offered him a piece of stockfish. But each time he moved forward to receive it, they stepped backwards, hoping to lure him beyond the compound before seizing and gagging him. At one point he raised an alarm and his would-be kidnappers escaped into the bush. In my childhood we were, as a general rule warned not to go close to strange men carrying sacks and long native baskets no matter what delicacies they might offer to us. The use of sacks for kidnapping was at least as old as Equiano's day. Thus he describes the 'stout mahogany-coloured' slave dealers who frequented their markets as carrying sacks with them. And as we have seen at one stage while he was being smuggled out of his village, he was put into a sack. An interesting aspect of this slave dealing business is that the Igbo did not just surrender themselves to it without protest or without taking some measures to restrict it. Hence Equiano's village always insisted on the dealers giving the strictest account of how they procured the slaves they had before being allowed to pass.[50]

Another striking description of Equiano's is the economic and social life of an Igbo village. On the economic side eighteenth century Igbo society was, according to him, a predominantly agricultural community. 'Agriculture', he says, 'is our chief employment; and everyone, even the children and women, are engaged in it'.⁵¹ This has remained the case. But when he says 'our land is uncommonly rich and fruitful and produces all kinds of vegetables in great abundance'⁵² one suspects that he was throwing a bait to the British industrial class whom he hoped to persuade to change from the slave trade to trade in the natural produce of Africa. This is not to say that there are no parts of Igbo land that are 'rich and fruitful'. The Anambra basin is an example. But had Equiano come from there he would have been used to seeing big streams, and then dried fish would not be such a rarity in his village as he claims in his *Narrative*. If he came from the present Abakaliki area which is also fertile, he probably would also have heard of the Cross River which is not so far away, and his kidnappers would not have moved him 'through dreary wastes and dismal woods'⁵³ as the vegetation there which early in this century was already savannah, would be close to assuming that form by mid-eighteenth century. The propaganda intent of this section of the *Narrative* is probably most clearly brought out when Equiano goes on to assert:

> We have plenty of Indian corn, and vast quantities of cotton and tobacco. Our pineapples grow without culture; they are about the size of the largest sugar-loaf, and finely flavoured.⁵⁴

This was the standard image of Africa painted by the abolitionist propagandists who, like Equiano, believed that the Negro lived 'in a country where nature is prodigal of her favours'.⁵⁵ Subsequent accounts based on scientific study rather than romantic propaganda have revealed that the African environment is very hard on its human occupants. This was particularly so in Igbo land. And if the fight which Equiano witnessed in their common was a land dispute, as suggested above, eighteenth century Igbo land was already becoming over-crowded and exhausted, with the remaining fertile bits becoming bones of contention amongst land hungry villages.

To supplement agriculture there was a sizeable volume of commerce. Markets were already fully developed as important economic and social centres. Says Equiano: 'We have also markets, at which I have been frequently with my mother'.⁵⁶ It was traditional in Igbo land for young children of about

Equiano's age to follow their fathers and mothers to the local market. The first sons would accompany their fathers, as they had to carry for these elders their stools and skin bags containing their drinking cups, snuff-boxes and so on. The other children helped their mother to move her wares, which were often many, varied and bulky to the market. This remained the case until the triumph of schools disrupted everything. In Equiano's day long distance trade was well developed and supplemented local trade. It was by the former that Equiano's part of Igbo land which lay in the far interior, got the luxury and rare goods which the Europeans brought to the coast in exchange for slaves. The items of long distance trade according to Equiano, included 'fire-arms, gunpowder, hats, beads and dried fish',[57] the last item being produced by the coastal peoples themselves. Like in Equiano's day, dried fish has continued to be 'esteemed a great rarity',[58] in different parts of Igbo land to which it is still being imported from Oron and Calabar (on the Cross River) and from Ijọ on the coast.

The dominant aspect of the long distance trade was the slave trade. Thus Equiano's village market was visited by the 'stout mahogany-coloured men' whom they called '*oye-Iboe*' meaning 'red men living at a distance'.[59] It can be assumed that Equiano had forgotten what these men were called. Jones says these men were 'red' because they rubbed preparations from camwood which he describes as 'the characteristic colour east of the Niger'.[60] There were five characteristic dyes east of the Niger. These were *uri* (indigo), *uhie* or *ufie* (camwood, which is red), *odo* (yellow coloured preparation), *nzu* (white chalk) and *nchara* (brown coloured dye). The first four were used for body decoration but traditionally not usually by men. Men robbed *uhie* and *odo* only if they were ill, as these two preparations were believed to be efficacious in cases of general bodily pains and debility, while *uri* was used as treatment for measles and pains in the joints. *Nzu* as bodily decoration was used mostly on children and by nursing mothers. *Nchara* had limited use, usually on ritual occasions. The five colours were also used in dyeing. It is difficult therefore to say how the passage in question should be interpreted. In any case it is most likely that Equiano's 'mahogany-coloured' slave dealers living at a distance were Aro traders. Apart from moving imported European goods into Igbo land from the coast, and taking slaves in return, the Aro also purchased *uhie, odo* or *edo* and *nzu* for sale in Ibibio land where these were also needed for ritual purposes. In any case there is evidence that *uhie* or *ufie* was a major item of export of Igbo land. Writing about the Fulani women of Raba, capital of Nupe, Laird and Oldfield said:

> Several mornings in the week they besmear themselves all over, from head to foot, with a red pigment prepared from red-wood brought from Eboe (Ibo) country. It is supposed to possess a tonic quality, and also to lighten the colour of the skin and correct the fector of perspiration...⁶⁰ᵃ

It is tempting to suggest that Equiano's long distance traders came to be associated with *uhie or ufie*, that is came to be 'red men' because they demanded for so much of this in Igbo markets that it came to be assumed that back home they used so much of it. As these men were most likely Aro traders this would establish that by the eighteenth century the Aro trading business was already fully established. This would destroy the case of British political and anthropological officers who in the 1920s, on the basis of some rather unsatisfactory study of Aro genealogies, dated the founding of the Aro community to sometime between 1700 and 1760.⁶¹

Early in this century uninformed European opinion at times gave the impression that trade in the African interior was entirely or at least mainly by barter. For Igbo land Equiano's *Narrative* at least assures us that monetary transactions were already established in the eighteenth century. He says that in his village there were 'some small pieces of coin ... made something like an anchor'.⁶² Here Equiano was probably describing the manilla currency. The currency situation in pre-colonial Igbo land has not been satisfactorily studied and may turn out to be one of those aspects of our history that may prove impossible of satisfactory reconstruction from oral tradition; especially as the matter was not tackled energetically and systematically before the general demise of the most authentic repositories of our tradition. Mr. G. I. Jones made an impressive start on this topic in his 'Native and trade currencies in Southern Nigeria during the eighteenth and nineteenth centuries' but then this was limited largely to the coast with occasional mention of the interior. In this regard it is instructive that Mr. Jones did not use Equiano's *Interesting Narrative*.

Using ethnographic data collected early in this century Jones delimited three currency zones in Southern Nigeria made up of the cowrie, the manilla and the brass rod zones. According to him different parts of Igbo land fell into different zones: the Northern, Isuama and Riverine Igbo coming within the cowrie zone, the Southern Igbo under the manilla zone and the North-Eastern and Cross River Igbo under the brass rod zone.[63] One can only assume that this is a rough and working delimitation and that in any case the ethnographic data referred to was neither systematic nor comprehensive. For amongst the Northern Igbo the manilla and the brass rods were in use: in the Otanchara clan, a Northern Igbo people, for instance, the manilla was in use and remained in use along with the cowrie for years after the establishment of British rule. The present writer used the cowrie in the 1940s but heard stories of the use of the manilla. Among the Nsukka, also a Northern Igbo people, the brass rod known locally as *echi* remained in use until about the 1940s. Equiano's account would thus appear to establish that the use of manilla as currency by the Northern Igbo was at least as old as the eighteenth century.

When Equiano reached Timnah which, from his description, was in the delta he discovered that the currency there 'consisted of little white shells, the size of the finger nail'.[64] This was certainly the cowrie shell. One would then ask whether Equiano's omission of the cowrie from his description of the currency of his village would mean that this currency was not in use amongst the Northern Igbo in his time, or whether this was another instance of his memory failing him. The later was probably the case. As Jones and other authorities have pointed out the cowrie probably got into West Africa long before European advent through the overland route linking the Eastern Sudan and East Africa[65] with West Africa. Professor Shaw's archaeological report on his finds at Igbo Ukwu show that there was a long established trade contact between Northern Igbo land and the East via this overland route. It is thus not unlikely that cowries came into Northern Igbo land along with the Eastern beads which were found in such large numbers in the excavated sites at Igbo Ukwu which have been dated back to about the ninth century A.D.[66]

Beyond this, there would appear to be another omission. Jones, in his article cited above, has shown that there was an 'earlier metal currency or currencies in which the unit was of iron' and which 'predated' manilla, and brass rods 'at least in Eastern Nigeria'. By the seventeenth century this currency had penetrated down to the coast and was being reported on by European travellers. In the seventeenth century Dapper associated it with a community he described as Moko on the Western side of Okrika. 'I think', says Jones, 'we can accept Moko as an Ibo or Ogoni community bordering Okrika and assume that the iron currency derived from the hinterland'. Jones would trace the place of origin beyond the Southern Igbo area as, he points out, 'there are nō iron deposits and with them iron-workings farther south than the Okigwi-Arochuku ridge'.[67] Thus the currency situation in the Igbo interior was probably much more developed by 1750 than even Equiano's account makes it. And it is only reasonable to assume that the Aro and other long distance traders did not recognize currency barriers; and since Aro trading business spanned the entire former Eastern Region and even penetrated the southern zones of the present Benue State and the south-eastern section of Kwara State, that they helped to move the different currencies identified by Jones forwards and backwards through most of the region. Though, no doubt, the strength and popularity of each currency varied from one part of this Aro trade area to another, it is doubtful that there were rigid currency zones.

To support this fairly well developed trading system described above, there were a number of village industries which produced various items for exchange. 'When our women', says Equiano, 'are not employed with the men in tillage, their usual occupation is spinning and weaving cotton, which afterwards they dye and make into garments. They also manufacture earthern vessels, of which we have many kinds'.[68] The first point that strikes one here is the fact that the industries which Equiano described as pursued in his village are all women's industries. To the uninformed this would seem to confirm the view of many early European visitors that African men were generally lazy and exempt from work, and spent their time drinking while the women carried the greater part of the burden of maintaining the family. On the contrary one should see it as reflecting the circumstances of Equiano's early upbringing which I emphasized above—his being a charge of his mother's who brought him up. He was likely to have spent most of his time with his mother in the company of women spinners and potters. He would therefore not be too familiar with such other crafts as basket-making, carving and the like which were the preserve of the men.

Of the two industries mentioned above by Equiano, pottery probably requires little comment. Its origin in Igbo society, or at least in Igbo land would appear to be very ancient indeed. Professor Hartle, archaeologist, has dug up in the Nsukka area pottery which have been carbon dated to about 2555 B.C. His description of these sherds talks of their looking very much like the unfired clay vessels still made and used in Nsukka today.[69] Many parts of Igbo land have very good clay for pottery which is now exploited for modern ceramics. Pottery as an industry was very important in Igbo life. Not only did it provide wares for household use, it also provided receptacles for ritual and religious purposes. For the latter type of pottery Inyi, now in the Awgu division would appear to have had the pride of place.

Equiano's reference to cotton spinning, cloth weaving and dyeing Mr. Jones regards as one evidence that Equiano came from a West Niger Igbo village under Benin influence since this industry, he claims, was better developed in the Benin empire, and in any case was not in existence in the Eastern Igbo area except where it was introduced by the Igala.[70] For now it suffices to point out that Mr. Jones presented no evidence whatever to prove his theory that the Igbo did not grow cotton, spin or weave it except where they came under the influence of the Igala. The fact remains that cloth-making was a widespread village industry in Igbo land. The records of the nineteenth century explorers of the lower Niger clearly show that Igbo woven cloth was an important item of trade on the banks of the Niger and Benue. 'At several of the market towns on the south side of the Binue, near the confluence at Igbegbe', wrote Dr. William Balfour Baikie,

> we have seen a peculiar sort of country cloth, ornamented by perforations, which were done during the weaving, and which, we were told, was made by the Igbo people.... We had made many inquiries about this race, but until our conversation with the Galadima could learn nothing satisfactory about them, but now we found they were the same as the 'Ibo'... These cloths are most probably manufactured in Elugu, that being the Igbo district nearest to Igara, and the cloth being found chiefly in the markets near the confluence.

Later Dr. Baikie was told by Odiri, the son of the Obi of Onitsha, 'that the fancy cloths about which we had been so often inquiring were made near Onitsha'.[70a]

It may also be pertinent to observe that up to as late as the

1940s cotton spinning and dyeing, if not weaving, by women remained a common village industry in many parts of Igbo land where it would be absurd of talk of cultural history in terms of Igala influence. The author remembers many women in the Ihube village-group of Otanchara clan in the present Okigwi Division who were accomplished cotton spinners and how the thread they produced competed imported thread stiffly. The women who used it in sewing said it was stronger. It was also cheaper and in any case it was just the right size for the locally made needles which were then in vogue. One of these women spinners, Madam Mgbọwụ, span with such easy dexterity that could only have come from immemorial custom. As for dyeing this was even more common in Ihube in the 1940s. The women bought the thread white and then dyed it blue or red or yellow according to taste and need. Chief Mbabuike Ọgujiọfọ who was old enough to be recruited as a court messenger in 1909, a year after the establishment of British rule in Okigwi, in 1962 assured the writer that this craft was even more widespread in the Otanchara area and many other parts of Igbo land before the British advent. Chief Agiriga Irechukwu of Ihube, who was a widely travelled trader in pre-British days confirmed this story. As already pointed out this industry is still a going concern in the Nsukka area which in the past would appear to have supplied a wide area of Igbo land with the famed, but incorrectly named, *akwa Uburu* referred to above. Just the other day the author visited the Edemani village-group in Nsukka where he saw the women spinning the cotton for this cloth with an effortless ease and dexterity that reminded him of the early forties when he used to watch Mgbọwụ in the home and in the market turning out yards and yards of thread while her attention was engaged in haggling or enthralling conversation.

The point is that contrary to Jones's belief, Equianọ was most likely describing a long established textile industry in a Northern Igbo village-group. Until recently cotton grew wild in many parts of Igbo land, but it would appear that the master spinners also made an effort to supplement this by deliberate cultivation. At least the writer noticed that in his childhood much of what passed for wild cotton grew in what his people called *ụkabia*— a piece of land farmed the last planting season and from which the major crops like yam, cocoyam and so on had been harvested. On this matter the report of Rev. J. C. Taylor, C.M.S.

173

priest at Onitsha is illuminating. On 29 July 1857 he entered in his diary:

> I took a short walk in the extensive corn and yam plantations, when I had a good opportunity of observing that cotton was planted to the same extent nearly, to be an after crop when yams and corn are removed from the fields. The people of Onitsha manufacture their own clothes, generally plain or fanciful white. European manufactured goods are not so commonly used here as in the lower parts of the river.[70b]

The attempt of Sir Ralph Moor early in this century to grow cotton on a large scale on the banks of the Nkissi river, east of the Niger, probably owed something to the fact that he thought it a viable proposition from seeing indigenously grown cotton on both sides of the Niger. Moor was particular in surveying the economic potentialities of the area under his control and sent out expeditions for this very purpose. It is likely that it was the report of some of such expeditions that helped to encourage the experimentation at Nkissi.[71]

All this evidence would appear to support the view that cotton spinning, weaving and dyeing was probably more widespread in Igbo land in Equiano's day than Mr. Jones would concede and than it was early in this century. The more likely thing is that this village industry declined as more and more of cheaply produced Manchester cotton was pumped into Igbo land in the nineteenth century in exchange for palm produce. It is unlikely that one can now find in the entire Otanchara clan a woman who can still spin cotton. Yet only about thrity years ago this was very much in evidence, and by 1900 much more so according to the accounts of Chiefs Mbabuike Ogujiofo and Agiriga Irechukwu. By the same token it is likely the industry was more widely practised in Equiano's day.

Later in his account, while describing the economy of the zone through which he passed, Equiano mentioned a third industry, this time a man's industry, which he remarked was also practised in his village. This was smithing. 'This first master of mine', he writes,

> was a smith, and my principal employment was working his bellows, which was the same kind as I had seen in my vicinity. They were ... covered over with leather; and in the middle of that leather a stick was fixed, and a person stood up and worked it.[72]

In the entire section relating to Equiano's early life in his village and his journey out of Igbo land, this passage is probably one of his most accurate descriptions. The smith's bellow in Igbo land remained precisely as Equiano saw and described it until the last one or two decades when modifications have come in through the impact of Western ideas.

Smithing is an ancient occupation in Igbo land. According to an Nri creation legend it was the first occupation in Igbo land or rather in the world. When Eri came down from heaven, the Nri claim, he found everywhere to be a morass. Then he appealed to Chukwu (God) who sent down an Awka blacksmith to dry the land.[73] The Awka were, and still are, the leading blacksmiths in Igbo land, if not in much of Southern Nigeria. They were followed by the Nkwerre and Abiriba. Neither Awka smiths nor the Nkwerre and the Abiriba were limited to iron. All, it would appear, handled brass. It was thus probably a smith from Awka or Nkwerre or Abiriba that Equiano served and described, for the material he worked on had 'a lovely bright yellow colour, and was worn by the women on their wrists and ankles'. Equiano on his side thought it was gold, but this was probably out of the question.[74] Unless we are to speculate that the Aro who kidnapped Equiano took him to Awka or Abiriba or Nkwerre before moving him to the coast, we should conclude from this account that by 1750 these smiths had already spread throughout much of Igbo land. In any case when the British came they found colonies of these smiths scattered all over Igbo land and even beyond. In addition to parts of Igbo land the Awka were active in Urhobo land, the Abiriba in Ibibio and the Nkwerre in Ogoni.

On the social aspect of life in eighteenth century Igbo land Equiano was rather scanty probably because writing for industrialized Britain where labour was regarded as a virtue, he wanted to debunk the idea then popular in anti-abolitionist circles that the Negro was naturally lazy and would not work unless forced to do so. As somebody put the prejudices against the Negro later what the Negro wanted most was 'to do nothing for six days in the week and to rest on the seventh'. It was probably in reaction to this wicked libel on his countrymen and in order to convince the industrialists that they stood to gain if the slave trade were abolished and Africa 'opened' up to European commerce, that Equiano was concerned to emphasize that his people 'are habituated to labour from ... earliest years. Everyone contributes something to common stock'; and that as they 'are unacquainted with idleness', they 'have no beggars'.[75] Thus the village square, the centre of Igbo social life, the place where many a protracted session of the village assembly were held to decide on matters of moment, made no appearance in Equiano's *Narrative*. This anxiety to portray his kinsmen as a people who are business-like and who despise idleness is further seen in his assertion that the proceedings of the village assembly 'were generally short'.[76] This, of course, they were not as the meeting provided the opportunity for the display of wit and eloquence, and every issue was argued out in detail and every point of view listened to. Equiano even placed little emphasis on his childhood sport, except to sustain his case that training in arms was taken seriously. Thus the only sport he mentioned was practising with 'darts, and bows and arrows'.[77]

But in spite of this preoccupation he had to boast of his people being 'almost a nation of dancers, musicians and poets' who celebrated every important event 'in public dances, which are accompanied with songs and music suited to the occasion'. The point here was not only that his people danced, but also that they danced for good reason, on important occasions. And even then the dancing offered opportunity for the rehearsal of 'some interesting scene of real life, such as a great achievement, domestic employment, a pathetic story, or some rural sport'. For instance the first 'division' of dancers made up of married men 'in their dances frequently exhibit feats of arms, and the representation of battle'.[78] Thus in Equiano's village dances were no mere meaningless surrender to the wild extravagances of tribal orgy, they were more or less puritanistic rituals designed to achieve a higher purpose in society. The important point here, however, is that Equiano satisfactorily recaptured the great part which singing and dancing played in the social life of an Igbo village. Not only was it relaxation, it was also a sort of social ritual, full of variety and inventiveness at times almost bordering on improvisation since it was 'generally founded on some recent event'.[79]

Another aspect of Igbo social life which Equiano touched on was marriage. For our purpose here a very important sentence is 'Both parties are usually betrothed when young by their parents'.[80] This refers to what has often been described in this century and by Europeans as child marriage. This practice persisted in most of Igbo land until about the forties of this century. In the Nsukka area it still exists though it is now very much on the wane, or at least so the elite who now look on it as disgraceful say. This practise made courtship very little known in traditional Igbo society. It gave protection and sense of social purpose early in life to girls. Not every child betrothal led to marriage, but most did. And according to our elders marriages in those days were, in spite of that, much more stable than these days when most people choose their spouses on attaining majority.

Another important though not fully revealing sentence was Equiano's statement that on the day of formal betrothal in the case of grown up, 'the bride and the bridegroom stand up in the midst of their friends, who are assembled for the purpose, while he declares she is thenceforth his wife, and that no person is to pay any address to her'.[81] This was a very important aspect of Igbo marriage ceremony. Since, as already said, there was very little courtship and the bridegroom made the approach indirectly through an intermediary—*onye ebe aku* now inaccurately called witness—it was assumed that the matter remained a secret between the three families—that of the bridegroom, that of the bride and that of the intermediary—until this public declaration. Yet so closely knit was the life of the village that nearly every grown up would know of the budding marriage. But nobody would discuss it openly and directly. If a bridgegroom mismanaged his approaches and the matter became a public talking point in the village, the intended marriage could miscarry. Assuming then that the matter had been discreetly handled, this open declaration thus became a necessity. But the matter was by no means as simple as Equiano made it. When it got to that stage, the bride who, all the while the marriage party were eating, drinking and cracking jokes, was with her mother in the kitchen would be called in by her father. He would serve her a cup of wine and tell her that the people there came to marry her but that since so many men were present, he and his brothers did not know who it was; therefore she should taste the wine and hand it over to her husband-to-be. Since in those days, and in fact even now, such parties held at night, and since before the availability of European lamps the room would be poorly lit and since the bride and the bridegroom would not have met too often before, there was thus a real danger of the girl tasting the wine and offering it to the wrong person—though obviously this wrong person would not

177

touch it—it became necessary that the bridegroom should make himself conspicuous either by coughing or standing up at the right moment as if he were going to ease himself. Then the girl would sip the wine and hand it over to him. The relations of the bride would then pretend as if that was the first time they knew who their brother-in-law was. The most elderly of them would then stand up, shake his hand and tell him something like this: 'Welcome our brother-in-law. All this time we have been in the dark. We have been passing you on the road without knowing. Please forgive us. From now on when we see you we shall know we have seen our own man. The same applies to you. This marriage will turn out well. Ours is a great family, we produce good children. We also know about your family. Welcome'. In the rituals of Igbo marriage this was probably one of the most important and critical, even though everybody knew it to be a formality.

For the rest Equiano's description of the stages in the protracted traditional Igbo marriage system is rather muddled. The number of visits which the bride paid to the family of the bridegroom varied from place to place. The ceremony of tying 'round her waist a cotton string'[82] is interesting. By the beginning of this century it had come to be known as *ijewe akwa*, tying cloth. With this ceremony the girl who hitherto had been going nude, except for the string of beads round her waist, would now be entitled to wear half a yard of cloth round her waist. But it was not performed as one of the rituals of marriage. It marked the attainment by a girl of adulthood though generally it had to be performed by the husband in case of those already married.

On religion, Equiano's *Narrative* does not successfully recpature the complexity and subtlety of Igbo belief. This is one of those aspects of Igbo society that would have changed least between Equiaho's day and the early part of this century. Rightly he points out that the Igbo believe in a Supreme Being, what he calls 'one Creator'[83] or what the Igbo call *Chukwu*, a contraction of *Chi Ukwu*—the Great *Chi* or Creator. But what his relationship was with the Igbo man in everyday life Equiano does not say. But maybe the otiose character of this *Chukwu* in Igbo cosmology and religious thought is reflected in Equiano's statement that the Igbo think 'he may never eat or drink'[84] for the Igbo make no sacrifice directly to the Supreme Being of their belief, but to lesser gods who may be described as the messengers of this Supreme Being and who manipulate the daily life of the average Igbo man. Of these gods Equiano says nothing.

Equiano says he never heard of the 'doctrine of eternity'[85] among the Igbo. But a close study of his description of what has been miscalled in this century as 'ancestor worship', would show a concept of eternity which, unlike the christian one, is closer to the stoic doctrine of cyclic return. In Igbo thought the boundary between the living and the dead is a very narrow one and death is a process by which the human soul passes from this world of the living to the world of spirits, while re-incarnation—probably what Equiano miscalls transmigration[86]—is the process by which the soul moves from the world of spirits to the world of the living. Death and child birth were the two processes of maintaining this endless communication between the two worlds. Implicit in this was a doctrine of eternity. If an Igbo elder were asked to describe the topography of the spirit-world, he probably would end up giving the topography of his village. The dead had their farm lands and play-grounds, their nights and days, their meal times, though at times they were believed to attend the same markets as the living—even if the latter could not see them. But somehow they still needed support from the living, hence, as Equiano said, before his people ate their food, they would make libation 'by pouring out a small portion of the drink on the floor, and tossing a small quantity of the food in a certain place for the spirits of departed relations'.[87] Furthermore within the first eight days of a person's death the living were supposed to feed him or her by taking cooked food to the grave every evening until he or she settled down. Equiano says he used to accompany his mother when she went to fulfil this ritual at her mother's grave. 'When she went to make these small oblations at her mother's tomb', Equiano writes, 'I sometimes attended her. There she made her libations, and spent most of the night in cries and lamentation'.[88] This practice continued till the 1940s at least. Also, as Equiano points out, the great ones of the land were buried with their personal effects for use in the next world.[89] They were also buried along with slaves to attend to them there; though probably in order to maintain his point that the Igbo treated their slaves well,[90] Equiano refused to mention this. Since the Igbo never thought this close contact, this coming and going, between the two worlds could ever be terminated, it could be said that they had a doctrine of eternity, a doctrine certainly more dynamic and humane than the christian one in which the traffic is one way, and men are translated from life through death to eternal damnation or eternal joy, but there is no traffic from these two equally awful eternal extremities to life.

Though Equiano said nothing of the minor deities who occupied such an important place in Igbo religion, he talked of his people having priests and magicians.[91] These priests were not the direct servants of the Supreme God—in Igbo religion there are no such people—but of the minor deities. Equiano says he does not know whether the offices of priesthood and medicine men were combined in the same persons or were separate.[92] Judging at least from the late nineteenth century and the early twentieth century on which we have information, the two offices were generally separate—the practice of medicine being a profession which anybody could learn. Though the particularly successful and effective medicine-men were supposed to be those who were endowed from birth for the profession. These are, at times, described as having had a call in almost religious terms. Herbs were said to 'speak' to them. But for the work of priesthood one had to have a calling, though invariably this calling ran in certain families. The only thing is that an older son who is considered a profligate might be side-stepped by the god in favour of his younger but much wiser and more sober brother.

Those who calculated the year in Equiano's village, people who, according to Equiano, went by the name 'Ah-affoe-way-cah'[93] were not just any priest or ordinary wise men as Equiano would seem to imply, but mainly those who held the *Isi Ani* (*Isi Ala* or *Isi Ajana*), the priesthood of the Earth Goddess. In a predominantly agricultural community like that of the Igbo the reckoning of the year was directly related to keeping track of the seasons in order to spot the right time for planting and harvesting, as a slight miscalculation could lead to famine and disaster. As this was also closely related to the observance of rules supposed to have been dictated in the beginning by *Ala* (the Earth Goddess), and *Njoku* (or *Ihejioku* or *Ifesioku*) the *Yam God*, this calculation had to be done and the announcement made by the conclave of the priests of the two gods, though at times in consultation with other elders who might also be expert in observing seasonal changes.

The medicine men and doctors did not only heal wounds and expel poisons or discover jealousies, as Equiano would seem to imply, they dealt with all the health and medical hazards a community could face. They even carried out minor operations like in cases of hernia. Healing by bleeding as mentioned by Equiano was a common Igbo medical prescription and has survived till date being used as auxiliary treatment in such cases as dislocation leading to serious swellings, abscesses, protracted stiff neck and even hypertension. Apart from curative medicine, Igbo medicine men were also concerned with the preventive side. Because they believed that most illnesses were caused by malevolent spirits and wicked men, for them preventive medicine came to mean largely helping to adjust relations between the living and the living, the quick and the dead. Hence Equiano says they were expert in discovering jealousy, for only jealousy would cause one man to harm another. This would also give some insight into the emphasis they would appear to have laid on discovering poisoning, according to Equiano. The Igbo Supreme God was basically just and would allow every good man to attain a grand old age—the ripe and proper age for making the transition from this world of men to the world of spirits. Because the Igbo believed this sincerely they came to see premature deaths as necessarily caused by wicked men and malevolent spirits. Thus when a premature death occurred they had to assure themselves it was not caused by a fellow man by resorting to some such process as described by Equiano.[94] If the result turned out negative, then suspicion shifted to either the dead ancestors or to the spirits. Here a diviner was consulted to say which ancestor or spirit was responsible, what was its annoyance and what action was necessary to ensure it did not continue causing such untimely deaths in the family. In spite of the much advertised success of christianity amongst the Igbo, these beliefs and practices remain part of Igbo life. The method described by Equiano for discovering poisoning leading to death, is still mentioned as being in use from time to time in some Igbo villages remote from centres of governmental and modernizing influences.

Equiano was not satisfied with merely describing 'the manners and customs' of his people, he also sought to deduce from the ethnographic picture which he painted a theory of Igbo origin. He felt this picture was so much like that presented by Jewish society under the Patriarchs that one could reasonably conclude that 'the one people had sprung from the other'. After some reference to the great authorities of the time who derived the Negroes from 'Aser and Afra, descendants of Abraham by

Keturah his wife and concubine' he writes:

> Like the Israelites in their primitive state, our government was conducted by our chiefs, our judges, our wisemen and elders; and the head of a family with us enjoyed a similar authority over his household with that ascribed to Abraham and the other Patriarchs. The law of retaliation obtained almost universally with us as with them ... we had our sacrifices and burnt offerings, our washings and purifications, on the same occasions as they had.[95]

Two comments are necessary here. The first is that this type of ethno-history has continued to dog researchers into Igbo history and society in this twentieth century. Archdeacon Basden, who made extensive recordings of Igbo ethnography, was inclined to write Igbo culture history in terms of Hebrew influence or the impact of what he called the 'Levitical code'.[96] Many other European commentators on Igbo society in this century have also sought to account for certain features of Igbo culture in terms of Jewish, or Egyptian, or in any case Middle Eastern impact. The other comment is that many sections of the educated Igbo have not hesitated to emphasize resemblances between their people and the Jews. Not only have the educated Aro traced their origin to the Middle East, but it has been argued that the word 'Ibo' is a corrupt and contracted form of the word 'Hebrew'. Just the other day a fairly well educated Igbo told the author that the phrase *Talitha cumi* which Jesus used in raising the damsel from death in the Bible story is the same as the Igbo phrase *teta kue ume* (awake and breathe)! More seriously, however, most educated Igbo have seen their historical vicissitudes in this century as paralleling only those of the Jews since the days of the exodus. What is important from the practical point of view, however, is that this widespread, though probably unhistorical, ideological feeling of oneness with the Jews, which as we have seen goes back to the ex-slave boy Equiano in the eighteenth century, provides some clue to the understanding of Igbo pyschology, motivation and drive.

From the foregoing rather brief analysis of Igbo society as seen through Equiano's *Interesting Narrative*, a number of conclusions emerge. Firstly, that aspect of Equiano's *Narrative* relating to his early life in Igbo land was not based entirely on his own recollections. He also depended on information gathered from other Igbo and African slaves with whom he was in touch. He also borrowed material from the contemporary narratives of slave captains who visited the West African coast. Secondly, aspects of the *Narrative* show how limited his knowledge of Igbo society was either because of his youth when he was kidnapped, or because of his early up-bringing in the company of women or because of the erosion of his memory by decades of slavery in the West Indies. Thirdly, in spite of these limitations, the *Narrative* provides fairly reliable ethnographic information on eighteenth century Igbo land. Fourthly, though it would be dangerous and naïve to postulate that Igbo society remained static from mid-eighteenth century to the early twentieth century, yet the amount of close resemblance which the author sees between Equiano's village of the 1740s and his own part of Igbo land of the early 1940s gives enough ground for assuming that Igbo society and culture, in spite of the slave trade, the economic changes of the nineteenth century and the ruthless assault of Europe in this century, enjoyed a large measure of stability and continuity during the period under study. Thus Equiano's *Narrative* though limited in scope and depth could be said to provide a base line for the study of traditional Igbo society.

Finally whatever the limitations of Equiano's description, there can be no doubt that he loved the society in which he drew his first breath and was proud to be Igbo. He was particularly proud of Igbo character. Thus he writes: 'The West India planters prefer the slaves of ... Eboe ... for their hardiness, intelligence, integrity and zeal.' These qualities, he believed, paid the Igbo well 'in the general healthiness of the people, and their vigor and activity; I might add too in their comeliness. Deformity is indeed unknown amongst us ... Numbers of the native Eboe, now in London, might be brought in support of this assertion.' The Igbo, he also boasted 'have no beggars' as they 'are unacquainted with idleness'.[97] One must observe that this love of and pride in his people must have been deep indeed that Equiano was able to retain such warm sentiments for a society which had rejected and sold him into slavery. Probably this was also a measure of his alienation from Europe which in spite of its much vaunted civilization treated him with unrelenting brutality and would not even permit him to be reunited with his kinsmen. There is no doubt that Equiano was an Igbo man to the marrow. Throughout *The Interesting Narrative* one sees evidence of that drive and confidence in himself, and some would add intelligence, which have continued to make his kinsmen the objects of secret admiration but of open hatred by many who come into contact with them.

NOTES

1. T. Hodgkin, *Nigerian Perspectives* (Oxford, 1960).
2. J. D. Omer-Cooper *et al.*, *The Making of Modern Africa*, Vol. 1 (Longman, 1968), pp. 123–4.
3. T. Hodgkin, *Nigerian Perspectives*, p. 5.
4. *Ibid.*, pp. 5–6.
5. Olaudah Equiano, *The Interesting Narrative of the Life of Olaudah Equiano or Gustavus Vassa The African*: Eighth Edition Enlarged (Norwich, 1794), p. 31.
6. Olaudah Equiano, *The Interesting Narrative*, p. 45.
7. *Ibid.*, p. 4.
8. *Ibid.*, p. 19.
9. *Ibid.*, p. 12.
10. *Ibid.*, p. 21.
11. *Ibid.*, p. 31.
12. *Ibid.*, pp. 85–6.
13. *Ibid.*, pp. 38–9.
14. *Ibid.*, p. 21.
15. Captain Hugh Crow, *Memoirs* (London, 1830).
16. Equiano, *The Interesting Narrative*, see the bottom of pp. 5 and 16.
17. See Philip Curtin (ed.), *Africa Remembered* (I.U.P., 1967), p. 61.
18. Equiano, *The Interesting Narrative*, p. 4.
19. *Ibid.*, pp. 4–5.
20. Chinua Achebe, 'Handicaps of Writing in a Second Language', *Spear Magazine* (Nigeria, August 1964). It is only fair to state here that Mr. Achebe did not try to discuss why he chose to derive Equiano from Iseke in Orlu. He wrote: 'Equiano Olaudah, better known as Gustavus Vassa, the African ... was an Ibo—(I believe from the village of Iske in Orlu division of Eastern Nigeria)'.
21. D. I. Nwoga, 'West African Literature in English' (Ph.D. Thesis, London, London, 1964), p. 127, footnote 97.
22. Equiano, *The Interesting Narrative*, p. 38.
23. Paul Edwards (ed.), *Equiano's Travels* (London, 1967), p. ix.
24. See Philip Curtin (ed.), *Africa Remembered*, p. 61.
25. Equiano, *The Interesting Narrative*, p. 20.
26. P. Edwards, *op. cit.*, p. ix.
27. Equiano, *The Interesting Narrative*, p. 8.
28. See Philip Curtin (ed.), *Africa Remembered*, p. 65.
29. A. E. Afigbo, 'Herbert Richmond Palmer and Indirect Rule in Eastern Nigeria, 1914 to 1919', *Journal of the Historical Society of Nigeria*, Vol. 3, No. 2, 1965.
30. Equiano, *The Interesting Narrative*, pp. 3–4.
31. *Ibid.*, p. 3.
32. My own *italics*.
33. *Ibid.*, p. 15.
34. *Ibid.*, pp. 16–17.
35. *Ibid.*, p. 31, *italics* added.
36. See Philip Curtin (ed.), *Africa Remembered*, p. 66.
36a. S. Crowther, A Few Notices of Onitsha, Idda, and Gbegbe, and of the overland route to Abeokuta and in S. Crowther and J. C. Taylor: *Niger Expedition, 1857–59* (Frank Cass Reprint, London, 1968), p. 422.

37. The material on the traditional role of women in Igbo warfare is based largely on information collected by the author from among the Northern and Eastern Igbo.
38. Equiano, *The Interesting Narrative*, pp. 15–16.
39. T. Hodgkin, *Nigerian Perspectives*, p. 245.
40. Talbot and Mulhall, *The Physical Anthropology of Southern Nigeria* (Cambridge, 1962), p. 5.
40a. Wherever reference is made to Equiano's *Narrative* in the discussion on the family compound and Igbo architecture it is to pp. 10–12.
41. Equiano, *The Interesting Narrative*, p. 4.
42. *Ibid.*, p. 5.
43. A. E. Afigbo, *The Warrant Chiefs* (Longman, 1972).
44. Equiano, *The Interesting Narrative*, p. 31.
45. *Ibid.*, p. 32.
46. F. Hives, *Justice in the Jungle* (London, 1932), pp. 84–6. *Italics* added.
47. Equiano, *The Interesting Narrative*, pp. 32–3.
48. F. Hives, *Justice in the Jungle*, pp. 68–9.
49. *Ibid.*, pp. 204–12.
50. Equiano, *The Interesting Narrative*, pp. 13–14, 33.
51. *Ibid.*, p. 14.
52. *Ibid.*, p. 13.
53. *Ibid.*, p. 38.
54. *Ibid.*, p. 13.
55. *Ibid.*, p. 12.
56. *Ibid.*, p. 12.
57. *Ibid.*, p. 12.
58. *Ibid.*, p. 13.
59. *Ibid.*, p. 12.
60. See P. Curtin, (ed.), *Africa Remembered*, p. 65.
60a. Extract from M. Laird and R. A. K. Oldfield, *Narrative of an Expedition into the Interior of Africa by the River Niger 1832–4 in T. Hodgkin: Nigerian Perspective* (London, 1960), p. 243.
61. See the Essay on 'Aro Legends of Origin'.
62. Equiano, *The Interesting Narrative*, p. 12.
63. G. I. Jones, 'Native and Trade Currencies in Southern Nigeria during the Eighteenth and Nineteenth Centuries', *Africa I*, 1958, p. 48.
64. Equiano, *The Interesting Narrative*, p. 41.
65. G. I. Jones, 'Native and Trade Currencies, etc.', *Africa*, I, 1968, p. 48.
66. See T. Shaw, *Igbo Ukwu: An Account of Archaeological Discoveries in Eastern Nigeria* (Faber and Faber, 1970).
67. G. I. Jones, 'Native and Trade Currencies, etc.', *Africa*, I, 1958, p. 47.
68. Equiano, *The Interesting Narrative*, p. 8.
69. D. D. Hartle, 'Archaeology in Eastern Nigeria', *Nigeria Magazine*, No. 93, June 1967.
70. See Philip Curtin (ed.), *Africa Remembered*, p. 65.
70a. W. B. Baikie, *Narrative of An Exploring Voyage Up the Rivers Kwora and Binue in 1854* (Frank Cass Reprint, London, 1966), pp. 287–8, 297.
70b. S. Crowther and J. C. Taylor, *Niger Expedition 1857–59*, pp. 29–30.
71. A. E. Afigbo, 'Sir Ralph Moor and the Economic Development of Southern Nigeria 1896–1903', *Journal of the Historical Society of Nigeria*, Vol. V, No. 3, December 1970.
72. Equiano, *The Interesting Narrative*, p. 34.
73. M. D. W. Jeffreys, 'The Umundri Tradition of Origin', *African Studies*, Vol. 15, No. 3, 1956.
74. Equiano, *The Interesting Narrative*, p. 34.
75. *Ibid.*, p. 14.

76. *Ibid.*, p. 5.
77. *Ibid.*, p. 42.
78. *Ibid.*, p. 7.
79. *Ibid.*, p. 7.
80. *Ibid.*, p. 6.
81. *Ibid.*, p. 6.
82. *Ibid.*, p. 6.
83. *Ibid.*, p. 18.
84. *Ibid.*, p. 18.
85. *Ibid.*, p. 18.
86. *Ibid.*, p. 18.
87. *Ibid.*, p. 9.
88. *Ibid.*, p. 19.
89. *Ibid.*, p. 22.
90. *Ibid.*, pp. 17–18.
91. *Ibid.*, p. 21.
92. *Ibid.*, p. 22.
93. *Ibid.*, p. 22.
94. *Ibid.*, pp. 22–3.
95. *Ibid.*, pp. 25–6, see also p. 20, where he writes again 'We practised circumcision like the Jews, and made offerings of feasts on that occasion in the same manner as they did. Like them also our children were named from some event, some circumstance, or fancied foreboding, at the time of their birth'.
96. G. T. Basden, 'Notes on the Ibo Country' in *The Geographical Journal*, Vol. 39, January–June 1912, pp. 246–7.
97. Equiano, *The Interesting Narrative*, p. 14.

6. Aro Origin Legends: An Analysis

Introduction

'Except for the Fulani', wrote G. I. Jones in 1939, 'no Nigerian people have produced more speculation about their origin than the Aro'.[1] Speculations on the origin of the Aro fall into two broad groups. In the first group are those produced by the Aro themselves as an account of their own history and social development. In the second group are the speculations produced by officials of the British colonial service in an attempt to understand and solve a many-sided riddle which they popularly described as the 'Aro problem'. On the surface these men were seeking to get to the root of the question of Aro origin. But in reality they were comparable to any of the factions in Aro Chukwu who were concerned not so much to attain an objective account of their traditional history, as to construct social charters that would serve their own purpose. In this sense these speculations are treated as legends of Aro origin and subjected to the same process of socio-historical analysis as the oral traditions collected from Aro Chukwu. In the first part of this paper only the traditions in the first group, that is those indigenous to Aro Chukwu are dealt with. In the second part the European speculations on Aro origin as well as the present writer's tentative suggestions on the matter are discussed.

This paper is a contribution to the study of the influence of local politics and social conflicts on oral history in a non-literate society exposed to rapid and wide-ranging changes. It does not seek to determine who the Aro are, where they came from, when and so on. The changes referred to in the last but one sentence were brought about by British rule. British 'suppression' of the Long Juju oracle and the need to expand the cultivation of food and cash crops made it necessary that the Aro, who lack land, should convert the virgin forest on which the Long Juju grove stood to arable land or some other use. This was a piece of land which for generations had not been claimed by any individual or group, but was probably the common property of all the Aro: at least the Long Juju which was located there was the common institution of the entire Aro community. With the need to establish exclusive ownership to this piece of land also rose the need to establish a claim to the Long Juju which was formerly located there. In the second place British rule placed a new premium on 'kingship' or 'chiefship' through the system of indirect administration. This meant that the position of Eze Aro which probably had attracted few contestants in the past became a prize which all leading families and individuals in Aro Chukwu contested. Finally British policy in the matter of slavery and especially missionary preaching which laid emphasis on the lost sheep, created tensions in Aro Chukwu society which had traditionally distinguished between the free and servile-born. These were the changed and revolutionary circumstances in which factions and interest-groups in Aro Chukwu struggled to find their feet by re-examining the question of their pedigree.

It is suggested here that any one who would seek to reconstruct Aro traditional history from all the rival versions of Aro origin, must recognize that he is dealing with at least three categories of traditions. First, there was that collected about 1914 during a dispute over the succession to the Aro 'kingship' which deals with the charter supporting that institution. Then there are those collected in 1917 during the contest over the right of ownership to the Long Juju grove. These deal with the question of title to land in Aro Chukwu. Finally, there are the versions collected in the 1920s during the rift between the free born and the slaves which deal with the place of the slaves in Aro Chukwu society.

Part I. The Aro on their Origin

Before relating and analyzing the different versions of Aro origin, it would be necessary to attempt to sketch briefly the traditional social and political structure of Aro Chukwu. This will help one to understand the discrepancies which exist between the rival versions, as well as the aims of the factions that have given them.

The Aro clan (or sub-tribe as it is at times called) comprises nineteen villages. Each of these villages was largely autonomous especially in matters which did not touch interests outside it. But unlike most Igbo clans or sub-tribes, Aro Chukwu had to some extent a form of more or less regular clan government and administration. According to Mr. Shankland who investigated Aro political system in 1933, the Aro were clan rather than village conscious. Even though each village had its own administrative and judicial machineries, 'the paramount power (in Aro Chukwu) was vested in the Nde Akpa Nkpo or clan council over which the Eze Aro permanently presided'. This council helped to give Aro Chukwu a greater sense of internal 'cohesion' *vis-à-vis* outsiders than would otherwise have been the case. But when Shankland went on to assert that the decisions of this Council 'were obeyed without question or remonstrance' he entered contentious grounds. Also according to Shankland the Eze Aro who presided over the Council 'was and is the head of the royal house of Aro and is always the oldest living free born tracing direct descent from Oke Nachi, the traditional founder of the royal line'. This family was said to be the senior lineage in Oror village. The other members of the council were the village heads of the remaining eighteen villages of Aro Chukwu.[2]

By the second decade of this century the nineteen Aro village, had come to regard themselves as falling into five 'patrilineages', that is into five groups or 'families' each of which believed that it descended from a single founding father or a closely related group of founders. The families or groups were as follows:[3]

Ada (Igbo) Group	Amaseri (Igbo) Group	Mixed Igbo and Ibibio	Unspecified or Amaja Group	Akpa Group
Utugugwu	Ugwuafọ	Obinkita	Isimkpu	Ugwu-a kụma
Oror	Ugbo	Amanagwụ	Atani	Agbagwụ
Amankwụ	Amaọba		Amangwu	Ujari
Amuvi				Amụkwa
Asaga				Amasụ
				Ibom

It is important to note even on the basis of legendary history that the villages tracing descent to Igbo founders had an easy chance of dominating the political, social and economic life of Aro Chukwu. The villages which claimed outright Igbo origin through Edda and Amaseri number eight. To them may be added the villages of the Amaja group—Isimkpu, Atani and Amangwu. The versions of the two factions, as will be shown later, agree to the effect that these three villages were founded by people (slaves?) captured by hunters from Asaga village in the

Edda group. In fact Oti Nwa Anichọ and his faction in 1923 went so far as to refer to Atani and Amangwu as descendants of Oke Nachi, the legendary founder of the Igbo group.[4] The *Amaja* group could therefore be included in the so-called Igbo 'family' group, and this would bring the number to eleven. Obinkịta and Amanagwụ, according to the tradition collected by Mathews in 1927 were described as part Igbo, part Ibibio.[5] The significance of this claim to be part Ibibio will be discussed later, but they should be included in the so-called Igbo group. At least their politics could be regarded as pro 'Igbo group'.

Following this analysis, therefore, in spite of the elaborate grouping of the nineteen villages into five so-called 'partrilineages' or 'family' groups, the structure of Aro Chukwu would seem to correspond to the standard structure of most Igbo village-groups which is based on what has been termed dual division. Under this system each village group is divided into an upper (*ndi elugwu*) and lower (*ndi agbo*), or into *Ikenga* and *Ihitte* categories. In Aro Chukwu this division crystallized into a division between the so-called Igbo group and the so-called Akpa or non-Igbo group. But since the so-called Igbo group is traditionally associated with slave status, or at least believed to have descended from slave ancestors, the two villages of Obinkita and Amanagwu have sought to escape the stigma of slavery by claiming Ibibio origin, or at least part-Ibibio origin.

Today neither the grouping unearthed by Mathews in 1927, nor the grouping postulated by the present writer above is popular in Aro Chukwu. In fact a well educated and enlightened Aro, himself well versed in the traditions of his people, warned the writer that neither of the above would make sense to an Aro man today. The current grouping is tripartite and as follows:

Oke Nnachi		Eze Agwu	Ibom-Isi
1. Utugugwu	7. Ugbo	1. Amanagwụ	1. Ugwuakụma
2. Oror[6]	8. Amaọba	2. Obinkita	2. Agbagwụ
3. Amankwụ	9. Isimkpu		3. Ujari
4. Amuvi	10. Atani[6]		4. Amụkwa
5. Asaga	11. Amangwu		5. Amasụ
6. Ugwuafọ			6. Ibom

It is suggested here that internal evidence, as well as evidence derived from comparison with the structure of other Igbo groups would tend to support the hypothesis of dual division. The manipulation of this organization which produced first five 'divisions' and now three 'grouping' is part of the process by which Aro Chukwu community has sought to attain stability in the changed circumstances created by colonial rule and the erroneous policies associated with it.

And now for the legends themselves. Apparently, in spite of the belief which was widespread amongst the British in Nigeria that the Aro were a remarkable people, no definite effort, at least none that has survived, was made before 1914 to delve into Aro history. British interest in the Aro in that period would seem to have been limited to ensuring that this people did not revive the cult of *Ibini Ukpabi* (the Long Juju) and the trade in slaves. These were the two 'crimes' which, the British claimed, had forced them to underake the expedition of 1901-2 against the Aro. In 1914, however, the occasion offered itself for such investigations in the fact that there was a dispute over the succession to the Aro kingship between one Mazi Ukwu Okoro of Utugugwu and Mazi Kanu Oji of Oror, the two villages being in the so-called Oke Nachi or Igbo 'family' of villages. Unfortunately only the version given by Ukwu Okoro of Utugugwu was recorded. But even that alone, in the light of the analysis carried out above, makes an interesting study. Said Ukwu Okoro:

> 'A chief of Ibibio whose name I do not know bought a slave called Agu from Enugu. The slave became wealthy and got plenty of children. When he found that he was stronger than his master he rebelled against him. People came from Akpa to fight for Agu, and a native doctor was brought from Edda to make war medicine. He was brought by Ndem, a grandson of Agu.
> 'Ndem's father is called Ezeke and is the founder of Utuhugu. Ndem had a son called Okpo who seduced the wife of the Edda doctor whose name was Nachi. Nachi making war medicine had to refrain from intercourse with women and thus his wife's pregnancy proved her unfaithfulness.
> 'When the woman named Okpo as her lover Nachi was angered and said he would make medicine no more but would go over to the other side and make medicine for them. This frightened Ndem and made him promise to offer Nachi anything he demanded for compensation. Nachi said he would wait until his wife gave birth before he declared what compensation he wanted. In due time the woman gave birth to a male child. Nachi was happy and then proceeded to ask Ndem to transfer to him the rulership over his people—the rulership to be vested in Oke, the new born child. When Oke grew up he was made

king. At that time he lived at Utuhugu but on account of the fight with the neighbours at Ugwuakuma Oke's family moved to Oror buying the land from Ibum'.[7]

On the surface this is an account of the origin of Aro kingship. But in reality it is nothing of the sort. The point of the story lies in the concluding sentence: 'At that time he (Oke Nachi) lived at Utuhugwu, but on account of the fight with the neighbours at Ugwuakụma Oke's family moved to Oror buying the land from Ibum'. In other words Utuhugwu, not Oror, was the original 'national' capital as well as the 'royal' village of Aro Chukwu. By this Ukwu Okoro of Utuhugwu was asserting the premier claim of his village to the Aro kingship over Oror. Here one may trace the beginning of the process which today has led to the tradition amongst the Aro that the kingship is not hereditary in one family, but rotates amongst the three so-called family groups—Oke Nnachi, Eze Agwu and Ibom-Isi.[8]

Also worthy of note is the way the rival candidates sought to protect the exclusive claim of the Igbo faction to the kingship. They did not allow the contest to degenerate into a bitter and protracted rivalry which would threaten the solidarity of the Igbo group to the advantage of the Akpa section. In fact Ụkwụ Okoro soon decided to retire from the contest in favour of Kanụ Ọji. Also he made sure that the Akpa group were excluded from all claim to the kingship by asserting that the first king of Aro Chukwu was the son of a union between the two main branches of the Igbo group. By this accident the 'alliance' of the two branches against the Akpa section became transformed into a 'blood union'.

Whereas the occasion for the first recording of this legend was an internal dispute within the Ada (Igbo) group, for the recording made in 1917 the occasion was a dispute between the Ada family group and the Akpa faction over the right of ownership to the virgin bush, *Ovia Chukwu*, the grove or forest which had once been the abode of the Long Juju. The dispute went to court and, before the arbitrator, Mr. A. E. F. Murray, political officer, the two parties fell back on traditional history and legend to elucidate and validate their claims. The two rival accounts of Aro origin which were told during the arbitration were thus clearly the results of deliberate manipulations of tribal history in an attempt to assert title to a piece of land. But still they make important contributions towards our understanding of the dynamics of Aro politics. It is important to note that in this matter only one of two claims could be valid in traditional law—either claim based on prior occupation, or claim based on conquest. Claim based on purchase would be irrelevant since in traditional law there could be no question of outright sale and purchase of land. The Ada group based its claim on prior arrival and title, the Akpa group on conquest. For this matter it was not necessary to assert more to establish either case.

Many people gave evidence on both sides but here we shall reproduce only the most representative and comprehensive case on either side. Chief Anicho Anyakoha of Amankwu (Edda group) giving the case for the plaintiff stated:

> 'The land Avia Chukwu[9] is common property of all the Aros. Utu Ugu and Eze Agu are the only two people who have any vestige of right to lay claim on the land.
> 'The Defendant is a stranger, he is one of the Iboms whom the Aros employed to fight for them.
> 'Eze Agu was the ancestor of Utu Ugu. He was the first man who owned Aro Chukwu. He found Ibibios there and fought with them. For this purpose he employed the Iboms. The Iboms came from a place called Akpa up the Cross River'.[10]

On behalf of the defendants, the Akpa group, Mazi Okoro Ezike stated as follows:

> 'I[11] came here from Akamba in the Ikom District. Utu Ugu employed us to fight for them. The people who were settled between the Government station and Ibom were called Loessien.[12]
> 'We drove them away and returned to settle down at Ugwuakuma. My grandfather was called Umachi, he killed Loessien, the Ibibio Chief.
> 'Umachi was a hunter. One day he was hunting from Ugu-Akuma and noticed the bush *Afia Chukwu* and the surrounding lands and thought it would be a good place to build a house, as Ugwuakuma was too small. He was the first Ibom man to settle there. After this he planted tombo trees on the land. The former inhabitants, the Ibibios, did not make Long Juju'.[13]

The arbitrator, Mr. A. E. F. Murray, made the award to the Akpa section on the grounds that their titles based on conquest had superseded that of the Ada group based on prior occupation. But this is not the only point which interests us here, especially in the light of later developments in the rivalry between the factions in Aro Chukwu and the influence that the rivalry, which accumulated acrimony as time went on, had on later versions of the legends. The point is that these accounts made no reference whatever to a fact which had been brought to light in 1914—the conditions or terms under which Eze Agu̲ (Eze Agwu̲) or Agu̲ (Agwu̲) and his descendants lived among or with the Ibibio. These accounts tend to assume that Eze Agu and his descendants were free men and had settled amongst the Ibibio to ply their trade. On this matter Mr. Murray argued:

> 'There is one important point to which very little reference is made, and this is the terms on which the Aros lived with the Ibibios before the advent of the Iboms. . . . The inference to be drawn from this is that the original Aros (Eze Agu and his descendants) who were undoubtedly a mercenary people, settled down amongst the Ibibios for purposes of trading in the same manner as the Hausas do at the present day. In all possibility they formed settlements and tried to make friends with the Ibibio inhabitants. When this failed they resorted to another device and called in the Iboms for purpose of exterminating them and driving them southward across the Enyong Creek'.[14]

But in the light of the claim made in the 1914 version that Eze Agu̲ was a slave purchased from the Enugu area, as well as in the light of the revival of this story in later versions of the legend, Mr. Murray's assumption is probably untenable. The key to the non-recurrence of this tradition in the versions given in 1917 is to be found in the application of certain principles of native jurisprudence to the issues of slave status and land ownership. It is noteworthy that in 1914 U̲kwu̲ Okoro had not only asserted that Eze Agu̲ was a slave, but had also gone on to claim that when Eze Agu̲ prospered he rebelled against his masters. The fact that the rebellion succeeded meant that Eze Agu̲ had effectively asserted his freedom and independence.[15] When he dealt with Nachi and the Akpa mercenaries, he dealt with them as equals. When the Akpa came Eze Agu̲ and his people were no longer slaves and their being in Aro Chukwu before the Akpa was a sufficient title to land. To counter this, the Akpa section did not need to base their non-recognition of the claims of Eze Agu̲'s descendants on grounds of the stigma of slavery for this would be irrelevant. All they needed to counter was the claim of prior occupation. And they did so by asserting rights of conquest.

The versions of the legend given in 1917 were adequate for the needs which they were designed to serve at the time. Soon, however, new situations arose, and to meet these it became necessary to embroider and modify the different versions. To understand this new situation[16] it will be necessary to give a brief historical background starting with an analysis of social 'stratification' in Aro society.

In the pre-colonial period the Aro, like their neighbours were slave dealers and slave owners. In fact it could be assumed, since they excelled all others in this region in the slave traffic, that the Aro kept more slaves than their neighbours. Being long distance traders they needed slaves as carriers and for currency. They also needed slaves as farm and domestic hands, for sacrifices on ritual occasions and during the burial of their prominent dead. These slaves, it is true, were not maltreated like slaves in Europe and the New World, but they had fewer social and political rights than the freeborn. They could not hold political office, could not be admitted into the secret organizations, did not participate in the running of the *Ibini Ukpabi* oracle, did not share in the ritual celebrations that went with Ikeji (New Yam) Festival, or in the Ǫtǫsi (Ǫfǫ) ceremony. The clear demarcation between the slaves and the free born was perpetuated by the fact that the slaves and their descendants were known as *ohu* (slaves) while the free-born were called *amadi*.

When the British occupied Aro Chukwu in December 1901 they were determined to arrest and punish the Aro nobility all of whom they regarded as belonging to the class of high priests who operated the Long Juju oracle. By this step, they hoped, they would spell the doom of *Ibini Ukpabi*.[17] As a result may prominent *Amadi* Aro were arrested and detained while many more went underground. For a long time the latter refused to come forward to take office as Warrant Chiefs. In the event when the British established a Native Court in 1902 to take charge of the local administration of the entire Aro District most of the Warrant Chiefs who represented Aro Chukwu on the court were men who traditionally had no right to represent their village in such matters. What was worse some of them were not even from the class of the *amadi*, but were outright slaves.[18] 'Before the coming of (the Colonial) Government' wrote T. M. Shankland in 1930:

> 'they (the Aro) had an organised judicial and administrative system for the clan, and it cannot but be regretted that after the Aro Expedi-

tion so great was the desire to destroy the Aro power that little of the indigenous system was permitted to surve'.[19]

After the first few years it would seem the policy of forcibly repressing the *amadi* aristocracy was partially abandoned. At least when in 1906 Chief Kanụ Okoro, the Eze of Aro (Aro clan Head) surrendered himself to the Government authorities at Calabar, after being in hiding for about five years, he was restored as the clan head of Aro Chukwu. But it is not clear whether he was appointed to membership of the Native Court.[20] In any case whatever the extent to which this policy of reversal went, up to 1923 and 1924 many of the leading political figures who worked as the recognized agents of the colonial administration were from the inferior class in Aro Chukwu society. One such figure was Mazi Ijeomanta Ijeoma Ebulu who after the Aro Chukwu Expedition became the uncrowned head of Aro Chukwu. Of slave status he had risen to be a prominent and wealthy slave merchant. When the British took Aro Chukwu he boldly came forward to welcome them and through the favour of the British administration became very influential in Aro Chukwu affairs. His son K. E. Ijeomanta was, later in 1926, to make a significant contribution to the argument over the founding of Aro Chukwu. On this matter Mr. E. J. Price, Assistant Dictrict Officer for the Aro District, wrote early in 1923 as follows:

> 'There is, however, a slave class (in Aro Chukwu) who have usurped in some cases authority under the disintegrating influences of the Aro Expedition and Government policy to such an extent that they are now reciters of native law and custom.
> 'Among this class can be found good men like Ijeomanta Ijeoma Ebulu who is an old man and no doubt is now influenced by younger members of his family such as William I. Ijeoma and Kanunta Ijeoma Ebulu'.[21]

According to the Assistant District Officer, the spokesman for this group was Chief Anichọ Anyakọha who in the twenties, as we shall soon see, was the reciter of the version of Aro legends of origin favoured by the socially handicapped groups.[22]

An analysis of the status and pedigree of the members of the Aro Native Court carried out in 1924 revealed that the Eze Aro was not a Warrant Holder. He was in fact in exile for crimes connected with reviving the Long Juju. Of the nine Aro Warrant Chiefs none was a traditional village head. If the investigating officer had gone a little deeper into the matter he probably would have discovered that many of them were in fact slaves.

This was a potentially explosive situation as the *amadi* could decide any day to seek to assert their rights against this class of *arriviste*, especially should they get some encouragement from official quarters. This was what happened about this time. By 1919 it had been discovered that the Warrant Chief System of local government was being applied in the teeth of severe opposition from the people. It was also discovered that the Warrant Chiefs were oppressive and corrupt. In 1922 Mr. S. M. Grier, the Secretary for Native Affairs, was sent to tour the entire Eastern Provinces where this system obtained. In the report which he submitted Mr. Grier proclaimed the Warrant Chief System a failure. He attributed the failure to, among other things, the fact that most of the Warrant Chiefs were not men who by tradition and native usage enjoyed the right to exercise political power over their people. As part of the general effort to correct the ills of the system the Government encouraged inquiries into native political organization designed to find out the traditional heads of villages who were to be encouraged to take the places of those Warrant Chiefs who had no traditional right to political leadership in their communities.[23]

At Aro Chukwu these disturbing inquiries coincided with a reformist movement under the championship of an organization called *The Aro Patriotic Society* which claimed that it aimed at 'the uplift and enlightenment of the town and people'. The members of the society were described as 'the Christian young men of the town'. According to Mr. E. McLachlan of the United Free Church of Scotland who championed the cause of this society before the District Officer,

> 'Those who comprise the movement are the great majority of the people, it is supported by about six out of every seven of the population and are drawn from seventeen out of the nineteen towns of Aro.'[24]

In spite of its claims of wide appeal, the movement was suspect in the eyes of the *amadi*. To start with most of the early Christians were slaves or at least people who carried no social weight whatever in their communities. They were in other words socially handicapped people. In the second place many of the Warrant Chiefs whose positions were threatened by the inquiries into the status and pedigrees of chiefs patronized the movement in a bid to find a political base for their power. There is thus every evidence that the weightier half of this society comprised the socially under-privileged, while its opponents were mostly members of the old aristocracy, the *amadi* who were striving to regain their positions of dominance and could achieve that aim only through the revival of the traditional usages.

> 'Recently,' wrote Mr. McLachlan, 'an attempt was made by those who called themselves 'free born' to regain their old fashions. The other section of the society (i.e. made up of those of slave descent) have combined to maintain their positions, to abolish as many of the old superstitious customs as possible and to induce a more civilized manner of living. They mention the juju *Otusi* which is blamed for many evil things . . .'[25]

It should be pointed out that the 'juju' '*Otusi*' against which these so-called reformers directed much of their assault is said to be the Aro equivalent of what in other parts of Igbo land is described as *Ọfọ*, the traditional staff of office, the symbol of truth and justice. The movement was then directed at the basis of the old order which if successfully overthrown would make nonsense of the search for people who by tradition were qualified to exercise rulership.

These were the totally confused circumstances in which the colonial government collected what to date are probably the most detailed accounts of the different versions of Aro legends of origin. In these accounts two interest groups, which no longer correspond entirely to the division between Ada (Igbo) family group and Akpa family of villages, tried to find a historical charter that would protect and consolidate their entrenched positions which each felt the other threatened. The *amadi* class who were in political wilderness under the Warrant Chief System sought to regain their position by calling the *ins* slaves, while the latter sought to blur the traditional distinction between the *ohu* and the *amadi* in the hope of destroying the claim of the *amadi* to exclusive political privileges in Aro Chukwu. In this latter rivalry Chief Anichọ Anyakọha of Amankwu (Ada group), a man of non-*amadi* descent was the spokesman of the threatened slave class, while Oti Nwa Anichọ of Ugwuakụma (Akpa group) became the spokesman of the *amadi* class. The fact that these two men came from rival villages gives the false impression that the conflict was, as in 1917, between the two dominant descent groups when in fact the matter at issue cut across this traditional division.[26] But as always on such occasions and in such matters the battle was fought out within the context of the social structure. Each party constructed a family tree which involved juggling with the origin of each member village.

> 'There appear to be two distinct parties in Aro', wrote Major Sealy-King who knew the nature of the conflict in question, '... (a) (Those who trace their descent from Kakakpu an Ibibio. (b) Those who trace their descent from Iruk-Nta who was an Ibo and apparently a slave. Both parties consider themselves free-born. The latter party is headed by Chief Oti Nwa Alicho'.[27]

Mazi Oti Nwa Anichọ opened this round of the debate with a written account of Aro origins dated 4 August 1922. In it he argued that the aboriginal inhabitants of Aro Chukwu were Ibibio. But unfortunately they had found themselves at war with a dissident branch of their line led by one Kakakpọ the ancestral father of Okoroafor Udo, the then village head of Amanagwụ (of the mixed Igbo-Ibibio group). Kakakpọ sent Okenachi, the head chief of Utugugwu (Ada Group) to invite their ancestors, Osim and Akụma, to come to his aid. Osim and Akuma took with them one Ezeobi, who later became the founder of the village of Agbagwu, (Akpa Group). On their way Osim and Akụma encountered and defeated the Nosi tribe who were at the time the owners and manipulators of the *Ibini Ukpabi* oracle. On reaching Aro Chukwu Osim and his brother attacked the Ibibio, quickly defeating and expelling them. However in the running battle Osim was killed by an Ibibio warrior. Enraged by this loss, Akụma seized Okenachi and wanted to kill him to revenge the death of his brother. Okenachi pleaded for his life and took the matter to Kakakpọ whose agent he was. 'To save Okenachi', claimed Oti Nwa Anicho, 'Kakakpo' surrendered all Aro land to Akuma and his children'. Again at the end of the war Kakakpo confirmed this total surrender of Aro land to Akuma and his descendants. Also Akuma and his warriors had captured from the Ibibio the villages of Asaga (Ada group), Amuvi (Ada group) and Amanagwu (mixed Igbo-Ibibio group). From Ugwuakuma, where Akụma lived, this warrior leader sent out his men to colonize the village of Ibom.

Some time later the people of Asaga (Ada group) went hunting and in the bush captured some people whom they brought to Okenachi at Utugugwu. But Okenachi ordered these captives to be taken to Akuma who sent them to found the village of Isimkpu (the group of unspecified descent). Also at the end of the war Akuma discovered he needed new raffia war caps and so sent Okenachi to Amaseri to invite Agwueke to come to Aro to weave war caps. This man came and settled. His descendants founded the villages of Ugbo, Ugwuafo and Amaoba. Later the authorities of Ugwuakuma chose a chief from Ugbo to rule over these three villages.

For some time Akuma dominated the affairs of Aro Chukwu. This angered Okenachi who apart from having invited Osim and Akuma, claimed that it was the charms he made that had made victory over the Ibibio possible and easy. He therefore protested to Kakakpo who 'gave over to him the remaining portion of his lands and said he (Okenachi) was to share authority over Aro with Akuma'. From that time, claimed Oti Nwa Anicho, 'Utugugwu represented by their ancestor Okenachi shared the rights of headship over all Aro with Akuma'.[28]

The import of this account is obvious. Even the account itself is entitled 'Aro History designed to show that Ugu-Akuma is head of all Aro'. Thus we are told that *Ibini Ukpabi*, the premier bastion of Aro Chukwu influence was captured not from the Ibibio but from Nosi, who had nothing to do with the foundation of Aro Chukwu. No other group could thus dispute control of this premier institution with Akuma's descendants. Also we are told that Kakakpo surrendered his title to most of Aro-land to Akuma, so also his title to political leadership. Thus when strangers came, like the mythical founders of Isimkpu, it was not Kakakpo that assigned them land on which to settle but Akuma. Later still, Kakakpo surrendered what little land and political power remained for him to Okenachi. In this account the slave class was assigned no part whatever in the founding of Aro Chukwu. Of the three heroes, Kakakpo was an Ibibio, Okenachi came from Amaseri, Akuma from Akpa, and all three are regarded as *amadi*. Soon however, this attitude broke down. The slave class became so vociferous in Aro affairs that it could not be easily wished away into oblivion. In another account given by this man in 1923, he made an effort to fit them in where he believed they ought to belong.

On 23 December 1922, Chief Anicho Anyakoha supported by

Toti Nwa Toti, Ijeomanta Ijeoma Ebula, Awa Okpara Eke, Ojim Emenike, Oji Udensi, Uche Nwaokereke and Ovia Okoro Obasi replied to the above account in a version they sent in, attached to a petition which they wrote to the Assistant District Officer, E. J. Price.

In their account they claimed Aro Chukwu was once occupied by an Ibibio community founded by one Okon Uku who was also the priest of *Ibritam* or Long Juju (Ibini Ukpabi). Okon Uku begat Uruk (sympathy). Uruk later purchased a slave from the Igbo country whom he called Uruk Nta after himself. In time Uruk Nta prospered and became impatient of control by his Ibibio masters. 'He refused to marry Ibibio women, but took his wives from the towns of Ihe, Ututu and Isu because they were Ibo races like himself.' This was much displeasing to his masters who soon had an opportunity to humiliate him.

Uruk Nta later told his son Nachi about the humiliation. Nachi moved him and his people from Obinkita where they were then living to Amanagwu and declared war on the Ibibio. Nachi retained the services of an Edda medicine man called Oke. Oke later asked for help from Nna-ubi, the head chief of Akankpa in the Ekoi country. Nna-Ubi raised a regiment which he christened Ibom and placed under the command of his two sons, Osim and Akụma. The regiment drove out the Ibibio but lost Osim who was killed by an Ibibio warror, and was buried at Oror.

At the end of hostilities Akụma and his Ibom regiment refused to leave Aro Chukwu as they were afraid to face the ire of Nna-Ubi at the loss of Osim. Instead they pressed for and got from Nachi 'part of the rights and title of *Otusi* or *ofor* and likewise rights over the juju called *Ibritam* by the Ibibio, *Ebulukpabi* by the Aro and Chukwu by the Ibo. They were also given rights over the market of Ncheghe'. 'From then on', Anicho Anyakoha and his group asserted, 'these war aliens came to assume the same status as the descendants of Uruk-Nta the original slave man and the father of the aboriginal Aros like Obinkita and Amanagwu sections'.

Oke, the Edda doctor, also asked to be rewarded for his part in the war and was 'conferred the right to succeed Nachi, the eldest son of Uruk-Nta.' After this Anichọ Anyakọha and his group went on to account for the foundation of the other groups of villages. In this the differences between their own account and that of Oti Nwa Anichọ are not very significant. But one noteworthy discrepancy is they do not concede that it became the right of Akuma to assign lands to later immigrants. This right and power remained in the hands of Nachi, the son of Uruk-Nta the founder of 'aboriginal Aros'.[29]

The significance of this account lies in the theory that through successful rebellion Uruk-Nta and his line had asserted and achieved their freedom. When the war ended it was Nachi, Uruk-Nta's son who had undisputed control over *Ibritam* (said to have been wrested from the Ibibio) and over *Otusi* or *ofor*. He later conceded some, not all, of the right to these key symbols of *amadi* status to the alien soldiers, thus making them also *amadi*. For his part in the war Oke, the Edda medicine man was not set up apart to raise an independent community. Instead he was absorbed into the community of the descendants of Uruk-Nta. We are told that as soon as this happened Aro kingship became hereditary in the family of Uruk-Nta stationed at Oror.[30] Anicho Anyakoha and his group were not, however, going to leave the moral of the tale in doubt. They went on to make it plain. Their deductions from their account deserve quoting at length as they give the clearest insight into the whole affair.

They maintained:

> 'In the beginning the juju Ebulukpabi was generally attended by all the citizens of Aro at the performance of its ceremony. It was the same with the *Otusi* or *Ofor* ceremony. There were, and there are still, specially nominated priests in each section who officiate at the ceremonial offering each year to invoke its blessings on behalf of each family, such priests were chosen in each family according to seniority rather than according to descent or pedigree. Only women were ineligible and that due to the fact that they are not reliable. There was no discrimination in favour of the so-called *Amadis* and against the so-called *Ohu* or slave born.
>
> 'Kakakpu was the last son of Uruk-Nta and it is his descendants who have tried to introduce the novel idea of discriminating against the so-called slave-born.
>
> '...
> ....
>
> 'The prohibition against burying dead persons of slave origin with copper rods and leopard skin, or wearing copper rings by women of slave origin in fattening houses is of recent origin and owed everything to the evil minds of men like Omenukwa of Asaga, Kanu Ehui of Amankwu and others.
>
> 'The title *Amadi* or free-born is vague in this respect, for there is no family in Aro that will give account of their blood as descended from

Okon Uku, the Ibibio founder of the place or from Uruk his son. Uruk-Nta was a slave, therefore every descendant of that line has no claim to the title of *Amadi*, neither have the mercenaries who settled after the Ibibio war'.[31]

Assistant District Officer E. J. Price fully appreciated the purpose of this story and the petition. He knew both were sparked off by the fact that the position of certain Warrant Chiefs of slave status was threatened. He mentioned some of these by name. They were Anicho Anyakoha, Kalunta Ijeoma Ebulu and John Kanu. Another signatory to the petition was William I. Ijeoma, a former court clerk.

> 'The petition', commented Mr Price, 'arises from their learning that the status of birth of some of them on the Native Court has been questioned. These are the classes of men who would be debarred from Court membership and authority, if the suggestions of the Secretary for Native Affairs are carried out'.[32]

But Oti Nwa Anicho and his group would not accept this theory that all Aro people were either all *amadi* or all of slave descent since every Aro including Kakakpo was either a descendant or Uruk-Nta and therefore of slave origin, or a descendant of Akuma, an alien mercenary. In their 1922 version the *ohu* were not mentioned at all. Now Oti Nwa Anicho and his group introduced the *ohu* element. But they refused to concede that this social class played a principal part in the founding of Aro Chukwu. The *ohu* merely fought as dependants of Kakakpo an Ibibio of free status. They did not lead the revolt as was claimed by the other group.

According to their new version, Uruk, an Ibibio, bought a slave from the Igbo country and called him Uruk Nta. Uruk had two sons, Obia and Ipia; later, Obia begat Kakakpo. On the death of Uruk his fellow Ibibio men sought to deny the children their legitimate political rights. Consequently Uruk Nta and all those loyal to Uruk's family declared war on the other Ibibio faction. When Obia died in the war Kakakpo became the leader of the Uruk faction. Kakakpo then sent for an Edda doctor called Oke to help him. Oke sent to the Ekoi country and got help from Nna-Ubi who sent an army led by his two sons-in-law Obi and Ovia, and his two sons Osim and Akuma. The Ibibio were beaten and expelled but Osim was killed. As a result Akuma and his troops refused to return home but asked for land on which to settle. 'Kakakpu gave him a portion of the land to dwell on with the same right as other citizens. They now live at Ibom and are free born'.

Oke the Edda doctor, they went on, also asked for some land as compensation for the role he played in the war and was given the area of Oror, Utuhugwu, Amankwu, Atani and Amanagwu. His descendants are still in these places and are 'considered Aros and free'. One man by name Ezejaka who was found under a palm tree after the fight was given the land of Isimkpu, Atani, and Amanagwu. 'His descendants are looked on as Aros and free'. The people who at present live at Ugbo, Amaoba and Ugwuafor originally came from Amaseri in Afikpo District. 'They also helped to drive out the Ibibios by making war hats and were given the above named lands to dwell on. They are free-born and Aros'. This faction then went on to assert that only the descendants of Kakakpọ had the right to attend the *Otusi* ceremony.[33] The descendants of Uruk Nta of course remained what their ancestor was—of slave status.

Another attempt, in the period covered by this study to attain a solution to the basic social rift in Aro Chukwu between the *amadi* and the *ohu* through the manipulation of Aro traditions of origin was made in 1926 by Mr. K. E. Ijeomanta already mentioned. This man was a missionary school teacher at Calabar and produced in 1926 in the Aro dialect of Igbo a 25 page pamphlet dealing with Aro history. Mr. Ijeomanta was a member of the *Aro Patriotic Society* and a citizen of Amanagwu village. Like his father he was not an *amadi* and his pamphlet was inspired by the desire to raise the status of the non-*amadi* elements in Aro Chukwu. He is said to have gathered his facts from an elderly Warrant Chief, Ọkpani Okoronkwo.

According to Mr. Ijeomanta's story, the original home of the Igbo people was the Nile valley. From there they migrated through the Sudan to the region they now occupy. Upon their arrival they started spreading out for more land. Uru was a leader of one of these waves of secondary migration which headed in the direction of the Cross River. Uru and his advance party ran into some Ibibio villages around Aro Chukwu and was captured. The rear party instead of seeking to rescue Uru headed towards Bende. The important point of this story is that Uru, the so-called ancestor of the slave class, was not a slave as such but a war captive.[34] Therefore his descendants cannot justifiably be regarded as slaves.

What does one make of these conflicting traditions and

accounts? Modern sociological analysis of oral traditions has suggested that 'they are not substitute for history and are at best regarded as systems in which a very limited number of items are manipulated to explain or justify existing institutions and social groups'.[35] This is probably an overstatement or in any case a limited view of the possible functions which oral traditions serve in a non-literate society.[36] But nonetheless if we apply this sociological approach to the different versions of the Aro legends of origin and combine it with a detailed analysis of the circumstances in which these were collected, we are better able to recognize the limitations of these accounts. Only in this way would it be possible to understand the wide divergences which exist between one account and the other.

Competition and rivalry are of the very nature of Igbo social organization. These exist between individuals, groups and even amongst the gods. This is one explanation for the fact that each ward of a village has its own square (*ama*) where it often holds evening markets, its own shrine of most local gods and even of the earth goddess, its own commons and all those other attributes which would enable it to lead a full life in case of enstrangement from the other units of the village. This pattern is repeated at the village level, thus making the village more or less autonomous in its internal affairs *vis-à-vis* other villages. The village-group is autonomous and independent, though not absolutely so, of the other member units of the clan or sub-tribe. It is not surprising that the rivalry and competition are carried on to the sphere of tribal lore, ideology, and history. Thus each ward, or village-group has its own version of the founding, expansion and growth of the village, village-group or clan.

This feature of Igbo society helps to explain the welter of versions of the story of the founding of Aro Chukwu which the British were faced with in the 1920s. The 1914 account 'established' that succession to Aro Chukwu kingship was hereditary in the villages of Igbo descent and that Utugugwu, the village of the informant, was the original 'home' of Aro kingship and therefore the first Aro 'national' headquarters. The versions of 1917 sought to tackle the question of how one could establish a valid claim to land by traditional law. The versions of 1922 and 1923 represented the attempt of Aro Chukwu society to grapple with the new social problems created by the continuance of a large and increasingly vociferous and prosperous slave population in a new era that preached social, moral and political equality between the free and servile-born. The 1926 version represented the effort of members of the new educated class, recruited from both groups, but mainly from the servile-class—an elite class which had learnt the christian doctrines of the equality of all men before God—to find a new rational basis that would offer equal opportunities to all. This was why it became necessary to make Uru not a common slave but a war captive. This was considered to imply a nobler status.

Over and above all these there is the more important tradition that the Aro are the final result of generations of blending together of three ethnological entities—Igbo, Ibibio and the so-called Akpa. All who have handled this matter have tended to take this story literally. Sir Herbert Richmond Palmer, the Lieutenant Governor of Northern Nigeria, said Akpa referred to the Jukun, Matthews said it referred to the Ekoi and through them probably to the Idoma or Jukun. It was in the effort to discover who were the Akpa of Aro legends that other authors, as will be shown in Part II, introduced such elements as the Portuguese, the Carthagenians, the Jews, the Fulani and so on into the story. G. I. Jones who has been among the most reliable of those who dealt with these traditions thinks there was in fact an Akpa group involved in the foundation of Aro Chukwu. In 1939 he thought it came from the tribe classified by Dr. Talbot as 'Ekuri-Akunakuna'.[37] In 1950 he traced the Akpa to an offshoot of the Agwa'agune without indicating whether these are one and the same people as the 'Ekuri-Akunakuna'.[38]

But it would appear that to adopt this literal interpretation is to miss the point of this aspect of the traditions. Both Capt. H. Webber and Mr. H. F. Matthews made attempts to map the areas of business operation of the various Aro 'patrilineages' that is of the Ada Igbo group, Amaseri Igbo group, Akpa group, mixed Igbo and Ibibio group and of the *Amaja* group. The results showed, in broad terms, that the so-called Igbo descent villages operated in Igboland, the so-called mixed Igbo-Ibibio villages mainly in Ibibioland, the so-called Akpa villages mainly in the region of Ekoi and beyond. 'It will thus be seen', concluded the anthropological officer, Matthews:

> 'How closely the spheres of influence corresponded with the places of origin. The Ibo people, namely those of Ada and Amaseri, covered the Ibo section; the Akpa mercenaries covered the country closed by the bend of the Cross River while some could be spared to assist in the

Ibo sector; the Ibibio-Ibo remnants covered the Ibibio sector bounded on the east by the Enyong Creek. There remained the small but important sector on the coast between Ibibio and Ibo, viz, Kalabari and their neighbours on the Bonny estuary and creeks. Here was one of the great outlets for the slaves which would be obtained up-country. This sector was duly provided for in the persons, whoever they were, who were brought in by some means and founded Isimkpu, Atani and Amangu. On the analogy of the other sectors it appears highly probable that they were Kalabari traders either captured by a hunting party sent out for the purpose or persuaded to come into the combine by its promise of much profit . . .'[39]

An application of the sociological method to this matter reveals that the spheres of influence did not correspond with the places of origin, but the places of origin later coincided with the spheres of influence. A lot of emphasis has been laid on the fact that Aro economic hegemony in this whole area rested on the reputation of the oracle *Ibini-Ukpabi* and on the use of Abam, Ohafia and Edda warriors to terrorize those who refused to fit into the Aro scheme of things. But this theory ignores the fact that in the beginning these methods were probably inapplicable. It is most likely that the Aro began in a small way to build up their business and that it was as their business grew and as they ranged farther afield, that they spread the fame of their oracle and probably came to build up an understanding with Abam, Ohafia and Edda warriors. In those early days, therefore, it was only imperative that the Aro should depend like other Igbo peoples on the traditional methods of securing safe passage from one village to another, from one region to the other. Describing this system in a recent article, Dr. Ukwu said:

> 'The long distance traders relied on covenants at the personal level, *Igbandu*, as the principal means of guaranteeing freedom of movement across the country and safety among strangers. By this the traveller established a ritual kinship with an influential member of the village group he was visiting or passing through. The parties were bound to do no harm to each other and the host protected his guest and generally acted as his agent *vis-à-vis* other members of the community. It was also his duty to have the departing guest escorted to the *Ogbugbandu* with the next village group and formally hand him over to the contact there. Thus the traveller was shuttled across the country by a relay of hosts'.[40]

This arrangement did not operate only at the personal level. It operated also between village-group and village-group.

After all, the *Ogbugbandu* mentioned by Dr. Ukwu was usually the midway point between the village-groups where representatives of both groups had mixed blood drawn from their veins and eaten this with kola nut and goat meat sacrificed for the occasion. This was taken to establish ritual kinship, making the two groups 'brothers'. Operated and sustained over a long time, especially under such a highly successful arrangement as the Aro evolved, this could easily lead to the two groups claiming descent from one founding father. And it is suggested here that this was probably how the Akpa-descent villages acquired 'Akpa' origin and so on for the others.[41] The cultural and linguistic gymnastics which Palmer, Meek and Matthews later went into in an effort to explain these matters are irrelevant to the case. The alien traits which they emphasize could easily have been acquired and probably were by the Aro through their long-ranging trade and oracle system which also entailed long periods of stay or even permanent settlement among the peoples they traded with. It is instructive that the villages trading towards the coast did not evolve putative kinship relations with the peoples of the coastal area. This was where the Aro met with the stiffest opposition and rivalry. Here they were often discriminated against and even cheated. The Aro trading in the region did not feel sufficiently 'at home' to claim to have a home there.

In this connection again it is relevant to mention a point which struck H. F. Matthews as odd at the time. This is that nearly all the names involved in the legendary drama that led to the foundation of Aro Chukwu are Igbo names. The only exceptions are Ndem, Loessien (Essien?) Kakakpo. These exceptions can be explained by the fact that most Aro people speak Ibibio, many speak Ekoi or Ejegham. Ibibio names are common amongst the Aro. Their business interest in Ibibio land and their location, on the boundary between Igbo and Ibibio explain these 'intrusions'. Another possible explanation is the Aro system of naming. An Aro man, it has been said, usually names his first son after his own father, his first daughter after his mother. His second son he names either after his uncle or after his wife's father or after a friend who was useful to him during his occupational wanderings beyond Aro Chukwu and whose memory he would want to commemorate. Many Aro married from outside Igbo land, mainly from Ibibio land, and the region of the Upper Cross River. In those areas too they had trusted friends. It was thus easy for Aro people to bear non-Igbo names. Such foreign names, therefore, are a false pointer to ethnic origin. But how does one explain the fact that the so-called Chief of the Akpa (whether Ekoi, or Akunakuna or Jukun) of Aro legends as well as his children bore Igbo names at the time of first contact between them and Okenachi the travelling doctor who hired them? In fact the whole tradition of hiring an Akpa fighting band might best be seen as an attempt to harmonize the later excessive dependence on Abam, Ohafia and Edda warriors with Aro history and éthos. This was not a later failing, the tradition would seem to say, but has been in line with Aro policy from the beginning of using others to fight their wars.

But all said and done one cannot but be impressed with the extent to which, judging from the legends, the servile class had by this century become integrated into Aro society in spite of their large numbers and the threat they must have posed to Aro values. This fairly close integration is shown in the fact that the slave class are portrayed as having been present at, and participated in, the foundation of Aro community. There may be some dispute as to what were their social rights, but there was none as to the fact that they were part and parcel of Aro Chukwu society. This is a testimony to the liberality of Igbo society, as to its capacity for handling the problem of slavery, an issue which in many societies is a perennial source of instability.

PART II: Foreigners on Aro Origin

If the accounts of Aro origin analyzed in Part I mirrored the strains and stresses in Aro Chukwu society during the first three decades of this century, British speculations on Aro origin also showed part of the attempts of the colonial government to deal with what they described as the 'Aro problem'. By the 'Aro problem', the colonial administration meant the question of Aro origin, the nature and extent of Aro influence in pre-colonial times and the use to which the colonial government could put that influence. Here, however, we are concerned with the first third of the problem—the question of Aro origin. Many British officers made determined, but in retrospect futile, attempts to reach an answer to this question. Of these the most celebrated theorist, and probably also the most pernicious and irrelevant, was Sir Herbert Richmond Palmer one of the most striking personalities of the Northern Nigerian political service during this period. We would not bother about these views if they had not had such an unfortunate effect on the study of Igbo history. We discuss them in some detail here to expose their utter baselessness and clear the way for more rewarding research. The analysis also gives us some insight into aspects of the nature of the colonial regime in Igbo land.[42]

Palmer's acquaintance with the Aro and Aro Chukwu was a very brief and shallow one. It derived from a roving tour of the Southern Provinces which he made on behalf of Lugard in 1914 as a prelude to the administrative reforms which were introduced along with the amalgamation of the two Nigerias. Palmer's own confessional notes or minutes on this matter dated 10th August, 1926, are very revealing and reward quoting at length. He said:

'When I visited Aro in 1914 the chief points that struck me were:

- '(a) That the Aros divided their world into four sectors just as the Jukons do.
- '(b) That they say they came from the Cross River and formerly spoke a different language.
- '(d) They were a hieratic caste like the Jukon and called themselves Inokun'.[43]

Palmer never visited Aro Chukwu again. But on the strength of this limited first impression and of other hypothesis which he had dreamed up to explain the socio-political situation that faced the Administration of the Northern Provinces in the region below the Benue, he evolved a theory of Aro origin. This theory at best ignored the various traditions of the Aro, and at their worst perverted the import of those traditions in order to attain a political objective which was dear to Palmer. Palmer waded into this problem fully only in 1921. In that year he produced very lengthy memoranda which dealt with the origin of the Aro people and launched the debate on Aro origin into an orbit where it came to engross the attention of the colonial administration for many years.

Reduced to its bare bones, Palmer's theory was this: the Aro, though Igbo speaking by the time British rule was imposed, are not Igbo. They are an off-shoot of the Jukun of Kororofa, and in that sense, belong to the same race as the Jukun, and the ruling aristocracies of Benin, Idah and Yoruba land. Palmer regarded this group as a Hamitic, and therefore alien, race endowed, unlike their 'wretched' Negro subjects, with innate qualities of rulership and therefore capable of evolving centralized political systems. Their political organization, according to him, usually has as its apex a divine king like the *Oba* of Benin, the *Oni* of Ife, the *Atta* of Igala or at least a hieratic aristocracy like the priestly class that manipulated the Long Juju at Aro Chukwu. Palmer based this grand hypothesis on questionable political, etymological and religious evidence.[44]

But before we go on to all this evidence it is necessary to summarize briefly Palmer's ethno-historical reconstruction of the evolution of civilization in pre-British Nigeria. In 1922, J. N. Brooke, a political officer in the Northern Nigerian Service, who had become a convert to the ideas of Palmer on this matter, summarized them for posterity. Here we give a summary of his summary.

Palmer believed that between two thousand and one thousand two hundred years ago, Egyptian influence spread 'right across the Sudan from Darfur to the Benue and Upper Niger by way of Lake Chad, the Yo and Shari rivers'. Then between 760 and 1400 waves of Hamitic adventurers founded Kingdoms in Bornu and Bagirmi, 'and perhaps also in the Kororofa and Jukun countries of the Benue basin'. From Kororofa and other areas under Jukun influence 'civilization spread to Hausa land, Kamerun, Yoruba and Borgu'. In any case, he said, from about 700 A.D. missionaries of culture ranged over all Nigeria penetrating 'beyond the more open bush country into the dense forests of Adamawa, the Upper Cross River (and Aro country), Yoruba, Benin, etc.'. 'From the generalized culture of these early Hamitic people', he maintained, 'sprang the Yoruba' Ife, the Nupe and the Jukun Wukari kingdom (the last of which the Attah of Idah and the Aro of Aro Chukwu in the Ibo country are off-shoots)'. The Jukun, continued Palmer, later established an Empire in the fourteenth century. This empire, he said, reached its apogee towards the end of the sixteenth century and was at that time 'one of the seven greatest kingdoms of the Sudan, possessing all the lower and part of the middle section of Hausa land'. He also claimed that 'their (Jukun) dominion extended south to the Cross River and even to the Atlantic'. Jukun power later declined and was eventually destroyed by Fulani and Munshi raids. When the Munshi (Tiv) came over the Sonkwala range and attacked Wukari, he went on, 'the Jukun of Kasimbila went south and became Ibo-speaking under the name of Aro Chukwu, they became the dominant caste among the Ibo'.[45]

The fact is that Palmer never entertained a shadow of doubt that the Aro were a Jukun off-shoot, or a colony of the Jukun cut off from their base after the Tivi were said to have seized the region they now inhabit and in so doing disrupted Jukun power by blocking their way to the sea. The Atlantic was believed to have occupied a vital place in the economy, and therefore political ascendency, of the Jukun state. It was through it, the northern pundits asserted, that the Jukun disposed of the slaves they caught in their wars of territorial expansion.[46] Palmer in fact never ceased to assert that the Aro were Jukun. In September 1921 he wrote in one of his interminable minutes on this matter:

> 'The country I wish to refer to, more particularly, is the country between the Benue and the sea ... the whole of this part of the country is dominated in an ethical and spiritual sense by one race—though that race is called by three different names—Jukun, Igala and Aro'.[47]

And now for the evidence on which Palmer based his recondite hypothesis. One set of evidence derived from the unproven assumptions which he entertained on the socio-political organization of the peoples of Southern Nigeria among whom were included the Igbo and his 'Jukun Aro'. According to him throughout Southern Nigeria the political analyst could discover 'two distinct kinds or forms of indigenous Native Rule' or political systems. 'The first, the oldest and most primitive' was by means of graded organizations which might embrace a group of villages, clans or a tribe, the heads of the organizations being the oldest and most respected men....' Some of the graded organizations were age-grade, some were secret associations, some partook of the characteristics of both. This form of rule, said Palmer, was the preconquest political system of the 'retrograde' autochthonous negroid peoples.

The second type of political organization was that based on kingship or centralized control of a sort. This type, he claimed, was 'imposed on the first in greater or lesser degree in various parts of the area under reference and it may be said while the first is Bantu the second represents the spread of Hamitic influence south of the Benue and the Niger'.

> 'The most conspicuous instances of this', he went on, 'are of course the Alafin of Oyo, the Oba of Benin and the Attah of Idah, while the Aro power in Iboland represents a compromise between the two

systems which in all probability originally came from the same source as the Attahate viz—the Jukun Kingdom of Kororofa'.[48]

If Aro political system 'identified' them as Hamatic and as specifically allied to the Jukon, so did etymological and linguistic evidence, Palmer argued. 'The word "Aro" in Aro Chukwu', he said,

> apparently means (a) Father or Nourisher (b) in a secondary sense the Sacred Spear. The Ibo word for God is Chineke, so that Chuku is doubtless only another dialectic variation of the defied ancestor of King Juok, Jukon, N'jokun or N'yaku (N'yakang).
> 'The root "Ar" in the sense of father or nourisher is peculiar to the group or clans of peoples found only in the Sudan, the group Zaghawa. The word for father in modern Zaghawa is "Kisar" which is the converse of the Hause word sarki ... The Kanuri king-name *Arki* is from the same root, and has the same meaning and is quite clearly the same word which is the first part of the Nubian king-name Ark-Amon (sustainer)'.[49]

The religion of the Aro, maintained Palmer, also showed them up as an off-shoot of the Jukun people, and also as Hamitic since it was the same as that of ancient Babylon:

> 'It appears', he said, 'that the real "Jukons" were a comparatively small aristocratic caste—who held their power mainly by spiritual and occult influence much like the Aro in Iboland ... It may also be noted that the so-called Long Juju of the Aros was simply a hoax box to control and make a profit of the Ibos. The real religion of the Aro presents an extraordinary similarity to that which obtains in the southern Jebels of Kordofan and among the Dinka and the Shilluks on the Nile, its "sacra" being a spear which when planted beside an altar ensures the presence of the N'yakang or Juok (i.e. the deified ancestor)'.[50]

On another occasion when he was pleading that the Christian missionaries be made to recognize the special claims of this his Hamitic aristocracy—the Jukun of Wukari, the Aro of Aro Chukwu and the Attah of Idah—he asserted:

> 'The position is briefly that the Igala religion, the Jukun religion and all the better side of Ibo religion are derived from Wukari and that the religion of Wukari is the Egyptian religion of Meroe, that is worship of Isis, Osiris and Ammon ... Considering that the Jukuns and the Aros are taught from childhood the Babylonian legends of creation—varied of course in details just as the Jewish legends vary from Babylonian—it is not surprising that the Jukun and the Aro regard Old Testament teaching as a rather absurd travesty of their own religon ...'[51]

These highly provocative ethno-historical speculations were passed on to the authorites of the Southern Provinces of Nigeria. After going through Palmer's memoranda, Colonel H. C. Moorhouse, the Lieutenant-Governor, Southern Provinces commented:

> 'I am afraid I have not studied the (Aro) question sufficiently to disprove or confirm Mr Palmer's statement... that the country between the Benue and the sea is "dominated in an ethical and spiritual sense by one race"... but I would say at once I am by no means convinced by the arguments put forward by him in this memo and the one previously submitted'.[52]

But whether Moorhouse believed it or not, the matter could not rest there. The issue had to be investigated. In fact these memoranda were promptly passed down to the Resident of Calabar Province who passed them down to the District Officer, Ikot Ekpene Division and from the latter officer they got to the political officer in charge of the Aro Chukwu District.[53] As Palmer's hypothesis passed down the administrative ladder on its journey to the officer in charge of Aro Chukwu, young officers absorbed sections of it which pleased or attracted them most. And soon those who were expected to confirm or disprove Palmer's thesis were heard reciting aspects of it. These recitations were made as confirmation of those sections of the hypothesis which had attracted these junior political officers. Palmer regarded his hypothesis as an organic whole which had to fall or stand as a piece. He took the 'confirmation' of any aspect of the thesis as a vindication of the whole theory.

It thus becomes clear that it was partly under the influence of the ideas expressed by Palmer in 1921 that political officers at Aro made an effort to understand the welter of conflicting versions of Aro legendary history which, as shown in Part I, the internal crisis in Aro Chukwu society threw up in 1922 and 1923. In 1921 Palmer had called the Aro 'Apa' a name which was also believed to be applicable to the Jukun. As already seen the versions of the legends given by the rival groups in Aro Chukwu in 1922 tended to emphasize the role of the so-called Akpa mercenaries as the dynamic element in Aro culture history. This impressed Palmer. Mr. D. A. V. Shute, District Officer, in analyzing Aro legends and social structure, in 1926 used a language that Palmer understood.

'The Aro political organisation of a king with a council of representatives of various towns', said Mr. Shute, 'is alien to Ibo and and Ibibio custom'.⁵⁵

Mr. Shute also came to parrot Mr. Palmer's view that the so-called Akpa or Apa elements were the culture carriers in Igbo society. 'At the end of the war (against the Ibibio)' he wrote on another occasion,

> 'either by force of arms or by superior intelligence the Akpas found themselves dominant over the heterogenous Ibo and Ibibio tribes among whom they found themselves, and who, had it not been for the Akpa strain to leaven the lump, would probably have remained much as Ihes and Ututu's today . . .
> 'Settlements of the Akpas were placed near the settlements of the inferior peoples to keep an eye on them and while respecting the customs and social organisation of these peoples the Akpas superimposed on them their own political structure'.⁵⁶

These ideas of a Hamitic group of culture carriers though certainly derived from Palmer impressed him as proof of his theory. It is therefore understandable that when in late 1926 the question of the role of the Aro in the Eastern Provinces, as well as their relationship with the Jukun was referred back to Palmer for reconsideration he was emboldened to instruct the Secretary, Northern Provinces to write as follows:

> 'I am to say that the passage of five years has not suggested to His Honour (H. R. Palmer) that any material modification of the views expressed in 1921 is necessary'.⁵⁷

At this point the Southern Nigerian Administration decided to ask Mr. H. F. Matthews, Anthropological Officer, to go into the question of Aro origin, the nature and extent of Aro influence etc. and advise the authorities. But Mr. Matthews was formerly an official of the Northern Nigerian political service and thus was not unaware of the romantic legends of culture heroes which the Northern pundits had put out and were pressing.

Matthews proceeded by collating, analyzing and reinterpreting all the materials on Aro origin which had accumulated in the archives of the Southern Provinces since this question was first broached. In the process he was expected to examine, criticize, reject or confirm each evidence on which people like Palmer who had advanced definite theories of Aro origin based their speculation. Mr. Matthews singled out three hypotheses for examination. These were Palmer's thesis which has already been stated at length; Talbot's hypothesis (advanced in his *Peoples of Southern Nigeria* published in 1926) that the Aro were probably the outcome of a union between the local inhabitants and early Portuguese explorers, traders and missionaries; and then the view contained in Aro legends that the Aro were a union of three ethnological elements—Igbo, Ibibio and a group of mercenaries called Akpa.

Matthews first dealt with Palmer's religious argument. On the issue of a spear cult he claimed he discovered that the use of spear as a sacred emblem was not originally common to all sections of the Aro 'confederation', but was at first limited to the Akpa-descent villages whom he asserted came from Ekoi. Those he called the original Aro, that is the Igbo element who are believed to have invited the Akpa group, had a religion which he said was the same as the religion found in the rest of Igboland. 'Any foundation which the spear cult may give for Jukun affinities', he argued, 'must therefore only apply to the Akpa mercenaries, that is to the tribes generally known as Ekoi'. The Akpa descent villages claimed that their ancestral father, Nna-Ubi, gave a spear to his sons Osim and Akuma before they left for Aro Chukwu. This spear they also claimed, 'is merely an heirloom and has no sacred significance'. The only time it was used on ritual occasions was during one of the sacrifices to the *Ọvọ Ukwu* of Ugwuakụma, during the New Yam (Ikeji) Festivals when it was 'planted at the entrance to the shed in which the sacrifice is performed'. This shed had 'no altar with or without ram's horns'. Matthews disputed the assertion that Akụma's spear had no sacred functions,

> 'seeing that the head priest, its custodian, has to be ceremonially installed before he assumes custody of it'.

At the time of Matthew's investigations the high priest designate was one Kalụ Enọ (Umọ?) who, Matthews said, adopted an attitude 'of passive uncommunicativeness both personally and in his influence on others'. Because of this attitude and because he had remained un-installed for four years Matthews thought the 'unwelcome delay (in his installation) (was) enforced by the lack of some ingredient for the ceremony'. This ingredient, he said, was a human being to be used for sacrifice.[58]

In the non-Akpa descent villages, however, Matthews also found in existence certain spears. These were in possession of two individuals—Chief Anichọ of Amankụ (Ada-descent village) and Okoro Ekuala of Amaọba (Amaseri-descent village). He found Mazi Okoro Ekuala's spear

> 'laid among rafters of an open shed, in the compound, which shelters various objects of a more or less sacred nature such as modern drums, a bell of European make, two small pillars, a bundle of offor sticks, nine skulls of horses sacrificed at past funerals of heads of the village and a collection of sheep's and goats' skulls with horns on them being the remains of sacrifice. The latter which was lying in a heap and with no apparent orderliness or arrangement, are the only objects I have noticed which would correspond at all with the rams' horns on the altar described by Mr Palmer.'[59]

Mr. Matthews believed there was something special about these spears because they were brought out 'only at funerals of very wealthy and important men' when they are 'carried round the towns and flourished, thrown up and caught before the commencement of the funeral play which included the sacrifice of slaves and horses and other livestock'.[60] Matthews was told that the two shrines he saw were called 'Nyamavia' (Inyamavia), 'an Ibo word meaning Juju for ensuring profitable trade'. Each village, each kindred and each trader or business man had its or his own.[61] Matthews then went into a detailed and profuse disquisition to show that the sacred spear occupied an important place in Ekoi religious ritual. Therefore the 'atrophied spear cult', which he said he found in Aro Chukwu he concluded must have been derived from that source—brought in by the invading Akpa, or preceding the invading Akpa through the Ibibio whom he considered an earlier off-shoot of the Ekoi. More realistically he thought it could have been borrowed by the Ibibio from the Ekoi whom 'they regard as their superiors in magical arts'.[62]

On the linguistic evidence for Palmer's Jukun thesis, Matthews pointed out the fact that the linguistic classification of the peoples of this region had not yet reached any degree of finality. The Ekoi, from whom he said the Akpa-descent villages of Aro derived, were classified as Semi-Bantu, whereas the Jukun were grouped as West Sudanic (by N. W. Thomas), the Bolewa (of Bornu and Gombe) as Central Sudanic. The Idoma dialect, he claimed showed close resemblances to the Ekoi language. 'It is possible', he concluded,

> 'that the Semi-Bantu speaking Ekoi were an originally Sudanic speaking tribe which has changed its language but retained the spear cult or more probably were a Semi-Bantu speaking tribe which acquired the spear cult from a ruling (Jukun?) caste'.[63]

If the former were the case then the Ekoi from whom Matthews said the Akpa descent villages derived would be an off-shoot of the Jukun and thus Palmer's thesis proved. If the alternative were the case, then any traces of Jukun culture found in Aro Chukwu must have derived from culture contact which took place during the heyday of supposed Jukun political and economic domination of the region between the Benue and the sea.

Matthews found Palmer's etymological evidence absolutely inapplicable. 'Inokun', he said, could not be derived from the same root as the Kanuri 'Kokuna' and 'Nokena' nor from the same root as 'Jukun'. 'Inokun', he correctly pointed out, 'is not the name the Aro collectively give themselves. It is the Ibibio name for them. The Ibibio language he said is of the Semi-Bantu division of Sudanic. He also correctly pointed out that 'the Aro really pronounce the name which they apply to themselves 'Arụ'. The Igbo word for spear is *Aro (Araw)*. So their name, he concluded, does not mean 'spear'. 'Chukwu', he also correctly pointed out 'is simply the Igbo word compounded from 'chi' (spirit), 'uku' (Great) just as 'Chineke' means the 'creator-spirit' and it (Chukwu) has no connection with a dialectic variation of 'Juok', 'Jukun' etc. meaning deified ancestor'.[64]

The theory that the Aro were a cross between the local negro inhabitants and the early Portuguese, Matthews considered very weak and not worthy of serious consideration. 'The arguments, cultural and linguistic', he said, 'which I have heard in support of Portuguese influence are fragmentary and not themselves weighty'. For one thing it was Matthews' conviction that Aro Chukwu community was formed earliest about 1700, a period of time during which the Portuguese were no longer an influence to reckon with on the Cross River.[65]

Matthews might feel that some of the 'facts' which Palmer adduced to prove his Jukun thesis were far-fetched and weak, but he was impressed with the argument that Aro Chukwu population 'certainly' contained 'elements of a hieratic caste' whose presence, in the words of D. A. V. Shute, 'leavened' the 'inert' 'Ibo-Ibibio' lump thus giving rise to the 'highly intelligent' Aro the British knew. Matthews' own hypothesis is derived from a literal interpretation of the basic 'facts' of Aro legends of origin. He accepted in principle the 'facts' that the Aro derived from a mingling of Igbo, Ibibio and Akpa elements. He accepted that of these the Ibibio were the aboriginal inhabitants. Later an Igbo community, made up either of purchased slaves or free settlers, came to live amongst the Ibibio. In time the Igbo, owing to their 'superior' intelligence, he said, came to assert themselves against the Ibibio. A war broke out and the Igbo called in Akpa mercenaries to do the fighting. During the war the Akpa wrested Ibritam or *Ibini-Ukpabi* from the Ibibio custodian, Loessien, who before he was killed stupidly revealed the secrets of the oracle. At the end of the war the Akpa were, of the three elements, the politically dominant. But soon they were supplanted by the 'intelligent' Igbo group led by Nachi 'the soothsayer' or 'medicine man' of 'superior intelligence' from Ada. It was Matthews' opinion that close investigation would also reveal that Nachi was probably a descendant of a hieratic caste that probably had settled at Edda for generations. Under the influence of Nachi, he argued, *Ibini-Ukpabi* was developed from a local oracle of little consequence to the famous oracle it was at the time of British advent. Matthews' literal approach to the legend was such that he regarded all the various and irreconcilable names mentioned in all the versions—Nachi, Ndem, Kakakpọ, Akụma, Obi, Ọka, Okwara, Okpo, and Ezejaka not only as historical personalities but also as contemporaries! He also regarded as historical events, the legends relating to the founding of the villages of Amaseri-descent as well as the Amaja group.[66]

The literal approach to the Aro legends is not the only interesting feature in Matthews' own hypothesis of Aro origin. Also worthy of note are the proofs he adduced to connect the 'Akpa' mercenenaries with the Ekoi tribe, the Ekoi with the Idoma, whom he said were subjects of the Jukun Empire and then the calculation by which he arrived at the conclusion that the Aro community was founded not earlier than 1700 or 1730, but most probably around 1750.

First the arguments linking the Akpa of Aro legends with the Ekoi. Matthews argued that *Idoma* is a term which the Jukun applied to non-Jukun people over whom they ruled. Among the Idoma, he argued, there is a people who call themselves Akpa and who, he said, are related to the Yatche in the then Ogoja Province. The name Ekoi, applied to the people described by Talbot in his book *In The Shadow of the Bush*, he said, was given to them by the Efik. The people, he claimed, called themselves *Akpa*. Matthews maintained that this was the name by which they were known at the time the war that led to the founding of

Aro Chukwu was fought. Therefore the Akpa of Aro Chukwu legends, he concluded, came from Ekoi. Then he went on to show that he found close resemblances between some 'Akpa' vocabularies collected from an 'Akpa-Aro' and some Ekoi words collected some time earlier by Talbot. He referred to the spear cult which was widespread and deep rooted among the Ekoi and traces of which he said he found in the Akpa-descent villages of Aro Chukwu. There were also the 'facts' that the Ekoi and the Aro practised the mummification of bodies of prominent men by drying, made use of 'the peculiar pictographic system of writing known as 'Nsibidi'.[67] This 'Nsibidi' in particular would seem, argued Matthews, to link the Akpa-Aro and the Ekoi with the Nile valley. He said it had been pointed out how close is the resemblance between this 'pictographic writing' and the 'characters found in ancient royal tombs at Abydos and in Ancient Egyptian rock drawings and designs'.

> 'This resemblance', he argued, 'appears to be beyond such explanations as mere coincidence. If this "Nsibidi" writing can be traced in other places which will form a link with Ancient Egypt, its origin will be ascertained. Considering the already clear connexion between the the Jukun and the tribes of the Upper Nile, research among the Jukun might be fruitful'[68]

In short, if, argued Matthews, the Idoma were once under Jukun rule, the Ekoi a branch of the Idoma and the Akpa-Aro an off-shoot of the Ekoi, then the Aro if not directly an off-shoot of the Jukun contained elements from a hieratic caste (through Nachi) and through other people who were once under a hieratic caste and must have inherited some of their qualities. But from Palmer's point of view all his so-called hieratic elements between the Niger-Benue confluence and the sea—the Aro, the Yoruba, Bini and Igala ruling elites—were all allied to the Jukun. Thus Matthews' theory was a 'confirmation' of Palmer's Jukun origin thesis through a circuitous route.

Then the arguments on which Matthews based his calculation that the Aro community was founded between 1700 and 1760. One derived from genealogical 'evidence'. He collected genealogies from seventeen different Aro elders. These were traced variously from Akụma, Nachi, Ndem, Kakakpọ, Obi, Oka, Akara, Ọkwara, Egbo and Ezejaka and varied in depth from four to eight. Matthews took an average of this which gave him a depth of six. On the assumption that an African generation lasted 25 years, this gave him 150 years. This meant for him that the 'Aro confederation' as he called it came into existence about 1760. But that was not all. He connected this 'evidence' with 'evidence' derived from ethno-history by the northern pundits. Some time earlier Mr. J. B. I. Mackay, the D.O., Idoma, had suggested that about 150 years before the establishment of British colonial rule 'there was a great upheaval which caused many clans to move simultaneously'. Palmer said this great upheaval was the breakup of the Jukun Empire. Mackay said it was the Tivi invasion which cut the Jukun commercial route to the sea, and forced the 'Apa' or Jukun in Kororafa and Idah and the tribes of Bauchi to move. Now Matthews said this great upheaval also affected the Upper Cross River and

> 'would account for the Ibo being pressed forward on the Ibibio with the resultant friction already related and also for the availability of Akpa mercenaries who were also feeling the pressure from the north and were seeking an outlet'.[69]

Combining these two 'facts' Matthews arrived at his celebrated conclusion that Aro Chukwu community came into existence not more than two hundred years from the date of his investigations.

A copy of Matthews's report was sent for comment to Mr. Palmer who passed it on to Mr. C. K. Meek, administrative officer turned anthropological officer, for criticism. Meek shared Palmer's views on the close connection between the Jukun and all the other so-called hieratic ruling aristocracies of the Southern Provinces. Not surprisingly therefore he could not accept those aspects of the report which tended to cast doubt on the 'fact' that the Aro were an off-shoot of the Jukun. On the linguistic side he considered it a mistake to link Bolewa and Jukun. He thought it was also a mistake to classify the Arago language as Semi-Bantu. 'The use of spear as a cultus emblem', he re-emphasized, 'has a wide distribution. But it seems to have been specially characteristic of Jukun chiefs'. He pointed out that mud pillars, which Matthews confessed to having seen in Aro Chukwu 'are characteristic of Jukun peoples, but are found also among the Ibo and in the Cameroons'. He said 'Nyamavia' (Inyamavia) contained a name 'Nyama' which was commonly used in the Benue for God. 'The name Akuma', he asserted, 'is certainly Jukun and is in fact the name of a Jukun cult the emblem of which is a horned mask'. He said it was 'common among the Jukun for people to be named after cults'. He considered the term *Akpa* 'a very widespread tribal designation, particularly among the Jukun peoples and those closely associated culturally with them'. He listed many Jukun peoples who called themselves *Akpa* or *Apa*. He traced the Long Juju or the *Ibini-Ukpabi* to the *Jukun*. The *Jukun* cults of *Yaku* and *Ayo* he said were, like the Long Juju, oracles. He referred to Talbot's story in the *Peoples of Southern Nigeria*, Vol. II that the Aro Chukwu priests were not expected to live more than seven years. This he likened to the Jukun practice which forbade the *Aku* to live longer than seven years. In short the Northern pundits saw in the report more evidence of Jukun connection that Mr. Matthews, with all his belief in a stratum of the Aro being a hieratic caste, was prepared to concede.[70]

Meanwhile Matthews had continued with the investigations, this time from the Edda end. He went to Edda hoping 'to solve the connection between Ada tribe and Okenachi and the ultimate origin of the Ada people'. He hoped to do this through comparing the rituals and symbols connected with the feast of New Yam, but he had found these to diverge greatly from what obtained in Aro Chukwu. Then he delved into Edda legendary history and came to the conclusion that the Edda were not Igbo because they 'adopted the prohibition of eating new yams before the feast day after they arrived at their present habitat from the Ibo village of Uturu (near the railways east of Okigwi)'. According to his own theory the Edda came from the east bank of the Cross River, from 'Egoribum' which Matthews said could be identified with Ibum in Ekoi, with the possible implication that the Edda were also an off-shoot of the Ekoi, like the Akpa-Aro. If this were so, he concluded, this would explain why Okenachi, the Edda 'doctor' was able to invite the 'Akpa' mercenaries to drive out the Ibibio. The Edda told Matthews that from Egoribum they came to Une and from the latter place to the district now occupied by the Ihe and Ututu peoples who live next to Aro Chukwu. There they were when one of them, Okenachi 'rose to prominence as a doctor and came to Agwu's assistance, to drive out the neighbouring Ibibio people by calling in the Akpa mercenaries from across the Cross River'.[71]

At Owutu Edda Matthews came across a tradition which claimed that Okenachi was a great-grandson of Uru and thus a great-nephew of Agwu (Agu) to whose help he went in the war against the Ibibio. Comparing this with the story told by Mr.

Ijeomanta in his pamphlet (see Part I of this essay), Matthews came to the view that it was probably an Edda invasion that the Ibibio beat off when Uru was made captive. 'This', he said, 'would be consistent with the state of flux of population in those days possibly due to the breakup of the Jukun hegemony'. The Edda said they lived near Aro Chukwu until they received news that some people called 'Ukwa Onyeocha' who were armed with guns were on their way to attack their general area. So they fled to their present habitat where they were sheltered by hills. 'Considering the interchangeability of the sounds "kp" and "kw" in local pronunciation', argued Matthews, 'Ukwa' may be a variant of 'Akpa'. When he referred this matter to Mazi Ubi of Ugwuakuma (Akpa-descent village), Ubi said that 'the Ukwa Onyeocha were identical with the Akpa mercenaries who had introduced guns to this locality' and that 'it was by means of this new arm that they drove out the Ibibio'. Mazi Ubi added that they got their arms from European traders at Calabar.[72]

With this crop of fresh 'evidence' which again he took literally, Matthews came to modify his conclusions on the foundation of the Aro Chukwu confederation. He discarded the idea that Akpa superiority or that of Okennachi derived from superior intelligence innate in a hieratic caste. Their superiority he now attributed to their possession of the new weapon *Uta Ọkụ* (fire bow) or gun.

> 'Thus', he said, 'the cause of Aro superiority in fighting was from the outset the monopolist possession of firearms rather than valour or fierceness of onslaught and this monopoly they retained more or less intact over the valley of the Cross River for a very long period until their prestige rested on their Long Juju, the monopoly of middlemen trade between the coast and the interior and the terrors inspired by such hired warriors as the Abams, Ohafias and Adas. Furthermore this preliminary superiority in arms seems clearly to have been the basis of Aro influence, followed by a hieratic hegemony *locally*[73] developed and only distantly, if at all, connected with Jukum cults'.[74]

From this it would appear that Matthews had broken with the Northern pundits—Palmer and C. K. Meek. But in his conclusion he wrote:

> 'I have been unable to connect the Aro with any tribe of outstanding dominance, such as the Jukuns were at their zenith, except through the Ekoi who may possibly have been an off-shoot or a dependency of the Jukun, but have not, now at all events, any noticeable superiority over the surrounding tribes'.[75]

Matthews was again back to the conclusions he had reached in his first report which Palmer and Meek saw as a confirmation of their Jukun thesis. He also got from his investigations at Edda other 'facts' which he believed buttressed his conclusion that the Aro confederation must have been founded in the second half of the eighteenth century. One 'fact' was that the 'Edda genealogies' he collected were, on the average, eight generations deep. This told him that the flight of the Edda from the neighbourhood of Aro Chukwu must have coincided with the upheaval that led to the foundation of the Aro community. The other 'fact' was the story that the war of the Aro confederation was fought with guns—probably blunderbusses. Mr. Matthews followed this so-called trace of evidence up to the Tower of London Amouries and in November 1928 wrote, saying:

> '... during my leave in England I made enquiries regarding blunderbusses and was referred to the Tower of London Amouries. There I noticed that all the blunderbusses were made of brass.
> 'I wrote the Curator of the Amouries and his reply supports my computation from Aro genealogies, viz that the foundation of Aro dates from later half of the 18th century. You will note that the dates on the Tower of London blunderbusses range from 1696 to 1840 and that blunderbusses *may*[76] have been discarded in appreciable numbers at the end of the 18th century and if so it is quite *likely*[77] that they were exported to Nigeria just as the old flint-lock muskets found their way to the Persian Gulf and Africa'.[78]

It was not until about February 1928 that Mr. Matthews gave what might be considered his final opinion on Aro origin. In a memorandum he wrote on that date, one can see Matthews struggling to free himself from the strangle-hold of the Jukun or hieratic caste thesis, but without much success. First he conceded that long before the foundation of the Aro confederation, Igbo land had been under the influence of Kororafa. Then he asserted that the rise of the Aro to a position of pre-eminence among the Igbo and Ibibio derived from the reputation of the Long Juju and the possession of superior weapons—fire-arms. The origin of the spear cult he said had been 'lost in the mist of a much more distant past'. Then came the rub. He postulated that the Akpa-Aro though originating in the Upper Cross River would appear to have settled near Calabar 'probably for generations as an outpost of Kororafa'.[79]

But if H. F. Matthews' faith in the Jukun or hieratic caste

thesis was somehow shaken at last, Palmer's never was. In a memorandum of 16 June 1928 on the Eastern Provinces, he persisted in propagating the idea that the Jukun, the Igala, the Aro, the Bini and Yoruba ruling aristocracies derived from the same hieratic Hamitic race who since 700 A.D. had been the culture carriers and heroes in the area later known as Nigeria. Because of this fact, he argued, much of Nigeria enjoyed cultural homogeneity with the result that:

> 'Linguistically and culturally there is no part of Nigeria where a line can be drawn and it can be said that here the North ends and the South begins. The inheritance of culture and ideas has been almost without exception through thousands of years from North to South and East to West. Tribe has followed tribe, cultural conception has followed cultural conception, but though the extremes visibly differ there is a distinguishable woof running through the whole while the web is mainly varied by environment'.[80]

It was while the efforts catalogued and analyzed above were being made at the level of basic research and interpretation to get to the root of the problem of Aro origin that popularizers went on spinning the legends of Aro origin which Jones mentioned in his article in 1939. One thing common to these theories was the assumption that the Aro were not Igbo, or at least that the 'active' and 'intelligent' section of them was not of local derivation. From this general assumption it became a matter of more or less feckless chance, whether the particular theorist thought the alien element was derived from the Phoenicians or the Cartheginians or the Portuguese, or the Jews expelled from Spain in the late fifteenth and early sixteenth centuries, or the Jukun or the Fulani.[81] Since there was no evidence one way or the other it would appear each author sought to attain originality by choosing a people which no previous writer had mentioned. The only minimum requirement was that such a people should be assumed to be Caucasoid. Rev. Basden refused to name any particular people but added a new element to the problem by claiming that the Aro told him that their founding fathers came with a 'book'.[82]

British colonial officers interested in this matter, in particular men like Palmer, Matthews, Meek and so on, probably left these shores feeling satisfied that they had solved the problem of Aro origin. But the modern scholar of the problem cannot be expected to share in this illusion. We now know better than they did some of the main characteristics of oral tradition. We also are more conscious than they were of the untenable assumptions and irrelevant political objectives which made them handle Aro traditions of origin the way they did. As a result we now know that the various syntheses which were produced by the Aro, by Palmer and by Matthews as contributions to the reconstruction of the story of the founding of Aro Chukwu are questionable as history.

Palmer's hypothesis deriving the Aro from the Jukun or some hieratic caste allied to the Jukun is unacceptable. In spite of its elaborate pretensions to being the result of researches carried out on the ground, it was largely an extension to this part of black Africa of the Hamitic hypothesis, then in the ascendant but now totally discredited, which provided the pet explanation for the history of civilization in Negro Africa. According to this hypothesis the Negro was the inert branch of the human family incapable of any cultural advance on his own except if he had acquired the 'eternal spark' through contact with the race then classified as Hamitic. Palmer's thesis thus amounted to this: the Igbo and the Ibibio left to themselves could not have evolved the Aro trade and oracle systems which were believed to have depended on the exercise of great intelligence and organizing ability. The Aro system therefore could only have arisen under the influence of Hamites. And since the Jukun were then considered as Hamites and 'were' the branch of this race nearest to the Aro sphere of influence, therefore Aro Chukwu must have been a Jukun colony or at least contained a stratum of population derived from the Jukun or allied peoples. In discussing the matter in 1939 Jones wrote:

> The main point they (the theories) seek to explain is the superior intelligence of the Aros.... Hence most of the theories about their origin say that the Aros are derived from a cross between white and negro stocks.[83]

In the second place Palmer's theory was designed to serve a definite political purpose. From about 1918 local government in the Eastern Provinces, became a vexed issue. The efforts made by Lugard to harmonize local government practices there with what obtained in the Emirates of Northern Nigeria had failed—owing to the inability of the administration to find a class of men who could play the role assigned to Emirs in the Northern Provinces. The issue of what to do with the local government system of the Eastern Provinces was being hotly debated at the time Palmer propounded his thesis of Jukun-Aro connection. This was in fact his contribution to that debate. What he sought to do was to convince all and sundry that the Jukun ruled from the Benue to the sea until their collapse about 1750. When their route to the sea was cut, their brothers or a colony of them in Igbo land, that is the Aro took over the political, religious and moral leadership of the Eastern Provinces. If this was so, and he believed it was so, then it was untrue to say there was no class of people in the Eastern Provinces who could be assigned the role played in Northern Nigeria by Fulani Emirs. The Aro were such a class, he said, being like the rulers of Benin, Yorubaland, Igala and Wukari, a class innately endowed with political and' moral leadership. 'The Jukun of Apa and Igala and Aro', he said,

> still dominate this part of Nigeria by intellectual superiority. The superiority and influence is (sic) there whatever the Government does. The practical position is whether Government is prepared to try the policy of giving these races legitimate outlet for their ascendancy, and use them as a 'contact' with the lower grade races or is going to pursue a policy of repression, or at all events non-support.[84]

Here Palmer's Jukun thesis could be likened to any of the versions of Aro traditions given by local Aro Chukwu factions. It was a manipulation of a few ethno-historical materials of questionable validity to achieve a purpose decided upon on other grounds.

Even more serious from the point of view of the scholar is Palmer's method of coming to the conclusion which he stated with such certainty and finality. Luckily for us he left a record of how, on the strength of little or no evidence, he went from questionable probability to questionable probability until he built up this grand hypothesis which has bedevilled the interpretation of the material collected from Aro Chukwu ever since. Writing on 4 January 1928 he said:

> I started from the tradition and widely held belief supported (in some measure) by old maps, that the Old Kororofa Empire or influence extended to the sea and the *inference* that, if that was the case, Jukun or Kororofa culture and belief must have influenced the people now known as Ibo and Ibibio. I also *thought* that since the Munshi are certainly a recent intrusion from the southeast into their present habitat, it was *probable* that before that time the influence of Kororofa on and their contact with the Cross River region was greater than it has been since.

My *impression* also certainly was that the founding of Aro Chukwu did not date back more than 150–200 years and I remember that on the question of where the immigrants came from I was told that they came from the Upper Cross River, which from further inquiries I *judged* to mean the neighbourhood of Ikom. I *conjectured*[85] that they might have been Akpa, i.e. Jukuns, especially as it was stated that their language, now gone out of use, was neither Ibo nor Ibibio.[86]

Mr. Matthews' own theory combined some of the shortcomings of oral tradition with those of Palmer's speculative ethno-history. His literal approach to the legends was certainly naive and unscientific. His belief that either the Akpa or Okenachi must have belonged to a hieratic caste and that their impact on the supposed degenerate Igbo and Ibibio sections of the Aro population explains Aro ascendancy, belongs to the same order of racist myth as Palmer's Jukun thesis. What remains to be assessed of Matthews' contribution to the debate is his dating of the foundation of Aro Chukwu. The only solid evidence he seemed to have was the depth of Aro and Edda genealogies. But this category of evidence from an acephalous society has been shown to be unreliable by those who have worked on it recently using more advanced methods and techniques than were available to social anthropologists at the time Matthews investigated Aro history. On this question of the value of genealogies in the Eastern Provinces Jones has recently written:

> There are some Nigerian communities, notably Benin, which are interested in recalling the names of their kings. The Ijo and other peoples of the Eastern Region are not. We can assume, therefore, when we encounter such a list... that it has been produced to satisfy a European demand in response to European stimuli.[87]

This observation is very applicable to the Aro case. Before the investigations of the 1920s the Aro were probably not used to reciting any king list. They had not the institutions for it, nor did the Aro monarchy play such a key role in Aro politics to inspire such practice. The king lists which Matthews worked with were necessarily improvized, designed to meet the requirements of the white man for the time. Also it is not known how many names were left out, how many of those included were fictitious or how many generations of the Aro lived and passed away without anybody actually holding the position of Eze Aro. Matthews attitude which treated the list he got as more or less reliable is in keeping with his literal approach to the other aspects of Aro oral tradition. The argument based on the unestablished date of Jukun decline as well as on the assumption that blunderbusses must have found their way to the Cross River region about 1760 is not worth pursuing. With regard to the argument based on Jukun collapse one might mention that it is doubtful whether the break up of an empire necessarily increases the pressure on its frontiers. Thus the mass population movements which were believed to have set the 'Akpa' (whoever they were) on the move and thrown the Edda on the Ibibio is not an established historical fact.

The Aro Chukwu community must be considered first and foremost as an Igbo clan. But being a border community and because of the nature of its occupation—long range trading and the manipulation of an oracle whose fame and influence took in a large portion of the territory between the Benue and the sea—it has absorbed many non-Igbo elements through marriage, domestic slavery and the other usual processes of contact and fusion. A comparison of the foreign traits in Aro Chukwu culture with those in the culture of other peripheral Igbo is revealing. The Igbo have always been open to acculturation. Their large scale acceptance of western culture even to the extent of near-total abandonment of their own is no new feature.[88] Among some of the peripheral Igbo, among the Onitsha and the Western Igbo for instance, pre-colonial acculturation went so far as to give rise among these communities to a tradition that they are off-shoots of the Edo who had influenced them most. With the Aro the wheel had not yet gone full circle: hence only two sections of the clan had come to develop legends of non-Igbo origin. Probably had colonial rule not come when it did to dam the stream of history which was already moving in that direction, the whole Aro community would at one time, like the Onitsha and allied Igbo communities, evolve legends of non-Igbo origin. However, it would appear that the cultural pulls from the Igbo home land and from the mythical non-Igbo 'homeland' had already reached a state of equilibrium largely owing to the volume of Aro business interests in both areas.

Secondly, in considering the foundation of Aro Chukwu we must leave aside the cataclysmic and dramatic elements centred around Uru, Urunta, Kakakpọ, Nna-Ubi, Osim, Akụma, Okenachi and so on. The study of early Igbo history is still in its infancy. But the little done has not so far revealed that Igbo society was organized primarily for war, or that the distribution of the Igbo over the area they now occupy was brought about by cataclysmic events involving the mass movement of populations. The indications are that the compelling factor was the pressure of population leading to the impoverishment of the land under occupation and therefore creating the need to search for virgin land. By and large by the time slave raiding became an important factor in Igbo socio-economic life by the eighteenth century, the Igbo would certainly have settled effectively more or less the area they now occupy. It is instructive that the much talked of slave raids and need for protection from raids were not stirring enough to necessitate a revolution in Igbo socio-political and military organization. This would tend to show that in Igbo land raiding and wars did not play a very important part in population dispersal.

Present hypotheses on Igbo dispersal produced by social anthropologists and ethnographers would seem to indicate that this was a slow, unspectacular and phased affair. According to this hypothesis wherever the Igbo people came from originally, it would appear that they settled first in the region enclosed by the Nsukka Awka, Orlu and Okigwi Divisions, of Colonial Nigeria. As population grew and the soil became exhausted, people left this nuclear centre for the Nsukka-Udi area and for the region towards the coast. The latter group gave rise to the present Oratta, Ikwerre, Etche, Asa, and Ndokki tribes. In time too another group left from the Isuama area. Another wave arising out of the latter then left in two groups; one prong settled the Ngwa area, the other the Umuahia and Ohafia-Aro Chukwu regions.[89] While this was happening in Igbo land the Ibibio were also spreading out. But they would appear to have started dispersing from a nuclear area bordered by Aro Chukwu to the north, Ika to the west and Oron to the south. Most likely, therefore, by the time the Igbo prong from Isuama to Umuahia and beyond got to the Aro Chukwu-Ohafia ridge in the final phase of Igbo dispersal, they ran into the northern Ibibio fringe already settled somewhere around the present boundary between Aro Chukwu and Ibibio land. This is perhaps the only meaningful explanation of the story that the Ibibio were the original inhabitants of Aro Chukwu.[90] Then again it was after they had settled down and established regular relations with their Ibibio neighbours, that this Igbo fringe developed contacts with the non-Ibibio beyond the Cross River. This would explain the introduction of the Akapa element into the story long after contact had been made with the Ibibio. This hypothesis of Igbo dispersal have been questioned by the present writer elsewhere. For one thing it has not yet received definite support from detailed linguistic studies, nor from archaeological evidence. But for the time being it is the most popular working hypothesis on the matter.

It is not possible yet to date these movements. One can only wait for the archaeologist to establish how old Igbo occupation is in each of these regions. Dr. V. C. Uchendu has recently postulated that movement out of the nuclear Igbo area took place 'as early as the fourteenth or the fifteenth century'.[91] But this estimate, this magic date, probably has no more value than earlier ones proposed by Talbot and others. From the linguistic and archaeological evidence mentioned in the earlier essays it is very likely that Igbo occupation of these parts is ancient indeed and that by the christian era the Igbo and the Ibibio had more or less settled most of the area they now occupy, probably thinly in places, but nonetheless effectively.

NOTES

1. G. I. Jones, 'Who Are The Aro?', *Nigerian Field*, Vol. VIII, 1939, p. 101.
2. C.S.O. 26, No. 29017, Intelligence Report on Aro Clan, Calabar Province, pp. 18–22.
   A. E. Afigbo, *The Warrant Chiefs* (Longmans, 1972), Chap. 1.
3. Here I have followed the analysis made in 1927 by Mr. H. F. Matthews, Anthropological Officer for Southern Provinces. On this matter the tradition is very much confused and conflicting. For instance the version given by Chief Oti Nwa Anichǫ and his group on 1/5/23 described Atani and Amangwu as belonging both to the Ada (Igbo) family of villages and to the so-called *Amaja* or unspecified family group. It is said they were called *Amaja* because they served the other villages of Aro as *messengers*. The significance of all this will be discussed later. Jones says that Obinkita and Amanagwų claim to be descendants of an Ibibio founder.
   See file A.D. 635, Aro Sub-Tribes (Enugu Archives).
   See Report by Matthews dated 11.7.27.
   See also The Aro People, Arodist 1/7/33 (Enugu Archives), Letter No. 277/22/1933 of 1/5/23 from Political Officer, Aro Dist., to Resident Calabar Province.
   Forde and Jones, *The Ibo and Ibibio-Speaking Peoples of Southeastern Nigeria* (London, 1950), p. 56.
4. Arodist, 1/7/33, The Aro People (Enugu Archives), Letter No. 277/22/1933 of 1/5/23 from Political Officer, Aro Dist., to Resident Calabar Province.
5. A.D. 635, Aro-Sub-Tribes (Enugu Archives), see Report by H. F. Matthews dated 11.7.27.
6. These are said to be mixed, though predominantly Oke Nnachi, thus Atani Agbǫ, for instance, is said to be Eze Agwų.
7. Arodist, 1/7/33, The Aro People (Enugu Archives), see the 'Legend of Aro

Origin told by Ukwu Okono in 1914, a candidate for the kingship of Aro but now retired in favour of Kalụ Ọji'.
8. See the second table above.
9. This would be *Ovia* in Aro dialect of Igbo.
10. Arbitration case No. 3/1917 enclosed in the file, Arodist 1/7/31, The Long Juju of Aro Chukwu (Enugu Archives), p. 1.
11. This should read 'My ancestors'.
12. This should be an Ibibio. In some versions, and even in the next sentence of this version, Loessien (which probably should be read Essien) is given as the name of the chief of the Ibibio whom the founders of Aro Chukwu met on the spot when they arrived.
13. Arbitration case No. 3/1917 enclosed in the file Arodist 1/7/31, The Long Juju of Aro Chukwu (Enugu Archives), pp. 7-9.
14. *Ibid.*, pp. 2-3. Mr. Murray would appear to subscribe to the view that his so-called 'Original Aros' belonged to the 'Fulani type'.
15. Based on discussions on traditional law with various Igbo elders in 1962 and 1963.
16. We are going on to discuss the versions collected in 1922. As mentioned earlier on Capt. H. Webber, D.O., collected some Aro traditions after 1914, the date is not certain. We know nothing of the circumstances necessitating his effort. Apparently he collected them at two different times. On the first occasion it would appear that the tempo of internal Aro Chukwu politics was at a low ebb. His informants would therefore appear to have had no interest in telling him Aro traditions. This is probably the explanation for the fact that Capt. Webber's first record of these traditions reads as follows:

> 'The Aro claim to descend from one Oke Nachi. He had nine sons from whom the different Aro families spring. No information can yet be obtained as to their place of origin all questions about which are answered by "We have always been here".
> It is difficult to guess from which faction Webber collected this version. One would be inclined to say that it was given him by an informant from the Ada (Igbo) group; but it is open to doubt whether this group would do the Akpa section the honour of assigning them descent from the so-called "original" Aro. It would appear that a little later and from a different informant Webber collected a version which made reference to the war with the Ibibio. According to this version—"The Aros sent to *Ebum*, the king of the Ekoyis in Oban, offering him all he could ask for to come and help them in overthrowing the Indokis (Ibibios). King *Ebum* agreed and sent a very large army under the command of his eldest son. They succeeded in annihilating the Indokis, but the leader was killed. The remainder were frightened to return and remained with the Aros receiving a very large grant of land. That is why Ibam (Ibom) the town they founded, has very much more land than any other Aro town"'.

This version was certainly given by an Ibom informant conscious of the land in question between the Ada group and the Akpa group.
There was a sequel to the Webber report. In 1922, Mr. E. J. Price, A.D.O., Aro Chukwu was asked to comment on it. In his reply he wrote 'I cannot confirm Capt. Webber's Report and believe it to be wrong... The account of the nine grand-fathers (i.e. the first account by Webber quoted above) is denied even by the men who say they were consulted by Capt. Webber'. Because of all these handicaps surrounding the Webber report, I have decided to leave out a consideration of it in the main body of this work. For the Webber report, see the file Arodist 1/7/33: The Aro People, Notes by Capt. H. Webber enclosed.

For Price's comments, see Letter t.4/1922 of 16/11/22 in Arodist 1/7/33, The Aro People.
17. A. E. Afigbo, *The Warrant Chiefs*. See chapter 2; C.S.O. 1/33, see copy of a letter from O.C. Aro Field Force dated 3/1/02. See also Report No. 8 from O.C. Aro Field Force attached to Despatch No. 440 from Moor to Colonial Office in C.S.O. 1/3 of 1901.
18. C.S.O. No. 29017, Intelligence Report on Aro Clan, Calabar Province, written by T. M. Shankland A.D.O. 1933, pp. 4-16. See also Covering Report No. C.P. 50210 by the Resident of Calabar Province, G. H. Findlay which is enclosed in the Intelligence Report (Ibadan Archives).
19. C.S.O. 26, No. 29017, Intelligence Report on the Aro Clan, p. 3.
20. Arodist, 1/7/31. The Long Juju of Aro Chukwu (Enugu Archives). See Report on the Long Juju by A. P. Chamley, D.C., dated 31.10.12. A survey made in 1924 showed that the Aro Clan Head of the time was not a member of the Native Court. See Calprof 14, File No. C.582/22 with the title Pedigrees of Chiefs, Calabar Province. See the analysis of Major Sealey-King dated 2.5.24.
21. Arodist, 1/7/33, The Aro People (Enugu Archives). See statements on Aro origin dated 23/12/22 and attached to letter No. 28/2/1923 of 11.1.23 from E. J. Price, A.D.O. Ikot Ekpene.
22. *Ibid*.
23. A. E. Afigbo, *The Warrant Chiefs*, see Chapter 5.
24. Arodist, 1/7/33, The Aro People (Enugu Archives). See letter dated 11/10/23 from E. McLachlan to A.D.O. Aro.
25. *Ibid*.
26. In 1923 among those who signed Anichọ Anyakọha's petition against the *amadi* were people from Obinkita and Amanagwu (the mixed Ibo-Ibibio group), Ibom and Amasu (Akpa group), Ugbo (Amaseri group) Utugugwu and Amankwu (Edda group).
Arodist, 1/7/33, The Aro People (Enugu Archives). See petition dated Aro Town 31.10.23 to D.O. Aro District.
27. Arodist, 1/7/33, The Aro People (Enugu Archives). See letter No. 277/22/1933 of 1.5.23 from Major Sealy-King, A.D.O. Aro District to Resident Calabar Province through D.O., Ikot Ekpene.
28. Arodist, 1/7/33, The Aro People (Enugu Archives). See account of Aro origin written by Oti Nwa Anichọ and dated Aro Chukwu 4.8.22.
29. Arodist, 1/7/33, The Aro People (Enugu Archives). See the account of Aro origin given by Chief Anichọ Anyakọha and Co., and dated 23.12.22.
30. *Ibid*.
31. *Ibid*.
32. Arodist, 1/7/33, The Aro People (Enugu Archives). See letter No. 28/2/1923 dated 11.1.23 from Mr. Price to D.O. Ikot Ekpene.
33. *Ibid*., see letter No. 277/22/1933 of 1/5/23 from Major Sealy-King to Resident, Calabar Province.
34. A.D. 635, Aro Sub-Tribe (Enugu Archives). See Second Report on Aro Chukwu by H. F. Matthews—undated.
35. G. I. Jones, *The Trading States of the Oil Rivers* (O.U.P., 1963), p. 24.
36. This is not the place to pursue this matter. But the present writer believes that the functions of oral tradition in a preliterate society go beyond the need to validate social structures, groups or institution. They could also serve as ideologies as well as represent a genuine attempt to construct a meaningful story of the past. The interpretation of the past in the light of the present and vice versa is not peculiar to oral tradition. It is also a characteristic of history in the best tradition of the word. It is this fact that makes Groce's famous dictum that all history is contemporary history meaningful and valid.

37. G. I. Jones, 'Who Are The Aros?', *Nigerian Field*, Vol. VIII, 1939, p. 102.
38. Forde and Jones, *The Ibo and Ibibio-Speaking Peoples of Southeastern Nigeria* (London, 1950), p. 56.
39. A.D. 635, Aro Sub-Tribes (Enugu Archives). See Report on Aro by H. F. Matthews dated 11/7/27.
40. U. I. Ukwu, 'The Development of Trade and Marketing in Iboland', *Journal of the Historical Society of Nigeria*, Vol. 3, No. 4, June 1967, p. 650.
41. In time the fame of the Long Juju and the fear inspired by the raids of the Abam, Ohafia, and Edda who were in alliance with the Aro, came to overshadow this earlier arrangement which survived in the form of legendary homeland for the various Aro sections in the areas they were dominant.
42. For details of this man's experience and some aspect of the extent to which he constituted a nuisance for the Administration of the Eastern Provinces in the 1920s, see A. E. Afigbo, 'Sir Herbert Richmond Palmer and Indirect Rule in Eastern Nigeria 1915-1928', *Journal of the Historical Society of Nigeria*, Vol. 3, December 1965.
43. File No. 15911, Vol. 1: Tribes of Nigeria—(i) Inter-Relations, (ii) Aro Chukwu, Jukun, etc. (Kaduna Archives). See Minute by H. R. Palmer, Lieutenant Governor, Northern Provinces (hereafter L.G.N.P.) dated 10.8.26.
44. See the following documents Arodist 1/7/33. The Aro People. See memo. by Palmer, L.G.N.P. dated 11/5/21 and attached to M.P. Np. P1195/1921 of 13.7.21 from Secretary Southern Province (S.S.P.) to A.D.C. Aro Chukwu. Loko-Prof. 159/1921—Tribes of Nigeria: Inter-Relations of (Kaduna Archives). See minute by L.G.N.P. attached to S.N.P.s circular No. 156P/1921 of 11.7.21.
Conf. No. 80/1920 Diocesan Synod of Lagos, see Minute by Palmer dated 28.9.21.
Loko-Prof. 159/1921: Tribes of Nigeria—Inter-Relations of. See Minute by H. R. Palmer dated 14/11/21, attached to No. 3014/1921/4 of 24/11/21 from S.N.P.
45. K.2442, Vol. 1, Jukons of Wukari, Historical and Anthropological, Notes On, (Kaduna Archives). See the entire file.
K.2012, Vol. 1, Ethnographic Notes on Tribes in Idoma Division, Benue Province (Kaduna Archives). See memo. by N. J. Brooke, dated 30 September 1922.
46. A later version by H. F. Matthews, Anthropological Officer, Southern Provinces, maintained that on the contrary, it was the expansion of the Atlantic trade that undermined Jukun power. The Jukun power, he said, was based on the monopoly of salt bearing lakes. When therefore European traders introduced salt through Calabar and up the Cross River, the Jukun power waned. The Tivi invasion was the occasion for rather more than the cause of Jukon collapse.
See the file Conf. 1928—Arodist 1/7/17, entitled Odds and Ends, etc. See M.P. No. 24/1927/47 of 16/2/28 from H. F. Matthews to S.S.P.
47. Conf. No. 80/1920, Diocesan Synod of Lagos, see Minute by H. R. Palmer dated 28/9/21. On another occasion he wrote 'There appears to me no doubt that the Jukun (of whom the Aro are a branch) originally belong to the stratum of Sulam Hamites called by Arab writers Zagawa—who in 891 A.D. were the ruling race in Kanem according to the geographer Yacubi'. See Arodist, 1/7/33, The Aro People (Enugu Archives), memo. by H. R. Palmer dated 1.5.21.
48. Arodist, 1/7/33, The Aro People (Enugu Archives). See memo. dated 1.5.21 by H. R. Palmer.
49. *Ibid.* He also argued in the same memorandum that the Aro called themselves

Inokun, and this name was etymologically related to 'Jukun', and to the Kanuri words *Kokuna* (a noble), *Nokuna* (council of nobles). '... in all probability', he contended 'the word "Jukon" is the same in root as the Kanuri "Kokuna" (a noble) and "Nokuna" (council of nobles) and also the name "Inokun" which is the real name of Aro of Aro Chukwu'.

50. *Ibid.*
51. Conf. No. 80/1920, Diocesan Synod of Lagos (Kaduna Archives), see memo. by H. R. Palmer dated 28.9.21.
52. Conf. No. 80/1920, see comment by H. C. Moorhouse attached to Letter No. 2532/9 of 17.12.21 from C.S.O. to S.N.P.
53. See Arodist, 1/7/33, The Aro People (Enugu Archives).
54. K.2202: Memorandum on objections to Ibo recruited labour being brought over into Northern Provinces (Kaduna Archives). Here he wrote 'His Excellency is aware that when the Ibo country was first occupied it was governed by a race who are not Ibos, but a branch of a race called Apa—who are by origin a Hamitic people and most nearly allied to the Jukon kings of Kororofa and the Bulala and other Kamem tribes from whom the early kings of Kamem and Bornu also sprang. These Aros as they are called are so far superior in intellectual capacity to the primitive Ibo tribes—that they gained an absolute moral ascendancy over them . . .'.
55. Arodist, 1/7/33, The Aro People (Enugu Archives). See 'Legend of Aro Origin, told by Ukwu Okoro in 1914, a candidate for the kingship of Aro but now retired in favour of Kalu Oji'.
56. Arodist, 1/7/33, The Aro People (Enugu Archives). Notes on the legendary history of the Aro People, attached to No. 593/1703/1926 of 2.10.26, from Mr. D. A. V. Shute, A.D.O. Aro to D.O. Ikot-Ekpene.
57. Conf. 80/1920, Diocesan Synod of Lagos, etc. See memo. No. 301/1921/54 of 28.12.26 from S.N.P. to C.S.O.
58. A.D. 635, Aro Sub-Tribes (Enugu Archives). See the Report entitled: Aro Origins and Basis of Widespread Influence dated 11/7/27 by H. F. Matthews, Anthropological Officer. Matthews, as shown, thought this 'ingredient for the ceremony' which was lacking was a human head. He arrived at this conclusion by reference to the fact that among the Ekoi, from whom, according to Matthews, the Akpa-origin villages derived, the ceremony of 'Eja' (New Yam Festival) was accompanied by human sacrifice. 'If this suspicion is correct', he concluded, 'the custodian designate (of Akuma's Spear) will not be installed so long as the ingredient is unobtainable and if at any time he is installed close inquiry into the reason for doing so after so long a delay would be advisable'.
59. *Ibid.*
60. *Ibid.*
61. The *Inyamavia* is said to be the Aro equivalent of or supplement to the god more generally known as *Ikenga* which ensured success in the professions—especially trade.
62. A.D. 635, Aro Sub-Tribes (Enugu Archives). See Report by H. F. Matthews dated 11/7/27.
63. *Ibid.*
64. *Ibid.*
65. *Ibid.*
66. *Ibid.*
67. It was in fact on 30.5.27 that H. F. Matthews first announced the discovery of the 'fact' that the Aro also used the 'Nsibidi' pictographic writing. He said: 'After preliminary denials it has come out that the Akpa-Aro do make use of 'Nsibidi' signs but to what extent is not yet known. But it forms another closer link with Ekoi culture.

'Mr. Palmer, Lieutenant Governor, Northern Provinces stressed the point that the Aros in their religious system have the cult of the spear which is erected near or on an altar which bears rams' horns. (This detail of rams horns, I have not yet seen). The significance of this is that the spear planted by an altar is an important household juju of the Ekoi, is a cult of the Jukun and cognate tribes in the north-east of Northern Provinces and forms a link with ancient Meroe and with the Shilluk and other tribes of the Nile valley.
'An article in the last journal of the Royal Anthropological Institute shows the striking resemblance of certain "Nsibidi" signs to those found in ancient rock paintings and pot designs dating back to early Egyptian times.
'Thus "Nsibidi" and spear cult from links connecting Aro, Ekoi and Jukun and related tribes with early Egyptian culture'. Arodist 1/7/17, Odds and Ends, etc. Confidential 1928 (Enugu Archives). See letter from Matthews to Resident Calabar, dated 30.5.27.
68. A.D. 635, Aro Sub-Tribes (Enugu Archives). See Aro origin etc., by H. F. Matthews, dated 11/7/27.
69. *Ibid.*
70. File Minutes dated 6.9.27 which is a comment by C. K. Meek on Matthews' Report on Aro Chukwu.
71. A.D. 635, Aro Sub-Tribes (Enugu Archives).'See Second Report on Aro by H. F. Matthews.
72. *Ibid.*
73. My own *italics*.
74. A.D. 635, Aro Sub-Tribes (Enugu Archives). See Second Report on Aro by H. F. Matthews.
75. *Ibid.*
76. My own *italics*.
77. My own *italics*.
78. Arodist, 1/7/17, Odds and Ends, etc., Conf. 1928. See M.P. No. 24/1927 of 5.11.28.
79. *Ibid.* See M.P. 24/1927/47 of 16.2.28 from Matthews to Secretary, Southern Provinces.
80. File 15911, Vol. I, Tribes of Nigeria, etc. (Kaduna Archives). See memo. on the Eastern Provinces by H. R. Palmer attached to 3014/1921/90 of 19.6.28.
81. G. I. Jones, Who Are The Aro?, *loc. cit.*, pp. 102–12.
82. G. T. Basden, 'Notes On The Ibo People, Southern Nigeria', *Geographical Journal*, January–June, Vol. 65, 1925, p. 37.
83. G. I. Jones, 'Who Are The Aro?', *Nigerian Field*, Vol. VIII, 1939, p. 101.
84. File 15911, Vol. 1, Tribes of Nigeria, etc. (Kaduna Archives). See memo. on Eastern Provinces by H. R. Palmer attached to 3014/1921/90.
85. All the italics in this quotation are mine. The italicized words clearly bring out how flimsy were the grounds on which Palmer based his theory.
86. File 15911, Vol. 1, Tribes of Nigeria, etc. (Kaduna Archives). See Minute by His Honour H. R. Palmer, L.G.N.P., enclosed in 3014/1927/67 of 4.1.28.
87. G. I. Jones, *op. cit.*, p. 25.
88. In his book, *The Missionary Impact on Modern Nigeria 1842–1914* (Longmans, 1966), Prof. Ayandele has gone so far as to describe this as amounting almost to a total destruction or disruption of Ibo culture. See pp. 157–8. However, the present writer considers this an exaggeration.
89. G. I. Jones, *The Trading States of the Oil Rivers*, p. 30.
V. C. Uchendu, *The Igbo of Southeast Nigeria* (Holt, Rinehart and Winston Inc., 1966), p. 3.
90. This could be taken to mean that after leaving Umuahia, the leaders of the prong did not meet any people until they had got to the general zone dividing Aro Chukwu from Ibibio-land. The story involving *Ukwa Onyeocha* who

were armed with guns certainly refers to a latter day event probably to an eighteenth century incident, to one episode in slave raiding in the Cross River valley.
91. V. C. Uchendu, *op. cit.*, p. 3.

7. The Eclipse of the Aro Slaving Oligarchy 1807–1927

At the beginning of the nineteenth century the Aro slaving oligarchy backed up, as it was, by the prestige of a widely famed oracle and a symbiotic alliance with the neighbouring warlike clans of Abam, Ohafia and Edda was, without question, the dominant commercial interest in the hinterland of what was the Bight of Biafra. By 1927 it was in utter disarray and its ascendancy a thing of the past. The process by which this disaster overtook the Aro has never been fully analyzed, nor has the changing response of the Aro to their deepening predicament. It is the intention of this paper to make a beginning in attempting to fill this gap in our knowledge. To this end it is argued here that, contrary to popular belief, the decline of the Aro began long before and continued long after the much famed expedition of 1901–2. That expedition was, no doubt, the severest single blow that expanding British interest dealt to Aro hegemony, but it cannot alone explain the decline and fall of that interest-group. It is also argued that the Aro fought hard to retain their long standing dominance in the economic life of the Igbo, the Ibibio and their neighbours, but were unable to refashion the basis of their ascendancy to suit the new situations which arose with the imposition of imperial interest and rule. It was this that constituted their failure and the triumph of the colonial government.

The nature and extent of Aro influence in pre-colonial times have been analyzed by various scholars, and there is no need to repeat it here.[1] But one point which has not always been fully emphasized or often recognized requires brief mention. And that is that Aro hegemony has to be seen in terms of two concentric rings of influence which were exploited with varying intensity. The smaller and inner ring took in the whole of the former Eastern Nigeria with the exception of the coastal states, then some parts of Southern Idoma, Igala and Tiv land. In this area the Aro dominated directly the distribution of foreign goods as well as the assembling of slaves for sale to the coastal middlemen. In this area too not only was the influence of *Ibini ukpabi* (the Long Juju of European records) very intensive, but the Aro were able to use their alliance with the warlike Abam, Ohafia, and Edda to great effect. Then there was the outer and larger circle which took in the whole of the area just delimited as well as the territories on the periphery of it—the coastal states, the Western Igbo and the Western Ijo, the border with the Cameroons and some more of the territory of the Igala, Idoma and Tiv. This was the sphere of influence of *Ibini ukpabi*. The people in this area did not worship the *Ibini ukpabi* like they worshipped their local deities, but they saw it as a supernatural agency that helped them out of their many perplexities, resolved their difficult land and other disputes, helped their barren women to become fertile, and enabled them to communicate with their prominent beloved dead. The Aro on their side saw it merely as another adjunct to their commercial activities, a convenient instrument for exploiting the superstition, stupidity and ignorance of their neighbours. They probably had no illusion about its being a mere hoax. There was a local Aro saying that 'An Aro does not tell a fellow Aro that *Ibini ukpabi* asked of him'. The point that is being made here, however, is that it was not everywhere the Aro operated or exercised influence that they acted as dominant middlemen traders. Along the coast for instance, where the people were even keener and more sophisticated traders, the Aro limited their activity to taking European goods from the coastal peoples in exchange for slaves and to being the agents of their oracle. In fact in such places they more often than not used local business men whom they could trust as the secondary agents of their oracle.[2] On the Niger and on the Cross River the story was the same for similar reasons.[3] When we talk of the eclipse of the Aro oligarchy, therefore, we have to bear in mind the decline and collapse of these two rings of influence.

The decline of the Aro oligarchy goes back to Britain's decision in 1807 to abolish the slave trade to the New World, and subsequently to take measures to prevent other nations from continuing to prosecute that then still lucrative traffic from which she had 'voluntarily' excluded herself. British success in this matter between 1840 and 1860 dealt the first blow to Aro interests. As is well known, the wealth and ascendancy of this oligarchy was based on the slave trade. The cutting off of the foreign demand for slaves created a crisis for all groups involved in the trade. For the Aro the system they built up over the centuries for prosecuting this business—the *Ibini ukpabi* oracle, the strategic settlements throughout south-eastern Nigeria, the alliance with the Abam, Ohafia and Edda—remained in full working condition. This meant that the Aro were still in a position to procure as many slaves as they did during the heyday of the traffic. The socio-economic consequences of this situation for the Aro are still to be fully studied. But there is evidence that the internal market for slaves expanded appreciably to absorb much of the surplus. Dr. J. S. Harris has ably analyzed the traditional openings which existed in indigenous society for the absorption of slaves.[4] To these were now added a new opening—the labour demands of the palm oil trade. In the interior, amongst the primary producers, a great deal of labour was required to harvest and process the palm fruits as well as to transport and market the products. Part of this labour demand was met through increased polygamy and the rearing of many children, the other part through the increased purchase of slaves. At the same time coastal society came to require more slaves than they probably ever demanded for local use in the palmy days of the foreign slave trade to meet their socio-economic needs. On this Harris has written:

> Vast numbers of slaves were still needed (by the city states), no longer for export, but to prepare and load the palm oil and kernels for shipment, to man the canoes which shuttled between the ships and the shore, to comprise the personnel of the up-river trading expeditions, and to work on the farm lands which supplied food for the coastal communities.[5]

Still it would appear there was a glut in the slave market. These local openings could never take in as much as the wasteful foreign trade did. And it must be explained that these were not entirely new openings. From local traditions all that happened was that they absorbed more slaves than hitherto. All said and done the abolitionist movement no doubt led to a fall in the price paid locally for slaves. In the days when it was possible to export these human merchandise, and when therefore the price of a slave was high, only very wealthy families could afford slaves who were killed to accompany their prominent dead in the journey to the other world. But from the 1850s it would appear to have become relatively easy for even the averagely rich or the not-so-poor to purchase slaves for their funeral rites or for those of their relations, while the very rich were able to afford many more. The result was thus most certainly an increase in the incidence of human sacrifice for funeral and general propitiation purposes, as shown by the events in Calabar which led to the rise of the Order of the *Blood Men*.[6]

Because of all these local openings for slaves the slave trading business of the Aro managed to survive the abolition of the American slave trade. The other bases of their ascendancy—the Long Juju and the alliance with the Abam, Ohafia and Edda were largely unaffected and for the time being unthreatened. In any case the Aro oligarchy remained fully in control of the interior—dominating there the internal slave trade and the distribution of imported goods. What other part the Aro played in the oil trade, apart from supplying the servile labour force needed by both the primary producers and the coastal middlemen for the purposes delineated above, is not known.[7] The Aro trade system was not suitable for handling the oil trade, it was geared mainly to the trade in human beings. In this matter the Aro do not seem to have been very adjustable. In a world given to rapid and bewildering changes, they quickly became anachronistic, and it was this professional anachronism that turned out to be their undoing.

The Aro oligarchy thus survived the first threat to their ascendancy, though probably with diminished earnings, not so much because of their ingenuity, but largely because they were beyond the reach first of the guns of the Preventive Squadron and then of the heavy political arm of the Consul for the Bights of Benin and Biafra. But this was not to be for very long. Slowly but steadily what has been described as 'the expanding European frontier' swallowed up the southern, western and eastern periphery of the Aro sphere of influence and thus came face to face with the inner ring described above. It was only then that the real crisis of the Aro oligarchy began.

The process by which this came about has been dealt with in detail by many scholars,[8] but can be briefly summarized here to refresh our minds and put the discussion in proper context. The crucial years were from 1832 to the 1890s. On the western flank European business men had started from 1832 exploring the trade of the Niger and by 1879 already had stations at strategic points on the river such as at Abo, Onitsha and Lokoja. Meanwhile in 1856 agents of the Church Missionary Society (C.M.S.) had established on the Niger and started the propagation of Christianity. To the south Britain started undermining the independence of the coastal states by means of the slave trade treaties from the later 1830s. By 1840, Bonny, the last of these states to enter into this kind of treaty, was brought into line. The Presbyterians established in Calabar in 1846 and began their attempt to evangelize the basin of the Cross River. To consolidate these gains of 'the expanding imperial frontier' Britain in 1849 appointed John Beecroft Consul for the Bights of Benin and Biafra. Through the exertions of the consuls and gunboats in the Oil Rivers, and of the commercial companies on the Niger, Britain was soon able to hand over the administration of the Niger waterway to Goldie's Company and to proclaim a protectorate over the Oil Rivers. With this the Niger Company started setting up a number of administrative posts to enable it exploit the trade of the Niger waterway and its immediate environs. In the Oil Rivers the Consuls also set up Consular Courts which aided by the gunboats sought to make British interest and dominance in this area secure. From 1891 this process of asserting, securing, and consolidating British interest was taken up more seriously with the establishment of a regular administration in the Oil Rivers under Sir Claude Macdonald. Meanwhile the missionaries had continued their work. On the Niger the C.M.S. were no longer alone. The Roman Catholics had arrived and established there in 1885. From Onitsha this missionary influence spread inland to Ogidi, Obosi, Nnewi and so on. In the Oil Rivers the C.M.S. had decided to back up the work of the Presbyterians by establishing at Bonny in 1864. On the Cross River the Presbyterians though slow and lacking in dynamism were making steady progress. In 1884 they explored the upper reaches of the river and established a station at Ikotana about 75 miles from Calabar. Four years later they moved up to Unwana, 30 miles further up from Ikotana, and established a station. In 1888 Miss Mary Mitchell Slessor moved up to Okoyong and stationed there.

 For the Aro the consequences of this steady and unrelenting advance and consolidation of 'the imperial frontier' were far reaching. On the one hand the work of the Royal Niger Company and of the C.M.S. and Catholics on the Niger tended to sever the western shore of that river—the Western Igbo and the

Western Ijọ—from the main centre of Aro influence. It is not yet possible, owing to lack of detailed research, to say how severely the influence of these agencies of the imperial factor damaged Aro interest, especially the sway of the Long Juju, but that it tended to curtail that sway there can be no doubt. Missionary preaching and the general conditions which the Niger Company sought to impose in the interest of trade were clearly antithetical to the regime of the Long Juju and there is evidence that the two interests came into conflict. Also as the Niger Company moved further into the hinterland especially up to Oguta it encountered the inner ring of the Aro sphere of influence where Aro economic interest was dominant. This intrusion of the imperial factor into the Aro area generated such bitter conflict between the two interests, that from time to time Sir George Tubman Goldie contemplated military expedition against the Aro. Writing in 1899 he said:

> The question of the Omotchuku's (or Long Juju) power has been constantly before me for the last twenty years. I believe that Sir Ralph Moor underates the extent of its influence, while I thoroughly agree with all that he says as to its detrimental effect on the regions under fetish control.
> If the Royal Niger Company had had a free hand, they would have made the overthrow of this power their first main concern on receiving the charter in 1886 but in view of the Aro country containing the markets of all the principal Oil Rivers (except Benin) any such action was for political reasons, inadvisable, and especially after the formation of the Oil Rivers Protectorate, now known as the Niger Coast Protectorate, within which the centre of the Juju system lies.[9]

In the Oil Rivers the entrenchment of British influence had also told severely on the ascendancy of the Aro oligarchy. Increasing christianization and general westernization not only undermined belief in local deities and cults, but also must have affected belief in the powers of the Long Juju. In this period, for instance, there was in some of these city states, a wave of violence against indigenous cults at times accompanied by the destruction of traditional religious images and totemic animals. This happened in Bonny, for example, in 1889. The more people who cast aside traditional religions and beliefs as superstitious rubbish, the fewer the people who were prepared to submit their problems to the Long Juju. This meant business set-back for the Aro. The consolidation of the imperial factor in the Oil Rivers in this period affected the business of the Aro oligarchy adversely in another aspect—in the slaving aspect. The British authorities were able to stamp out human sacrifices on funeral and ritual occasions throughout these states. Through British help the Blood Men of Calabar stopped the lavish sacrifice of slaves on the death of prominent free-born Efik.[10] Previously these sacrifices had claimed a large number of slaves most of whom were supplied by the Aro. The abolition of the practice meant that the demand by coastal society for slaves from the interior declined. From then on the 'Houses' wanted new slaves either to replace those who died from natural causes, or to further the expansion of their trading enterprise. But unfortunately for the Aro, however, through the advance of the imperial frontier towards the hinterland, the business of the 'Houses' had little opening for great expansion. As a result the demand for slaves for deployment as business agents and representatives became slight indeed. The slaves also benefited in other ways from the improved conditions which colonial rule brought. They came to enjoy easier conditions and better treatment and thus came to enjoy longer life expectancy. This again meant that the demand for slaves to replace those who died otherwise than through human sacrifice could not have been great either.[11] At the same time, on the eastern flank, that is on the Cross River, the influence of the Protectorate Government and of the Presbyterian Mission tended to sever the territory on the left side of the river from the main centre of Aro influence. Thus by 1891, in all directions except from the north, the territories within the two rings of Aro sphere of influence were being gradually clipped off by advancing imperial frontier.

The encroachment of the imperial frontier on the Aro sphere increased with the establishment of Macdonald's administration in 1891. From the beginning this administration pursued a deliberate policy of gradually detaching from the Aro, communities among whom they enjoyed economic and oracular influence. Reporting an instance of the successful application of this policy in 1900 Sir Ralph Moor wrote, no doubt gleefully, as follows:

> The work that has been lately done in the hinterland of Opobo District has, owing to the indefatigable praiseworthy efforts of travelling D(istrict) C(ommissioner) James resulted in friendly relations with the Quas and the road opened from Azumini to Inen and hence to Eket in the Old Calabar District. Mr. James has been able to detach the Qua tribe from the Aro tribe and made them

friendly to Government. This has rather increased than otherwise, the suspicions of the Aros and on all occasions when escorts march on the road from Azumini to the north they are flanked by parties of armed Aros watching their movement.[12]

Going hand in hand with this policy was a more general one which sought to get the area under Aro influence hemmed in on nearly all sides by territories under the direct control of the protectorate administration. In 1902, just after the Aro Expedition, Moor graphically described this policy and its implementation. According to him on coming into existence in 1891 the Government of the Oil Rivers Protectorate directed all its energy and limited resources towards establishing control 'over the tribes of the coast who acted in all cases as middle-men'. But no sooner was this ambition achieved than was it realized that 'there could not be definite and stable Government control until such a time as the country of the producers was dealt with and Government established therein'. As a result it became the declared policy of the Government to conquer 'the territories to the east of and within the loop of the Cross River on the eastern side of the Protectorate and to establish control through the territories on the west which at the time consisted only of Warri and Benin countries'. By 1899 control of the territories within the loop of the Cross River had been secured, while the conquest and occupation of the 'western territories' were achieved with the liquidation of Nana of the Benin River (1894) and Oba Overami of Benin (1897). With this, said Moor, 'there remained that portion between the Cross River and the Niger, with the exception of the area of the coast middlemen tribes'. This was the region dominated by the Aro and thus it could be said that by 1900 the Aro sphere of influence was hemmed in to the west, south and east by a hostile imperial power.[13]

Along with this policy of virtual encirclement was the systematic organization of local administration designed, it was claimed, to meet the needs of the conquered peoples in the new era. Prominent in this new system were the establishment of Native Courts, the creation of administrative districts with the headquarters where the District Commissioners lived with all their subordinate staff. The colonial authorities believed that the peoples who were coming under their control had lived in a condition approximating to the Hobbesian state of nature and that to provide an instrument for the regular and equitable administration of law was the best way to maintain order and fight the 'beneful' influence of the medicine men, the juju men and the oracles which they said had tyrannized over the peoples for centuries. Whether the administration was right or wrong in this belief, is not now the matter at issue. The fact is that the institutions of local rule which it established, especially the native courts, turned out to be among the most effective counter measures against the Aro and their Long Juju. They provided an alternative and parallel means for securing redress. They were cheaper in many respects than an appeal to the Aro oracle. A few shillings were enough to secure the intervention of a native court. Whereas it took months to consult an oracle, at most a man did a full day's journey to reach the court under whose jurisdiction he lived. The court offered a man an opportunity to argue out a case with his adversary face to face, unlike the oracle whose proceedings were shrouded in mystery. The Native Court had its shortcomings, but we shall see how these worked to the advantage of the Aro later.[14] Just as the native courts were incompatible with the Long Juju, the new roads and administrative headquarters undermined the Aro trade routes and the strategic location of Aro settlements. Since these roads did not necessarily follow the old trade route, and the administrative headquarters as well as the native court centres were not established at or by the side of the Aro settlements, traffic gradually but steadily moved away from the Aro trade route network.[15] The effect of this development on the ascendancy of the Aro oligarchy got worse as more and more territory came under British control. The climax came later with the Aro Expedition and the increasing British mastery of the interior.

Also as the British moved into the interior they were accompanied, and at times preceded, by coastal traders. These men were already reconciled to the new line of trade while the Aro were not. For this they had the support and encouragement of the colonial government. They also had more capital, had reorganized their trade system to suit the oil trade, and were on the whole considered more honest and straight-forward than the Aro. The result was that the interior producers welcomed them and preferred direct dealings with them to having to do so indirectly through the Aro. In a number of places the people passed local laws forbidding the Aro to trade directly with the coastal middlemen, and in at least one case where this law was infringed imposed heavy fines on the Aro delinquents.[16]

In the midst of all these tribulations a strange thing happened to the Aro oligarchy. In 1899 a group of '136 refugees from the Long Juju fled to the Government for protection'. According to Sir Ralph Moor's story they were the wretched remnants of a much larger party of about 800 who had gone from the region of the Niger to consult the Aro oracle about 1894 or 1895. The Aro had detained them at Aro Chukwu, sold some of them into slavery and used some for human sacrifice. 'In this way' said Moor,

> the party of 800 gradually dwindled down to the miserable residuum of 136 who were the most wretched and emaciated body of people I have ever seen grouped together. They were evidently regarded as unfit for purposes of sacrifice or even to be disposed of as slaves and it must be due... to their miserable condition that they had the opportunity of escaping.

After having escaped they made their first appearance to the political officer stationed at Eket who sent them to Brass through Bonny. From there they were sent to the Agent General of the Royal Niger Company who helped them to return to their various towns and villages around Aseh Creek and Aboh.[17] It is however unlikely that people went to consult the Long Juju in such large groups. What is more likely is that these were people who had gone at different times through the process of consulting the *Ibini ukpabi* and had been condemned to be sold into slavery but could not be disposed of by the Aro owing to the ruinous shrinkage of their market for slaves. They must have already been marched into Annang (the Qua or Kwa of early colonial records) hence, as Moor said, they were able to take the opportunity of the panic caused by an expedition into the Annang territory by the Niger Coast Protectorate troops, in 1899, to make good their escape. The important point, however, is that in one form or the other these people had seen through the hoax of the *Ibini ukpabi* oracle, and with the encouragement of the Government undertook extensive campaigns against it on returning home. Said Sir Ralph Moor:

> Since this event the refugees have been talking freely in their country and have exposed to all the tribes around the fraud of the Long Juju with the result that the profit of this nefarious form of priestcraft will gradually be curtailed.[18]

This incident, no matter how it came about, constituted a severe damage to the reputation of the Long Juju and the economic system of the Aro oligarchy. And if my reconstruction of the event above is correct, then one can only conclude that the Aro were beginning to lose control of the situation.

The Aro felt very keenly the continued shrinkage of their business as a result of the relentless advance of the imperial frontier. In 1896 they spurned all attempts to bring them to a peace parley with Moor's government until the latter had given up the policy of encouraging European traders and coastal middlemen to penetrate the interior to deal directly with the primary producers. The only arrangement they were prepared to accept, they insisted, was that

> they (the Aros) be left to act as middlemen (in the interior), that is, when the Efik men take up goods to the market of the upper Calabar River, they should not go beyond Budeng, they (the Aros) will meet the Efiks at this place and buy all the goods they have from them to sell again in the interior.[19]

The Aro statement of their grievances against the Government of the Niger Coast Protectorate is a clear indication of how severely they had been affected by the establishment of that government and the policies which it pursued. Summarizing these complaints in 1899 Moor wrote:

> The Aros have also definitely formulated complaints against and objections to the Government stating that:
>
> (i) Since the establishment of the Government their monopoly in the trade of potash has been broken and all natives are enabled to carry it throughout the territories.
> (ii) They are now unable to obtain rifles and cartridges as formerly since Government is prohibiting their import.
> (iii) Their trade in slaves has been to a great extent ruined as the Government has put an end to human sacrifice and prevents, as far as possible, the exchange and sale of slaves.[20]

On another occasion the Divisional Commissioner, Opobo, Mr. Murray, reported as follows:

> I saw an Aro man at Azumini and he informed me that the stopping of human sacrifice striking at their slave trade, the difficulty of obtaining gun caps, and the great falling off in attendance of the big waterside chiefs at the Aro Long Juju meant such a large pecuniary loss to the Aro tribe that all the families have assembled and sworn to prevent the Government from advancing any further into the interior.[21]

But as the last quotation shows the Aro did not just meekly complain against the advance of the imperial frontier. They sought to halt that advance believing it was the only way to preserve their ascendancy. In this period their main response to the threat which the Protectorate Government posed to their interest was to instigate and organize the local populations among whom they plied their business to resist the advance of the Government into the interior. Their strategy was to persuade the local people that it was not in their interest to deal directly with the white men and the coastal traders. In places they succeeded in this way in instigating the people against the Government. They were successful in this regard among the Annang as among the Ikwo and Ezza tribes on the right side of the Cross River.[22] Political officers stationed at New Calabar (Degema) also attributed the resistance they encountered at Elele and its neighbourhood to the 'wicked' machinations of the Aro.[23] Specific instances of the efforts of the Aro to fight back will help to illuminate the character of this conflict and some of the many forms it took.

On the Niger, behind Oguta, the Aro relying on the terror inspired by their oracle were able to disrupt the trade of the Niger Company in palm oil and kernel. As a result of their counter strokes the palm oil available for purchase by Company's agents fell from 250 to 110 puncheons a month at Atani. The effect on the kernel trade was even more drastic. They stopped the women from cracking the nuts by the simple process of 'placing' on them 'a juju' which they said would strike with sterility any woman who cracked kernel for sale to the Company.[24] It must be said, however, that it is possible that part of the reason for the decline of the trade here was the notoriously bad native policy of the Company. On May 28 1899 the Obinkita Aro who dominated the trade of Annang territory held a meeting in an Annang village to which they invited representatives of all the neighbouring villages. At that meeting they warned the people of the drastic consequences of not supporting the Aro in their fight to ward off the white man. According to paid agents of the Government who attended the meeting

> the Iga people told the Aros that they were tired of fighting, that the white men were too strong for them and they intended to make peace. The Aros replied that they could do as they liked, but that the white men and Aros would soon have a fight and when they, the Aros, had proved the stronger all towns who would not help them would then have to reckon with the Aros and Abams.[25]

In February 1901 Acting Travelling Commissioner, Mr. Gardiner, reporting on a tour he made from Akwete into the Annang village of Ine‧ig said:

> The natives in the different towns along the road seemed inclined to be friendly, but all expected dashes in the shape of gin, tobacco etc.—this was toll for keeping the road open for white man. It was necessary to give them dashes, and will be for the next 4 or 5 months at any rate, as there are a number of Aros settled in some of the towns and living there and they are instigating the Quas against the white men, telling them not to let us pass. So that if we do not give them presents when we call at their villages, some of them will close the road again. I slept at Ese Obong. Chief Udo here, who is the son of the late chief, has succeeded him. (The late chief was a great friend of the Government.) I had a long talk with him, and he says the Aros are troubling him, because he allows the Consul to pass and also lets him sleep in his house. That his father used to do the same and that was why he died. He will also die if he continues to allow the white man to pass etc.[26]

Where such blackmail and subtle pressure failed, the Aro resorted to more violent methods by calling in their Abam, Ohafia and Edda allies to attack and sack the villages friendly with the Protectorate Government. In April 1901, for instance, the Aro and their allies attacked the village of Mbiabong and its neighbours ostensibly because this people had killed a leopard and refused to surrender its skin to the Aro but in reality, claimed Leslie Probyn the Acting High Commissioner, as a reaction against the continued falling off of their business.[27] Similarly on 21 November 1901 the Aro and their allies attacked and nearly wiped out the village of Obegu. They would also have attacked Akwete but for the prompt intervention of the troops of the Protectorate.[28] The people in this area were already under the influence of the Protectorate Government. They not only welcomed the Bonny and Opobo traders who came to deal with them directly, but they also sought to exclude the Aro from the trade of their land. Not surprisingly this angered the Aro whose business fortunes were already on the wane.[29]

After reviewing these and other similar instances of Aro resistance to the advance of the imperial frontier Sir Ralph Moor concluded that:

> the Aro are directly opposed to the opening up of their country or the establishment of any administration therein as they recognise that their Long Juju business will then be done away with for it has been

seriously crippled in recent years by the action of the Government in preventing the people of Opobo, Bonny and New Calabar from appealing to the Long Juju.³⁰

He therefore resolved to deal with the Aro oligarchy militarily. The upshot, after long delays, many postponements and protracted preparations was the Aro Expedition of 1901-2 which not only captured Aro Chukwu but patrolled and overawed a large section of the territories of the Igbo and Ibibio-speaking peoples. This expedition has been dealt with elsewhere in some detail by the present writer.³¹ We are here concerned with its consequences for the ascendancy of the Aro oligarchy.

The success of the expedition was a deadly blow to Aro hegemony. For generations after generations the Aro had enjoyed virtually unchallenged economic supremacy among the Igbo, the Ibibio and some other neighbouring hinterland groups. Through the alliance with the Abam, Ohafia and Edda the Aro had also enjoyed an equally unchallenged military prestige. Not only could they make the services of these warlike clans available to any village or village-group that so requested and paid for them, but they were also able to use these warriors as instruments for enforcing their own demands and avenging wrongs done to, or indignities inflicted on them. They had for generations paraded themselves and been accepted by their neighbours as the agents of the supreme manifestation on earth of the High God, *Chukwu*, which they could manipulate to protect and serve their interests and against which all mortals were powerless. They had also claimed that it was this High God, *Ibini ukpabi*, whose special protection made it possible for them to deal directly with the white man whom they portrayed to their neighbours as an evil being whom these neighbours should avoid direct dealings with at all cost.³² And what was more, ever since the two frontiers—the Aro and the British imperial—came into contact in the 1880s the Aro had boasted to all around their ability to deal with the British threat. Now all this boast, all this bragging, all this ancient reputation for military and supernatural power had proved pathetically unequal to the expedition of 1901-2. Not only had the Aro been unable to protect their neighbours and traditional friends, they had proved unequal to the task of defending and protecting their homeland. And as a result the abode of their *Chukwu* had been *desecrated* and blown up by the white man.³³

It is not surprising therefore that many of the surrounding peoples who hitherto had either supported the Aro in their quarrel with the British, or had sat on the fence, now decided to throw in their lot with the British, at least until something else happened to justify their doing otherwise. The reaction of the various peoples in and around the Ediba District on the Cross River to the news of Aro defeat was characteristic. Just a few days after the capture of Aro Chukwu, the officer in charge of this station reported that:

> The political aspect of the District has altered in a most marked degree .... due, beyond all questions, to the success of our war now waging against the Inokun (Aro).
> At the beginning of the quarter the majority of the towns evinced no particular regard for the white man, ...
> However, as I have just mentioned the war against the Inokun people has brought them to their senses. ... I have received visits from the towns of Ebom, Afafani, Annang, Ismudon, Ekuri, Ugep, Abayong and all Afikpo towns, they one and all came to express their friendship with the white man and hoped that we would not make war on them, and if the Government desired anything done they would be only too willing to assist in any way possible.[34]

On the whole about 6,000 square miles of territory were covered and subdued during the operations carried out by the Aro Field Force. But the shattering effects of the event were not limited to this relatively small area. They spread far beyond.[35] And whereever this was the case it affected the ascendancy of the Aro in various ways.

Firstly, many people began taking the invincibility of the white man for granted with the result that they came more to treat the Aro with scant respect, and to listen more readily to overtures from the Protectorate Government. Secondly, the whole area subdued by the Aro Field Force was carved up into administrative divisions and districts, with native courts established at strategic points. The effects on the Aro of the introduction of this administrative pattern into the interior were similar to their effects along the coast; the only difference was that having now penetrated to the seat of Aro power, they were more far-reaching. Thirdly, many more of the primary producers came to deal directly with the white men and the coastal traders only to discover that not only were the white men not evil spirits as they had been made to appear in Aro propaganda, but that it paid better to deal with them and the coastal middlemen face to face. This fact made the advent of the British and the overthrow of the Aro monopoly welcome in many places. Commenting on one of Colonel Montanaro's reports on the progress of the Aro Field Force, Sir Ralph Moor wrote in February 1902:

> From the report it will be seen that the people of Oloko are glad that Aro power is broken and are looking forward to a gradual improvement in their trade position in consequence of Government intervention.[36]

Fourthly, the government of the Southern Nigeria Protectorate mounted a widespread campaign against the Aro and the ancient basis of their influence—especially against the *Ibini ukpabi* oracle which they portrayed as a hoax, and against slave dealing. Wherever they formed a district or set up a native council or court, they held meetings with the leaders of the people to warn them against the Aro, against slave dealing and against the 'empty tricks and pretences' of medicine men and oracles, especially against the Long Juju. They assured the people they had destroyed all traces of the latter and would deal severely with anybody who sought to revive it. To one such meeting held at Aro Chukwu, the headquarters of the oracle, and which the High Commissioner addressed himself, chiefs and elders were invited from villages within a radius of ten to fifteen miles.[37]

Also at such meetings and at meetings of native courts the administration took steps to ensure that the Aro did not

> continue acting as they did when they were the dominant power.[38]

This was to be achieved partly through making the local people realize and exercise their powers and prerogatives as hosts over all travellers or settlers in their midst, especially over the Aro who were advised to understand that like all other travellers and traders they were only guests wherever they stopped for the night and not 'members of a conquering race'. On this matter Leslie Probyn, the Acting High Commissioner, said in 1903:

> By native law each town must make reasonable arrangements for the accommodation of strangers, this includes travelling traders such as the Aros. Those who visit such towns must conform to the orders of the local authority, they are guests in a sense—that is they visit the town by implied invitation but only on condition they pay their way. They are like all guests subordinate to their hosts ... but some of the Aros insist on being treated not as visitors but as members of the conquering race. Thus must be stopped.[39]

Another way to make the Aro recognize their changed circumstances under the new regime and behave accordingly was to force them to realize that they are only tenants-at-will in the villages where they founded settlement. 'The Aros like all other natives', continued Mr. Probyn in the same minute

> can only reside permanently in a place if they acquire permission to do so from the native rulers of the place. There is according to native law no right to settle in a place, this can only be done by the permission of the town, such permission is invariably given to those who are ready to recognise the town as befriending them but is refused to any who will not give proof that they will be orderly law-abiding inhabitants.[40]

All political officers in the areas conquered by the Aro Field Force ('in the country under Aro dominion') were asked to educate the native councils and courts under their control on these matters and to get them to pass by-laws impressing on the Aro that 'their right as traders will be supported only on' the condition they 'remember that they are guests and as such must conform to the legitimate rule and requirements of towns through which they travel' or in which they settle.[41]

And finally, the conquests of the Aro Field Force lay the greater part of the territories of the Igbo and the Ibibio open to missionary work. The details of the missionary invasion of this region which followed the expedition are not yet known. But what happened at Aro Chukwu itself can be taken as example. Immediately after the expedition missionary propagandizing started at Aro Chukwu led by one Dr. T. B. Adams whose example was soon followed by other missionary agents.[42] Some elements of the Aro Chukwu population, in particular the slave class who would seem to have out-numbered the freeborn known as *amadi* were greatly impressed by the power of their new masters, the proclamation against the slave trade and slavery and, probably because of these, decided to identify themselves with the white man who in conquering them had also liberated them. By 1904 many of these were already christians and had contributed money and materials to build themselves a church. When in that year Dr. Robertson and Dr. Rattray of the Calabar Mission visited Aro Chukwu, these new christians 'showed them round the town of Obinkita and took them to various sites any of which they offered to the (Presbyterian) mission'.[43] There were also many freeborn who followed suit. In 1907 it was reported that:

The head chief of all the Aros, who was the chief formerly in control of the Long Juju at Aro Chukwu, is one of those most favourable (to the missionaries). He had already announced to the other chiefs his intention to rule in God's ways. He has been the most keen in asking the missionary to come. A new church will be built and he offers to build a house for any missionary who comes.[44]

How genuine was the conversion of the head chief, Chief Kanu Okoro, we do not know. It was only the previous year (1906) that he surfaced after going into hiding in 1901 during the Aro Expedition, and was reinstated on condition he was prepared to conform to the requirements of the new situation. He probably 'embraced' christianity as a tactical move in the game rather than out of conviction. A few years later he was to be convicted, as we shall see later, for reviving the Long Juju. But if men like Kanu Okoro were not genuinely converted, there were others who probably were and this fact caused a rift in Aro society. Reporting to the Presbyterian authorities on his visit to Aro Chukwu in 1907 the Rev. Mr. John Rankin said:

> The people are a stalwart race, far in advance of (the) Efik. The majority are very anxious for help. *A section is strongly opposed to the point of persecuting those who under the influence of Miss Slessor and others have already begun to live in God's fashion.* This opposition seems to be one of the hopeful signs as proving that there will be no indifference.[45]

But this split among the Aro meant that Aro ascendancy could not be maintained on the old basis without the fear that somebody would give away the secret. As we shall see later it was an Aro that gave away to the colonial government the fact that the Long Juju oracle had been revived under the direction of Chief Kanu Okoro. Within other villages, village-groups and clans throughout the whole area formerly under Aro dominance there were similar splits between the converts to the new ways and the traditionalists. And the former, nearly always anxious to appear to live according to the latest mode introduced by colonial rule, were often ready to betray the traditionalists to the white man's government. This development made all slave dealers and votaries of oracles like the Aro *Ibiniukpabi* unsafe.[46] All said and done the Aro lost heavily in consequence of the success of the Aro Field Force in 1901–2.

The Southern Nigerian Administration was elated by the achievements of the Aro Field Force and saw the expedition as spelling the doom of the Aro as slave dealers and agents of the

Ibiniukpabi. Aro Chukwu was captured on 24 December 1901, on 3 January 1902 the Officer Commanding the expedition, Colonel Montanaro, wrote triumphantly:

> I have blown up the Long Juju and utterly destroyed all traces.[47]

In the same jubilant mood, the Acting High Commissioner, Leslie Probyn, wrote about a year later:

> During the year 1902 the Protectorate was freed for ever from the evils of slave raiding and slave dealing on an organised scale.[48]

And then referring more specifically to the work of the Aro Field Force and the 'fall' of the Aro oligarchy he wrote:

> The military operations which were brought to a successful close in 1902 destroyed the system of slave making ... and the dreaded (Long Juju) oracle ceased for ever to exercise its baneful influence.[49]

Ever since, these claims conveying the erroneous impression that the Expedition of 1901–2 destroyed without trace Aro influence between the Niger and the Cameroon border, have been echoed by historians and publicists.[50] Nothing however, could be further from the truth.

The truth is that the Aro responded to the challenge of their conquest and subjugation in two principal ways. Some of them exploiting British ignorance of the extent and organization of their trade and oracle system sought vainly to retain their ascendancy on the old basis. Others, no doubt the more amenable to change and therefore the more adaptable, sought to exploit the new circumstances and opportunities created by the establishment of colonial rule. Some combined the two ways, either pursuing them simultaneously or abandoning the one after it have proved to be a blind alley and taking up the other. As will become clear from what follows the two ways evoked stiff opposition and hearty denunciation from the colonial regime. It would appear there was something inherent in Aro methods which kept their business beyond the pale of what the government of the Southern Nigeria Protectorate considered lawful and respectable. No Aro adopting either of the two ways described could cast aside overnight the predatory instincts and sharp practices which had characterized their way of life in the pre-colonial days when they were, as one eminent Igbo historian has described them with pardonable exaggeration, 'the economic dictators of the hinterland'[51] of the Bight of

Biafra. Here we shall first deal with their attempt to maintain their ascendancy on the old basis.

The operations of the Aro Field Force were hardly over before the Aro revived slave-dealing on a large and organized scale. So basic was slave running to their livelihood. The expedition was brought to a close about the end of the first quarter of 1902, but by June British political officers in charge of the Cross River Division, to which Aro Chukwu was then attached, were already complaining loudly about the revival of Aro slaving activities just on the north-western fringe of the area effectively subdued by the Field Force. And before the end of the year the Government again found it necessary to mount another expedition against this centre of Aro slaving interest. The centre in question was Uzuakoli. Representatives from this village-group were among those addressed by Sir Ralph Moor at Aro Chukwu in January 1902.[52] Again on 26 March 1902 a similar meeting was held at Bende, with representatives from Uzuakoli attending, at which all the neighbouring villages were similarly solemnly but sternly warned by Leslie Probyn 'that buying or selling slaves was prohibited'. In spite of all these, 'on April 11, i.e. the second market after the meeting, slave dealing commenced there', and prominent Uzuakoli and Aro traders were implicated in the crime.[53] The dealers moved their human wares either through Enna, Edda, Biakpan and the Cross River to Calabar, or through Ibeku, Olokoro and Ikwerre to New Calabar (Degema)[54] where, in spite of the anti-slavery policy of the Government, there was still some demand for slaves.

In point of fact the Aro had little difficulty in continuing with their slave dealing business at Uzuakoli. The operations of the Field Force had been concerned primarily with the areas which subsequently were constituted into the Ikot-Ekpene, Aba, Owerri and Bende Divisions. This left the northern and north-western portions of the Aro sphere of influence largely untouched and unsubdued for a time. Thus not only were the Aro able to continue operating under-ground in the areas effectively occupied by the Government, but also in the as yet unconquered territories they were able to continue to exercise a measure of their old influence openly. Uzuakoli lay on the north-western fringe of the area effectively conquered by the Aro Field Force. It was one of the traditional seats of the *Agbagwu* trade fair system which played a prominent part in the marketing and trading life of the Igbo people and which the Aro had exploited to great advantage in the days of their ascendancy.⁵⁵ According to one tradition, in the pre-colonial days this fair had rotated between Bende and Uzuakoli.⁵⁶ But with Aro Chukwu and Bende now conquered and occupied by the white man, the Aro and other slave dealers decided to shift the seat of the fair permanently to Uzuakoli which lay close to the area not yet under alien control.

It was only through the use of paid local spies that the Government was able to discover to its chagrin that the Aro Expedition had not successfully destroyed for all time the basis of Aro power. The question then arose as to what to do to clean up this 'nefarious' centre of Aro enterprise. Giving an opinion on this matter the Acting Divisional Commissioner for the Cross River Division, Lieutenant Richard Morrisey said:

> To stop this market the following propositions occur to me: 1st, destroy the town; 2nd, occupy it. Either of these courses would mean the creation at some town further north of a new market and it appears to me that unless we are prepared to go on further into the country we should not weaken the Bende garrison, which may be required elsewhere at any moment, by occupying Ozu-Akoli. In short the town should be destroyed, with the exception of a small portion of it whose peoples profess friendship and who seem to realise the risk of punishment which the inhabitants of the larger portion are running.⁵⁷

An alternative policy was to attract the *Agbagwu* market back to Bende or in any case establish there a rival market under the direct influence and control of the administration and to prevent the Aro, at least the Aro Ụnọ (*Home Aro* as opposed to the *Aro Ụzọ*, the *Aro of Dispersion*) from attending the Uzuakoli market. 'Bende', it was argued in support of this alternative policy,

> shared at one time with Uzuakoli ... the honour of being the largest slave market in the Protectorate. Large settlements of the Ndoti, Isimkpu and Aro Oru tribes were here and the Bende people simply thrived on the fact of their being chosen as the spot for this traffic. The slave trade by law is now a thing of the past, and it is most important to induce the Aros, Abiribas and Nkwerri people to return to the (Bende) market which should now be a large produce market. The Bende people themselves are most willing to please.... (I) spoke very strongly to the Aros about the market at Ozu-Akoli. They must return to the market at Bende. We know they were still selling slaves at Ozu-Akoli and also that the Aros were going there instead of to Bende. This must stop. When the Aro-Oru, the Elugu and Ohaza (ra)

find that the Ndoti and Isimkpu etc. do not go to Ozu-Akoli they would come to Bende if they wish to obtain goods such as cloth and tobacco. They knew very well there would be no interference with legitimate trade at Bende. I warned them that if they continued avoiding Bende and keeping the people away the Government would probably consider the advisability of stopping their own people from going to Ozu-Akoli. It was, they knew, a slave market, produce and chop could be got more easily at Bende as anywhere else if the people were allowed to come. Besides the temptation to many of them would-- be too great and then we did not want them to run risks of getting seven years imprisonment.[58]

The advocates of this policy felt, however, that should it fail it would still 'serve no good object driving the market away from Uzuakoli' since as long as it was there it would be possible to exert 'a certain amount of control' over it. The Government could, for instance, pretend that it did not know that slave dealing was going on there while at the same time using paid spies to 'obtain (such) information as would lead to the capture of any Aros, Abiribas or other natives found in possession of slaves bought at Uzuakoli since 1 April 1902'. This would 'enable the District Commissioner to make such an example of any offenders caught that the demand for slaves at Uzuakoli market will cease any way from our sphere of influence on account of the danger attaching to the people who insist on buying slaves'.[59]

Or better still, it was urged, the more important thing to do was to destroy the *demand* and consequently the *supply* for slaves. Most of the slaves bought at Uzuakoli were taken to the Delta states. A means therefore should be found of hunting down the coastal 'demanders'. This would destroy the main market for slaves and force the Aro to take up an honourable occupation. On this point, Mr. R. Granville, District Commissioner argued:

> It is quite evident that the demand for slaves, both male and female still exists on the waterside and I think the conviction of a 'demander', the more prominent the better, would do more to stop the traffic than the conviction of a comparatively unimportant supplier.
> If it was possible to introduce a system by which all heads of houses were compelled to register their house-holds, and when this has been in force for some little time it was publicly proclaimed that all unregistered persons who had joined the houses after a certain date, unless born in the house, could come before a commissioner and claim his freedom, it would owing to the increased risk largely lessen the demand and consequently the supply.[60]

After some hesitation, it was decided to 'destroy the town', probably in consequence of the triumph of Richard Morrisey's view that 'further parleying with these people will have little result for good'.⁶¹ In fact as a result of pressure from Richard Morrisey, the officer commanding the troops in the Cross River Division drew up a plan of operations against Uzuakoli as early as August 1902. According to the plan a force made up of three European officers, one European N.C.O., one political officer, one medical officer, 104 native riflemen and 18 native artillery men would attack the town and destroy it in two days.⁶² But before this plan could be implemented, there was trouble in Ibeku and Olokoro to deal with which a much larger force under Major W. C. E. Heneker was used. Lieutenant Morrisey was the political officer attached to the expedition. At its successful conclusion he persuaded Major Heneker that the time was opportune to deal with the new nerve centre of Aro slave dealing business—Uzuakoli. The purpose of this subsidiary expedition which apparently was undertaken without authorization from Calabar was conceived almost in the same grand manner as the Aro Expedition of 1901–2. 'Lieut. Morrisey', wrote Major Heneker in his final report:

> ... asked me if I did not think that the time was propitious to visit Ozu-Akoli and give a final blow to the slave trade, and I cordially agreed with him. Our prestige was very high just then in the surrounding country and all wrong doers were trembling in their shoes and fearing a visit. The chiefs and real natives of the town had sent into Bende assuring the District Commissioner that they had no hand in the war and were harbouring no refugees. There appeared the chance of ... ridding the country of several of the participants in this black traffic.⁶³

What followed was rather melodramatic. The people around Bende had learnt the futility of opposing the troops of the Protectorate by force. The thing to do was to make a show of submission, feed the troops until they departed and then revert to the same practices that had brought about the military visitation. Thus as Heneker's column approached Uzuakoli, the chiefs and their people met them outside the town, escorted them to the village square where they had built a temporary camp. Then 'some 600 women danced round the camp for three hours as a sign of joy' at the 'visit' of the troops. The next day Lieut. Morrisey, under a threat to destroy the town and seize the chiefs, forced the village-group to surrender 51 people said to have been carrying on the slave trade. Most of these were said to be foreigners and some of them were caught 'red-handed with slaves in their possession only caught three or four days before'.[64] The threatened blow had come and passed, Uzuakoli was not destroyed, the *Agbagwu* market was not moved to Bende, the Aro had not been prevented from visiting the Uzuakoli market, and no measures had been concerted to destroy the little that remained of the market for slaves in Oil Rivers States. As the administration soon found out the Aro slaving business was not yet finally destroyed. That was not to be for a long time, and even then was not to be achieved by means of military promenades.

Mr. Frank Hives who served as District Commissioner at Bende long after the expedition of 1902 against Uzuakoli, has left us a vivid account of how he had to face and again deal with the problem of Aro slaving interests at Uzuakoli. From the experience of his predecessors at Bende he had learnt that it was futile tackling the problem by means of military patrols. Instead he relied on paid spies to spot out slave dealers, report these to him and then he would hunt down and punish them. On occasions he had to track them down to Uzuakoli, at other times he had to ambush them with good effect on their way from the *Agbagwu* market.[65] In the annual report on the Colony and Protectorate of Southern Nigeria for 1907 the Government was still vociferously complaining against the 'pernicious influence' of the Aro in the Okigwi Division and elsewhere. Referring specifically to Aro slave dealing the report said:

> These Aros are continually seizing and selling people and are most difficult to find out.... They cause the same trouble around Abakaliki.[66]

But by the time this report was written open slave raiding and trading were already out of the question for the Aro and all other devotees of the business. The Ezza patrol (1905), the Onitsha Hinterland column (1908) and the Ahiara Expedition (1906) had already done much to bring what was left of the Aro sphere of influence under colonial control. With this the Aro had to modify their methods and tactics. From now the slave trade became a very precarious enterprise which had to be conducted underground. It was probably because of the increased difficulty of open slave dealing, and probably because the Aro thought the colonial authorities had relaxed their vigilance that

Ibini ukpabi oracle was revived at Aro Chukwu from about this time.

The Aro had in fact not sat idly by while the British administration sought to undermine popular faith in their oracle. They had mounted a counter propaganda of their own. *Ibini ukpabi*, they claimed, knew in advance the plans of the colonial administration to capture Aro Chukwu and dynamite its abode and long before the operation started had wisely left the ravine and the bush it had inhabited for centuries. It had already found a new abode and would make itself manifest in due time.[67] The British political officers knew of this counter propaganda and suspected that the Aro were eager to revive the oracle somewhere around the Bende Division. They had in fact been on the alert, expecting such a revival since early 1902 when the female elders of Aro Chukwu requested from Moor for permission to revive *Chukwu* and control it themselves. When Frank Hives became District Commissioner at Bende he quickly came to the conclusion that it was erroneous for anyone to believe that the Long Juju had been destroyed and 'stamped out of existence—discredited by the failure of its supposed powers to protect itself'. He believed that since most of the Aro priests, including the head priest escaped capture in 1901-2, they must have re-established the oracle at some other place 'keeping its site a secret as long as possible, and moving it whenever there was suspicion that the secret was becoming too widely known'.[68] The extensive inquiries which he made about what had happened to it, he said, merely led to the oracle being set up and dismantled so often. But it was not until after 1906 that the oracle was re-established on a grand scale.

As already mentioned briefly above, it was only in 1906 that Chief Kanu Okoro, the traditional clan head of all the Aro went to Calabar 'and gave himself up asking that he might be reinstated'. This the Government did without suspecting that the action was going to lead to a great deal of trouble. As soon as he settled down, Kanu Okoro held a big meeting of his people during which he told them that:

> he had come back to Aro Chukwu and that he had got permission from the Government to restart the Long Juju, and that anybody wishing to hold the Long Juju had first of all to obtain his permission and to pay him money for it.[69]

Apparently there were some of his hearers who felt that they had

had enough trouble from the Government and did not want to risk any further military visitation. This was especially so with the representatives from Obinkita, the village which appeared to have suffered most damage at the hands of the Aro Field Force.[70] The dissenting faction insisted that a written permission should be obtained from the Government before the oracle could be revived. Eventually about August 1909 the Aro Chukwu chiefs sent a petition to the Government praying to be allowed 'to resume the worship of their ancestral God, Chukwu'. But the petition merely gave the Provincial Commissioner, Eastern Provinces, the opportunity to put in writing a warning which he had issued to Aro leaders in June 1907 to the effect that:

> he could under no circumstances recommend the re-establishment of *the Long Juju* in *any shape or form*,[71] that he trusted no one would be foolish enough to start Long Juju in some secret place as it was sure to be discovered and trouble bound to ensue, and that he hoped the matter would not be brought up again.[72]

He ordered that this warning be read to the chiefs when assembled in the Native Court.

But if the Aro were dismayed by this reply, they were not deterred from carrying on with their preparations for reviving the oracle. They did so with such success that by 1912 when the oracle had to be 'smashed' again by the colonial administration, it was claimed by the District Commissioner in charge of Aro Chukwu that 'it was practically as strong and as far-reaching a juju as it was before the Government took over the country' in 1902. It was also claimed that 'practically every Aro Chukwu chief partakes in the holding of this juju and the profits thereof'.[73] The discovery of the oracle was made possible by the fact that after two tours in the Aro sub-district, the District Commissioner, Mr. Chamley, had successfully wormed himself into the confidence of some of the christian natives who then revealed the secret to him. When he followed up the information he discovered four centres where the oracle had been re-established, and on the whole caught 26 prominent Aro in the act of holding the Long Juju. Also 22 boys given by clients for sacrifice to the Long Juju but who were to be sold into slavery were recaptured. The spatial distribution of these boys, given below, shows how widespread was the influence and authority of the revived oracle.

Okigwi District —6
Udi District —5
Bende District —5
Onitsha District —2
Abakaliki District—1
Orlu District —1
Okwoga District —1
Unidentified —1

It was to this point that Mr. Chamley wanted to draw attention when he wrote:

> All the children, it will be seen, have been drawn from practically all the districts in the Eastern Provinces, north and west of Aro Chukwu.[74]

But of course the sway of the revived oracle went beyond the Eastern Province as Onitsha and Okwoga, from which three of the boys came, were then in the Central Province.

Once again the question arose as to what to do to destroy the oracle finally. The first thing was to make an example of those caught red-handed in the act of working the oracle. Three of them were sentenced to death as they were found guilty of murder. They had sacrificed one Aba to the Long Juju. Chief Kanu Okoro, the man behind the revival of the oracle and who had made so much money from the racket was sentenced to three years imprisonment with hard labour and then to deportation, while the others were sentenced to six months imprisonment. The four sites where the oracle was being worked were razed to the ground. Then came the issue of ensuring that the oracle was not revived again. This was tied to the question of how to keep a close control on all the Aro people, and how to purify or close down the Uzuakoli market which had continued to serve as the most important single centre for the sale and purchase of slaves. On this issue Chamley was clear what was to be done. 'I may say', he wrote to his superiors:

> that I am perfectly sure that practically the whole of the Slave Dealing in the Eastern Provinces is done through the Long Juju and the Aro, people being brought from all parts of the Eastern Province to the Uzuakoli market and there sold. *Until all Aros not residing in Aro Chukwu district are made to return to Aro district, and until the Uzuakoli market is done away with so long in my opinion will Slave Dealing in the Eastern Province prosper.*[75]

But Chamley's superiors would not agree with him. Horace

Bedwell, the Provincial Commissioner, for instance, considered the suggestion of getting all the Aro quarantined in the Aro district as 'impracticable' and 'absurd'. 'Mr. Chamley's suggestion of bringing all Aros into Aro Chukwu district', he said

> is not practicable. Even if it could be done a further order would have to be given that they should never leave the district which would render it absurd.[76]

What of the old suggestion that the Uzuakoli market should be destroyed which Chamley now revived? Mr. Bedwell also considered it impracticable. He conceded the close connection between the Aro slaving business and that market. But at the same time he pointed out that:

> This market is the largest and most important in the whole of the Province ... (Its) removal ... would merely have the effect of at once locking up a very large trade and of removing the illicit portion to some other place.[77]

He, however promised to 'take steps to try and purify the market' now that all around Bende who had heard what happened to Chief Kanu Okoro and the other culprits 'are for the moment afraid of being suspected even of any connection with the Juju'. It is not known whether anything was eventually done in this respect.[78] Bedwell did not believe that slave dealing and the Long Juju could be stamped out by military patrols and the detonation of high explosives. Only education and enlightenment could do it. On this he pointed out rather helplessly:

> I would like to believe, as Mr. Chamley does, that the juju is now destroyed, but I do not think that a practice as old as this can be eradicated in what historically speaking is a few minutes. ... Until the belief people have in the juju is outgrown we shall always be presented with the possibilities of its revival and be confronted with the difficult task of reducing the slave dealing coincident with it.[79]

Bedwell was right and Chamley wrong. In fact the very next year, 1913, information was brought to the Government that the Long Juju had been re-established, this time not in the Aro district, but in the Okigwi Division, at Isiagu now on the railway line.[80] Then two years after this, 1915, Okoroafo Akakpo, one of the men who let on the secret of the oracle to the Administration in 1912, reported another move to re-establish the oracle at Aro Chukwu.[81] One may ask why it turned out to be so difficult to destroy the Long Juju and scotch the slave trading business of the Aro even after the British had taken effective control of southeastern Nigeria and established functioning administrative institutions at the provincial, district and lower levels. There were many reasons for this.

One of these was that for a long time the British did not understand the intricacies of the Aro system. They were given to the idea that slaves necessarily had to be recruited by violent methods—by wars and slave raid and thus thought that once law and order had been imposed and villages stopped from going to war with their neighbours that slave dealing would suffer a severe set-back. But in the area in question wars and raids had never occupied a prominent place in the list of methods used in procuring slaves. Those who were not enslaved through the oracles were 'spirited' away by very subtle methods or sold into slavery by their own people either for committing heinous crimes or for being afflicted with deformities considered to derive from a divine curse. As the British 'menace' increased the Aro resorted more and more to these subtle methods, in particular to dealing mainly in children who could easily be enticed away with such then rare delicacies as sugar, stockfish and so on, or gagged and carried covered in native long baskets with the least trouble, or dressed up and made to look like the children of their captors while being moved to the slave market. In this regard it is noteworthy that all the slaves rescued after the second destruction of the Long Juju in 1912 were children between the ages of three and nine years. Frank Hives who served for many years in these parts and played a large part in tracking down Aro slavers has described these methods lucidly in his reminiscences: *Juju and Justice in Nigeria*, and in *Justice in the Jungle*: so also has Jack S. Harris, a social-anthropologist who worked among the Ozuitem people of Bende in the 1930s.[82]

If the methods for recruiting slaves were such that the British could not easily discover and suppress, so were the methods of disposal which the Aro were now forced to adopt. The earlier method was to parade the slaves in the open market for those who cared to price and purchase. But no sooner did the British penetrate the interior than this method was discarded. Even as early as 1902 it was discovered that most of the slaves sold at Uzuakoli were not displayed in the open market. Speaking on this matter that year Mr. Grenville, District Commissioner Aro district, said:

Comparatively few slaves are actually exposed in the market for sale, in fact on the last visit my spy made he only saw 10, 7 of whom were heavily chained, but a system of selling in houses has been introduced. Buyers when transporting their slaves to the various destinations also clothe them better than formerly to make them uniform with the rest of the party and therefore less conspicuous when passing a Government post.[83]

Mr. Hives' subsequent experiences in the Bende District confirmed these observations. One of the slaves whom he rescued when at Bende was in a caravan which he, Hives, had seen earlier but did not suspect was a slave caravan. Also when subsequently he went into Uzuakoli to track down slave dealers, he found them in private compounds rather than in the open market.[84] This became more and more the case as British control took a firm root and the risks of the business increased. 'Every attempt so far made', confessed Horace Bedwell in 1913, 'to detect this illicit sale of people in the Uzuakoli market has failed'.[85]

The survival and persistence of the Aro system for so long also owed a great deal to the loopholes in, and the shortcomings of the colonial administrative set up. It is true, as mentioned earlier, that the establishment of the district headquarters and native courts as well as the network of main roads which came with the establishment of colonial rule were subversive of the Aro system. This became more and more so as time went on, especially as it came to be believed that British rule had come to stay. But at the same time the shortcomings of the colonial system played into the hands of the Aro. The fact that the motor roads did not necessarily run along the old Aro routes, that the district and native court centres were not necessarily located at the once strategic points where Aro settlements had grown—these meant that a certain volume of traffic in slaves and 'pilgrims' to the Long Juju continued for a long time without attracting undue attention from the Government. While the produce trade 'flowed' along the newly made roads, the slave trade and oracle business 'flowed' along the old and tried bush tracks. This fact helped the Aro in another way. It was along these old bush tracks that their settlements mostly lay. This made it easy for the news of the presence of any white man or his suspected agent on this route to be passed on in advance from settlement to settlement to prevent those dealing in or keeping slaves being surprised. Furthermore the villages in all this area were and are situated so close to each other and there was so much coming and going between village and village that it was quite easy for news of the visit of a white man or his other suspected agent to precede him.

Along with these was the fact that there were so many traditional functions which the colonial system could not perform. There was no provision under this alien regime for 'telling' the future or 'holding' discussions with ones departed relations or for dealing with the psychological problems associated with barrenness, sudden and premature death and so on. It did not attempt to tackle the problem of disposing of people deformed because of divine curse. The courts established under the alien regime were often considered ineffective by the elders—at least in the matter of disposing finally of unrepentant criminals. At worst these criminals were sentenced to imprisonment. But in prison, according to Abakaliki elders, they not only got 'fit and fat', but learned a few more tricks from their fellow criminals and the white men and came home only to become greater nuisances to their people.[86] When the people found themselves still faced with these problems to which the colonial regime appeared to have no answer, they invariably turned to the tried and tested old methods. This meant either selling the unwanted person to the Aro or consulting the Aro oracle. This helps to explain, to a great extent, the survival until even the middle forties of this century of the organizations associated with such other oracle as *Igwe-ka-Ala* at Umunneọha and *Agbala* at Awka.

In 1912 when Chamley 'smashed' the Long Juju for the second time, he captured along with the manipulators of the oracle a number of its visiting clients. The statements of these men at the trial of the accused persons help to illustrate the point being made here. One of these men, Obasi Nwezi, said:

> I am the chief of Ilago in Onitsha. I came down here because I lost two of my wives. I have now got another wife and I wanted to find out whether she would be spared and whether she would have a child.[87]

Another client, Awa, stated:

> I am a native of Uku in Bende District. The accused Oji Obona took me to Udo Elekwa to sacrifice for me that I may get a child and live.[88]

And still another client said:

> I am a native of Ndoni in the Onitsha District. Uku Agu brought me down here because my father is sick and I have nothing to eat. He said that a visit to the juju called Mufu would solve my problems.[89]

These were all problems for which it was felt the colonial regime had no solution. As long as this mode of thinking persisted, people were bound to continue to have recourse to the Aro oracle and similar institutions.

And what was more the Aro attempt to maintain their ascendancy on the old basis was closely linked with their second major reaction to the establishment of colonial rule. The nature of this reaction and how it helped to sustain the one already discussed will now be examined.

Early in the confrontation between them and the expanding imperial frontier, some of the *Aro Uzo* (*Aro of Dispersion*) had enlisted in the service of the British invaders, not so much because they were anxious to see the triumph of British imperialism, but because it paid them in many ways to serve this rising power. The Aro were in a good position to perform this task. Their trade routes spanned the whole region. They enjoyed a privileged position as travellers because of the protection which the fame of their oracle and their alliance with the Abam etc. assured them. They thus knew the region inside out. Also even though the British knew about some of the tricks of the Aro, and at times wanted not to use them as guides, it was not always easy to avoid using them. For though the early British claimed one could always distinguish between the 'intellectual' and 'Hamitic' Aro and the other 'degenerate natives' from mere physical traits, it was in fact not possible to do so. Commenting on this fact Frank Hives who faced this problem in an acute form as one of the early political officers posted to Bende said:

> We usually had to depend upon an Aro guide, though he always swore he was not an Aro at all.[90]

Through being so close to the colonial power the Aro were able to know well in advance what the next stage was in the plan to subdue the country, by what method this would be done, how it would affect them and so on. As a result they had the opportunity, while pretending to show British officers and/or their agents the way, of either leading them away from the target or warning their fellow Aro about the intended move as well as advising them on the best line of response to adopt. It also gave them the opportunity to extort money etc. from both the colonial power and other local non-Aro peoples. The former paid them for 'showing' them the way, the latter for either warning them in advance of the 'visitation' or for giving 'expert' advice on how to deal with the threat or for leading the officer and his troops away from their village.

Being close to the colonial power redounded to the advantages of the Aro in another way. In the early days of British penetration of the interior, when the white men were held in great awe, those who led them about the country were able to share in this awe and prestige. Among the natives who did this work the Aro were the most prominent. In some astounding cases the Aro were able to claim in certain interior villages that the white men were the agents of their dreaded oracle. With this they were able to levy blackmail all around. Mr. Hives has left us a lucid description of how this operated. From having followed the troops around for some time the Aro came to know that any village which the troops were to visit, or just pass through, whose inhabitants met the patrol promptly and peacefully in the market place or town square and provided food for the soldiers as required was spared. But one whose inhabitants took to the bush was treated as hostile and destroyed. When therefore the troops of the Protectorate were about to visit a village, the Aro guides made this fact known to their colleagues who then preceded the troops by a few days 'levying heavy fees upon the inhabitants in the way of slaves (generally females) and brass rods promising that when the payment was made they would order their servants, the troops, not to molest them'. Those who succumbed to the blackmail were advised to meet the troops in the market square with music and dancing, 'and to have ready for them quantities of yams, fowls, a few goats and a large number of pots of water'. The upshot was that the village would not be sacked and the food supplied would be paid for. But a village which tried to 'open eye' (i.e. pretended to know it all and therefore refused Aro demands) was told that the troops which were heading towards it served the wicked white men and 'would kill the males, enslave the young females, loot all the houses and destroy all the town by fire' unless ambushed and wiped out on their advance into the village. Here the result invariably was that the village was sacked and consigned to the flames.[91] 'It was some time', confessed Mr. Hives

> before I discovered why we were welcomed with open arms in some towns while from others we met with strong opposition which caused us many casualties.[92]

Very few things came amiss to the Aro. Even the institution

of the native court they were able to put to some use. Owing to the difficult circumstances of the early years of colonial rule which need not be dealt with here, the British did not find it easy finding the right men to appoint as members of the native courts, that is as warrant chiefs.[93] The Aro put this British difficulty to good advantage. As people who knew the villages well, they would be paid by the Government to help find the men to be made chiefs. And after these men had been appointed warrant chiefs the Aro would extort money from them for helping to make them 'big chiefs'.[94] And after these courts had become firmly established some Aro went into league with the more disreputable of the chiefs and converted the courts into instruments for making money. The Aro would drag their unsuspecting neighbours to court over trifles or on trumped up charges. The chiefs would extort money from the victims in the form of presents and tribes and share the proceeds with their Aro allies. The same chiefs would then 'intervene', plead with the Aro to accept a settlement out of court and to this the Aro would 'reluctantly' agree, or better still the Aro would simply move to another town and the case would lapse from the non-appearance of the plaintiff. This was a common feature of native courts situated close to villages which had Aro settlements. Where the chiefs were not amenable to their plans, the Aro sought to undermine the chiefs' influence with their people through pointless and endless litigation. In the Okigwi Division (then made up of Orlu and Okigwi districts) these practices lowered the moral tone of the courts so much and caused such social disruption generally that some of the more reputable chiefs raised a hue and cry against the Aro.[95] In December 1919 the Divisional Officer, Okigwi, H. de B. Bewley reported:

> I attribute this state of affairs in Okigwi and Orlu Districts mainly to the influence of the Aros. They have a large settlement at Ndizuogu on the Orlu-Okigwi boundary and have secured a footing in many towns in both districts. They are utterly unscrupulous unadulterated liars, and responsible for most of the slave dealing that takes place ... A deputation of the leading warrant chiefs in Okigwi with one accord begged to be allowed to exclude all Aros from their court. According to them it is impossible to decide cases in which they are involved. They tell lies and buy witnesses. If they are decided against they seek to undermine the chiefs. It is proposed to open a new Native Court in Orlu District at Akokwa, the Orlu chiefs are unanimous in their desire that Aros should be excluded from it.[96]

In the great days of the slave trade the Aro had been largely responsible for meeting the needs of the peoples of the hinterland of the Bight of Biafra for imported European goods. Their monopoly of this business had indeed been one of the main bases of the widespread influence and respect they commanded amongst their neighbours. They did not abandon this trade with the imposition of colonial rule. What, however, they could not maintain, in spite of their attempts in that direction, was their monopoly of it. But for the first few years of colonial rule they enjoyed a great advantage over their neighbours in the prosecution of the trade. For one thing it was not separated from their slaving business. If anything it was closely wound up with it. It could travel along the same route as the slaves who were usually made to carry the goods. And what was more the British believed at first that only by using the experienced middlemen—the Aro and the coastal traders—could they hope to effect the commercial revolution which they were working towards in this part of the world. So much so were the British committed to this idea that even while the Aro Expedition was still going on, one of the political officers attached to one of the columns of the Field Force, started issuing 'books' (signed papers meant to confer right of free passage) to prominent Aro traders permitting them to trade. The wily and resourceful Aro immediately sought to put these papers to maximum use, they would appear to have thought that it would help them to preserve their hegemony in spite of their defeat by the Field Force. They fanned out into most of the areas covered by the Aro Field Force brandishing these papers and claiming that:

> they have been given permission by white men to trade and that they have been told so long as they trade, provide chop and carriers, they will be left a free hand in the country.[97]

The message had an electric but untoward effect wherever it was broadcast. At Oloko, for instance, the people were coming to the conclusion that the Aro were finished with, and were about to throw in their lot with the colonial government by surrendering all prominent Aro refugees in their midst when they received this news. Their reaction was to hold back in the belief that the Aro had made their peace with the white man and that it was unwise to alienate them.[98]

The officer, Woodhouse, who issued the 'books' to the Aro received a reprimand for his hasty action, but the policy of encouraging the Aro to trade was persisted in. A few months after this the political officer at the newly created district headquarters of Bende, in enunciating his policy towards this people, said:

> Every encouragement should be given to the Aros to trade now that they have fallen into line with Government. The great idea is to make the Aro interest himself in the produce trade, in which by his intelligence he will remain as the middleman of the interior in trading and buying oil instead of as hitherto slaves. In the process of this trade he will be displaying goods to the natives, which hitherto they have not seen, and therefore have not had their desire whetted sufficiently to develop the riches in palm oil and kernels that lie at their door. The desire to possess will then show the necessity to work, which I trust will be followed by a corresponding large increase of trade.[99]

At first it appeared the Aro responded enthusiastically to this policy. Mr. E. D. Simpson, Assistant District Commissioner at Aro Chukwu, soon reported that the Aro were 'exceedingly satisfactory to deal with, being clean, courteous and obliging. . . . They are at last beginning to trade, after much urging and with success'. The Aro Chukwu market he described as 'well-attended by all the people around' and as 'increasing daily in size'.[100] This policy, and the Aro response to it for a time helped to buoy up the Aro oligarchy. They grew rich from distributing imported goods and in this had initial advantages in experience and capital. It also enabled them to cover up much of their other illegal dealings in slave trade and the promotion of *Ibiniukpabi* oracle. British awareness that the Aro were also engaged in substantial legitimate traffic limited the extent to which they went in seeking to destroy those aspects of Aro business life which they disapproved of. Their dilemma over what to do with the Uzuakoli market was a case in point. They were, as already shown,[101] held back from closing down the market partly because they feared destroying the legitimate side of Aro business enterprise. Ruminating on this dilemma in 1913 Horace Bedwell pointed out:

> The slave trade they (the Aro) are engaged in is only an adjunct, though a very large and important adjunct, of a genuine trade.[102]

With the colonial government hamstrung by this consideration the Aro oligarchy was able to continue, for longer than would have been otherwise possible, fighting a losing battle to maintain its ancient ascendancy.

But after two decades, or so from the British occupation of Aro Chukwu, it had become clear that the dominance of the Aro slaving oligarchy was already a thing of the past. The adverse effects on Aro interests of missionary influence, colonial rule, the penetration of the interior by the coastal middlemen, the new roads and new ways of maintaining law and order which we have already analyzed, increased with time. The dominant export of this region had for long been palm produce rather than slaves. This needed no special organization to carry it on. Nor did it require much capital. The result was that many people went into it. The Aro, denied in this the advantages which they enjoyed in the slave trade, were overshadowed by the interior producers who came to the trade with no prejudices and who lived in the heart of the palm belt. Christianity, western education, and general progress in political, social and economic matters undermined many of those traditional beliefs and notions on the exploitation of which the Aro had erected their ascendancy. Though to all intents and purposes by the end of the second decade of this century the Aro oligarchy had already suffered eclipse, it remained a force which continued to obsess the much long-obsessed officials of the colonial government. In this later period British obsession with the Aro nearly led to this oligarchy of slave dealers being set up as the political rulers of Igboland. How this idea came up and was eventually scotched can be easily summarized.

In 1921 Sir Herbert Richmond Palmer, the Lieutenant Governor of the Northern Provinces, a keen believer of the Hamitic hypothesis, produced a series of disquisitions on the interrelationship of the main tribes and ruling families of Nigeria. In these essays he came to the conclusion that the ruling families of Yoruba land, of Benin, Igala, and Jukun all derived from the same hieratic family and that the Aro were also derivatives of this family which he identified as Hamitic in origin. All the members of this family except the Aro, he argued, had been recognized by the colonial government and their power and position augmented under the system of indirect rule. As a result in Yoruba land, Benin, Igala and Wukari there was peace and quiet, there was also administrative and economic progress. But in the then Eastern Provinces (later Eastern Nigeria) there was unrest, uncertainty and administrative stagnation because the ancient ruling race or clan, the Aro, was being smothered by an unwise local government policy based on misguided missionary propaganda and promptings. It was the Government's policy of non-recognition of Aro political power, he said, that had driven the Aro to 'chicanery and crime', to slave dealing and Long Juju priest-craft. It was the same everywhere in the Western Sudan, Palmer claimed, that the ruling families were not officially recognized and given political power.[103]

The Palmerian thesis was not based on any convincing ethnographic or historical evidence and for the same reason was difficult, if not impossible, to disprove. Colonel Moorhouse, the Lieutenant-Governor Southern Provinces, whose comments on this thesis have survived, was not convinced by it. Declaring himself not qualified to confirm or disprove Palmer, he tried to dismiss the idea in a practical and businesslike manner. 'It is possible', he contended

> that our policy which deprived the Aro of his power has driven him to 'chicanery and crime' and that we have lost a golden opportunity of utilising in the Aro what might have been a power for good in the Administration of the Ibos.... In any case to attempt to restore the power of the Aro now would be out of the question.[104]

This should have been the end of the matter. But it was not, as the problem of how best to govern the Igbo and their neighbours was at the time the foremost question occupying the attention of the colonial government in the region east of the Niger. As people discussed this matter and sent up their views to government, Palmer's suggestion that the Aro held the key to the problem came up time and again. Early in 1922 Frank Hives Resident of the Owerri Province, asserted that 'the Aros were and are now to a great extent the power in the Ibo country' and then 'regretted' 'that their power could not have been made use of for good when the country was first opened up'.[105] A little later the same year the Secretary for Native Affairs, S. M. Grier, toured the Igbo and Ibibio provinces to investigate the local government problems of the day and at the end came up with a report in which he positively claimed that in pre-colonial days the Aro controlled the territory east of the Niger, and that they 'divided it up into districts which were ... to a great extent ruled by representatives sent out from their towns'. These representatives, when they attended the meetings of the villages and clans, claimed Grier, 'gave advice which was invariably taken'. He, however, was 'inclined to agree with those who believe that it is impossible' to make use of them in the administration of the region.[106] It was at this point that the Government decided to go into this matter in full with a view to finding out what Aro power was like in the past and how it could be used in the administration of the Igbo and their neighbours. This became all the more necessary when the Hon. W. A. G. Ormsby-Gore, after his visit to West Africa, reported in 1926 that the Ibibio and the Igbo were formerly under the Aro and that the break up of Aro power by the British had 'left the vast mass of the people freer but leaderless'.[107] The decision to appoint an anthropologist to investigate this matter was the closest the Aro came to a vision of political power. When the investigations of the anthropological officer, H. F. Mathews, in 1927 failed to uncover any evidence to support investing the Aro with political power over the Igbo, Ibibio and Ogoja, that vision vanished.[108]

It would appear that after this event the colonial administration lost interest in the Aro. At least it is very significant that the Women's Riot of 1929 was not blamed on them. Had such a major upheaval occurred in the Eastern Provinces before 1927, 'Aro machinations' surely would have been put forward as a convenient explanation. Probably it is a measure of the extent to which the slaving oligarchy had been eclipsed that the colonial administration, usually obsessed with Aro intrigues, did not resort to this pet explanation to account for the Riot. The Aro had fought and lost a protracted war, lasting over a century, to maintain their privileged economic position between the Niger and the Cameroons frontier. Theirs was an ascendancy based, not on any quality of mind or body peculiar to them as a people, but on the historical accident that they were able to exploit the peculiar socio-political circumstances of this region. At the time colonial rule was imposed, the people of Awka, Nkwerre and Umunneoha were rising to challenge and limit Aro economic and oracular sway. The British termination of the conditions which had encouraged and sustained these forms of activities destroyed the local hegemonies built upon them. In the final analysis, the eclipse of the Aro oligarchy meant the triumph of christianity and christian values, the almost total extinction of the internal slave trade, and the admission of the primary producers of the interior to a free and fair participation in the economic opportunities offered by contact with Europe.

NOTES

1. See for instance Simon Ottenberg, 'Ibo Oracles and Intergroup Relations' in *Southwestern Journal of Anthropology*, Vol. 14, No. 3, 1958. G. I. Jones, 'Who Are the Aro?', in *Nigerian Field*, Vol. III, 1959.
   K. O. Dike, *Trade and Politics in the Niger Delta* (Oxford, 1956).
   J. C. Anene, *Southern Nigeria In Transition* (Cambridge, 1956).
2. Based on oral information collected from various old men in the Coastal States in 1962/63.
3. G. I. Jones, 'Who Are the Aro?', *loc. cit.*
4. J. S. Harris, 'Some Aspects of Slavery in Southeastern Nigeria', in the *Journal of Negro History*, Vol. 27, No. 1, January 1942.
5. J. S. Harris, 'Some Aspects of Slavery etc.', *loc. cit.*, p. 38.
6. K. O. Dike, *op. cit.*, pp. 153-62.
   G. I. Jones, The Political Organisation of Old Calabar, in Forde, D. (ed.), *Efik Traders of Old Calabar* (London, 1956).
7. This question is one of those aspects of Southeastern Nigerian history which subsequent research will help to elucidate. There is an indication that some of the Aro took an interest in the oil trade early enough and used to ship produce down the Cross River to Calabar. If this was so, it is strange that it escaped all mention in the records of this period, even in the reports of Commercial Intelligent Officers who reported on at least one occasion on the trade of the Cross River.
8. K. O. Dike, *Trade and Politics in the Niger Delta* (Oxford, 1956).
   J. E. Flint, *Sir George Goldie and the Making of Nigeria* (Oxford, 1960).
   G. I. Jones, *The Trading States of the Oil Rivers* (Oxford, 1963).
   J. C. Anene, *Southern Nigeria in Transition* (Cambridge, 1966).
   O. Ikime, *Merchant Prince of the Niger Delta* (London, 1968).
   A. Ryder, *Benin and The Europeans 1485-1897* (Longmans, 1969).
   S. M. (now T. N.) Tamuno, 'The Development of British Administrative Control in Southern Nigeria 1900-1912'. (Unpublished Ph.D. Thesis, London, 1962.)
   J. F. Ade Ajayi, *Christian Missions in Nigeria* (Longmans, 1965).
   E. A. Ayandele, *The Missionary Impact on Modern Nigeria* (Longmans, 1966).
9. See Goldie's letter dated 16 November 1889 enclosed in No. 255 of 15/12/99 from Colonial Office to the High Commissioner and Consul-General, Niger Coast Protectorate, C.S.O. 1/14 of 1899.
10. K. O. Dike, *Trade and Politics, etc.*, Chapter 8.
    G. I. Jones, 'The Political Organisation of Old Calabar' in Forde, D. (ed.), *Efik Traders of Old Calabar* (London, 1956).
11. Oral information collected from Calabar, Bonny, Opobo and Degema in 1962/63.
12. Moor to C.O., No. 16 of 24/1/1900 in C.S.O. 1/13, Southern Nigeria Despatches to C.O.
13. Moor to C.O., memo. concerning the Aro Expedition. See C.S.O. 1/13 of 1902, p. 587, etc.
14. For a full discussion of the shortcomings of the Native Courts, see A. E. Afigbo, *The Warrant Chiefs*.
15. For the effects of the road revolution on trade in this region as for the criteria determining the establishment of District and Divisional Headquarters in the early days of colonial rule, see U. I. Ukwu, 'The Development of Trade and Marketing in Iboland' in the *Journal of the Historical Society of Nigeria*, Vol. III, No. 4, June 1967.
16. Oral information obtained at Obegu, Akwete, Elele, Opobo, Bonny and Calabar in 1962/63.

17. Niger Coast Protectorate Annual Report, see despatch No. 167 of 3.10.99 from Moor to F.O. and C.O. in C.S.O. 1/13 of 1899.
18. *Ibid.*
19. Letter No. 24 of 13.11.96 from D.C. Old Calabar to the Commissioner and Consul-General in Calprof 6/1, Vol. III.
20. Moor to C.O., No. 141 of 9.9.99 in C.S.O. 1/13 of 1899.
21. See Extract from the Report of Mr. Murray, D.C., Opobo, dated 3.7.99 in C.S.O. 1/13, Vol. II, pp. 465–6.
22. H. L. Gallwey, Acting Consul-General to F.O., No. 162 of 10.10.98. See Extract from Mr. Murray's Report on Opobo dated 3.7.99 in C.S.O. 1/13 of 1899, Vol. II, pp. 465–6.
    Moor to C.O., No. 79 of 23.3.1900 in C.S.O. 1/13 of 1900, Vol. 12.
23. See Extract from Quarterly Report on New Calabar District for Quarter ending 30.6.99 in C.S.O. 1/13, Vol. II of 1899, p. 467. See also Moor to F.O., No. 141 of 9.9.99 in C.S.O. 1/13 of 1899.
24. Moor to F.O., No. 141 of 9.9.99 in C.S.O. 1/13 of 1899.
25. See Extract from Quarterly Report on Opobo District for Quarter ended 30.6.69 in C.S.O. 1/13 of 1899, pp. 465–6 in Vol. II.
26. See Report No. 1/01 in Calprof 10/3, Vol. II.
    The cynical insinuation of the Aro here is that they or their oracle killed Chief Udo's father for his pro-British policy and would do the same to Chief Udo for a similar 'crime' against them.
27. Acting High Commissioner Leslie Probyn to C.O., No. 200 of 6.7.01 in C.S.O. 1/13 of 1901. See also in Enugu Archives, the file C.S.E. 1/11/4, entitled 'The Menace of the Aros'.
28. See Gallwey's letter to the Chief of Staff, Aro Field Force, dated November 1901 and attached to No. 401 in C.S.O. 1/13 of 1901.
29. Oral information collected from Akwete and Obegu in 1962/63.
30. Moor to F.O. and C.O., No. 141 of 9.9.99 in C.S.O. 1/3, Vol. II, p. 453, etc.
31. A. E. Afigbo, 'The Aro Expedition of 1901–1902. An Episode in the British Occupation of Iboland'. *Odu*, New Series, No. 7, April 1972.
32. Based on oral tradition collected in 1962/63 during an extensive field research among the Igbo and the Ibibio.
33. F. Hives and G. Lumley, *Juju and Justice in Nigeria* (London, 1930), p. 21.
34. Report on Ediba District for the Quarter ended 31.12.1901 in Calprof 10/3, Vol. II.
35. A. E. Afigbo, 'The Aro Expedition of 1901–1902. An Episode in the British Occupation of Iboland', *loc. cit.*
36. Moor to C.O., No. 52 of 4.2.02 in C.S.O. 1/13 of 1902.
37. Moor to C.O., No. 17 of 14.1.02 in C.S.O. 1/13 of 1902. Supplemented with information collected from Bende Division in 1962/63.
38. Minute M.P. 3402/03 of 12.10.1903 by the Acting High Commissioner Leslie Probyn on 'The Aro People' in the file Aro Dist. 1/7/33 in the Enugu Archives.
39. *Ibid.*
40. *Ibid.*
41. *Ibid.*
42. E. A. Ayandele, *The Missionary Impact on Modern Nigeria etc.*, p. 114.
43. D. M. McFarlan, Calabar: *The Church of Scotland Mission 1846–1946* (London, 1946), p. 117.
44. *Ibid.*
45. *Ibid.*
46. See A. E. Afigbo, 'Revolution and Reaction in Eastern Nigeria: The Background to the Women's Riot of 1929' in the *Journal of The Historical Society of Nigeria*, Vol. 3, No. 3, December 1966, for a detailed discussion of the

conflict between the new converts to christianity and their non-christian neighbours.
47. Report No. 12, by the Officer Commanding the Aro Field Force, attached to Despatch No. 3 of 3.1.02 from Moor to C.O. in C.S.O. 1/13 of 1902.)
48. See Report enclosed in Despatch No. 361 of 29.7.03 from the Acting High Commissioner to C.O. in C.S.O. 1/13 of 1903.
49. *Ibid.*
50. See for instance Alan Burns, *History of Nigeria* (7th Edition 1969, Arthur Norton Cook: *British Enterprise in Nigeria* (Frank Cass), D. M. McFarlan, *op. cit.*, p. 105.
51. K. O. Dike, *op. cit.*, p. 38.
52. Based on oral tradition collected from Uzuakoli and Oloko in 1962/63.
53. Report No. 9 of 12.6.02 from the D.C. Cross River to the Acting High Commissioner in Calprof 10/3. See also Report of 10/6/02 from Mr. Granville enclosed in Lieutenant Morrisey's letter.
54. Report of 10.6.02 from Granville enclosed in Morrisey's Report No. 9 of 12.6.02 in Calprof 10/3.
55. See U. I. Ukwu, 'The Development of Trade and Marketing in Iboland' in *J.H.S.N.*, Vol. III, No. 4, for more details on the place of the *Agbagwu* fair in the trading life of the hinterland peoples. I do not, however, agree with Ukwu's attributing of the origin of the Agbagwu fairs to Aro initiative.
56. See Report on Bende, undated, in Calprof 10/3.
57. Report No. 9 of 12.6.02 from the D.C. Cross River Division in Calprof 10/3.
58. Report on the Bende District, undated, in Calprof 10/3.
59. *Ibid.*
60. Report of 10.6.02 from R. Granville enclosed in Morrisey's Report No. 9 of 12.6.02 in Calprof 10/3.
61. Report No. 9 of 12.6.02 in Calprof 10/3.
62. Report of a tour of the Cross River Division dated 1.8.02 in Calprof 10/3.
63. Report by Major W. C. E. Heneker, Commanding Ibeku—Olokoro Expedition, dated 26.12.02 in Calprof 10/3.
64. *Ibid.*
65. F. Hives, *Justice in the Jungle* (London, 1932), pp. 201–12; 213–24.
66. Annual Report on the Colony of Southern Nigeria (Lagos, 1909), p. 20.
67. Based on oral information collected in 1962/63.
68. Hives and Lumley, *Juju and Justice in Nigeria*, pp. 21–2.
69. Report on the Long Juju dated 31/10/12 in the file, 'The Long Juju of Aro Chukwu', Arodist 1/7/31 Enugu Archives.
70. See Report of 10.6.02 from Granville enclosed in Morrisey's Report No. 90, of 12.6.02 in Calprof 10/3 for the lost of the Obinkita Aro at the hands of the Aro Field Force.
71. His own italics.
72. Conf. E. 74/09 of 16.9.09 from the Provincial Secretary, Eastern Provinces in Arodist 1/7/31, Enugu Archives.
73. Report on the Long Juju dated 31/10/12 in Arodist 1/7/31, Enugu Archives.
74. *Ibid.*
75. *Ibid.*
76. No. E. Conf. 136/1912 of 28/12/12 from H. Bedwell, Provincial Commissioner, Eastern Province, in Arodist 1/7/31.
77. *Ibid.*
78. An attempt was made to clear this matter up at Uzuakoli. That town was visited at least three times by troops in connection with slave dealing. The first visit was that of Lieutenant Morrisey and Major Heneker in 1902. But after that it has not been possible to connect any specific white man with the

subsequent visits. In the absence of written records the present writer has not been able to determine whether one of these subsequent visits was that promised by Bedwell in 1912. The matter is still receiving attention.
79. No. E. Conf. 136/1912 from H. Bedwell in Arodist 1/7/31.
80. Conf. No. 693/1913 of 9.12.13 from D.C. Arochukwu in Arodist 1/7/31.
81. Statement by Okoroafo Akakpo of Abagu dated 20.9.15 in Arodist 1/7/31.
82. Hives and Lumley, *Juju and Justice in Nigeria*.
Hives, *Justice in the Jungle.*'
J. S. Harris, 'Some Aspects of Slavery in South-eastern Nigeria' in *The Journal of Negro History*, Vol. 27, No. 1, January 1942.
83. Report dated 10.6.02 from Granville enclosed in Lieutenant Morrisey's Report No. 9 of 12.6.02 in Calprof 10/3.
84. F. Hives, *Justice in the Jungle*, pp. 201-12, pp. 213-24.
85. No. E. Conf. 136/1912 from H. Bedwell contained in Arodist 1/7/31.
86. For this aspect of the matter, see A. E. Afigbo, *The Warrant Chiefs*.
87. See statements by crown witnesses in Rex. V. Udo Elekwa and six others in Arodist 1/7/31.
88. *Ibid*.
89. *Ibid*.
90. F. Hives, *Justice in the Jungle*, pp. 169-70.
91. *Ibid*., p. 169, supplemented with oral information collected during a field research in 1962/63.
92. F. Hives, *Justice in the Jungle*, p. 170.
93. A. E. Afigbo, *The Warrant Chiefs*.
94. Based on oral information collected in 1962/63.
95. Conf. 15/15/19 of 18.12.19 from H. de B. Bewley, Divisional Officer Okigwi in the file, 'Remarks by F. P. Lynch, etc.' C.176/19, Enugu Archives.
96. *Ibid*.
97. Moor to C.O., No. 27 of 16.1.02 in C.S.O. 1/13. See also the attached Report from Lt. Colonel Festing.
98. *Ibid*.
99. Report on Bende, undated, in Calprof 10/3.
100. Report on Arochukwu District for the Quarter ending 30 June 1902.
101. See the paragraphs above which deal with the question of how to purify the Uzuakoli market.
102. No. E. Con. 136/1912 from H. Bedwell in Arodist 1/7/31.
103. Minute dated 28.9.21 by H. R. Palmer in the file: Diocesan Synod of Lagos, Conf. No. 80/1920, Kaduna Archives. See also memo. on the Eastern Provinces by H. R. Palmer attached to 3014/1921/90 of 19.6.28 in the file: 'Tribes of Nigeria—Inter-Relations 1591', Vol. I, Kaduna Archives, see also the file Lokoja Province Papers No. 159/1921, Kaduna Archives.
104. Comment by H. C. Moorhouse on Palmer's Minute attached to No. 2531/9 of 17.12.21 in the file: Diocesan Synod of Lagos Conf. No. 80/1920.
105. Owerri Province, Taxation and Native Courts Ow. 126/22, see para. 12.
106. See Grier's Report (paras. 55 and 58) in the file, Remarks by F. P. Lynch, etc. C. 176/19, Enugu Archives.
107. W. A. G. Ormsby-Gore, Cmd. 2744, *Report on a Visit to West Africa* (1926), p. 19.
108. See H. F. Mathew's first and second reports on the Aro in the file A.D. 635: Aro Sub-Tribes.

8. Igbo Land under Colonial Rule

Introduction:
　Owing to the present state of research into the history of the Igbo-speaking peoples, it is probably too early to attempt a definitive assessment of the impact of colonialism on Igbo society. A number of scholars, for example the late Professor J. C. Anene, the present writer, Dr. S. N. Nwabara, Dr. V. C. Uchendu, Dr. F. K. Ekechi, Dr. W. E. Ofonagoro and Mr. Johnson Nwaguru[1] have investigated aspects of the problem of British rule in Igbo land and thus enriched our knowledge of this period of Igbo history. Yet, it in no way belittles their achievements to concede that large sections of the problem remain to be investigated, especially the economic, social and psychological. And even with regard to the political aspect, probably the most intensively studied so far, there are many areas of Igbo land where definitive work is yet to be undertaken.
　The present essay in no way attempts to make good these shortcomings in current research into the history of Igbo land under colonial rule. It is a preliminary appraisal of the nature of British colonialism, its impact on Igbo society and Igbo responses to the challenges it posed. It depends largely, though not entirely, on a reinterpretation of published evidence and proceeds from the perhaps pardonable assumption that even though the details for different parts of Igbo land may differ, the broad trends are by and large similar.
　The argument is simple and may well be stated, to start with. It contends that colonial rule was a stunning and crucial experience for the Igbo, partly because of its aims and partly because of its methods both of which occasioned far-reaching changes in Igbo society. Then it argues that though colonial rule transformed Igbo society in many respects, it did not destroy Igbo identity or cultural soul. The Igbo have remained 'Igbo' in their attitude to and style of life; that is, while changing they were able to preserve their 'ethnic essence' because they were astute enough to use in their own way, the new institutions and

values introduced by colonialism. Thus, were it possible for an Igbo elder who died about 1850 to come back to life today, he would find the institution of the church strange, but he would understand why in many an Igbo village-group some sections would have Roman Catholic churches and others Protestant churches. Similarly he would find the western system of education strange, but he would understand why a man who had successfully put his child through this system 'has mouth' (*nwe ọnụ*) in village politics. In other words, it is a gross exaggeration to say that Igbo society and culture disintegrated or collapsed under colonial rule for, to a greater extent than has so far been recognized, the Igbo have sought to use institutions and techniques acquired through the link with the outside world established by colonial rule to maintain those values and styles of life which are intrinsic to their separate identity.

The Imposition of British Rule:

In British imperial law and by the accepted international conventions of the period, Igbo land became part of the British Empire when on 5 June 1885 the London Gazette ponderously announced to those who were equipped to hear it, that Her Britannic Majesty had taken the so-called 'Niger Districts' under her 'gracious protection'. Igbo land lay more or less at the centre of the Niger Districts. Had it been possible at that time to make this claim and its implications known to the staid and culturally arrogant elders of Igbo land, it would have provided them with the occasion for a good and prolonged laugh. And for over a decade or so after 1885, this claim continued to ring hollow as the different autonomous Igbo village-groups remained sovereign and independent each in its own affairs as well as ignorant of the political and legal claims and pretensions of Her Britannic Majesty and her consuls. This was still the period when Igbo elders could amuse themselves by contemplating the pun in the use of *Onye ọcha* for a white man and *onye ahụ ọcha* for a leper.

But at the same time these years were ultimately to prove crucial to the outcome of the imminent confrontation between British imperialism and the Igbo. For while the latter gloried in their remoteness from the coast which was being harassed and terrorized by British gunboats and consuls, as in their presumed ability to meet all foreseeable contingencies, the British gradually encircled them and established on their southern, western and eastern borders bases from which the subsequent assault would be made. Many years later Sir Ralph Moor in a memorandum on the process by which the British imposed their rule on the Protectorate of Southern Nigeria, argued that he and his predecessor, Sir Claude Macdonald, had made it their policy to tackle the problem of overthrowing the independence of the indigenous states gradually from the periphery. Firstly they would subdue the trading states of the Oil Rivers, imposing a new political, economic and moral regime on their peoples. Secondly they would subdue the peoples of the lower, middle and upper Cross River up to Ediba which lies opposite Afikpo. Thirdly they would conquer and occupy Itsekri and Edo land.[2] By the time all these were achieved the Igbo and their Ibibio neighbours found themselves out-flanked and virtually encircled.

The overthrow of the authority and independence of the Igbo village states was accomplished in two main ways—by so-called treaty and by war—though the distinction between subjugation by treaty and subjugation by war must not be pressed too far. Writing in November 1901 Sir Ralph Moor had said 'the natives must be made to understand that the Government is their master and is determined to establish in and control their country'.[3] This arrogant attitude had been at the root of British policy towards the peoples of their so-called 'Niger Districts' since 1885. It was the justification for the gunboat politics and diplomacy which by 1891 had brought the trading states under effective British control. In effect under the regime proclaimed by the British in 1885 only but a very thin line separated so-called peaceful negotiation from shooting war. This point needs to be further elaborated upon in view of the oft repeated claim that British rule in some of these communities was based on peace treaties.

In the first place negotiation properly so-called, leading to a peace treaty in which a people surrender their sovereignty and territory to another can take place only between two parties who at the beginning of the talks recognized each other as sovereign and equal, and as having the right to break off the negotiations or even to refuse to negotiate at all without incurring the threat of military chastisement or blackmail. But as already shown nearly a decade or so before the British got to the borders of Igbo land, they had proclaimed the people as subjects of their empire. In effect the treaties to which some Igbo groups were made to append their 'marks' were not treaties properly so-called because they did not result from negotiations conducted according to the above principle. Before the talks leading to their signature began the British had already arrogated to themselves the status of rulers, or 'masters' to use Moor's word, and saw the Igbo as their subjects.

In the second place the terms of a treaty with such far-reaching consequences for the future of one of the negotiating parties should be the result of discussions and bargaining between the parties. But this was not so. The terms were decided well in advance by the British, reflected only the British point of view, protected only British interests, though in their wisdom the British believed that indigenous interests were also protected. It was the contravention of this second principle that made some of the terms and claims of the treaties farcical and absurd. One example of this kind of absurdity could be given. Even though it is on record that invariably it was the British Officer who went to an Igbo community and invited its leaders to sign a treaty of friendship etc. with Britain, Article I of each of these treaties in all cases read:

> Her Majesty the Queen of Great Britain and Ireland & C, *in compliance with the request of the chiefs, and people of* .... hereby undertakes to extend to them, and to the territory under their authority and jurisdiction, Her gracious favour and protection.[4]

The contravention of the principle mentioned above also accounts for the fact that these treaties contained the same provisions in the same words no matter the Igbo state in question. This could not have been the case if each autonomous Igbo community had really been offered the opportunity to negotiate the terms under which it would allow the British into its territory.

In the third place the invitation which the British extended to an Igbo village to go into a treaty of protection with them was not in fact an invitation to choose between being annexed and not being annexed, but an invitation to choose between being annexed without bloodshed and being annexed by the opposite method. In effect the Igbo villages were not being invited to negotiate the end in view, but the means to an end already unilaterally decided upon by the British. That this was so is proved by the fact that in each case where the invitation was turned down, or it was considered unnecessary or not feasible to issue such an invitation, war naturally followed. The most outstanding instance of this in Igbo land was that of the Aro. Beyond that there was the case of Ihie and Asa who in 1896 refused to sign the treaty because it would involve them in the abolition of cherished customs. In his report on this matter A. B. Harcourt said 'I warned them of what the consequences would be if they continued in the practice'.[5]

A fourth reason why the distinction between the extension of British rule by treaty and by war should not be pressed too far is that, with regard to the form and character assumed by British rule, it did not make any difference whether an Igbo community was annexed by treaty or by war. In either case colonial rule meant for the village-group that:[6]

(i) It could not have access to any outside power except through the British.
(ii) Its juridical powers were severely curtailed. For instance its judicial institutions could exercise no authority whatever over 'British subjects and their property' or over other foreigners entitled to British protection.
(iii) It could not go to war with any neighbouring community to assert what it considered its legitimate rights since it was compelled to submit to British authorities all disputes with a neighbouring group which the two parties could not resolve amicably.
(iv) It was committed to subordinate its political institutions to the colonial power. As these treaties put it, each 'treaty town' was expected 'to assist the British Consular or other officers in the execution of such duties as may be assigned to them; and, further, to act upon their advice in matters relating to the administration of justice, the development of the resources of the country, the interest of commerce, or in any other matter in relation to peace, order, and good government, and the general progress of civilization'.
(v) It had to allow 'the subjects and citizens of all countries' to trade freely in its territory.
(vi) It had to allow christian missionaries to proselytise and practise their religion freely in its territory.
(vii) It had to abolish all customs and practices which the British found objectionable.

Had there been any real difference between annexation by treaty and annexation by war, then those communities which are usually said to have negotiated the terms under which they surrendered their sovereignty and independence should have been able to secure for themselves better conditions and wider areas of initiative than those which were conquered, thereby losing all rights.

With our argument thus established, the next thing is to examine briefly the application of these two different sides of the same policy-coin to Igbo land. In the period before 1900 British political penetration of Igbo land took place on two fronts. The first was the front stretching from Bonny to Opobo which brought the British to the Southern frontiers of Igbo land. The second was the Cross River which took them to Afikpo and Ikwo, the north-eastern frontier of Igbo land washed by that river. Between 1885 and 1899 the Royal Niger Company controlled the Niger waterway which should have led the protectorate administration straight to Onitsha and Asaba. From 1900 when the charter of that company was withdrawn, however, the administration came to exploit the access into Igbo land which the Niger waterway offered. As a result Oguta, Onitsha and Asaba became bases for advance into the Igbo interior. On the whole, therefore, there were three fronts along which British advance into Igbo land took place. Of these, the Bonny-Opobo front was certainly the most important.

In any case it was along that front that the first significant encounters between the administration of the Niger Coast Protectorate and the Igbo took place. By 1890 or so the states of the Oil Rivers had ceased to pose a serious threat to British imperial pretensions. In fact to such an extent had these states accepted British imperium, that British consuls came to see it as part of their legitimate duties to champion and advance the interests of coastal traders, especially of the Bonny and Opobo, in Southern Igbo land. Thus when in 1890 the Bonny traders complained of encountering, at Akwete, resistance to the expansion of their business, the Acting Consul, Annesley, mobilized his ill-trained and ill-disciplined constabulary for the purpose of teaching that Igbo state how unwise it was to stand in the way of the British or their friends. This first encounter between the British and an Igbo state in the Bonny-Opobo front ended in a victory for Akwete. Annesley and his forces, popularly known as the 'Forty Thieves', were routed with a number killed.

The following year, 1891, the administration of the Protectorate was put on a regular basis with Sir Claude Macdonald as High Commissioner and Consul-General. Among other things a regular force was raised as an instrument of British interests in the interior. In October the same year Macdonald took up again the unsettled dispute with Akwete. He visited the village state himself and discussed the outstanding issues with its leaders. Either because they were charmed by Macdonald's so-called diplomatic approach or because they were aware that in place of a lone consul they now had to deal with a whole administration, the Akwete elders proved conciliatory. They were in fact prepared to pay ten puncheons of oil as compensation for the Bonny trading establishments which they had burnt down in the course of the previous year's rumpus. The amicable contact which Macdonald established in 1891, matured the following year into a treaty of protection between Akwete and the protectorate administration.

From this British toe-hold at Akwete, officers of the protectorate started scouring the peripheral towns of Southern Igbo land, especially villages in Asa, Ndoki and Ngwa offering the people their usual alternatives of treaty or war, or, to use the delightfully alliterative phrase of General Faideherbe, 'peace or powder'.[7] Mr. Roger Casement, Acting Vice-Consul, was in Obohia in 1894 preaching this message. The following year Acting Vice-Consul G. R. Digan was in Obegu for the same purpose and succeeded in getting the elders of this village state to append their marks to one of his treaty forms. In 1896 the 'Akwete expedition' under J. R. V. Tanner and Mr. A. B. Harcourt traversed most of Southern Ngwa spreading the now stereotyped propaganda of the administration and collecting treaties of protection from village-states which allowed themselves to be bullied or blackmailed into appending their marks to the treaty forms. 1896 produced a particularly rich harvest of such treaties. Among the signatories that year were Oza, Obohia, Ohuru, Ohanko, Akanu, Ozata, Umuodo, Alaoji, Abala, Abaki, Mpopoiha, Akrika, Ogwe, Amupu, Ukebe, Ihie, Azumini, and Umuiku Iko. In 1897 Umunka-Aro, Asa and Obete signed similar treaties, to be followed in 1898 by Umuagbai, Azuogu, Maraihu, Okpuntu, Aba, Ihieoji, Umuocham, Ohabiam, Nnentu, Abayi and Umumba.

With these towns and villages on the southern fringe of Igbo land annexation through treaty was more or less the order of the day. Why this was so one cannot say for certain, but a few explanations could be hazarded. The Igbo communities here were in very close contact with the city states of the coast and thus through the Bonny and Opobo traders must have become fully briefed on the strength of the white man, including the fact that he was not over punctilious as to the means he adopted to achieve a desired end. In this regard the story of how Jaja of Opobo was tricked and done out of his kingdom was well known. In a place like Obegu there is extant a tradition to the effect that Chief Ananaba, the head of that village state at the time, went into the treaty of 1894 precisely because he was anxious to avoid suffering the same fate as Jaja. The British on their side soon found that the Jaja episode was well and widely known in the immediate hinterland of Opobo and Bonny and that it tended to undermine their credibility. From the same sources and in a similar manner these southern Igbo towns knew that to refuse to sign the treaty was to invite British invasion. The four decades or so of British gunboat politics in the Oil Rivers provided an awesome warning.

Furthermore, these villages knew that they had not only to reckon with the British but also with the coastal traders who had more or less become reconciled to their lot under the consuls. The coastal traders had in fact got to the point of using British power and influence to secure free and safe passage into such sections of their immediate hinterland which hitherto had been closed to them. The war against Akwete in 1890 already cited is a case in point. Even beyond that some of the coastal middlemen were now prepared to fight and die in the process of advancing British influence in the interior. Their leading citizens like Chief Cookey Gam of Opobo and Chief Dikko of New Calabar became employees of the Protectorate administration and operated, though ineffectively, as British Political Agents in southern Igbo land. Also in 1898 Opobo citizens enlisted in a motley levy raised by F. S. James, Mr. Murray and Mr. Roberts for an attack on the town of Ihie which had refused to allow the middlemen free passage through their territory. This role which the Bonny, Opobo and New Calabar traders now found for themselves under the new dispensation, on occasions helped to complicate the situation for the British. Because the coastal traders had become British agents, propagandists and employees, they became at times objects of suspicion by the southern Igbo towns. And it is not unlikely that some of the annoying problems which the British encountered in these villages derived partly from the opposition to the Opobo, Bonny and New Calabar traders who had meanwhile become the vanguard of British expansion.

Oral tradition also suggests that the ease with which some of the southern Igbo towns signed treaties with the British derived from their anxiety to use the opportunity of British expansion to free themselves from burdensome entanglements with their neighbours to the interior. Before British penetration in the 1890s the region of southern Igbo land was economically dominated by Aro traders and oracle agents. The result was that many of their dignitaries were indebted to Aro businessmen. A case in point, uncovered by Mr. Johnson Nwaguru, Archivist and a native of Ihie, was that of Chief Ananaba of Obegu. It is said that this man was ready to go into a treaty with the British because he hoped that by so doing he could renounce his enormous debts to the Aro and escape what would otherwise have been the obvious repercussion—an Abam raid.

However, when we talk of the readiness of these southern Igbo towns to enter into treaties with the British, that 'readiness' must be understood only in a relative sense. There is abundant evidence in the records and oral traditions of the people that there was usually some resistance to the signing of some of the treaties. And in any case the complex social and political circumstances of these towns were such that the British did not understand. This meant that on many occasions the advance by treaties ran into unforeseen and at times, insoluble problems leading to the adoption of the only other logical course— military expedition and blackmail. One or two examples could be given here. Reference has already been made to the fact that these towns at times sought to seize the opportunity of the British advance to throw off Aro economic control. Thus after going into a treaty with the British in 1892 the people of Akwete sought to force the Aro out of the trade of their land. Their ruling secret society, the *Qkonko*, passed a law banning all strangers from attending the market of *Ajala Qnwo* where they would have direct dealings with the Bonny and Opobo men. A wealthy Aro, Okori Torti, who ignored this law was subjected to a heavy fine.[8]

Similarly the town of Obegu whose Chief was heavily indebted to the Aro, and whose traders accused the Aro of profiteering sought also to exploit the advent of the British to push Aro businessmen out of their town. To this end they looted the wares of the Aro in their market and chased the men away. Furthermore relying on their treaty with the British the Obegu tried to escape time-honoured obligations enjoined by custom. They refused to surrender to Ihie, a neighbouring village state, one of their men who had murdered an Ihie man. Yet by tradition they were expected to do that, and in any case a few years before their treaty with the British Obegu had secured from Ihie an Ihie man who had murdered their own man. These complications in local politics, some of them the direct outcome of British presence, at times made the advance by treaty virtually impossible. On occasions the whole thing led to a situation in which one town adopted an overtly anti-British and anti-treaty attitude simply because its neighbour, a traditional or new-found enemy, had signed a treaty with the British. In the case discussed above, the Ihie (in spite of their own treaty with the British) joined hands with the Aro and all other villages opposed to Obegu and Akwete and organized an attack on Obegu, Akwete and the British. This type of complex local situation is part of the explanation for the fact that by the time they had finished annexing the towns of the southern fringe of Igbo land, the British had come to lose faith in the efficacy of advancing by treaty negotiations.

If advance by treaty into Igbo land made some, albeit slow headway on the Bonny-Opobo front, it made none whatever on the Cross River front. This was partly because the Afikpo and Ikwo were in no way disposed to entertain the messages and messengers of the Protectorate Government. These people had a warlike tradition in which they gloried and the institution—fairly well-integrated age-grade organizations—with which to prosecute wars. There was also the fact that depending on the Cross River waterway the British tended from the first to adopt there the same gunboat tactics which they had used to conquer or terrorize the Oil Rivers states. For one thing this meant that on the Cross River the British had the unflattering image of bullies and military blackmailers, an image which undercut the application of diplomatic methods. Yet advance by bombardment from the gunboats had severe limitations on the Cross River since the upper reaches of that river occupied by the Afikpo and Ikwo among others, were navigable by launches drawing up to 6' 6" for only a small fraction of the year. This meant that for the greater part of the year this method was inapplicable. But the British were already compromised by it. We thus had a situation in which the people could toy with the British by pretending to be of 'good behaviour' during the high water but defied them during low water. Finally by 1899, that is about two or three years after the British had bombarded their way close to Afikpo and Ikwo, the problems of this front came to be seen as just an aspect of the difficulties being encountered on the Bonny–Opobo front. It thus came to be argued that the real solution was to be found on this southern front. As a result the whole question of advance through Afikpo and Ikwo came to be subordinated to advance along the Bonny–Opobo front.

What was this great obstacle on the southern front? It was the Aro resistance to British penetration which the Aro saw as a threat to their trading and oracular business. As soon as the British moved into the hinterland of the Oil Rivers States or got as far up the Cross River as Itu, they had run into the ubiquitous Aro, but it was not until about 1896 that they came to see the Aro as holding the key to their penetration not only of Igbo land, but also of Ibibio land. From that date British officers operating beyond New Calabar, Bonny, Opobo and on the right bank of the Cross River started trying to get the Aro to append their marks to the usual treaty forms.

But this was not to be for various reasons. First, it appeared that British and Aro interests were in conflict to such a degree that they were unnegotiable except if the Aro were prepared to subscribe to a self-denying pact which would not only undercut their commercial activities, but also end their exploitation of the Long Juju Oracle. But this the Aro were not prepared to do. Second, the British had no clear idea who the Aro were, what was the basis of their influence and how far it went. In fact until about 1926, when the researches of the anthropologist H. F. Matthews came to their aid, they did not arrive at a clear appreciation of the nature and extent of Aro influence among the Igbo and the Ibibio. Meanwhile arguing from the ubiquity of the Aro, their commercial power and the fame of the Long Juju oracle which they manipulated, the Protectorate Government not only came to believe that the Aro ruled the Igbo and Ibibio interior, but that they inhabited the whole hinterland of the Oil Rivers lying between Onitsha and the Cross River. In the light of this erroneous belief the Government came to see every opposition to British penetration of the interior, whether beyond New Calabar, Opobo and Bonny or on the upper Cross

River, or beyond Oguta where the Royal Niger Company reported running into a mesh of local intrigue, as engineered and master-minded by the Aro. It was in this context that the eruption of the Ikwo on the right bank of Cross River came to be seen as one other incident in the anti-British campaigns of the Aro.

On many occasions the British were correct in reading Aro intrigue into the resistance they encountered. As already shown, the Aro were involved in the tangled events which obstructed treaty collection in the Ngwa, Asa and Ndoki region. The same was true among the Annang of the Kwa Ibo area and so on. But by applying this single explanation to all difficult situations which faced them in the interior the British often lost the opportunity of dealing with each case on its own merits. They also came to lose faith in advance by treaty. The thing to do, they came to believe, was to tackle the problem at the root—beat the Aro militarily and capture their 'imperial' headquarters. This conclusion was reached about 1899 and after that date we came to hear next to nothing about peaceful penetration. Every effort was now concentrated on the expedition against the Aro. With this all advance into the unknown interior temporarily ceased as attention was turned to collecting military and other intelligence from the bases already established beyond New Calabar, Bonny and Opobo, and on the Cross River. Indeed in this period the Aro Expedition was seen as the war to end all wars in Igbo and Ibibio lands, and it was organized on a scale befitting such a grand 'final solution'.

By 1900 the Royal Niger Company had lost all political power in Nigeria. Consequently its lower Niger territories (from Idah to the sea) were passed over to the Niger Coast Protectorate which was renamed the Protectorate of Southern Nigeria. The government of the latter thus inherited posts like Asaba, Onitsha, and Oguta where British influence was already consolidated by the Company. These came to constitute the third front of advance into Igbo land. And the plan of Aro Expedition showed this. According to the final plan of attack, there were to be four columns deployed as follows—two on the Cross River with bases at Itu and Unwana, one at Akwete on the Bonny-Opobo front, and one at Oguta on the Niger front. The expedition was launched on 28 November 1901 and lasted until May 1902. At the end of it 6,000 square miles of territory had been brought under British control, and that within the short period of five months.⁹ This immediately showed the superiority of advance by overt military action over penetration by treaty. It is not unlikely that this discovery had much to do with the fact that from then on the extension of British rule in Igbo land came to depend entirely on open war usually called punitive expedition or on the demonstration of military might usually described as military patrols.

There was probably another reason for the increased reliance now placed on military conquests or demonstrations. The Aro Expedition revealed that contrary to expectation there was no state of any great consequence in Igbo land with which if a treaty were negotiated, a sizeable territory would be brought under British control. On the contrary each tiny village-group was an autonomous polis which had to be dealt with separately. This of course raised the question of how best to economize badly needed time and manpower for other equally pressing administrative problems. To advance mainly by treaty would require a large army of political officers carrying wads of treaty forms tramping up and down Igbo land haggling with village elders who might not share, with the British Officers, the sense of urgency demanded by the job. On the contrary a patrol of 50 well-trained soldiers, armed with a maxim gun and repeater rifles, and led by a commissioned officer aided by a political officer, could in a week or so terrorize a whole district into surrendering their arms of precision and 'accepting' British rule.

In the light of these arguments, military expeditions which should have been the medicine of British imperial expansion in Igbo land, became its daily bread. As a result long after the Aro Expedition, in fact up to about 1917, military columns were marching up and down Igbo land terrorizing villages. One may not believe it, but it is true to say that it is virtually impossible to enumerate all the military expeditions and patrols which operated in Igbo land in the process of bringing the people under British rule. In 1902 there were among others, expeditions against Afikpo, Oboro and Uzuakoli, in 1903 the Umunneoha Expedition, in 1904 the Onitsha Hinterland Expedition and the Akwete-Owerri patrols, the Asaba Hinterland Expedition; in 1905–6 the Ezza, Ikwo, Noria, Ovoro, and the Ahiara (Bende-Onicha) Expeditions. In 1907 there were four, in 1908 the Niger-Cross River Expedition and so on till 1917 when Lenwe was conquered and the Awgu Division created as part of the effort to bring this people under control. In a real sense the imposition of British rule was a stunning experience for the Igbo. It was the first time in their history that an alien army marched through their land. The second time was to be when the Nigerian Army did so between 1967 and 1970 in pursuit, they said, of rebels.

But probably more rewarding than the enumeration of these expeditions and patrols, is the examination of the pattern of Igbo resistance to this massive British military challenge. From the currently available evidence[10] one discerns three main patterns of Igbo resistance to the British military challenge, and they will be dealt with here in an order which goes from the most overtly militant to the least so. Thus we have as our first pattern the response of those communities which were not prepared to go into any diplomatic negotiations with the British, and would not in fact receive British emissaries, but from the beginning reached out for their guns and matchets as their response to the presence of the white man in their territory. The second pattern emerges from the response of those communities which negotiated and talked with the British and their emissaries, hoping to keep them at bay by long and tedious palavers but which resorted to armed resistance only after they had become convinced that the British were determined to have their way at all cost. We have our third pattern from those communities which for reasons which will be dealt with later did everything possible to avoid armed encounters with the British, relying instead on magic and the intervention of their gods to drive the British back into the sea.

The first pattern is what we may describe as letting the guns talk. Our first example of this comes from the response of the West Niger Igbo to the threat which the advent of the white man posed to their society. This goes back to the days of the Royal Niger Company. Between 1881 and 1883 this company, then known as the United African Company, had established a trading post at Asaba following a treaty with the chiefs of the town. From Asaba it sought to penetrate the rest of the West Niger Igbo communities in search of trade, and at the same time made a pretence of exercising some sovereign rights over the people. This aroused the deep rooted hatred of the people for alien control as a result of which the leagues of youngman (*otu okolobia*) in the various village-groups came together and formed the *Ekumeku* secret organization, which was an underground movement of resistance to the British—trader, missionary and administrator alike. The term *Ekumeku* is untranslatable into English, but brings to mind such words as 'invisible', 'whirlwind', 'devastating', 'uncontrollable' and so on. The *Ekumeku* was able to obstruct the Niger Company's agents in the region beyond Asaba with such success, that the Company was forced to take the field against them in 1898 and impose an uneasy peace which lasted until 1900 when the Company was relieved of all political and administrative responsibility in Nigeria.

The Southern Nigeria Protectorate which now became responsible for the administration of Asaba and its hinterland inherited this obscure and explosive situation. As the British threat to the political independence and cultural identity of these Igbo village-groups grew in intensity with the establishment of Native Courts, the selection of local chiefs as agents of British rule and the establishment of mission stations, the cause for which the *Ekumeku* stood became more popular among the youths who were anxious to distinguish themselves in war in the tradition of their fathers. The society also became more ruthless in its treatment of opponents, especially of local people who were considered traitors because they served either the administration or the church or the traders in one capacity or the other. The *Ekumeku* would not negotiate or talk with the British administration or their agents partly because it was a secret organization whose members were supposed to be faceless and anonymous, and partly because the administration represented that alien control which the society was determined to root out of the West Niger area. The result was that the leading members of the West Niger Igbo communities would not answer to calls from touring political officers either because they were members of the organization, or because they feared severe reprisals from the society. In the same manner Native Court writs were openly and contemptuously ignored, while periodically these courts, mission houses and the compounds and properties of people who showed themselves conciliatory towards the British were wrecked and looted.

The British on their side did not understand the origin and character of the movement. At one time they thought it arose from these communities not having effective political institutions for settling inter-town disputes. As a result they dotted the entire area with Native Courts. At another time they thought it derived from these courts not being properly supervized and thus from the lack of effective contact between the people and the government. Consequently they urged closer supervision of the courts and more frequent tours by political officers. With this failure to understand what the movement was about, the British could not establish contact with it. The result was that meaningful peaceful negotiation never entered into the relationship between the *Ekumeku* and the Southern Nigeria Protectorate. In the event the guns had to 'talk' first in 1902 and again in 1909. Eventually the Ekumeku society was broken by repeated military defeats, incessant prosecutions and imprisonment by the Native Courts, proscription under the Unlawful Societies Proclamation No. 16 of 1905, and the use of the Collective Punishment Ordinance to discipline whole communities which entertained the activities of the society.

Our other example comes from the large and warlike Ezza group of the North-Eastern Igbo. By 1902 the British administration had established effectively at Afikpo to the south-east of the Ezza as well as in Obubra Hill further up the Cross River and from these places were making efforts to reach some understanding with the Ukawe, Qkpqsi, Ikwo and Ezza peoples around. But from the beginning the Ezza would not hear of the white man or go into any negotiations with his messengers. In March 1905 Major Crawford Cockburn, the District Officer for the Obubra Hill District, penetrated into the territory of the Ezza and their allies, escorted by a detachment of troops. The Ezza and their Achara allies ambushed and killed some members of the escort. Exploiting their ancient warlike reputation and the fact that they outnumbered most of the communities lying between them and Obubra, they either persuaded or bullied these to go into an alliance with them against the British. When the administration of the Cross River Division sent emissaries asking their representatives to come to a parley and state Ezza's grievances against the British they chased the emissaries out.

The Ezza used these emissaries to let the British know what they thought of the administration. Firstly, they asked the messengers to tell the British that the Ezza had heard how the Southern Nigerian Protectorate defeated the Aro and occupied their towns. This, they said, in no way overawed them for, they boasted, the Ezza were more powerful and more warlike than the Aro. Secondly, they asked the emissaries to tell the British that the Ezza people had never been ruled by an alien and would not now be ruled by one. In the whole wide world they recognized only the Heavens above and the Earth below. Midway between these two great forces the Ezza ruled supreme. Finally they told the messengers that if the British sent any more emissaries, the Ezza would cut off their heads and return these through the hands of those towns friendly with the administration. In this situation it was impossible to negotiate.

The result was that the British administration sent a military expedition against the Ezza who met force with force. Between 15 March and May troops of the Southern Nigeria administration were fighting in and around Ezza. The latter were beaten in various battles which lasted from 25 March to 16 May. The Ezza were greatly handicapped by the fact that their territory is open savannah land and this exposed them unduly to the devastating fire of machine guns. Furthermore, they were armed mainly with matchets, their traditional weapon, and could do harm only if they came close enough. But this opportunity they never had. Still it took days to break their resistance. As to their spirit subsequent events showed it was not broken.

The second pattern combined diplomacy and war. It has often been said that war is the continuation of negotiation by other means. The resistance of certain sections of Igbo land to the British threat conformed to this witty dictum. There was, for instance, the case of the Aro trading oligarchy which is probably the best known and the most written about of British encounters with Igbo resistance movements. By 1896 the British had consolidated their rule in the trading states of the Oil Rivers and the immediate hinterland and by so doing reached the southern outskirts of Igbo and Ibibio land where the Aro trading interests was the most important single force to reckon with. The Aro were determined to keep British interest out of this region to preserve their dominant role in the distribution of imported goods, to ensure the continuation of the slave trade which the British were anxious to abolish and to preserve the regime of the *Long Juju* on which so much of their influence and prosperity rested. The Aro saw British influence in three forms:

(i) the Opobo, Bonny and Efik traders who now started penetrating farther and farther into the interior to increase their profit and earnings which the activities of European traders in the area under effective British rule had diminished;

(ii) the missionaries who preached not only salvation but also social revolution through the abolition of many traditional institutions and usages;

(iii) the British political officer with his Native Courts and all that which would create conditions favourable to the Opobo, Bonny and Efik traders as to the missionaries. It was these three groups the Aro were determined to keep at bay.

Among the Igbo the Aro are noted for sweet, tortuous and double talk, a trait which could be useful in diplomacy, and the Aro used this to the fullest in their confrontation with the British from 1896 onwards. Both among the Southern Igbo (Ikwerre, Ngwa etc.) and among the Annang, British officers engaged in establishing friendly relations with various groups encountered Aro traders and agents from 1896 on and discussions on Anglo-Aro relations were held. On every occasion the Aro showed themselves prepared to talk and in this way the Protectorate Authorities were able to know what were Aro objections to the extension of British influence. But at the same time the Aro took other measures to instigate different communities to resist British advance. Where these methods failed they threatened the people with visitation from their Abam and Ohaffia allies. On the Cross River, in particular, the Aro showed a willingness to negotiate with the British agent, Chief Coco Otu Bassey, the conditions on which friendly relations between them and the British could be established. They were even prepared to attend in 1897 a meeting arranged by Coco Bassey on the orders of Sir Ralph Moor, the High Commissioner, to iron out existing differences. Eventually Moor defaulted as he was preoccupied with Benin affairs. The Aro delegation stayed at Itu 'for about a fortnight during which they were entertained at the expense of Government'. In spite of what may be considered the shabby treatment from the High Commissioner, they were ready to attend a similar meeting in 1898 on the initiative of the Protectorate Government.

But this preparedness to talk notwithstanding, the Aro remained implacable in their resistance to British penetration. By 1899 it had become clear to Moor that the Aro could not be brought under his administration by diplomacy. After this relationship between the two took a turn for the worse. The British began planning for a military expedition against the Aro who on their part intensified their efforts among the Annang, the peoples of the Upper Cross River and elsewhere to detach those who had gone into treaties with the Protectorate Government from the British alliance, to cajole or bully fence-seaters into militant resistance to the coastal traders, and the British and the missionaries, and to build up a wide-ranging alliance of offence and defence against all alien intruders. Some of those who proved unresponsive to Aro overtures were attacked and looted with the help of Abam and Ohaffia head-hunters. By mid-November 1901 the British were ready to take the field against the Aro who appear to have been well-briefed on the warlike preparations against them through their network of spies and agents. Then just a few days before the expedition set out the Aro led a band of Abam warriors to the town of Obegu and sacked it. They also threatened the town of Akwete, which was a sub-district, but were deterred by the presence of British troops. At Obegu the raiders took time to destroy the government rest house and to break the water casks which District Commissioner Douglas had assembled for the use of the Aro Field Force. Was this a pre-emptive strike on the part of the Aro? Or was it an attack provoked by developments in local political and economic relations unconnected with the impending expedition? Probably it derived from all these causes. In any case within a few days of the Obegu raid, on 28 November 1901, the Aro Field Force started operations against the Aro whose home town was captured on 24 December the same year.

The other example is provided by the resistance of the Afikpo village-group. In the course of the widespread demonstration of British power which followed the capture of Arochukwu, one of the columns of the Aro Field Force had penetrated as far north as the Afikpo village-group. The people who were badly shaken by the disaster that had befallen the Aro thought it wiser to submit than to resist. In fact while fighting was still going on around Arochukwu, they had sent emissaries to the political officer in charge of Ediba district to protest their loyalty and friendship to the British. Similarly when the column that came into their territory said the government would want to establish an administrative centre at Afikpo and asked for land for this purpose, the people promptly obliged.

The operations connected with the Aro Expedition ended in the first quarter of 1902. But by August the same year the Afikpo had gone back on their agreements with the Protectorate Government. They would not allow a government post to be established in their territory and would not even receive messengers sent to negotiate with them. They went so far as to attack those of their neighbours, like the village-group of Anoffia, which showed pro-British leanings and to ambush British reconnoitring parties and touring officers who visited their general area. So militant and defiant had the Afikpo become that none of their neighbours who were friendly with the government would take messages from the white man to them. According to one British officer, the chiefs and the peoples of these towns had grown so 'timorous and nervous' in anticipation of attacks from the Afikpo that 'they were living on the roads ready to run in the case of attack'. In anticipation of British reaction the Afikpo took measures to fortify and guard all the major approaches to their town, including the Cross River landing place through which they suspected the British might want to infiltrate troops.

On 28 December the British expeditionary force against Afikpo set out from Unwana. Making use of the intelligence collected from some frightened women of Ndibe town, the troops out-flanked the main defending Afikpo forces and attacked them from the rear. In the grass land terrain in which the battle took place, the Afikpo found themselves gravely handicapped in trying to crawl through the grass to get close to the British forces using repeater rifles and field guns. The result was that they suffered appalling losses. Still, said the commanding officers, they showed 'great courage'. Even after having been dislodged from their entrenched positions, they retreated to the defence of their homes. At this point the troops deployed the millimetre field gun and with its devastating fire scattered the Afikpo forces and seized their main towns. Once again after a period of diplomatic manoeuvring, the guns had been brought in to decide the issue.

The third pattern combined diplomacy and magic. Much of the information on which the reconstruction of this pattern of resistance is based comes from oral tradition collected by the author. Magic had always occupied an important place in the armoury of the African warrior, and the Igbo warriors of the first two decades of this century who had the unenviable duty of defending their communities against better armed British forces, had to rely on this to a large extent. The result is that magic played some important part even in the first two patterns of resistance sketched above. There are copious traditions about the efforts made by the famed medicine men of the different communities to stir up local gods and the ancestors against the British. Some towns would not rely on local doctors and magicians alone, but would travel long distances to invite more widely famed medicine men to strike the invading troops blind, or to scatter them with swarms of bees, to make their guns backfire or make the Igbo warriors bullet-proof. The fact is that since the gods and the ancestors were regarded as forming part and parcel of the society, they were called upon to help defend it against the alien invaders.

As already mentioned even in those communities in which the resistance to conquest was overtly militant there were attempts to harness the occult forces which ruled the Igbo cosmos to the defence of the old order. Among the Ezza, for instance, this effort not only preceded the fighting, but went on for years after the British had consolidated their presence in the entire Abakaliki Division. This was revealed by an incident which happened in 1918 and was recorded by Robert Cudjoe, a Ghanaian (then a Gold Coaster) who worked at Abakaliki as an interpreter. On one night there was a heavy rain during which thunder struck the soldiers' camp causing extensive damages and some casualties. According to Cudjoe some die-hard Ezza resisters who were his friends rejoiced openly before him, attributing the disaster to the work of their medicine men and the intervention of their ancestors. They were confident, they said, the white man would eventually be driven out of Abakaliki by these occult forces.

But apart from the above, there were many Igbo communities whose resistance to conquest consisted of making a diplomatic surrender to the British forces while devoting all their energies and resources to mobilizing the unseen forces of their society to do their fighting for them. The scholar working on this topic will hear from the elders of many Igbo communities how their people made a show of surrendering to the invading forces only subsequently to expel them from their communities through inflicting on the troops all kinds of epidemics. Some say the soldiers were forced to move camp either because they were attacked by jiggers or swarms of crabs and toads, or by diarrhoea and vomiting, or by some such malady.

There was for instance the case of Uzuakoli. This village group was visited by a military expedition towards the end of 1902 because the British said it was the den of slave dealers. But just before the troops entered the town, the elders consulted and decided not to offer open resistance. If the British had been able to conquer the Aro, the Abam, the Ohaffia, Edda and so on, they argued, they did not see how their town could fare better than these anciently famed warrior clans had done. Thus as the troops entered the town, they were met by bands of dancing women who said they were happy the white man at last thought it fit to visit them. Meanwhile the men had erected shades for troops in the central local market and provided food and water.

This diplomatic surrender, however, did not save Uzuakoli from humiliation. The leading elders were called out, bound hands and feet and left in the sun until all the Aro and other slave dealers in the town had been surrendered. If this were not done, they were informed, the town would be razed to the ground. Now to treat the elders in this brutal fashion was bad enough. But among the Igbo there is nothing more humiliating than to be forced to surrender strangers within your gates to their enemies. The stranger, *mbịanbịa* or *ọbịa*, was entitled to protection even at the expense of the life of his host.

All the Aro and other slave dealers were surrendered and were subsequently led away by the troops. After this, said my informants, Uzuakoli assembled all the reputed medicine men from the neighbourhood who prepared some medicine and buried it in the town square. This medicine proved so powerful, they say, that till today no white man can prosper at Uzuakoli. To the action of this medicine, they attribute the fact that all the British mercantile firms which early in this century established at Uzuakoli subsequently pulled out because their produce buying and all other business failed. The economic historian would attribute this to the fact that Umuahia, just twelve miles away to the south, is a more strategic centre for assembling the produce of the neighbourhood and so expanded at the expense not only of Uzuakoli, but also of Bende, the Divisional headquarters. Many more examples of resistances like Uzuakoli's can be given from other parts of Igbo land, especially from the Onitsha, Awka and Orlu areas visited by the Onitsha Hinterland Column of 1904 without any show of open resistance to the invading troops.

In summing up Igbo resistance to British military conquest, one observes that the pattern of resistance adopted by each community could be related to the structure of their society and the circumstances of the time. In communities like those of the West Niger Igbo, where the resistance was championed by a secret society, it is understandable that negotiation played little part. Also the Western Igbo had first to deal with the worst and most ruthless kind of white man before coming under the Protectorate of Southern Nigeria. The Niger Company's record of dealings with the peoples of the Lower Niger is probably one of the blackest in our history. It can therefore be understood if the Asaba hinterland would have nothing to do with them and if the people carried this policy of non-fraternization even to their dealings with the colonial government. It was not easy to distinguish between the Niger Company's agents and the European political officers. They were all whites and at times made similar demands. It is also pertinent to mention that these communities had a long tradition of resistance to alien rule and control from Benin. The existence of the well-organized associations of warrior young men which fought the British can be accounted for in terms of this earlier resistance which had taught the people the basic lessons of how to deal with the 'alien' imperialist. The influence of Benin had thus helped directly and indirectly to rationalize the social organization of these communities and the process of mobilization.

With regard to the Ezza the circumstances were similar. The need of this community for land was insatiable and this meant that for centuries the Ezza had been engaged in fighting their non-Igbo neighbours from whom they seized all the land they needed. This created a fighting tradition which not only ensured that the young men were well organized for offence and defence, but which also made the people proud. With such a tradition they could not be brought to surrender their independence by negotiation.

The Aro on their side could afford to indulge in endless negotiations even when they had no intention of giving in to British demands. This was because at the time the British were talking of the Aro as if Arochukwu lay just beyond Akwete or Itu, it lay in fact beyond easy reach of the forces of the Protectorate. There was therefore time to talk and they talked for five years. Also as expert traders the Aro were used to long and tedious haggling which did not always have to lead to the realization of the desired goal. The Afikpo on their side first tried diplomacy when they thought the British had not come to stay. When they discovered their mistake, they organized for war and their society, with its different grades of young men's associations inured to war and head-hunting and with each grade anxious to achieve some fame, was well placed to fight back and they did.

With those who tried tactical surrender while mobilizing the occult forces against the British, there were also good reasons. They had watched many of their neighbours make heroic stands and lose. This taught them that they could not beat the white man militarily. In this regard the abject military defeat of the warlike Cross River and North-Eastern Igbo communities, which were anciently famed for war and had the organizations for waging it, was sobering to many. There was also the fact that many of these other Igbo groups were not as well-organized for war as the Eastern and Western Igbo. Young men's societies were not that cohesive, nor had they recent and intoxicating traditions of martial achievement. In the light of all these they tended to rely more on their native doctors and the unseen forces that ruled their world.

Igbo resistance to British conquest lacked epic events like those that marked the Asante campaign, the Benin expedition and Lugard's Burmi campaign in Northern Nigeria, though that is not to say that it was lacking in heroism, resourcefulness and doggedness. In fact on this matter the picture of the Igbo which emerges from the available records is that of a heroic and determined people. In 1902 Major H. L. Gallwey, political agent Aro Field Force, reported that 'not only did the Aros have no intention of allowing the white man into their country, but... they thought they were strong enough to prevent him ever getting there'.[11] The following year, 1903, that is after the might of the British had been demonstrated in the Aro campaign, an Igbo village state told Bishop James Johnson 'Go tell the white man, we are ready for him'.[12] It was surely not without cause that after his peregrination through Igbo land the Bishop remarked that the fighting spirit of the people 'is not easily broken (despite) the vastly superior strength of the foreign power that has assumed to itself the Government of the country'.[13] The oral traditions reveal that each village state, until it actually came face to face with the might of the imperial power remained very confident in its military might and rather contemptous of the white man. This is probably the explanation for the fact that when the British conquered village 'A' its neighbours at times accounted for British victory in terms of 'A's stupidity in not taking the one precaution or the other, rather than in terms of British superiority.

The fact that the British occupation of Igbo land was accomplished through almost innumerable little military campaigns is to be explained not by Igbo lack of fighting spirit, but by the lack of the institution or the tradition for large scale military combinations. The absence of an Igbo state comparable to Asante or Benin meant that there was no authority to muster Igbo resistance to British conquest into one mighty heroic stand. The fragmentation of authority and society meant that each autonomous unit fought its own war of independence on its own and lost it in its own way too. But in the long run this fact was to be a source of strength to Igbo resistance to British conquest. It meant there was no single authority whose defeat would place all Igbo land at the feet of the alien conqueror. Every bit of territory, therefore, had to be fought, or bargained, for separately. This took more time and more energy and was very exasperating to the British. Long after the much fancied Fulani, Kanuri and Yoruba empires had settled into a smug acquiescence in British rule, the British were still wheeling military columns round and about Igbo land in pursuit of 'naked savages'.

Administration and Politics

The structure of colonial administration in Igbo land was not basically different from what it was in either Yoruba land or among the Edo and Ibibio-speaking peoples; or for that matter in Northern Nigeria. But with regard to the politics which took place within that structure, especially, at the level of local government, Igbo land presented peculiar problems and challenges which in time won for its inhabitants an undeserved reputation for ungovernability—if not for anarchy. Here we shall examine first the emergence of the administrative structure and then its performance.[14]

To present the matter simply, we shall see the history of the colonial administrative structure in Igbo land as falling into two main epochs. The first covers the period from 1891 to 1905, that is the years of the Oil Rivers (from 1893 Niger Coast, and from 1900 Southern Nigeria) Protectorate. In much of this period questions of administrative structure and policy were decided upon almost entirely on the basis the political, social and geographical realities of the Oil Rivers coast, with these decisions being subsequently extended to the Igbo and their Ibibio neighbours of the hinterland without a definite effort to adjust structures and policies to the different circumstances of these peoples.

This first epoch was that of Divisional Administration pure and simple. By this is meant that all the areas brought under control or thought to have been so, were grouped into divisions each of which was more often than not further divided into districts. Each divisional administration was directly responsible to the local head of the colonial government who until 1900 was designated Commissioner and Consul-General but who after that date was called the High Commissioner. By 1896 or so there were three such Divisions in the Niger Coast Protectorate. These were the Eastern, Central and Western Divisions with headquarters at Calabar, Bonny and Warri respectively. The Eastern Division overlooked Ibibio land or could be better described as the coastal base of that territory. It was from there that British penetration of Ibibio land and the Cross River area was largely accomplished. For Igbo land the important Divisions were Central and Western. The Central Division formed the springboard from which the British jumped into most of East Niger Igbo land. Akwete, the first Igbo village state to be made an administrative headquarters (in 1897 when it became a sub-district with a Vice-Consul in charge) was part of the Central Division. The Western Division, on its side could be regarded as the coastal base of the portion of land between the Niger and Yoruba land, that is including the West Niger Igbo. We could see here the beginning of the process which ended in the administrative and political partition of Igbo land first, between the Western Region and the Eastern Region, second, between the Mid-West Region and the Eastern Region and third, among the former Mid-West, the former East Central and the Rivers States.

In 1900 when the Niger Coast Protectorate acquired the lower Niger waterway, that is from Idah to the coast, which was formerly under the control of the Royal Niger Company, a number of administrative changes became necessary, leading to some adjustments in the boundaries of the divisions. First the Cross River Division was created, with headquarters at Ediba on the left bank of the river. This meant detaching the affairs of the upper Cross River from those of the Eastern or Calabar Division. With the conclusion of the Aro Expedition and the administrative consolidation which followed, the Cross River Division came to comprise Arochukwu sub-District, Bende District, Afikpo District and Obubra Hill District. The other important aspect of this reorganization from the point of view of the Igbo was the setting up of administrative headquarters near Oguta and at Asaba, these coming under the Central Division which also embraced the Akwete sub-district. From this grouping of Igbo sub-districts and districts along with non-Igbo districts and sub-districts it is quite clear that the colonial administration never considered administering the Igbo only in ethnically homogenous units. This remained the case until the end of colonial rule when the policy was passed on as a legacy to the nationalist rulers of Nigeria who have ennobled that lack of policy into a policy for preserving national peace and integrity. Meanwhile as military expeditions and patrols scoured and scourged Igbo land, many more administrative headquarters were set up at important Igbo centres. Particularly noteworthy was the fact that towards the end of this epoch Onitsha replaced Asaba as administrative headquarters. As more Igbo territory to the east of the Niger was conquered, the advantages of Onitsha as a commercial centre had become more and more manifest, while the artificial importance which the Niger Company had vested on Asaba started waning.

The epoch of purely Divisional Administration came to an end in 1906 with the amalgamation of the Protectorate of Nigeria with the Colony and Protectorate of Lagos. This affected the structure of colonial administration in Igbo land just as it did in Ibibio and Edo lands. The most important administrative innovation of this phase was the provincial system. The fact is that in the very early days of British colonial rule in these parts, it was considered necessary that each European officer should have wide enough powers to cope with the many emergencies which were bound to arise in connection with the imposition of British rule. To this end divisional, and even district political officers had wide powers and were given direct access to the head of the colonial administration. Secondly, in those early days the extent of territory under effective control was very much limited which in turn meant that the divisions were few in number and that the Commissioner and Consul-General could easily have direct access to them. In fact at no point during the first phase demarcated above did the divisions number more than four. In this situation it made sense that each divisional officer should have access to the highest local head of British colonial administration. In fact, this arrangement had the extra advantage that the Commissioner and Consul-General (from 1900 High Commissioner) knew of all important developments in each division.

But as more areas of Southern Nigeria came under effective control these arguments tended to lose their force. It became necessary to curtail the powers of divisional officers as emergencies tended to become few and far between. To this end a senior officer had to be placed between the divisional officer and the High Commissioner to serve a number of purposes. He saved the High Commissioner from being inundated with administrative minutae from the divisions which now grew in number. He also ensured that divisional officers cleared with him all important actions they contemplated taking. This arrangement was good for the divisions also since it tended to speed up administration more than would have been possible if all the many divisions of this new period had to obtain clearance on every important matter from the High Commissioner. On the other hand it put a rein on the misuse of power by the divisional officers.

It was probably these considerations that led to the introduction of provincial administration into the new territory which emerged as a result of the 1906 amalgamation. Under this system all the divisions of the colony and Protectorate of Southern Nigeria were grouped under what would today look like three monster provinces—Lagos or Western, Warri or Central and Calabar or Eastern Provinces with headquarters at Lagos, Warri and Calabar respectively. For our present purpose only two of these provinces—Central and Eastern—come into the discussion. The Central Province included, in addition to the Edo and Western Ijọ, Urhobo and Itsekri, the Igbo-speaking peoples west of the Niger area as well as much of what later became Onitsha, Udi and Nsukka Divisions. The rest of the Eastern Igbo were included in the Eastern Province.

Below the Province there were the Districts. In the course of the reorganization many more districts were created in Igbo land. The administrative units situated in the Igbo areas included Bende Arochukwu, Afikpo, Abakaliki, Ụmụduru (later Okigwe) Owerri, Aba, Ahoada which were in the Eastern Province: and Onitsha, Agbor, Asaba, Ọka (later spelt Awka) and Aboh which were in the Central Province. The last three units were mere sub-districts.

With the amalgamation of 1914 the provincial system was extended and given a specifically Lugardian interpretation. Lugard considered the three pre-1914 provinces of the South rather cumbrous and inconsistent with the drive for efficient administration. He believed that the relatively smaller provinces of the North were much more satisfactory from this point of view. Consequently he split the Western, Central and Eastern Provinces into nine new provinces, with the Igbo being divided between the so-called five eastern provinces—Warri, Benin, Onitsha, Owerri, Calabar and Ogoja. In some sense this was a slightly neater arrangement since no Igbo group east of the Niger was included in any province west of the Niger. But that is probably all one can say for the new arrangement from the point of view of giving the Igbo political and administrative unity under the new dispensation as was the case with many other peoples.

The West Niger Igbo came under Benin and Warri Provinces and were given two administrative divisions—Aboh in Warri and Asaba in Benin. At first there was no province devoted entirely to the Igbo. The Onitsha province, though predominantly Igbo, contained many non-Igbo peoples—like the Igala and Idoma. Thus the Onitsha Division included Igala elements, the Okwoga Division was the administrative centre of the Nsukka Igbo and then the Idoma. The Awka and Udi Divisions of Onitsha Province were entirely Igbo. The Owerri Province again, though predominantly Igbo, included the eastern Ijọ, Ogoni, Abua and so on who were not Igbo. It started off with four Divisions—Owerri, Aba, Degema and Okigwi, with the non-Igbo elements in the Degema Division. In time two other Igbo divisions—Bende and Ahoada—were carved out of these four earlier units. The Abakaliki and Afikpo Igbo were included in the Ogoja Province which started off with only three Divisions—Ogoja, Abakaliki and Obubra.

Subsequent reorganizations amplified this situation. The redemarcation, in 1918, of the boundary between the Northern and Southern Provinces got the Onitsha province disembarrassed of its Idoma and Igala elements. Onitsha thus became, except for the small Eteh enclave in what later became Nsukka Division, the only province which was entirely Igbo until 1947 when the Rivers Province was created to cater mainly for the non-Igbo elements of the old Owerri Province. But again this arrangement still saw a large slice of Igbo territory—the Ikwerre with centre at Port Harcourt—being carved out of the main Igbo core. Here was the beginning of the present Rivers State. However, to go back to the reorganization of 1918 and of the years immediately after, Onitsha Province in time emerged with five Igbo Divisions—Awgu which was created in 1917 after the Lenwe military expedition, Awka, Nsukka which started in 1918 (after the break up of the Okwoga Division) as Obollo Division but in 1922 acquired its current name, Onitsha and Udi. The Arochukwu, Ututu and Ihe Igbo were included in the Calabar Province.

A few things might be said about the personnel who ran this administrative system. The top echelon comprised white officers who up to 1899 were known as Vice-Consuls and from 1900 as Commissioners. With the reorganization of 1914, officers placed in-charge of provinces came to be called Residents (instead of Provincial Commissioners as hitherto); while those in charge of divisions and districts came to be known as Divisional and District Officers. These white officers were supported by a cadre of African staff. For the first three decades or so of colonial rule in Igbo land, the African staff were made up almost entirely of aliens, that is non-Igbo educated Africans—Efik, Ijọ, Sierra Leonean and Gold Coast elements. These men occupied positions as low down in the administrative hierarchy as the Native Court Clerk service. In fact they dominated all junior and middle range positions which demanded a certain degree of literacy in English. The explanation for their dominance was that the missions started working amongst them about half a century before the British penetration of Igbo land. By the time the latter event took place, therefore, they had raised a generation or two of men who could read and write English of sorts and who were in great demand for staffing junior positions not only in the government but also in the missions and commercial firms as clerks, interpreters, messengers, technicians, teachers, police, labour gang drivers and so on. Only the Onitsha and Asaba Igbo amongst whom the missions started work from the 1850s had by 1900 or so produced educated sons who could compete with these 'aliens' for the junior government positions in Igbo land.

The first thirty years of British colonial rule in Igbo land thus saw the Igbo being also subjected to what might be called the sub-colonialism of an educated non-Igbo African elite. Those were the golden days of the Pepples, Jajas, Hallidays, Shaws, Cudjoes and so on who through the control of the junior colonial service established petty tyrannies and ran a reign of terror and blackmail virtually without the knowledge of the

European staff. Their depredations which survive very vividly in oral traditions are hardly referred to in the surviving official records. Some of them, especially the district interpreters, the chief and court clerks wielded so much power and arrogated to themselves so much authority that they survive in oral traditions as district commissioners. The positions which these men built up for themselves started being seriously eroded only from about the 1930s when educated local Igbo youths, helped by pressure from their chiefs and peoples, began edging their way into the junior administrative service.

The division of Igbo land into districts, divisions and provinces turned out to be an event of reolvutionary proportions for the people. For one thing it was the first time in their history that any area as large as the district, division or province was being administered as a unit. Hitherto the largest administrative and political unit was the village-group, with the clan (Jones's tribe) being largely a cultural and ideological union of autonomous village groups. Through the impact of district, divisional and provincial administrations, the Igbo came to have a vision of areas of social and political co-operation larger than the village-group or even than the clan. From sharing the same district and divisional officers, as the same resident (or Provincial Commissioner), neighbouring Igbo groups developed that new sense of inter-relatedness which towards the twilight of colonialism blossomed into those Divisional and Provincial Unions which played a vital role in the social, economic and political development of Igbo land.

But, to give the full picture, it is needful to point out also that while creating new unities, the district, divisional and provincial idea also introduced its own divisive element. People incorporated into one district, division, or province invariably saw themselves, in true Igbo fashion, as counterpoised against, and in rivalry with, those in the next district, division or province, just as in traditional Igbo culture every lineage was counterpoised against, and in rivalry with its neighbour, as was also every village with its neighbouring villages, every village-group with its neighbouring village-groups and every clan with its neighbouring clans. In Igbo land today, for instance, one of the greatest divisive factors is the distinction between the old Owerri and the old Onitsha province Igbo. For, unfortunately, the boundary between these two provinces appeared to have run along the lines of minor but significant cultural differences.

Contrary to popular misconception this administrative boundary did not coincide with the dialectal boundary for the Udi, Nsukka and Awgu whose dialects are closer to Owerri, than to Onitsha, were included in the later province But just like in traditional culture, these ideas of contrapuntal relationships and rivalry were also in many respects a blessing in disguise, since they made for happy mutual emulation and healthy competition in development.

If, as already contended, the divisional and provincial system was revolutionary for the Igbo, the system of local administration which buttressed it was probably even more revolutionary, for it was at this level that British colonialism got involved in a head-on collision with Igbo culture and values. In Igbo land, as in many other parts of British colonial Africa, the system of local government was that popularly known as Indirect Rule. It was indirect rule in the sense that it sought to use indigenous Igbo institutions for the government of the Igbo. Unfortunately, however, so subtle and complex were indigenous Igbo institutions of government, and so uninformed and impatient for quick results were the British, that the effort led to many mistakes on the part of the government and to untold hardships for the people.

As already pointed out, the British formulated their basic ideas for the government of the Niger Coast Protectorate at a time when they had effective control only of the communities of the Oil Rivers whose institutions they understood only in part. It is thus not surprising that the version of indirect rule which the British first applied to Igbo land (i.e. from 1900–12) was that elaborated in the dim light of only a perfunctory knowledge of these coastal societies. This version was centred around an institution known as the Native Court. According to the theory of the system the Native Court comprised the traditional chiefs of the communities which fell within its jurisdiction. It was also a multi-purpose governmental institution in the sense that it exercised judicial, legislative and executive powers. Finally the Native Court was to be a medium through which what was best in British civilization would combine with what was best in Igbo civilization to give birth to a new Igbo culture. Thus in exercising its legislative and judicial powers, for instance, the Native Court was to apply Igbo customary law modified to agree with British sense of justice and natural law. But the snag lay in the fact that while the British knew what was their sense of justice and their conception of natural law they knew next to nothing about Igbo custom. Similarly while the Igbo knew their own custom they knew nothing about that elusive thing called British sense of justice nor did they know what the British thought natural law was.

The first Native Court to be established in Igbo land would appear to have been that instituted at Akwete in 1897. By that time the basic structure and practice of this system of rule as it obtained up to 1912 or so would appear to have been established. There were at this time two kinds of Native Courts—the Native Council which was a Native Court sitting at divisional or district headquarters where it was presided over by a white political officer, and the Minor Court which was a Native Court sitting at the divisional or district antipodes and which therefore had to be presided over by any of the African members elected by his comperes for a period of three months. Each court had a clerk who recorded the proceedings and issued the numerous writs (patterned after those of the British courts) without which its proceedings and actions would be null and void. The British saw the establishment of Native Court as the logical follow-up to the annexation of any group whether by treaty or by conquest.

The above system elaborated on the coast, when extended to Igbo land, ran into almost innumerable problems a few of which only can be mentioned here. In the first place Igbo village-groups had no chiefs of the kind who, without violating indigenous political practice, could be made to occupy the position mapped out for members by the law establishing the Native Courts. As a result, even assuming that it was possible to discover all the titular heads of Igbo village-groups and to appoint them members of these courts, they would immediately become artificial political figures, suspect to their people and unable to exercise any real influence or authority unless supported at each turn by the punitive capability of the colonial power. But what was worse, it was not possible in most cases to discover the titular village-group heads and to appoint all of them members of these local government bodies. This was so partly because of ignorance and suspicion on both sides. On the part of the Igbo they misunderstood the British demand for their chiefs partly because they had no such personages and partly because they were suspicious of the new rulers. The result was that on many occasions Igbo communities pushed forward nonentities, common rogues or slaves as their chiefs in the belief that these were going to be killed or enslaved. One can thus imagine the consternation in the villages when these scums of society came back to their people with certificates or warrants appointing them chiefs over their betters.

On occasions when the titular village heads were discovered, they were found to be too old to be able to carry out the duties expected of chiefs in those rough early days of colonialism. The British also soon found that there were too many autonomous village-groups in Igbo land and that if all the village-group heads were recognized as chiefs colonial local government would soon be in the hands of a whole army of elders who could not all be effectively supervised or adequately remunerated. Yet the British insisted on the close supervision of all native functionaries since they believed this category of people were incapable of doing anything efficiently except if closely supervised by white officers. Furthermore the colonial officers, anxious for quick and big returns, were often too impatient to make the detailed inquiries which would lead to the appointment of other than slaves and rascals. Consequently they on occasions used the rule of the thumb and appointed either those who had been useful to them or who appeared to them to possess commanding presence and ability. Yet, it must be said, that in spite of these difficulties some of those who were appointed members of the Native Courts turned out to be traditional village heads—though, on a number of occasions, this apparently happy coincidence came about by mistake.

Apart from the difficulties associated with the selection of the personnel of the Native Courts there were others. One had to do with the conduct of those who had by whatever the process come to be appointed Warrant Chiefs (as the members of these courts were called). They saw themselves, as their people also saw them, as holding new appointments under the colonial government, rather than as the representatives of their communities performing the same functions as the village councils did before the advent of British rule. Because of this they waxed tyrannical as well as corrupt. Another problem had to do with the conflict between the Native Courts and Igbo traditional law and custom. The colonial government expected these courts, as already said, to follow traditional law and practice as long as these were not in conflict with British ideas of justice and natural law. But the members and their people in general tended to see the Native Court as the white man's institution not necessarily bound by indigenous custom. Its general paraphernalia, procedure and so on convinced both members and non-members that it was an alien institution. As a result its decisions and legislations were often seen as being necessarily in conflict with the peoples cherished ways and so were resisted.

The fact is that indirect rule, as practised in Igbo land before the amalgamation of 1914, represented the imposition on the Igbo of an institution elaborated for the communities of the Oil Rivers. On closer analysis the Native Court is seen to have been designed to bolster up the authority of the heads of houses of the coastal Ijo and Efik whose position and authority were at the time being undermined by many novel forces. These house heads had in the eighteenth century and early nineteenth exercised fairly extensive powers over their peoples and slaves and had played a key role in assembling local goods for sale to visiting white merchants and collecting from the latter wares for distribution in the interior. The new colonial government hoping to consolidate what remained of this authority and to use it decided to organize the house heads into councils. It was this contrivance for the coastal states among which some sort of chieftaincy obtained that was imposed on the Igbo of the interior whose institutions were significantly different. Nor was this the only measure designed originally for the coast which was imposed on the Igbo. Another classic case was the extension of the House Rule Proclamation (after 1906 Ordinance) to the Igbo among whom House Rule did not obtain.

The year 1912 appeared to hold out promises of new beginnings for Igbo land in the area of local administration for it saw the appointment of Sir Frederick (later Lord) Lugard as the head of a new administration which was to include both the Colony and Protectorate of Southern Nigeria and the Protectorate of Northern Nigeria. Lugard had a wide-ranging African experience derived from service in East and West Africa. There was thus a chance that he was aware of the variegated political traditions and systems of African peoples. Furthermore his African service had been broken by a spell in Ceylon and thus there was also a chance that he would come back to Africa with fresh visions and fresh ideas. But these apparent promises of 1912 were to be disappointed leading, in Igbo land, to terrible mistakes and a bloody tragedy. The fact turned out to be that Lugard had already been ensnared by a particular interpretation of indirect rule, that is by the version of it which he, and those who succeeded him in Northern Nigeria from 1906, had evolved in the Fulani emirates. The key to this version was the use of a big chief as the centre of the system. Other important features included the separation of executive from judicial powers at the local level and the imposition of direct taxation as the main source of revenue for paying the personnel of the local government and the cost of local development.

When Lugard came back to Nigeria in 1912 he judged the local government system of the Southern Protectorate by the above emirate standard and not surprisingly found that it fell far short of his expectations. In the two year period 1912-14 he spent time pouring vitriolic criticism on the Southern system and with the amalgamation proceeded to replace it with the Northern system. This he did by extending to the South the Native Courts, the Provincial Courts, the Native Authority and the Native Revenue Ordinances of Northern Nigeria. But Lugard and his Ordinance immediately found themselves running against the intractable political realities of Igbo land. The result was stalemate. If indirect rule in Igbo land before 1914 was never a very tidy affair, it became even untidier with the administration of these rather excessive doses of Lugardism.

The confusion which reigned in Igbo land following the attempt to implement these Lugardian reforms can easily be illustrated with a discussion of some of the conditions which arose with the application of the Native Courts and Native Authorities Ordinances. Lugard hoped to reform the Native Courts of Igbo land by reducing their membership which he considered too high. He believed that a few court members, each of them representing a larger unit than the village-group and sitting more often as a member of the bench, would be under more effective European supervision and would more quickly evolve into tribal chiefs. One of these, he hoped, would then evolve into a paramount chief or at least a district head. To this end he issued, early in 1914, orders instructing the political officers to drastically reduce, each in his division, the number of chiefs recognized by government as court members. However, for administration pure and simple a much larger number of chiefs were to be recognized. In application the order ran into serious trouble and was promptly abandoned. But still the tradition of keeping the number of chiefs low, irrespective of the demands of the people for the recognition of more chiefs survived. As a result many village-groups, some of them those who formerly had their own warrant chiefs, had by the 1920s no recognized chief of their own. They were thus brought under the authority and influence of Warrant Chiefs from neighbouring, and therefore rival, village-groups whose control they openly resented or even ignored.

As part of the same programme of reform of the Native Courts, Lugard instructed that instead of rotating the presidency of the courts, as was the case formerly, a permanent president should be appointed for each. Through official support and encouragement, it was hoped, each such president would grow into a sort of 'chief of chiefs', wielding authority not only in his own village-group but also in those of his chiefly colleagues. Again the application of this policy had not as much as gone even half-way, when it ran into the stiff resentment of the chiefs and their people who considered the whole idea alien to their culture. Consequently it had to be abandoned.

Similarly, the objective of Lugard's Native Authority Ordinance, as applied to Igbo land, was to speed-up the evolution of powerful chiefs. The point was that to Lugard the ideal Native Authority was the chief, as in the emirates, rather than the chief-in-council or the council of chiefs. So anxious was Lugard to implement this policy that he ordered the creation of paramount chiefs and sole native authorities in Igbo land. Chief Idigo of Aguleri, for instance, came to be appointed a subordinate native authority, while Chief Igwegbe Odum, an Aro fugitive from justice, was made the paramount chief of the Ajali Court area in Awka. As each of these appointments soon failed to justify Lugard's hopes, the experiment was eventually abandoned. Yet to the ambitious ones amongst the warrant chiefs this tradition died hard as each of them, from material and prestige reasons, schemed and strained to be made a paramount chief.

The Native Revenue Ordinance which would have imposed direct taxation on the people was not even introduced under Lugard because his residents and divisional officers opposed the move. They considered it impracticable because that ordinance contemplated conditions which did not exist in Igbo land. They also feared widespread disturbances among the Igbo.

Probably what is important for our purposes here is not the details of these reforms, many of which were not tried at all, and many of which were tried and abandoned. Instead what is important is the general situation which Lugard's period of office (1912–19) created in Igbo land. In this regard a few developments are worthy of emphasis. Firstly, Lugard's rule saw the end of the era when administrative questions were seen in the light of coastal realities and were dealt with as if the Igbo had evolved the house system of rule like the Ijọ and Efik. But then it ushered in the period during which administrative issues in Igbo land were seen and tackled in the light of ideas and systems formulated for the Muslim emirates of Northern Nigeria. This era lasted from 1914 to 1951. Secondly by the time Lugard's term came tó an end the structure and practice of local government in Igbo land was in a very untidy state. In spite of an effort at uniformity, few aspects of the system were actually uniform. Nobody knew for sure whether official effort was to be directed towards the artificial creation of petty tyrants known as paramount chiefs, permanent presidents and native authorities. As part of this confusion the European service was divided between those who pressed Lugard's ideas and those who considered them pernicious and out of touch with conditions existing in Igbo land and some other places. Some officers in the latter group felt slighted by the disparaging things which Lugard said about the pre-1914 system and by the way he set about changing it without consultation with them.

Thirdly, it was not only the system or the European officers who were affected by what had happened between 1900 and 1919. The people, who themselves were the guinea pigs, were also affected. For one thing, as time went on, the Warrant Chiefs and the Native Court staff became more corrupt and more oppressive. Also as time went on those who were not Warrant Chiefs saw that court membership was a lucrative job contrary to their earlier fears. As a result many people came to scheme for appointment as warrant chiefs. Some of these came from the senior lineages of their village-groups who now started feeling that it was their birthright to represent their unit in such matters. Some were simply ambitious, go-ahead men who wanted to exploit every opportunity to line their pockets.

No sooner did Lugard retire from Nigeria than the administration came to suspect that all was not well with the system under which the Igbo were being governed. Two reports by the Department of Native Affairs in 1922 and 1923 confirmed this suspicion, and showed that the system was inefficient, corrupt and oppressive. They traced the root of the problem to the fact that the system was untraditional. In their view the Igbo should be governed through their indigenous institutions, that is a proper indirect rule should be instituted. To this end, they recommended that effort should be made to ensure that all who held native court warrants were traditional village-heads and that Native Court boundaries coincided with ethnic boundaries. From 1924, the greater part of administrative effort in Igbo land was directed towards this end. The investigations, which were to prepare the way for these reforms, were making a rather indifferent and uncertain progress when about 1925 it came to be decided that direct taxation was to be imposed as part of the projected reforms. The arguments, which were Lugardian in any case, were that the taxation would provide the revenue for the local administrations in Igbo land to do positive good through public works and development; that the process of assessing and collecting the tax would encourage the traditional leaders of the people to come forward and assert their authority.

Unfortunately these largely theoretical arguments did not work out as nicely as they sounded. The Igbo hated direct taxation for various reasons—it sounded like tribute to a conquering power, it made holes in their pockets, it was untraditional and was preceded by the counting of adult males and the assessment of wealth which they both feared and misunderstood. These fears and misgivings were not yet dispelled when it came to be believed that because the colonial government had successfully taxed men in 1928, it was about to embark on the taxation of women also. The upshot was the Women's Riot of 1929-30 which rocked large sections of Igbo and Ibibio land and frightened the British to the extent that they used machine gun and rifle fire against unarmed women. Scores of women demonstrators were left dead and many more wounded. If the Riot failed to achieve the abolition of direct taxation, as the women had hoped, it at least brought home to the colonial administration the utter bankruptcy of the system of local administration which obtained in Igbo land before 1929. It did not, however, shake the faith of the government in Indirect Rule as a system.

On the contrary, it came to be argued that the failures and difficulties which had dogged the steps of the British in Igbo land derived from the fact that the indirect rule applied there was, to use Professor Ayandele's phrase, 'counterfeit indirect rule'. If it had been proper indirect rule, it was contended, the result would have been uninterrupted political and material progress as was believed to be the case in the Northern Provinces. Therefore, the Riots induced not a change of policy but a change of approach. The hitherto erroneous belief that indirect rule in Igbo land must necessarily mean chiefly rule was abandoned. By experience and through research it came to be realized that political power in an Igbo polity was diffused throughout the entire social organism rather than concentrated in a single family or individual or institution, and that the closest approximation to a sovereign authority in an Igbo community was the council of elders. Between 1930 and 1938 or so the administration spent most of its time and energies investigating for each area the character and composition of these councils, as well as constituting clan councils and clan courts into the new instruments of indirect administration in Igbo land.

For the first few years of this reform optimism reigned in official circles. Annual and occasional reorganization reports carried glowing accounts of how enthusiastic the elders and their people were about the new system, how the latter had helped to resore the confidence of the Igbo in the British and how far all this eased the problems of tax collection and assessment. Some particularly sanguine officers even believed the new system had helped to end corruption and other baser forms of the abuse of power in local government. But it soon became clear that this optimism was misplaced. The new Native Authority Councils and Courts were no more traditional than the Warrant Chief Courts. The clan never was, in pre-British days, an administrative and political unit, yet that was the role it was made to fulfil after 1930.

From this fact other problems arose. Firstly, since each member village of a clan had to be represented on the new clan councils, and courts, these bodies became rather unwieldy, impossible to direct and supervise. The administration complained that meetings were noisy and the members at times too ignorant or apathetic to respond to the instructions and guidance of the political officer. Some people who, under the British rule, had become somewhat used to one man representing a village-group or even a clan ridiculed a system in which everybody was a chief. The members themselves were sadly disappointed when they discovered that because of their numbers what they got as remuneration for their pains was always paltry. Yet they had rejoiced initially at being called upon to be court or council members because they hoped to gain as much material reward and prestige from membership as the warrant chiefs had enjoyed from being members of the abolished Native Courts. To supplement their paltry official takings, they resorted to taking 'presents' from clients and all. So it did not take long before the old cries of inefficiency and corruption went up again. And to make matters worse, the Second World War came in 1939, just as the new institutions were being brought into existence. The war depleted the available British staff and this in turn led to inefficient supervision and inadequate guidance.

Still the administration pressed on courageously, though fruitlessly, along its chosen path. It encouraged the clan councils to federate so as to pool their financial resources and be able to undertake visible development projects. Some federated, giving rise to such units as Mbano and Mbaise. But many refused to federate owing to local jealousy and limited political vision. The administration also gradually came to abandon its insistence on every council or court member being an elder. Educated youths, if chosen by their people were admitted. By 1948 or so this latter policy became what was known as the 'Best Man Policy'. This meant a further, and more drastic reorganization of personnel of the courts and councils. The policy allowed villages to choose their representatives according to any criteria acceptable to them, rather than necessarily on the basis of traditional rights to political office or leadership; that is they could choose the man they considered best qualified to represent them. In effect this was the end of the idea of indirect rule which was understood to mean rule through traditional rulers. In crowded and rowdy village-group meetings, held in the presence of district officers, people chose their 'best men', known in parts of Igbo land as *Eze Okacha mma*.

But this turned out to be only a stop gap for by 1951 the whole pretence of using traditional machinery in one form or the other had to be abandoned as unworkable. Among the reasons for this was the breakdown and ineffectiveness of the post-1930 system, popularly known as Native Administration. Another reason derived from developments in the arena of nationalist politics. The educated elements who constituted the vanguard of the nationalist agitation did not find enough scope for action or employment in the Native Administrations. Also, in principle they regarded indirect rule or native administration with suspicion as a special device for slowing up the political evolution of the African colonies. As a further concession to this group the colonial administration imported a modified version of the British County and Local Council system under which members were chosen by election. It was under this system that Igbo land attained internal self-government in 1957 as part of the Eastern Region of Nigeria. Later still the County Council system failed—most of them being hopelessly corrupt and uncertain as to what their duties were precisely.

Thus at the level of local government the history of Igbo land under colonial rule was a checkered and turbulent story, as systems evolved for areas of dissimilar social and political conditions were imposed on the people in the name of a uniform system of indirect rule. Though the Native Courts and Councils were closer to the people than the district, divisional and provincial institutions, they still failed to meet all the vital needs of the people for governance and social development. By and' large they dealt with events which took place in that fringe zone where the new British ways touched on the people's life. This left out those large areas of indigenous life which were largely successfully kept beyond the ken of the overly harassed colonial administration. Over such areas the traditional village councils, the age-grades, secret societies, oracles and medicine men, which the British wanted to drive out of existence, ruled supreme.

Economic Changes

As in the political sphere, colonial rule introduced many changes into the economic life of the Igbo. But it is not generally recognized that many of these changes were the results more of the general conditions imposed by colonial rule than of deliberate economic planning by the British. In fact, in most of its economic attitudes the colonial regime could be described as conservative rather than radical, except probably in the matter of currency changes. In the area of transport and communication where the regime again adopted radical and drastic policies, the initial intention was more political and administrative than economic. It is this which explains the fact that the most vital roads in colonial Igbo land originated as links between administrative headquarters (provincial and divisional headquarters) rather than between the leading market and production centres. It was largely through sheer persistence and by the superiority of the facilities they offered, that these roads came in time to be the main arteries of commerce in Igbo land. Still the importance of many of the main centres which they link remains even today artificial and political rather than organic and economic.

With regard to its economic policy in Igbo land, therefore, the colonial government could be said to have followed faithfully, almost till the passage of the Colonial Development and Welfare Act after the Second World War, a policy defined by Sir Ralph Moor in 1899 as one of 'supervision and control'.[15] By this he meant firstly, creating the general conditions of peace and improved communication which would enable the people to harvest their natural resources for sale to European mercantile companies; and secondly, laying down and controlling the conditions under which these resources are collected and marketed. To examine the application of this policy to the Igbo and its impact on their society, we shall discuss briefly the following items each of which is large enough for full-blown research: transport and communication, the currency question, the produce trade, agriculture and changes in land-holding, and the slave trade under colonial rule.

As already mentioned above, the transport and communications revolution in Igbo land, that is the displacement of the old and tortuous bush-paths by modern roads and railways, originated largely as a political and administrative event. The major roads in each division came into being in the first months of the establishment of the division, and were designed firstly to link the divisional headquarters to the Provincial headquarters and to older divisions and secondly to link the divisional headquarters to the Native Court centres. Through the need to recruit and supervise mass labour gangs for constructing the roads, the European officer in charge of the division was also offered the opportunity to spot the leaders of the various communities and associate them with his government, as well as to give the people as a whole a first taste of the meaning of *pax Britannica*. The administrative character of these roads becomes all the more manifest when it is emphasized that the headquarters which they linked were chosen not from economic considerations, but for political and health reasons—geographical centrality, availability of good water supply, fresh air and so on.

Since much of the labour for the construction and maintenance of these roads (until 1927 at least) was political labour, that is was unpaid for, the building of the roads did not even offer the usual economic opportunity for injecting capital into a community through public works. By the time payment for road labour was introduced, the most important of the network of modern roads in Igbo land had been constructed. When therefore Alan Burns in his *History of Nigeria* claimed that:

> Thousands worked for the government (on these roads), and were paid in money with which they were able to purchase for themselves both necessaries and luxuries, returning to their villages... to show off recently acquired fineries to their less sophisticated brothers[16]

it can only be assumed he was not writing for Igbo land or for those other portions of Southern Nigeria where direct taxation was not introduced until 1928.

With the railway, however, the situation was different. It was the discovery of coal at Enugu and the need to evacuate it cheaply after mining, that led to the construction of the railway that traversed Igbo land. Again, though railway labour came partly from conscripts raised by chiefs and partly from volunteers, it was paid for. This meant that unlike the roads, the construction of the rail line from Port Harcourt to Makurdi offered an opportunity for injecting some money into Igbo society with the usual recognized economic benefits—rise in purchasing power, more returns for producers of food, the expansion and reinforcement of the cash nexus and so on.

But no matter how they came about, the transport and communications revolution had far-reaching economic consequences for the Igbo especially with the increased availability of wheeled traffic from the 1920s. At first the advantages, especially from the new roads, lay in the fact that they tended to shorten distances between the towns they linked as well as increase the safety of travellers. On the old bush paths it was relatively easy to cut travellers off from their base and destination unless they took the elaborate precautionary steps demanded of traders and long distance travellers in the pre-British days. But on the new roads frequented by the agents of the new administration and along which such centres of authority as the Native Courts, divisional headquarters, police and military posts were situated, travellers were relatively safer, with the margin of safety increasing as the colonial regime got more deeply entrenched. All this meant increased flow of goods from regions of over-production to regions of great need.

With the railway there was another economic impact which became immediately obvious once the line traversed Igbo land. This was the fact that the European commerical companies which hitherto hugged the coast and the river banks, because they wanted cheap transportation, now penetrated the Igbo interior establishing posts and depots at vital points on the railway line. As a result the railway stations and halts became produce buying points of varying degrees of importance. Among such points were Port Harcourt which in addition was the port of evacuation, Aba, Ụmụọba, Ụmụahịa, Uzuakọli, Ovim, Afikpo Road, Agbani, and Eha Amufu. Each of these became, as it were, a 'port' with the surrounding towns and villages as its hinterland. They served as centres for collecting local produce—mainly palm oil and palm kernel—and for distributing the new cash currency, stockfish, tobacco, kerosene, cloth, enamel wares, metal gadgets, gun powder, spirituous drinks and so on. This meant that where hitherto only a small class of seasoned traders could get to the distant markets where local produce was sold to the big middlemen and imported goods obtained, now most people had this opportunity brought more or less to their door steps. The increased participation in the distribution and assembling of goods which this implied certainly quickened the tempo of economic life and increased the flow of goods. Also by reducing the distances travelled by people to get to important assembling and distributing centres, the penetration of the interior by the European firms meant a saving for the Igbo in labour which could be deployed in other areas of economic and social activity. Unfortunately owing to the very perfunctory manner in which the colonial government kept its statistics and owing to the general illiteracy of the Igbo at the time, leading to the absence of personal and family diaries and records, these significant changes cannot easily be quantified if at all.

Still, it must not be thought that the economic transformation occasioned by the transport and communications revolution was immediate, at least not for all portions as a study of the conditions in the 1920s and 1930s will amply demonstrate. In Southern Igbo land the road and rail revolution soon established itself. Here the effect of it on the produce trade was enormous, and the story of the growth which the revolution occasioned is probably best told in the rapid rise and expansion of Aba and Umuahia as important commercial centres. In this region the road and railway systems found no great difficulty in establishing themselves partly because they were not in competition with any long established system of water or river transport and partly because much of the land here is rolling plane. With reference to the question of river system, the only important river that washes Southern Igbo is the Imo which was not navigated to any great extent in the past and still is not. With the penetration of the interior by European, Bonny and Opobo trading interests, it was found to be navigable by large canoes only up to Owerrinta on the Aba–Owerri road. This point also became an important produce buying centre and expanded fast. It is likely that it would have outdistanced Aba and Owerri on either side of it but for the fact that these two places were in addition administrative headquarters and thus had the prestige and advantages which that status conferred.

The fact that most of Southern Igbo land is rolling plane was of importance in this regard as it occassioned a revolution within a revolution—the bicycle revolution. It is because of the nature of the terrain that the men and women of this zone used the bicycle in a radically new way, as the main means for moving produce to the rail-heads and other buying points. They were thus able to bring to the rail-heads the products of the remotest parts of their area untouched by motor roads. Even with the expansion and improvement of motor traffic, the bicycle has remained for this zone a vital means of transport—not only for moving goods but also for moving men from place to place. And the people have developed the art of riding bicycles to a fine point. The average man or woman from this part of Igbo land can still be seen transporting eight or more four-gallon-capacity tins of oil on his or her bicycle with practised ease. The bicycle revolution embraced the southern portions of what was the Okigwi Division where the great Obowo people live. The Obowo, depending largely on their bicycles, have extended their trading activities to as far north as Awgu, and to some parts of the Cross River plain where they have excited jealous envy from local traders for their intelligence and hardiness as businessmen.

In Northern Igbo land the situation was slightly, if not radically, different. Here the land is hilly, which meant that bicycles had only very limited use. Thus until the widespread use of motor traffic, the movement of produce remained largely the affair of carriers. The roads for long were not in great use. Thus for parts of Nsukka it could still be said in October 1934 that 'except on the P(ublic) W(orks) D(epartment) road motor traffic is scarce at present, but all roads are in constant use by foot passengers and are much appreciated by market-goers and other local travellers'. This meant that three decades or so after the establishment of British rule in Igbo land, some parts were nowhere near a reasonable exploitation of the advantages offered by the new roads. Another important point regarding the limited exploitation of these roads in Northern Igbo land, which hardly obtained in Southern Igbo land where the land was well drained or at least the soil different, was the fact that many of the roads were dry season roads since they traversed clayey soils which became easily water-logged in the rains. In the Nsukka Division in 1929, for instance, out of a total of 210 miles of roads maintained by the Native Authorities, only 124 miles were all season roads where 86 miles were dry season roads.[17] The percentage of dry season roads would be even much higher in the Abakaliki and Afikpo Divisions judging from the nature of their soil.

There was also another important factor which for a long time prevented the full impact of the road and railway revolution from being felt in Northern Igbo land. This was the competition between the railway and the ancient river systems of these parts. The Anambra and Niger river systems drain Northern Igbo land to the west while the Cross River drains it to the east. Trade on these river systems was long established indeed, and force of habit kept many of the traders looking that way in spite of the arrival of the railway. To the force of tradition was added the fact that, because river transport was cheaper than railway transport, the European businessmen who had their posts by the rivers could afford to offer higher prices than their counterparts on the railway. It was these factors that made the impact on Igbo economy of the rail line north of Okigwe quite limited indeed. Parts of Awgu, Udi and Nsukka Divisions and all of Onitsha Division looked towards the Niger, while the trade of the Abakaliki and Afikpo Divisions flowed towards the Cross River. Every year the annual report of the Nsukka Division carried a wail for the European factories at Eha Amufu because they were not worked to capacity as a result of competition from the above river systems. Competition from the latter was, however, only the beginning of the woes of the railway in Igbo land. The critical point was to be reached only much later when the Igbo used the roads and the five-ton truck not to feed the railway, as enjoined by the economic pundits, but to compete it.

Just as the innovations in transport and communication came to be appreciated and exploited only slowly, so it took time for the British coinage to assert itself against indigenous and earlier forms of currency—salt, cowries, brass rods, copper wires, manillas and so on. British coinage was introduced officially into the Niger Coast Protectorate in 1898 and equivalent rates worked out between it and those other forms of currency so as not to occasion a sudden breakdown in business transactions. Naturally the Igbo, like their other Nigerian neighbours, resisted the introduction of the new coinage partly out of habit and partly because it was not seen to have the ritual and other associations which over the centuries, had been built up around the old forms of money. But as in other matters the British forced the change down our peoples' throats, using threats and economic arguments to advance their position. The Aro expedition of 1901-2 had as one of its aims the introduction of the new coinage into the Igbo interior. The troops and carriers involved in the expedition were paid in British coins and they in turn forced the people to accept the new coins in payment for all the purchases they made or services they exacted. Every other expedition followed this example while the Native Courts which were scattered all over Igbo land did everything possible to force litigants to pay fees and fines in the new coinage. All those who worked for the government, the trading houses and missions were also paid in the new coin. For all these reasons the new coin started gaining ground against the old currencies.

In spite of its advantages, not the least of which was the fact that it had the backing of the all-powerful colonial administration, it took the new coin over four decades to drive out the old currencies. The reasons for this were many. Firstly, the new coin could not give as low units as the cowry, for instance, could give. The lowest unit of the cowry was the single cowry shell which made negotiation and calculation very exact. But the lowest unit of currency introduced by the British was the $\frac{1}{2}$d more popularly known in the records as the nickel. Now by the 1930s or so when the value of the penny had fallen somewhat, it was worth 30 heads of cowries, i.e. 180 cowries. This meant that the nickel was worth 45 cowries—still a very large unit as far as the Igbo were concerned. Secondly, the old currencies continued to carry ritual associations which kept them in demand. For example they were for long the media for meeting the financial side of marriage contracts. They were also required in sacrifices and so on. In the Nsukka area, the brass rod remained the legal tender in marriage contracts until the late 1930s. The cowry did not disappear from local financial negotiations until the late 1940s.

A great deal is often claimed for the introduction of European currencies into Africa. But with our closer knowledge of pre-colonial African societies and the role of cash in their economies, many of these claims now ring hollow and old fashioned. The present writer has discussed this matter with many Igbo elders who attained manhood in late nineteenth century (i.e. pre-colonial) Igbo land and experienced the currency changes introduced under British rule. And it is striking that none of them has said that English coinage is superior to indigenous coinage because it is easier to carry—one of the arguments which the colonial regime used to justify the change. They have all, on the other hand, complained against the relative rigidity of British coinage. They have also attributed to it the crisis of mounting inflation which they were subjected to when they came to be forced to pay ½d for items for which formerly they paid one 'head' of cowries or less.

In the area of currency change, as in the improvement of transport and communication, the colonial government at least took positive steps to alter existing conditions for the better. But with regard to the produce trade, the main bastion of the export economy of the Igbo, the government did next to nothing to improve existing conditions. The palm trees from which the palm oil and kernel were extracted grew wild over much of Igbo land, with particularly heavy concentrations in Southern Igbo land which along with Ibibio land belong to the palm belt of West Africa. Furthermore the Igbo had, long before the European advent, evolved fairly efficient methods for extracting the oil and the kernel. The result was that by the time European rule was imposed, the industry was already sufficiently well established to meet the demands of the commercial companies for oil and kernel. Here, more than elsewhere, was an ideal situation for the application of Sir Ralph Moor's modest policy of 'supervision and control'. There was little positive the new-comers could teach the Igbo concerning the industry.

Direct British intervention in the area of produce industry thus remained to the end very peripheral. At first this was limited to two areas—stimulating the people's taste for European products and luxuries so that the desire to make the money with which to purchase the imported goods would drive them to pay more attention to the commercial exploitation of their palm groves; and then encouraging them to preserve their palm groves by discontinuing the tapping of palm trees for wine since trees so tapped hardly ever bear palm fruits. To these ends, the government encouraged the commercial firms and the coastal middle men to penetrate the remote villages to display European fineries. They also made the Native Courts to pass bye-laws against the tapping and felling of palm trees. The companies, especially the United Africa Company and John Holt & Co. Limited, responded by establishing produce buying stations along the main river systems and the railway where they stocked and displayed an odd assortment of European wares. From these stores local middlemen bought consignments which they took to the areas remote from such company depots. The campaign against the tapping of palm trees for wine proved largely ineffectual as it took no account of the people's established habits and tastes.

The next significant action taken by the colonial government in connection with the produce industry was not exactly calculated to benefit the Igbo producers of palm oil and kernel. This was the introduction of produce inspection in 1928. For decades the European companies had complained against the tendency amongst the producers and the middlemen to adulterate the oil and kernel through the addition of waste matter, or in the case of palm kernel through soaking it in water so that the kernels would swell up and give a false impression of their actual size. There is no doubt that the middlemen and the producers resorted to such tricks on occasions. But investigation conducted by the present writer indicates that they did so as a response to similar tricks played on them by the European firms. Such tricks, it is claimed, included tampering with the sizes of otherwise standardized casks and bushels so that they could hold much more produce than the accepted standard measures on the basis of which payments were made. Whichever was the case the government decided in 1928 to come to the rescue of the European traders by introducing produce inspection which was designed to ensure that a given measure of oil or kernel did not contain more than a given percentage of waste matter. At the same time the government abolished the buying of produce by measure in favour of buying by weight.

Both innovations exposed the Igbo produce dealers to worse exploitation than hitherto. The poor middleman had to bribe the produce inspector or the latter would reduce all his strivings to nullity by declaring his produce adulterated. This in turn told on the primary producer who had to be bullied into accepting low prices because his or her produce 'contained' too much waste matter. Similarly the introduction of buying by weights entailed hardship for middleman and producer alike. At the time most producers and middlemen were illiterate. This meant that while most of them could say when a cask or bushel was full, only very few could tell the weight registered by their produce when it was placed on a scale calibrated in stones, pounds and ounces! The middlemen and producers reacted to these innovations at first by holding back their produce hoping that these innovations were only temporary. But after months of such holding back action, they came to realize that they really had no alternative to conforming with the demands of the law in this regard.

From the 1930s the government made some effort to influence the future of the produce industry through the Native Administrations (N.A.s). On the one hand they got the N.A.s to establish nurseries for palm seedlings from which local farmers were supplied at between $\frac{1}{2}$d and 1d for each seedling bought for planting. The effort proved largely nugatory partly because it was not prosecuted energetically and partly because the people were not convinced as to its necessity. They still had enough palm groves, had their traditional methods of raising palm trees which they continued to find satisfactory, and in any case were not aware of the competition from Malaya which the colonial government blamed for the depression of the produce industry in Nigeria. If anything, the producers and middlemen blamed the erratic behaviour of the produce trade on the 'wicked' white man who, if he were 'less wicked', would make more money available so that the price of oil and kernel would rise. Added to these were two points made by Mr. L. T. Chubb in his *Ibo land Tenure*. The one was that no Igbo man had the amount of land to make palm plantation profitable. The other was that the plantation trees did not necessarily give better yield than trees raised in the traditional manner.[18]

The other measure which the government took in this period to improve the lot of the produce trade was the introduction of oil mills and presses as well as nut cracker machines. The arguments for this were typically European, ignoring in its totality the African point of view and situation. Among other things it was contended that these new gadgets would speed up the processing of palm fruits, save labour, and improve the quality of the oil and kernel. No doubt this was so, but the would-be revolution in the produce industry soon ran into a series of unsuspected troubles arising from the local situation.

The most important of these was the determined opposition of the people. On the one hand the women did not want to hear of the new gadgets which they saw as a threat to their entrenched rights. By custom most of the palm trees belonged to the men who also cut the fruits when they were ripe. But the women picked the fruits from the stalks, pounded these in the mortar and extracted the oil. The man claimed whatever oil was in excess of that needed for household use, while the woman took the palm nuts for her pains. She cracked these and took the proceeds from the sale to meet her own needs. Now the establishment of the oil press and nutcracker would offer the men the opportunity to circumvent the women and claim all the proceeds by carrying the bunches of palm fruits to the press. Furthermore the women were concerned that shortsighted and listless menfolk, and there were such, could, in the bid to make as much money as possible from their palm groves, forget or refuse to leave any bunches from which would be extracted the oil needed for household use. Thus a situation could easily arise in which ancient families with palm groves would subject themselves to the indignity of buying palm oil from the market—a situation which an Igbo proverb aptly describes as *onye nwere nkwa, ya na-akwa n'afọ* (drumming on your belly when you have a drum).

Furthermore, decades of the developed oil trade had brought into being its own chain of interest groups who would be thrown out of job if the new gadgets gained ground. Apart from the primary producers whose interests were discussed above, there were the chains of small, middle range and big business men who collected and treated the oil and kernel and moved them to the big produce-buying points on the railway or the river banks. A detailed study of the structure and organization of this chain of middlemen has been carried out by Dr. E. W. Ardner for the Mbaise area.[19] The introduction of the oil press and nutcracker would throw most of these people out of job, leaving only the owner of the press and cracker who would become part producer and his own middleman. Beyond the economic side to such mass unemployment there was the social one—the fear that so many young men thrown out of job would resort to crime as a means of gaining their livelihood.

The argument regarding the saving in labour which the

machines would bring about did not appeal to the people either. Much of the produce season fell into the dry season when little farm work was done, and thus was welcome as a form of diversion and hobby. Because of the opposition which these considerations engendered, the hand press, the oil mill and the nutcracker, though in time introduced to a number of places in Igbo land, failed to revolutionize the oil industry during the period under study. To the end of colonial rule annual reports continued to complain of Igbo resistance to these new gadgets.

If the administration did so little to change the face of the produce industry in which it was so keenly interested because of its importance in international trade, it can be understood if it did nothing at all to promote or improve the cultivation of those crops which formed the bulk of the food eaten by the Igbo. The Botanical Gardens, and after them the Departments of Agriculture established by the government, concerned themselves with experimentation in the growing of cash crops like coffee, cocoa and so on even though eventually these remained peripheral to Igbo cash crop economy. They also spent much time and energy on forest reserves and the preservation of timber, even though by so doing they kept the people perpetually agog since these policies were seen as aimed at expropriating the people. But no record has yet come to light that the government showed any interest in the improvement of yam, cassava and cocoyam cultivation, either through the introduction of better species, or through designing more efficient tools. As a result Igbo agriculture, in so far as it touches on the production of local staples, has remained basically what it was at the time European rule was imposed. The major changes remain the introduction of new food items brought about by increased travel and quicker communication. Thus rice has become an important product for local consumption and local trade. A wide variety of beans and cereals also came to be introduced from the North.

On land as an economic factor, British rule had an impact whose importance has grown with the passing of years. By introducing the idea of deliberately experimenting with the plantation of new cash crops, for instance cocoa, the colonial regime created among the Igbo the new desire to acquire land on freehold terms. Hitherto all land had been either family property (like *ala ulo*, compound land) or community (village) property (like *ala agu* or *ikpa*), neither of which could be alienated in perpetuity from the unit in question. But under the economic and legal impact of colonialism there came into being, as Mr. L. T. Chubb put it, 'a growing class of African capitalists anxious to acquire secure tenure of land for plantation purposes'. Through the pressure of such men, Chubb found during his investigations in 1946 or so, that in different parts of Igbo land (in the Onitsha, Awka, Awgu Divisions and elsewhere) land deals had taken place which purported to confer on individuals freehold titles over specific plots of land on which they had paid rather paltry sums as purchase fee.[19a] The incidence of this practice has since multiplied, but still by and large the traditional system of land tenure remains the dominant one.

To round off this discussion of the economic changes undergone by Igbo society in consequence of colonial rule, one has to deal with the question of the abolition of the slave trade. On all accounts the internal slave trade was still an important and paying economic engagement at the time British rule was imposed. Not only were slaves still being recruited and sold by the Igbo to the Igbo, but slaves were being imported into and exported out of Igbo land. They were needed not only for sacrifice or for burying titled men, but they were in demand as farm and household hands, carriers and to form buffer settlements on lands under armed contest. The use of slaves in burying the prominent dead and in sacrifice to the gods soon died out with the establishment of British rule because of the heavy penalties attached to it and because it was a practice easily discovered. It, in fact, became government practice to be particularly alert on festive occasions and whenever prominent men died. Neither of the two events could be kept secret since each was accompanied by the prolonged firing of Dane guns or even cannons. Furthermore as part of the campaign against human sacrifice and the recruitment of slaves generally, the government waged a relentless campaign against the leading oracles and shrines in Igbo land. The Aro Expedition of 1901-2 was seen in part as a campaign against slave dealing.

But the other openings for the deployment of slaves were such as could not be easily detected by the British. Furthermore the avenues for recruitment and disposal were equally many and subtle. And in any case some of the leading oracles and shrines which had played important roles in the recruitment of slaves died hard in spite of British vigilance. The *Ibini Ukpabi* of the Aro, the *Igwe-ka-Ala* of Umunneoha and the *Agbala* of Awka had to be destroyed over and over again, the first time in the first decade of this century when British rule was being imposed, and the second time in the second decade of the same century when British rule had already taken root. Some of the difficulties with the campaign against the slave trade have been investigated in some detail in the essay on 'The Eclipse of the Aro Slaving Oligarchy'.[20]

The important point for our purpose, however, is that even though the enterprise declined as colonial rule took firmer and firmer root, it continued to be a source of livelihood to some Igbo business men until probably the 1940s. The records clearly show that prosecution for slave dealing continued to feature prominently in the proceedings of the Provincial Courts. Oral traditions however make it clear that prominent slave dealers remained defiantly active until the 1940s. There was, for instance, the story about an Aro slaver (died in 1969), who about 1942 or 1943 sold his carriers in the open market. He had got them to agree with him not only to transport his wares to the market, but to help whoever bought the wares move them to where they could find transport. But it turned out that the so-called wares were bales of worthless rags and dried banana leaves, and that when the Aro man's customers pretended to be pricing the wares by which the carriers stood, they were in fact pricing the carriers. As a result when any of the bales was sold and the carrier in charge of it went to deliver it, he was in fact delivering himself as a slave to a new master! But for the most part, however, slave dealing under British rule took the form mostly of the sale of little children, especially little girls. The latter went as wives especially into Ijọ houses where slave marriage was greatly in favour as a way of augmenting the population of the houses. By the 1940s this practice had become so widespread that in places '*iga di n'Ijom*' (being married into Ijom or Ijọ) had become synonymous with being sold into slavery under the guise of marriage.

Social Change Under Colonial Rule

There is probably no doubt that, looked at in terms of the total time-scale of Igbo history, British colonialism which lasted only a little more than sixty years, could be dismissed as a brief interruption. But in terms of the degree of the changes which it induced in the life and culture of the people, it was an event of far-reaching importance. If also there is no doubt that

Igbo society, like any other social organism, was capable of undergoing internally induced changes, it is equally obvious that many of the transformations which the Igbo underwent under colonialism cannot be accounted for in terms of developments already taking place in their society at the time of the imposition of British rule.

This issue of the transformation of Igbo society under colonialism is one that has interested many students of Igbo society who have debated with great skill the explanation for the relative ease with which the Igbo embraced, or were made to embrace, new fashions.[21] In this brief and general essay no effort will be made to probe the issue in great detail or to produce a sovereign solution to any of the nettling problems. Our attempt will be limited to a discussion of firstly the main factors making for social change, and secondly the extent to which Igbo society changed under colonial rule. Here we shall try and distinguish three important factors which on close analysis can be seen to have influenced the social life of the Igbo more drastically than any others. These are: the christian missions and the school, urbanization and increased travel, and finally the new economic opportunities created by colonial rule.

Thanks to the researches of Professors J. F. A. Ajayi and E. A. Ayandele, of Drs. S. N. Nwabara, F. K. Ekechi and E. A. Udo,[22] we now have a clearer picture of the missionary penetration of Igbo land, though there are still a number of details about it which remain to be worked out, especially for the Udi, Nsukka and North-Eastern Igbo areas. In any case there is no need to retell the story here. Depending on the findings of these works we can now make a number of observations on the spread of christianity in Igbo land.

One of these is that the missionary assault on Igbo land was launched along three main axes—the River Niger, the Opobo-Bonny and the Cross River axes. Of these the Niger axis was the earliest, going back to 1856 when the Church Missionary Society (C.M.S.) established a station at Onitsha. But the advance from this front, though reinforced in 1885 when the Catholics came in led by the Holy Ghost Fathers, made little progress before 1900 for a number of reasons. For one thing the Niger was not, for nineteenth century Europe, so much a highway of advance into Igbo land as the southern gateway into the Central Sudan (Hausa land) which was the loadstar of European adventurers for much of the nineteenth century.

There was also the fact that the method of converting Africans through their kings and chiefs adopted by the missions for the greater part of the nineteenth century was unsuitable for Igbo land where there were no kings and chiefs powerful enough to drag their peoples along with them into the christian fold. For the Eastern Igbo area the fact that the missions settled first at Onitsha would also appear to have been a handicap, for Onitsha had a long tradition of conflict with most of her neighbours. In the event nearly half a century of christian enterprise in and around Asaba and Onitsha, did not succeed in carrying the christian message into the heart of Igbo land. When Father Shanahan came to the field in 1902 he described the Catholic mission among the Igbo as 'consisting mainly of a few handfuls of slaves bought by the Fathers at 2s 6d each from slave ships passing down the river'.[23]

On the Opobo-Bonny and Cross River axes the missions ran into a belt of Ijọ and Efik-Ibibio peoples amongst whom they had to at least obtain toe-holds before going into Igbo land. By the time this was achieved Igbo attitude to the white man had hardened as a result of unhappy encounters with the political and military arms of British interests. In the event penetration along these fronts had to await the military conquest of Igbo land, even though as early as the 1870s the C.M.S. in the Oil Rivers had started collecting ethnographic and political information on the Igbo as part of the preparation for penetrating their territory from the south.

This leads us to the second assertion that in Igbo land, unlike in Yoruba land generally, the Cross followed the flag. After the Aro Expedition of 1901-2, for instance, the government invited the missions to establish at Aro Chukwu, Bende and Owerri and within three years or so they did that. In fact before that expedition there was a government ruling against missionaries and traders penetrating the Igbo interior because it was considered unsafe. After a careful study of this matter Dr. Ekechi has spoken of a 'conversion explosion' in Igbo land following British conquest.

The third assertion is that the success of the christian missions in Igbo land was, like in many other parts of Africa, brought about not so much by preaching 'Christ Crucified' as through the parade of the advantages of literacy over illiteracy, that is through the school. In the earlier phase of christian evangelism in Igbo land, the missions had hesitated between advance by direct preaching to the elders, appeal through social services like medical clinics and orphanages and the establishment of christian villages. Practical experience and hard thinking soon showed that these methods could not work the magic of converting the Igbo to christianity in large numbers. In the event the decision of the missions to use the school as their instrument of proselytization became a turning point in the history of christianity in Igbo land. Through the schools the missions exploited to some advantage the burning desire of the Igbo to become as expert as the British in the manipulation of their physical world. In effect the Igbo were not converted to christianity, they were ensnared for christianity by the school.

For now, however, our concern is the role of christianity and the school in social change in colonial Igbo land. The key to this question lies in an appreciation of the fact that the pre-colonial Igbo polity was not an Erastian state. On the contrary it was a community in which the worldly and the other-wordly, the political and the religious were closely bound together. As a result political, social and economic life were underpinned by a religion centred around the worship of a pantheon of gods and the veneration of the ancestors. Even such an apparently simple question as the young of both sexes going nude until puberty, was not just a matter of irrational attitude to garments, but was bound up with the traditional codes regulating morality and sex behaviour which were underpinned by religious sanctions. The insistence by christians on all age groups wearing dresses, was thus for the Igbo a much more fundamental issue than it was for the missions. In the context of Igbo culture conversion to christianity was not just a question of new ideologies for old. It also involved exchanging one form of social life for another.

In this process of changing the fundamental basis of society, the school played an important part because it was the instrument for mobilizing support for christianity and by the same token for withdrawing support from the old social order. This role was all the more crucial because those recruited for christianity through the school were by and large children, that is the younger generation who had not yet been fully inducted into the culture and lore of the nation. The result was that they brought to christianity fewer trappings of the indigenous culture than would have been the case if most of the early converts were elders who had become the embodiments of the traditions of their fathers. The first generation of Igbo christians thus had limited attachment to their traditional culture, and, in fact, from the beginning tended to pitch themselves against it. As a result, while time and death thinned down the ranks of the defenders of the old order, the ranks of the christians were progressively being augmented. This is a point which has not always been stressed in discussions on the spread of christianity in Igbo land.

Another point related to it is the fact that at the same time many of those first sent to school, and therefore to church, were either slaves or *osu* (outcasts). These were people who, because of their social disabilities, had a grievance against traditional Igbo culture and society. They saw the new christian body which was forming as an alternative to the Igbo society whose constraints they were happy to escape. A study of the early history of christianity in Igbo land reveals that it was marked by waves and waves of iconoclasm in which invaluable works of art and culture were destroyed by the new zealots. Now it is not unlikely that some of the ferocity of this iconoclastic campaign can be explained by reference to the social class of many of the early christians. The resentment of this class is by no means completely abated. One of their number was recently reported as saying that there is *nothing* in Igbo culture to be proud of.

Furthermore, the school dealt severe blows on indigenous Igbo culture not only because it was the instrument through which a large fraction of the younger generation of Igbo men were indoctrinated against the society and its values, but also because it tended to withdraw them physically from participation in those celebrations and social processes by which the values of the group were transmitted from generation to generation. The fact is that school children left home early in the morning for the school where they spent most of the day being indoctrinated as well as taking part in physically exhausting exercises and games. They came back late in the day too worn out to follow their non-school going colleagues in much of what they did. The scholars followed this routine for five days in the week (Monday to Friday) and spent the Sunday in church. In practical terms this meant they spent the active part of their days in school and church activities and thus had little time to devote to the calls of the age-grades, secret societies and other traditional rites even if they had been qualified and inclined to participate. Whereas the Igbo week was so arranged as to enable the young to work in the farm, do household chores and still find time to answer the calls of these institutions, the school week was not. In this regard Saturday was little use. The school children spent its morning hours washing their dresses for church and school, while the evening hours were spent in the church premises learning catechism and practising as choristers.

And what was more, it did not take time before the value of the school, as a means of getting ahead in the new world ushered in by the colonial rule, was proved beyond all reasonable doubt. The children, whether outcasts or not, who were used as guinea pigs to probe the import of that institution, within a few years learnt enough English and Arithmetic to be employed as clerks, messengers etc. in the government and commercial firms, and as teachers and agents in the schools and churches. In these jobs they acquired a new economic power and social status far beyond the wildest imagination of their parents and elders, thus becoming objects of admiration and envy. The result was that even those who initially scoffed at the idea of sending their beloved children to school, gradually came round to wish to do so. For example the grandmother of E. Kalu Uku of Aro Churkwu who was an uncompromising opponent of the new ways, decided that it was wise to send the young boy to school in order to enable him get on in life. 'Remember, Kanu', she advised, 'that you have only to learn enough to be able to make your way in this new world' while taking care 'not to let yourself go to church'.[24] There must have been many like this grand old woman who hoped that it would be possible for their children to eat the, to them, sour grape of Western education without having their teeth set on edge. But one after the other they discovered their mistake. So inextricably linked were the school and the new religion that all who even as much as toyed with the one got infected with the other.

Probably second in importance to the missions and the school as instruments of social change were urbanization and increased travel. Urbanization was unknown in pre-colonial Igbo land. The people lived in villages, village-groups and clans with the result that respect for religion, law and custom was induced partly by the sanctions of reward and punishment and partly by the influence of the family, elders and near-kinsmen. This also made it possible for peoples' lives to be organized around such gods and institutions as were important to the community. There was also hardly anything like living in anonymity or living an individual existence to the extent that is possible today in urban centres. If one were not known by name his family and lineage were and so could be got at when the need arose through the head of the family or lineage. But in urban conditions of existence one is released from all these intricate and intimate links which tend to hinder the development of rugged individualism. Also in urban environment one comes across people who have ideas, styles of life and behaviour, techniques etc. which are quite different from those obtaining in one's village, and therefore one stands a chance of learning things new—that is both good and bad.

It was by introducing these conditions that urbanization proved such a potent instrument of social change in Igbo land. The urban centres which were important in Igbo land—Onitsha, Asaba, Agbor, Aba, Port Harcourt, Umuahia, Enugu and so on arose more or less from similar circumstances. They grew up around those points which were important under colonial rule either as commercial or political centres or both. Port Harcourt, the most important of them all, came into being as a port and railway terminal for the evacuation of the produce trade of the former Eastern Region and of Enugu coal. Aba, though important commercially in the pre-colonial era as the point of inter-section of many trade routes, rose to pre-eminence as an administrative headquarters which was its main advantage over Akwete which was also an important centre for trade and was for a few years an administrative headquarters. Umuahia and Enugu rose first as economically important towns—Umuahia for produce and Enugu for coal—before becoming administrative headquarters. By the nineteenth century Onitsha was important as a commercial centre but acquired new and increased importance as the headquarters for a division and a province.

The fact is that each of these towns or points acquired a new importance as soon as it became the administrative capital of either a division or a province. For one thing it meant that a European officer or two, with all the usual accompaniment of military, police and court messenger detachments, clerks, interpreters and so on took residence there. At times too, the white missionary, looking for company and/or protection from the political officer came to settle there or at least nearby. With the missionary came his own retinue of catechists, church agents, teachers and so on. At once the town in question, even if hitherto it had been 'bad bush', became the Mecca of all the surrounding villages which came under the jurisdiction of the division for which it was capital. To it came chiefs and elders to answer the calls of the political officers, carriers and labourers required to move the loads of officers going on transfer or on tour and to clean the environs, church elders seeking for instruction from the missionary, and litigants appealing from Native Courts in the 'bush' to the political officer or his court.

In addition, the attempt to supply the economic needs of the population at the divisional capital led to much coming and going between the villages around and the headquarters. In time adventurous spirits from the neighbouring villages and beyond came to settle there more or less permanently to meet these needs on a regular basis. With places like Port Harcourt, Aba, Umuahia and Enugu this migration of population increased with the construction of the railway between 1913 and 1915. The railway brought in many non-Igbo elements who were needed to work the trains and maintain the subsidiary services. The coming of these people created new needs which were met partly through increase migration from the villages and partly through the old settlers broadening their outlook and expanding their business. In the case of Enugu the opening of the coal mines attracted plenty of population from all over Igbo land most of whom came to work as miners. It was in these different ways that modern urbanization came into Igbo land.

In these centres Igbo elements found themselves compelled to adopt styles of life quite different from what they came with from the villages. Invariably those who went to the towns were young men some of whom had been to school and so embraced christianity of sorts. On the other hand if they had not been to school and church, they could not bring their traditional gods with them either because they were too young to set up their own individual shrines or because it was impossible to transport these gods without breaking some essential taboos and so on. In the event they found themselves living their lives outside the immediate shadows of these gods and their priests and in time started adopting church-going habits which appeared quite popular in the towns. And with church-going went the acquisition of new mental and moral attitudes including the tendency to condone even such serious moral deviations as prostitution or even to benefit from the services it offered.

Also the nascent urban settlement looked up to the European officers and their servants for example whether with regard to the forms of houses they put up, or even how they ran their homes or even how they dressed for work or on ceremonial occasions. Through these sons abroad, as through the teachers in the rural mission stations, the new fashions in architecture, household organization, dress and personal hygiene filtered into the villages. Dr. E. A. Udo has recaptured vividly how the *manse* helped to revolutionize the life of villages, even to the extent of influencing our women's conception of their duties in the family.[25] Throughout the colonial period, he has rightly pointed out, the average European officer could retain a retinue of household servants—cook, steward, 'small-boy', gardener, 'wood boy', 'water-boy', 'mail-boy' and so on. The result of this was that both the white officer and his wife were relieved of all household chores. The white woman, therefore, when she was not running little local clinics for the sick, or Sunday schools for children or knitting classes for the girls, led a life of apparent idleness. The school girls, who were close enough to observe her daily routine came to assume that the educated and civilized housewife should normally carry no household duties. It is this pernicious example of the colonial days that still accounts for the large retinue of 'house-boys' and 'house-maids' found in the average educated African home.

But it must not be thought that the Igbo simply surrendered themselves to the new and enticing ways of the urban centres. On the contrary they carried to these towns those aspects of their village or traditional culture which could be accommodated with the demands of the new environment. Of these the most important was the 'lineage organization'. In the urban centre the smallest Igbo 'lineage' was the village-group and this provided the basis for organizing group activity. This helps to explain why, in the context of urban politics, an Igbo would normally refer to any person from his village-group as a 'brother' or a 'sister'. For mutual encouragement, support and control people from the same village-group or even clan (or divisions, for distant urban centres) tended to settle in the same part of the town, or at least to meet frequently on Sundays to discuss common problems and to 'pull the ear' of any member who was bringing shame to their 'town'. This tendency for people from the same village-group to stick together was all the more so since new migrants invariably came under the shelter of older migrants from the same village-group or so. It was this sort of informal organization of the first and second decades of this century which in the third and fourth decades blossomed into the formal 'patriotic' and 'improvement' unions which became so popular among the Igbo. By the 1940s these unions had become a main channel through which change and modernization flowed from the towns to the remotest corners of Igbo land.

It was not only the urban centres which grew up in Igbo land that influenced the life of the Igbo. Equally important were urban centres in far away places like Yoruba and Hausa lands. It is here that we see the importance of the increased opportunity for wide-ranging travel which colonial rule introduced. Some Igbo elements, especially long distance traders and purveyors of specialized skills like the Aro, Nri, Umunneoha, Nkwerre and Awka had travelled extensively among the Igbo and their immediate neighbours (Edo, Ijọ, Ibibio, Ogoja, Igala) in the pre-colonial period. But never before did Igbo businessmen have as much opportunity for travel as they had under colonial rule. By the second decade of the century venturesome spirits from among the Igbo were already making their presence felt among the Yoruba and the Hausa. By the 1940s what had begun first as a trickle was becoming a raging storm and causing disquiet on the part of the host communities.

However for our purpose what is important is that this long-ranging travel, and residence amongst the other ethnic groups of Nigeria caused important changes in Igbo way of life. New items of food were brought in, new ways of preparing old items (like the making of *moi moi* from beans etc.) and new forms of dress, (like those of the Yoruba and Hausa) were imported. Also the farther away from home the Igbo travelled, the larger the unit on the basis of which they organized their lives in the new centres. In urban centres within Igbo land village-group unions might be sufficient for protecting one another and local pride, but in far away Kano and Lagos it was the Igbo State Union that was important, even though beneath that umbrella were the Divisional and Town Unions. Colonial rule thus seems, to some extent, to have brought ideological and a quasi-political unity to the Igbo in the Igbo State Union. However the chequered political fortunes of the Igbo since independence culminating in the Biafran experiment seem to have disrupted that unity. This is so to the extent that many geographically peripheral Igbo now consider it more honourable and profitable to claim for themselves a new ethnic origin and identity as part of the nationalistic process of cleansing themselves of the sin of 'Igbo-ness'.

The main social changes induced by the new economic forces

unleashed by colonialism can be easily summarized as they are not radically different from those already mentioned above. But before we go on to them we must emphasize a point made earlier, that colonialism did not in fact drastically change the economic structure of Igbo land, not even with regard to the oil trade in which Britain was most interested. The main economic innovation of British colonialism was the opportunity it offered for a man who had no land, or decided to ignore his holdings in land, to earn a living through securing salaried employment. The salaried servant who neither farmed nor traded was a new kind of economic and social animal in Igbo experience and was appropriately named *Onye ọrụ Beke*. This phrase has a triple meaning which has not always been recognized. The salaried worker, whether he worked for the mission, or commercial firm, or government, was *Onye ọrụ Beke* because firstly he worked for the white man who paid him, secondly he did the same kind of work as the white man and thirdly like the white man he depended for his livelihood on salaries rather than on farming, trading or the manufacture and marketing of household, farm and decorative wares.

The impact of this development on society was quite far-reaching. It vested a new value on raw cash as such and the Igbo came to say '*Ego Beke na-ekwu okwu*' (the white man's money talks). The fact is that hitherto people made money and accumulated wealth in order to marry many wives, raise a large yam barn, buy admission to the revered title and secret societies since it was from these that prestige and status derived. But with colonial rule money came to have value for its own sake and to convey status even when not invested in the purchase of status in the traditional manner. Through the salaried servant colonial rule tended to give a new value to raw cash and through that to provide new criteria for assessing social worth.

It was partly this new value placed on money that helped to bring about the decline of the anciently-famed and the once highly-sought-for secret and title societies. It is true that money invested in the purchase of membership of these societies could be recouped through sharing in the fees paid by subsequent entrants. But this was a slow process of recovering invested capital, let alone of making profit on it. Under the colonial regime there were new and more profitable avenues of investment by which one could multiply one's capital quickly and accumulate the money that would 'give him mouth' in his community as well as give him access to new luxuries and gadgets. Therefore why invest in the title and secret societies? The result was that young men who earned money which they could have used in buying status traditional style, now looked elsewhere and invested it either in trade, or real estate or the education of their children or in company stocks. Starved of new entrants and of money these societies declined, losing political and social sway.

Also part of the political and social power of elders in pre-colonial Igbo society derived from their control of the primary means of production—land. The erring member of the lineage who thought he could dispense with the elders during the harvest season, could be made to mend his ways during the farming season when it came to assigning farm land and conducting the necessary rituals to ensure a fruitful harvest. Hardly any Igbo trader during the pre-colonial period lived entirely on the proceeds of trade. Most people depended to varying extents on land and thus had to be amenable to the control of those who 'held' (i.e. had responsibility for placating) the land. But the salaried civil servant, mission worker and mercantile clerk or messenger who depended entirely on his salary was more emancipated from traditional control than anybody ever was in the days before British rule. He could thus not only live his own life, but also introduce new ways without undue concern for what the elders would say or do or both.

Finally we come to the question of the extent to which Igbo society was transformed under colonialism. This is an issue which has at times been misunderstood. Writing in 1966 the late Professor J. C. Anene talked of the disintegration of indigenous society under colonial rule.[26] Professor E. A. Ayandele and Dr. F. K. Ekechi would also appear to subscribe to the same thesis at least in so far as they seem to explain the success of the christian missions in Igbo land after 1900 in terms of the collapse of indigenous society under the shock of military and political defeat.[27] In this regard Dr. Ekechi has talked of the 'massive Igbo response to christianity being generated by the social and political disruption that accompanied the establishment of British colonial rule'. Also he maintains that British penetration by force led to a 'breakdown of law and order resulting from the weakening of the mechanisms for preserving internal order'.[28]

A close study of the subject reveals that the political organization of the Igbo village-group never broke down or got disorganized under colonial rule, much as its area of competence was curtailed by the establishment of an all-interfering central government. As already pointed out, these institutions continued to operate in some form in those areas of the peoples' life outside the gaze of the colonial authority. The colonial government itself from time to time became aware of this fact. And it was the conviction that the traditional political institutions still functioned which inspired the administrative reorganizations of the 1930s. When in 1951 the idea of Native Administration was abandoned, it was not because the indigenous institutions of the Igbo had collapsed, but because they had successfully resisted being remoulded to meet the so-called modernizing needs of the colonial government. Even today these institutions remain alive and vigorous in the context of village-group politics. In spite of the heavy paraphernalia of modern government, the greater majority of the Igbo are kept on the path of lawful conduct not only by the police and the army, but also by traditional controls exerted at the village-group level.

If Igbo institutions did not collapse on the morrow of British conquest as was maintained by Anene, it follows that Igbo avidity for christianity did not derive from what Dr. Ekechi has called 'a crisis of social identity'. It is more likely that the Igbo became christians not so much because they felt they had lost their old identity, as because they found themselves in a world in which the old identity was no longer enough and they sought to supplement it by acquiring aspects of the identity of their conquerors. This would help to explain the fact that Igbo life under colonial rule was in some aspects a happy synthesis of the old and the new—a situation which the British found disquieting. Writing on the cultural situation in Igbo land in 1939 Mrs. Sylvia Leith-Ross said:

> Such a tremendous load has been suddenly put upon shoulders not yet ready to carry such a burden that it is no wonder the bearer falters, turns back, or rests a while in the familiar world of his own customs before resuming the christian path. The only real surprise is the fact that he does not seem to know that he is doing so, so that with no strain nor conflict, he can attend communion and believe in 'medicine', keep, until he is found out, a 'church' wife and several 'native marriage' wives, tie up preciously in the same corner of a handkerchief his rosary and the shaped bit of 'iron for juju' made for him by an Awka blacksmith, plant side by side in the garden round his new cement and pan-roofed house the hibiscus of 'civilization' and the *Ogirisi* tree of pagan family rites.[29]

This situation which Mrs. Leith-Ross described nearly four decades ago has not changed much, except in so far as more and more of the old culture is being revived and incorporated into the bit of already imbibed christian and western culture. Thus during the Nigeria-Biafra war, the Nigerians were fought not only with modern automatic weapons imported from the West but also with the spell of the guild of 'medicine' men. The title and secret societies have not only lingered on, but are showing signs of rejuvenation as the Igbo having lost the civil war, do not want to lose their identity.

Thus while talking of the Igbo having embraced christianity and Westernism with enthusiasm, one must not mistake this as meaning that they deserted their ancestral culture in all its forms. There is thus no reason to talk, as Professor Anene did, of the disintegration of indigenous society. Again it is not only that elements from the two cultures were, as Mrs. Leith-Ross said, interwoven 'with such facility that it is impossible either for him (the Igbo) or for others to see the joins', but that even this happy wedlock between the two cultures did not proceed at the same rate all over Igbo land.

The areas which by the 1940s had felt the impact of colonialism and christianity to a visible extent were largely Southern Igbo land which is the region of the densely populated palm belt, and the areas around Onitsha. In these places the explanation for the rapid change lay as in the case of Owerri province, in the pressure of population on the land which forced younger sons to seek to make a living by other ways than by farming. This led to the patronage of the schools and of salaried employment as of migration to urban centres. Around Onitsha and Awka the explanation probably lay partly on population pressure and partly on the length and intensity of christian activity.

But beyond these areas there were such places as the Anambra flood plain, Nsukka and the fertile lands of the Cross River plain, that is Abakaliki and Afikpo, where the rate of change was much slower. Here the density per acre is relatively low and the soil rich, which means that the people were under no particular economic pressure to abandon the land and take to the schools or urban towns. Also missionary penetration of these parts was late and slow. By 1934, for instance, there were only two schools in Nsukka where one could read up to standard six. For the rest the other schools in the division were hedge schools of the lowest type, poorly staffed and poorly equipped, with some of them no more than six years old or less. In the Abakaliki and Afikpo Divisions the situation was similar. Here part of the explanation lay in the fact that the area came largely within the sphere of influence of the Presbyterian Church which never had a dynamic expansion programme. The Catholics had also penetrated the area, but without stiff competition to spur them on, they had not achieved much either.

The Nsukka area—with its aggressively alive *Odo* and *Omabe* masquerades, guilds of titled men swinging their *Ọdụ atụ* happily to village meetings and markets (and almost to church), its child marriages and puberty rites—does not fit into the usual, picture of an Igbo land that lost its social and cultural identity with colonial conquest. Nor does Abakaliki with its *Ezeputa* and *Odozi Obodo* secret societies, its yam and horse titles and its unrelenting insistence that the farm is a better institution for educating the young than the mission school.

NOTES

1. J. C. Anene, *Southern Nigeria in Transition 1885–1906* (Cambridge, 1966).
   A. E. Afigbo, *The Warrant Chiefs* (Longmans, 1972).
   S. N. Nwabara, 'Ibo Land: A Study in British Penetration and the Problems of Administration 1860–1930' (Ph.D. Thesis, Northwestern University, 1965).
   V. C. Uchendu, *The Igbo of South East Nigeria* (Holt, Rinehart and Winston, 1965).
   F. K. Ekechi, *Missionary Enterprises and Rivalry in Igbo-land 1857–1914* (Frank Cass, 1971).
   W. E. Ofonagoro, 'The Opening up of Southern Nigeria to British Trade and its Consequences: Economic and Social History 1881–1916' (Ph.D., University of Columbia, 1971).
   J. Nwaguru, *Aba Division Under British Rule* (Emugu, 1973).
2. Moor to Colonial Office, No. 381 of 24/11/01 in C.S.O. 1/13.
3. Moor to C.O. No. 38 of 24 November 1901 in C.O. 520/10, quoted in Anene, *Southern Nigeria*, p. 220.
4. For an example of these treaties see Anene, *Southern Nigeria*, Appendix C, p. 333, the treaty with Opobo.
5. Calprof 8/2 Reports, see Reports dated 3.11.95 by Tanner, 1896 by A. B. Harcourt and 5.7.96 by A. G. Griffith on the Akwete Expedition.
6. Sir E. Hertslet, *Map of Africa by Treaty*, 3 Vols. (London, 1909). See Vol. I for some of the Treaties in Igbo land.
7. Quoted in S. H. Roberts, *History of French Colonial Policy*, 2 Vols. (Oxford, 1929), see Vol. I, p. 302.
8. Based on field information. See also A. E. Afigbo, 'The Aro Expedition of 1901–1902', *Odu* New Series, No. 7, April 1972, pp. 18–19.
9. On the Aro Expedition. See A. E. Afigbo, 'The Aro Expedition of 1901–1902', *Odu* New Series, No. 7, April 1972, pp. 3–27; S. N. Nwabara, 'Encounter with the Long Juju etc.', *Transactions of the Historical Society of*

Ghana, Vol. IX, pp. 79–89; J. C. Anene, 'The Southern Nigeria Protectorate and the Aros', *Journal of the Historical Society of Nigeria* (hereinafter J.H.S.N.), December 1955.

10. In addition to the works mentioned above see also P. A. Igbafe, 'Western Igbo Society and its resistance to British rule: The Ekumeku Movement, 1898–1911', *Journal of African History*, XII, 3, 1971; A. E. Afigbo, 'Trade and Politics on the Cross River', *Transactions of the Historical Society of Ghana*, Vol. XXII, Part I, July 1972; A. E. Afigbo, 'The Establishment of Colonial Rule (in West Africa) 1900–1918', in Ajayi and Crowder (eds), *History of West Africa*, Vol. II (Longman, 1973).
11. Quoted in F. K. Ekechi, *Missionary Rivaltry etc.*, p. 116.
12. Quoted in F. K. Ekenchi, *op. cit.*, p. 126.
13. Quoted in F. K. Ekechi, *op. cit.*, p. 258.
14. For sources, see E. E. Afigbo:

    (i) *The Warrant Chiefs*.
    (ii) 'The Native Treasury Question Under the Warrant Chief System in Eastern Nigeria 1899–1929', *Odu* IV, I, 1967.
    (iii) 'Revolution and Reaction in Eastern Nigeria, etc., *J.H.S.N.*, III, 3, Dic. 1966.
    (iv) Chief Igwegbe Odum, 'The Omenuko of History', *Nigeria Magazine*, 90, 1966.
    (v) 'The Warrant Chief System: Direct or Indirect Rule', *J.H.S.N.*, III, 4, June 1966.

    J. C. Anene, *Southern Nigeria*.
    M. Perham, *Native Administration in Nigeria* (Oxford, 1937).
    S. N. Nwabara, 'Ibo Land, etc.'.
15. For the early economic policy of the Southern Nigeria Administration. See A. E. Afigbo, 'Sir Ralph Moor and the Economic Development of Southern Nigeria 1896–1903', *J.H.S.N.*, Vol. V, 3 December 1970.
16. A. Burns, *History of Nigeria* (George Allen and Unwin Ltd., 1969), 7th edition, p. 217.
17. O. P. 320/1929, Annual Report, Nsukka Division for 1929, para. 63.
18. L. T. Chubb, *Ibo Land Tenure* (Ibadan University Press, 1961), p. 51.
19. E. W. Ardner, 'A Rural Oil Palm Industry', *West Africa*, 26 September 1953, p. 900, *West Africa*, 3 October 1955, pp. 921 and 923.
19a. L. T. Chubb, *Ibo Land Tenure*, pp. 23–31.
20. See Chapter 7 of this book.
21. Probably the most extended investigation of this matter so far is that by Professor S. Ottenberg, 'Ibo Receptivity to Change', in *Continuity and Change in African Cultures*, edited by W. J. Bascom and M. J. Herskovits (Chicago, 1958), pp. 130–42. See also, V. C. Uchendu, *The Igbo of South East Nigeria* and F. K. Ekechi, *Missionary Enterprise*, etc.
22. J. F. A. Ajayi, *Christian Missions in Nigeria 1841–1891* (Longmans, 1965).
    E. A. Ayandele, *The Missionary Impact on Modern Nigeria 1842–1914* (Longmans, 1966).
    S. N. Nwabara, *Ibo Land*, etc.
    F. K. Ekechi, *Missionary Enterprise*, etc.
    E. A. Udo, 'Methodist Contribution to Education in Eastern Nigeria 1893–1960' (Ph.D. Thesis, Boston University, 1965).
23. *A Short Life of Bishop Shanahan*, by the Holy Ghost Fathers, Onitsha Diocese, p. 22.
24. Mary Easterfield, 'Seeds in the Palm of your Hand', *West African Review*, December 1952, pp. 1365–9, January 1953, pp. 49–51, February 1953, pp. 141–3, March 1953, pp. 265, 267.

25. E. A. Udo, 'Methodist Contribution to Education, etc.', pp. 69–94.
26. J. C. Anene, *Southern Nigeria*, pp. 250, 257.
27. E. A. Ayandele, *Missionary Impact*, etc., pp. 156–8.
    F. K. Ekechi, *Missionary Enterprise*, etc., Chapter VIII.
28. F. K. Ekechi, *op. cit.*, p. 147.
29. S. Leith-Ross, *African Women* (London, 1939), pp. 292–3.

9. The Impact of Colonialism on Igbo Language: The Origins of a Dilemma

Introduction
Scientific interest in the study of the Igbo language began quite early in the nineteenth century in missionary circles in Sierra Leone where knowledge of African languages was seen as a necessary tool in the bid to evangelize the continent. By the middle of the century this interest had come to take deep root.[1] Between 1852 and 1900 over ten works had been published in the language, mainly by missionaries and their aides. Most of these were primers and grammars, a few were word lists and collections of proverbs, while the remainder were translations of sections of the Bible into various dialects of the language.[2]

This trend continued, or rather in fact broadened out, with the British conquest and occupation of Igbo land and the increased evangelical work which followed in the wake of the new political settlement.[3] By 1936, therefore, the systematic study of the Igbo language was about a hundred years old. Yet Miss M. M. Green could in that year say, with justified pessimism and much cogency, that

> A bird's eye-view of the present Ibo linguistic situation is not . . . an inspiring prospect.[4]

Nearly four decades after the above statement of Miss Green's, a student of the language could still assert with even more justified pessimism and equal cogency that the Igbo linguistic situation is deplorable. This is particularly so when the present state of that language both as an academic discipline and as a living vehicle of discuss and of Igbo culture, is compared with that of Yoruba and Hausa; two languages which scholars at one time regarded as standing the same chances of growth with the Igbo language.

The fact is that languages like Hausa and Yoruba have now outdistanced Igbo as academic disciplines and living media of discussion, as can be seen from a survey of the teaching and research programmes of Centres of African Studies, Institutes and Departments interested in African Linguistics not only in this country but in Europe, America and Russia. Hausa and Yoruba have surpassed Igbo not only in structural growth and in the evolution of a literary dialect, but also in the machinery and mechanism for ensuring unhindered growth. Reporting on this matter recently Mr. M. N. Okonkwo, himself a student of the language, observed that

> giant strides have been made in the study of the other two main languages of Nigeria—Yoruba and Hausa. Comprehensive schemes for the study of these languages have been worked out. A permanent committee made up of educated men, indigenous language experts and ordinary people versed in local customs has been formed for each of the languages. These committees strongly backed by the governments concerned with the languages encourage enthusiasm and scholarship in these languages. They work hard for the improvement of the study of these languages and (the) production of standard literature in them.[5]

With the Igbo language the situation is different. That language has been plagued by many problems, some of which are inherent in it, some of which have been imposed on it, but neither of which is insoluble if only central direction and co-ordination could be assured. We shall now take the main problems one after the other and show how each arose. We are doing this in the belief that an understanding of the history of each of these problems will contribute something towards any effort to find the only rational and satisfactory solution to them: that is the evolution or formation of a literary dialect of the language. Unless the Igbo language evolves such a dialect enjoying a pan-Igbo acceptance, it will never become the effective vehicle for expressing Igbo genius and group identity.

The Dialect Question:
The Igbo language is dialect-riven. To European and other alien linguistic scholars this is the supreme fact of the Igbo linguistic situation. Stated broadly and baldly in this manner one can only observe that this is neither a profound nor a surprising discovery. All languages before they develop literary dialects enjoying national status and recognition are dialect riven. This was true of European, as it is of African, languages. Even the Hausa and Yoruba languages whose pre-eminent position in our national life today other linguistic groups now

envy, were at one time dialect-riven. Furthermore even those languages which have evolved national dialects still show traces of their earlier dialectal divisions in what is now at times euphemistically described as 'provincialisms'.

With this observation one would pose the opposite view that the supreme fact in the Igbo linguistic situation was Igbo political fragmentation. That the Igbo-speaking peoples never came under the umbrella of one state or evolved any state with a sway covering a substantial fraction of Igbo land is now accepted by all students of Igbo political sociology. On the contrary the Igbo lived in tiny villages and village-group communities each of which prided itself in its political autonomy and separate identity. This autonomy and separate identity at times found expression in a separate dialect, or at least a distinctive way of mouthing the language: if not at times also in different words and phraseologies for the same objects and concepts. Thus, for instance, the Ihube village-group of the Otanchara clan in Okigwi Division would say *iye* for *yes* while their next door neighbours, the Ngodo village-group of the Isuochi clan in the same Division would say *eh-yi*.

'Vernacular literature, in Africa as elsewhere', argues Professor Westermann, 'is dependant on the centralization of cognate languages into one written dialect'.[6] From what we know of the history of many languages, political unity or centralized political control is probably the most effective agency for standardizing a language or levelling its various dialects into one 'national speech'. This is so for many reasons. The clan that achieves political dominance amongst a people becomes the object of envy and admiration not only by the conquered but also by those on the periphery of the state. The initial reaction of these two groups might be that of resentment and rebellion, but when the state achieves stability, resentment and hostility tend to give way to admiration and identification. The dialect of the clan becomes the prestige dialect which all those anxious to rise in the state learn to speak. In a literate society the epics and sagas of the people come to be written in the dialect of the dominant clan. In some cases the ruling aristocracy of the state might even take positive steps to ensure the dominance of their tongue. The absence of a pan-Igbo state or of an Igbo state controlling a sizeable fraction of the Igbo people was perhaps the greatest single obstacle to the emergence of an Igbo national dialect.

It is often pointed out, and correctly too, that though fragmented the Igbo communities were not disparate and isolated units. On the contrary there were myriads of Igbo institutions and practices which encouraged pan-Igbo travel and kept a sizeable fraction of the elite in contact with distant parts and peoples of Igbo land. Among these institutions and practices were the oracles, *Igbandu*, professional and associational guilds, title and secret societies all of which, according to Dr. V. C. Uchendu, tended to confer on some of the people pan-Igbo citizenship.[7] Some linguistic scholars starting from the above undisputed historical fact have argued that these institutions and practices encouraged dialect levelling in pre-colonial Igbo land. Says Dr. Ida Ward:

> The individualism of their social organisation has meant that widely different dialects have developed in the country in the past.... This does not mean however that there have been no dialect levelling influences in the past.... It is probably true to say that there is no such thing as 'pure' Ibo. As in the case of all languages, influences of one kind or another have made themselves felt. In the past the Arochukwu, trading over the whole country, founded settlements in many areas, and these have radiated Arochukwu linguistic influences. Similar settlements have been made by the Nkwerri traders. Big slave markets such as those at Bende, Uzuakoli, Akwete, Bonny must have had Ibo from all parts of the country congregated in them and these probably left some traces behind...[8]

This is, however, a doubtful proposition and was not based on a practical demonstration of the influences which the Aro, for instance, were said to have left on various Igbo dialects. Dr. Ward's thesis would appear to be based on an insufficient knowledge of the politics of Igbo communities in the pre-colonial days. In those far off days when most neighbouring communities lived in a state of what Mr. G. I. Jones has aptly called 'suspended conflict' which could at any moment warm up into active conflict, ability to speak the dialect of every region through which a trader or diviner passed was one of the surest passports to personal safety and success in the professions. Thus it is unlikely that the coming and going which obtained in pre-colonial Igbo society, the regular fairs at Uzuakoli, Bende, Uburu and so on necessarily worked in the direction of promoting the emergence of what might be called a 'national' dialect. I still remember an uncle of mine, Diribẹọfọ Mgbeke, who was a long distance trader of the old type and he had a perfect mastery of the dialects of all the regions to which he traded. He used to recount with pride how he escaped many land pirates by merely speaking their dialect and claiming blood relationship with the one or other of their eminent families where he was well known. Even to this day a wise and gifted trader can make a good bargain in an Igbo market by merely abandoning the so-called 'spoken union' for the particular dialect of the seller if he was clever enough to discern what the seller's dialect is early in the haggling process.

Whatever the case was, however, the fact remains that when the study of Igbo language began, linguists found the diversity and proliferation of dialects baffling and frustrating. 'The diversity of dialects', cried Mr. R. F. G. Adams and Dr. Ida Ward in 1929, 'is ... so bewildering that much work must be done before an investigator can hope to speak of the Ibo language as a whole'.[9] It is one of the sad facts of the primitive state of Igbo linguistic studies that even till date no one can say with certainty how many dialects of the language there are. The anthropologist, Mr. N. W. Thomas who attempted the first panoramic survey of Igbo cultures was of the view that Igbo language had at least twenty different dialects. This has been disputed by other authorities. Professor Westermann argued that Thomas probably 'exaggerated' the proliferation of dialects in the language since, in his view, 'a number of small variations in pronunciation and expressions between two places do not necessarily constitute a dialect'.[10] Westermann, however, offered no opinion on how many dialects there were. Nor has any sustained effort been made to work out generally acceptable criteria for demarcating Igbo dialects. Since this basic work has not been done, it is not surprising that no comprehensive dialect survey of the language has been made even though the need for such a survey was recognized, and a plea for it entered, as early as 1936 by Miss M. M. Green.[11]

If by 1936 the dialect situation in Igbo language was baffling to trained linguists it was even more so to the amateur missionary linguistic scholars of the nineteenth and early twentieth centuries who started the business of reducing Igbo to writing and forming a literary dialect out of its many dialects. It was not only that these missionaries were untrained but that their interest was not in linguistic science and the development of the language as such. Commenting on this matter in 1929 Adams and Ward said:

So far as we are aware previous investigators such as Bishop Crowther, Rev. J. Schon, Rev. J. Spencer, Archdeacon Dennis and Mr. N. W. Thomas have only considered the language as subsididary to their chief work. The result has been that dialects have been dealt with piecemeal.[12]

To say this is not to try to underrate the contributions of the missionaries in particular to Igbo linguistic studies, but to seek to understand the limitations of their approach and the problems which those limitations created in turn. Another factor responsible for the piecemeal approach of the missionaries was the fact that starting work in Igbo land long before colonial conquest, they stationed first at Onitsha and Bonny, that is on the periphery of Igbo land.

One result of this, and an unfortunate one at that, is that they began their study of Igbo language with dialects of Igbo which were heavily influenced by other languages, rather than with what might be called the language of the Igbo heartland—what Dr. Ida Ward called the Central Dialect of Igbo, or what other writers have called the Owerri Dialect.[13] By the first decade of this century when Igbo land was conquered and thrown wide open to the missionary, the administrator, the scholar and the trader, various primers and grammars and word lists had been published in these peripheral dialects of the language. And as each dialect was reduced to the cold and magical inky immortality introduced by the West, it acquired a new prestige. It also developed the new ambition to become the literary language of the Igbo people. Furthermore by the time the entire Igbo land was thrown open to the missionaries, these peripheral Igbo zones had seen over four decades of missionary evangelization and Western education. As a result they had raised a significant crop of men trained to read and write in English and in their own dialect of Igbo. It was with these men that the missionaries now made their assault on the presumed darkness and heathenism of the Igbo interior. As these men went along, they carried with them the primers, grammars, dictionaries and word lists written in their own, especially the Onitsha, dialect of Igbo.

It was at this point that the future of the Igbo language reached the cross-roads and took a turning that led to the present confusion in the matter of evolving a literary dialect. As they went into the interior, in fact as they penetrated a few miles beyond Onitsha and Bonny, the missionaries discovered that they had entered an entirely new dialect area. As they later discovered the Onitsha dialect in which most of the religious tracts had hitherto been written did not extend more than 'five miles to the south and twelve miles to the east ... and is only used on the west of the Niger by trading and educated classes at Asaba'.[14] The crucial decision that needed taking was whether to stick to Onitsha as the literary dialect of Igbo in spite of its limited territorial spread. As shown above it already had many advantages over the dialects of the interior. As Miss Green put it, it 'had acquired prominence with the missions both because the early settlements were on the Niger at Onitsha and because the sounds are easier for Europeans than those of the more southern peoples'.[15]

But these were not the considerations that weighed with the missionaries. Their concern was to reach the largest number of the people in the shortest possible time, if need be each group in its own language and dialect. And just as they had embraced the study of vernacular languages because they believed it would be easier to evangelize the people in their native language, than in a foreign one like English, German or French, so they, especially the C.M.S., now decided to jettison the peripheral Onitsha dialect, though not without some acrimonious internal controversy, in favour of another that would give them access to the hearts of the teeming millions of the interior. Thus far this decision may not be condemned. Had they adopted the Owerri dialect which was spoken by a larger number of people than Onitsha was, they might have been on the road to forging a literary dialect for the Igbo.

It is, however, only fair to concede that this opinion is based on information and knowledge which were not available to the Church Missionary Society at the time they took their decision. In 1939 Dr. Ida Ward undertook a linguistic tour of Igbo land:

> in order to examine a number of Ibo dialects from the point of view of sound usages and constructions in order to find out if there is a dialect which could be used as a literary medium for African writers and for school publications, which would be acceptable over a wide area of the Igbo country and which might form the basis of a growing standard Ibo....[16]

At the end of the tour she came to the conclusion that the Owerri type, or what she called the 'central dialect' met such a need. Not only was it spoken in the large Owerri Province, she contended, but

Some of the Northern dialects, including Nsukka, Eke, Udi, as well as a number of what may be called borderline dialects (which are mainly in the Onitsha Province) show more affinity with the central Ibo type than with the Onitsha dialect.[17]

This, however, was unknown to the missions in the first decade of this century. Probably convinced that all the dialects had as limited territorial scope as the Onitsha dialect, they decided on a compromise solution which led to the formation of the 'Igbo Esperanto' known as Union Igbo, an entirely new and artificial dialect spoken by nobody and therefore lacking any inherent powers of growth. 'Such a type of language' argued Dr. Ward, 'which is not a natural growth cannot easily be expected to develop'.[18] Yet the process by which this artificial dialect was built up makes an interesting historical study illustrating, as it does, that olympian evangelical optimism which teaches that with faith the christian could move mountains. The terrifying assignment of marrying a multiplicity of Igbo dialects to produce a national literary dialect was given to Archdeacon Dennis. The really staggering aspect of the assignment was that the dialect was going to be created in the process of translating the entire Bible from English into it (i.e. into the dialect that did not yet exist).

After a preliminary and necessarily hurried peregrination through those sections of Igbo land where the white man could then travel in safety, Archdeacon Dennis betook himself to Egbu in Owerri with a team of aides representing five dialects of Igbo, then regarded as the key, dialects. These were Onitsha, Owerri, Bonny, Arochukwu and Unwana.[19] The work began in 1905 and was completed in 1912, the Igbo Bible being issued in 1913. At the end not only the Bible but the Prayer Book was translated into this new dialect. For that, or in fact for any time, this was a great achievement, an everlasting monument to Archdeacon Dennis as a linguistic scholar, a theologian and a missionary. His was probably one of those very rare occasions in history that the ambitious animal, man, deliberately set out to create a language—it would in fact be wrong to call it a dialect as nobody spoke or wrote it. 'Obviously' Miss Green has written in amazement and admiration,

> the making of Union Ibo was a difficult and delicate task involving questions of inter-group jealousy and prestige as well as purely linguistic considerations, and as such it certainly commands respect.[20]

Probably precisely because it was such an unprecedented achievement, the Union Igbo ran into trouble from the start. The reasons for this are many. As already mentioned, having no natural born speakers, there were no people to champion its spread. In the end it remained the language in which the Bible and the Prayer Book were *read* rather than *discussed*. No sooner did people finish reading the Bible in Union Igbo, than they relapsed into their various dialects to discuss what they understood from the reading. This tendency was further encouraged by another factor. Discussing this matter Dr. Ward pointed out that for many decades the C.M.S. which manufactured, and championed the cause of Union Igbo which was based more on Owerri than on Onitsha dialect was forced to depend on Onitsha teachers for reasons already mentioned. This, she said, led to the inconsistency of

> the teachers using Union in reading lesson but probably not as a medium of instruction. Here they naturally tend to go back to their own dialect.[21]

But that was not all. Union Igbo was a creation of the Church Missionary Society. The other Protestant Churches were prepared to adopt it, at least in so far as they used the same Bible, as well as the same or more or less similar Prayer Books. But the Roman Catholic Mission would not. Unfortunately for the Igbo the bitter and senseless rivalry amongst the churches extended to the linguistic question. As a result the R.C.M. at first stuck to the Onitsha dialect with the result that school children as far away from Onitsha as Okigwi and beyond were taught to say '*yịọlụ ayị ayịyọ*', in place of *rịọra anyị arirọ*, only to be laughed at by their non-catholic brothers. After some time, however, when the Roman Catholics discovered that the importation of Onitsha dialect into the Owerri Province and beyond hindered their work, they turned round and issued primers in both Onitsha and Union Igbo.

Union Igbo has been criticized on many other grounds by linguistic experts like Miss Green and Dr. Ward especially on grounds of its structural and grammatical forms. No comprehensive study of the structure and grammatical forms of Union Igbo has been carried out. But it appears to me that criticisms of this 'Igbo Esperanto' on such grounds as inconsistencies in the use of Owerri and Onitsha forms etc. can only be considered to be beside the point. It was deliberately designed to be an amalgam of all the leading dialects, a compromise in which every dialect would receive and make concessions. When all criticisms of this great if unsuccessful effort have been made, it would still be necessary to point out, as Professor Westermann did long ago, that

> What Dennis did is not essentially different from what happened in European languages, when out of a number of dialects, one written language evolved, which bore and bears features of more than one dialect.[22]

The only difference was that the C.M.S. tried to launch the Igbo into this orbit of history through the efforts of one, though a highly gifted, man and in less than a generation if not in fact overnight.

Archdeacon Dennis's was the bravest and most historic effort to create for the Igbo a national dialect though, as Miss Green points out, it is debatable whether it should 'be regarded either as a mitigating factor or an added complication'.[23] It would appear, however, that if a central authority had come to his aid, the subsequent unhappy situation which developed might have been avoided, and linguistic unity imposed by inspired leadership. When Union Igbo is criticized, it is not always recognized how close it came to success. At one point in the search for an Igbo national dialect, the Education Board in Lagos resolved to adopt Union Igbo 'as the literary dialect of the Ibo languages'. It also recommended that the grammar of the Union Igbo should be made to approximate as much as possible to that of Owerri dialect on which Union Igbo was largely based. Professor Westermann suggested how this central direction could be exercised. 'It is evident', he said,

> that a committee will have to sit at regular intervals to enrich the language, i.e. decide whether a certain word or expression shall be admitted into Union Igbo or not. This committee shall consist of real experts who are broad-minded enough to leave room for a free and natural growth, development and enrichment of the language.[24]

But the colonial government had neither the will nor the inclination to implement these recommendations. Later still in 1939 Dr. Ward came out with a bold suggestion that the Owerri dialect, because of its territorial spread, should be adopted as the literary dialect of Igbo. But this view was not followed up by the colonial authorities. Later we shall come to the reasons for this lack of interest in the language question by the colonial power, or even by the national government that succeeded it. After the 1930s the issue of a literary dialect of the Igbo language hardly excited the minds of many again. In the 1940s and with the spread of literacy in English the question more or less lost its cogency and we enter the era of drift in the question of evolving a literary form of the language.

The Question of Orthography:

The Igbo, like many of their neighbours, did not evolve an indigenous script with which to reduce their language to writing before the advent of European rule. Nor did their territory lie within the area of West Africa which was influenced by Islam and the Arabs who spread the use of the Arabic script as they went. For a time in this century scholarly attention was drawn to *Nsibidi*, an indigenous sign-writing which flourished on the Cross River basin and in the Eastern Igbo area. This has not been studied in detail, but its use was severely limited. Though it served important functions, as will be shown below, it did not evolve into a script for writing indigenous languages in the same way as the Roman or Arabic script did. As a result in the nineteenth century the missionaries found themselves faced with a *tabula rasa* as far as reducing Igbo language to writing was concerned. This problem was in no way limited to Igbo. It was one which the missionaries faced in most of Africa and Asia. Not surprisingly they sought a universal solution to this widespread problem. For the Igbo this global approach to the problem in time turned out to be unfortunate.

The missionaries appealed to the famous German linguist and Egyptologist, Carl R. Lepsius, to adapt for them the Latin alphabet for use in writing African and Asian languages. In some respects Lepsius could be compared to Archdeacon Dennis—at least in his optimism and confidence. Believing that he knew practically every sound in human language, he set out to evolve 'one orthography for all languages of the world so that any one who knew this alphabet would be able to read any language correctly'.[25] Through the use of diacritic marks and the combination of certain alphabets to produce new sounds unknown to European languages, Lepsius was able to design an orthography which by and large met the basic needs of the missionaries in Africa and Asia. This he published in 1855 as *The Standard Alphabet*.

The nineteenth century translations of sections of the Bible into Igbo used this Lepsius alphabet. But soon many modifications were made and by 1908 when the New Testament was being translated into Igbo the alphabet was drastically modified especially through dropping many diacritic marks. It was this modified version of the Standard Alphabet that was used in printing the Igbo Bible in 1913. As Professor Westermann put it, these modifications were such that almost the only uniformity between the Bible orthography and the Standard Alphabet was the use to some extent of diacritic marks. Nor was it only in writing the Igbo language that such changes were made in the orthography recommended by Lepsius. Similar changes were made in the process of actually writing other Nigerian or even African languages. Thus where Lepsius had used sub-script horizontal lines to produce new sounds out of such vowels as 'o' and 'e' it soon became the practice to use vertical lines or even dots for the same purpose. Yet under the Lepsius system a dot under a vowel was supposed to give it an entirely different value.

Thus by the first and second decades of this century, the Lepsius alphabet had broken down in its actual application to the writing of Igbo and other African languages. But this was not the only complaint against the Standard Alphabet. Linguists pointed out, for instance, that it was not capable of representing all the essential sounds in African languages. It had only six vowels, yet as experience later revealed, it required eight to represent effectively all the significant sounds in Igbo language. And finally the fact that it made extensive use of diacritic marks was considered another serious handicap. It was argued that these marks were apt to be left out in writing and this would constitute as much a spelling error as the omission of a letter, that diacritic marks are likely to be altered, that they give a blurred outline to words thus impairing legibility and straining the eyes. In printing, it was further contended, diacritic marks 'are apt to break off, and they wear out more quickly than the letter itself, so that more frequent renewals are necessary'. The very use of diacritic marks over some letters, it was concluded, was proof that the particular symbols 'are unsatisfactory from a practical point of view'.[26]

For these reasons the International African Institute set out to design another orthography for writing African languages which would avoid most of the pitfalls of the Lepsius alphabet. The designers of this new script were practically as ambitious as Lepsius had been. According to them their aim was

> the unification and simplification of the orthography of African languages.[27]

By this they hoped to clear the confusion which at the time reigned in the writing of African languages and to enable native Africans to make a smooth transition from reading one language to another through ensuring that any letter used in writing an African language would have the same or similar value when used in another language. They also wanted to find distinct symbols for all vital sounds in each language and to dispense with the cumbersome diacritic marks. For the Igbo language the introduction of this so-called new Africa orthography meant the near total elimination of diacritic marks except for 'i'. Also two new vowels were added.[28] For these reasons the new orthography was loudly praised by its sponsors. They pointed out that it brought out an important feature of the Igbo language which the old script had concealed—the existence of vowel harmony in the language. By vowel harmony they meant the principle by which in Igbo open vowels go with open vowels and closed vowels with closed vowels except in compound words. It happens, argued Miss Green, that the Igbo language possesses the system of vowel harmony which once it is grasped is

> a veritable lifebuoy for the would-be learner. On the other hand a failure to grasp it is a source of constant confusion.[29]

To evolve this orthography which was paraded as being in accordance with the latest discoveries in linguistic science was one thing, to get it widely accepted as the script for writing Igbo language was another. The first attempt to do so was made in 1929 when Professor Westermann was invited to Nigeria to advise the Government on linguistic questions. After extensive discussions with all interests concerned 'it was unanimously decided that the alphabet recommended by the Institute should be adopted for the writing of Igbo'.[30]

But any hope that this unanimous decision would be implemented by all concerned was soon dispelled. While the colonial government and the Roman Catholic Mission quickly switched over to the new Africa script, the Protestant Missions stuck to the old one. And soon an argument was raging as to whether the new script had any real advantage over the old. Among other things it was argued that the short-comings of the old script had been exaggerated, that the new script introduced new letters which would confuse the Igbo and aliens alike and which, since they were not found in the standard Latin alphabet, would require the redesigning of type faces etc. to meet the needs of printing and typing materials in Igbo language. This difference between the new Africa alphabets and Latin alphabets which were used for English, it was further argued, would impede the spread of the English Language amongst the Igbo. And what was more, the Protestant Missions maintained, they already held large stocks of Bibles, Prayer Books and primers written in the old script, and to suddenly discard these would entail such staggering financial losses as they could not bear. The late 1920s and early 1930s were a period of slump in world trade and this meant that the colonial government was in no position to underwrite the losses which the changeover would entail for the missions.[31]

Coming to the side of the Protestant Missions later in the fight against the new orthography were the Igbo State Union and the Society for Promoting Igbo Language and Culture. Why these two bodies teamed up against the new Africa orthography are by no means quite clear. One has the suspicion that the new orthography stank in their nostrils of wicked imperialism. Alternatively it might be said that the religious affiliation of the leading spirits in these two Igbo organizations holds the key to the answer. The Society for Promoting Igbo Language and Culture apparently wrongly attributed the introduction of the new script to Mr. R. F. G. Adams, the Chairman of the Igbo Language Bureau, and Dr. Ida C. Ward who did an epochal work on tones in Igbo Language. For instance while boasting of the success of the Society in killing the new orthography, Mr. F. C. Ogbalu the current chairman of the Society and one of its leading spirits said:

> The Society has accomplished much right from its inception in 1949; it successfully fought the Adam/Ward orthography, buried it and finally substituted the now accepted Onwu Orthography—which was its sole invention.[32]

At one stage in the acrimonious debate some leading members of the Society rather paradoxically argued that:

> After all what matters is the substance or subject matter and not necessarily the orthography which is merely a medium through which the student presents his knowledge on the subject.[33]

Thus the introduction of the new script led to deadlock and confusion where it had been expected to produce clarity and growth in the language just as the creation of the Union Igbo had caused confusion in the question of a central or literary dialect. All through the thirties, forties and fifties, the matter could not be settled to the satisfaction of all and the two scripts were being used side by side.

In the fifties the debate which seemed to have died down in the preceding decade was revived with greater virulence in consequence of the appointment of the Ọnwụ Committee to study the question and recommend a satisfactory script which would then be imposed on all sides by the Government of the then Eastern Region. Incidentally Dr. Ọnwụ was one of the leading members of the Society for Promoting Igbo Language and Culture. From all indications the Society was determined to save the old orthography in some form. Mr. F. C. Ọgbalụ advocated the final 'h' as a way of avoiding the excessive use of diacritic marks which was one of the main criticisms of the old script. He spoke very eloquently and persuasively on the matter. Those of us who were his students at St. Augustine's Grammar School, Nkwerre, honestly believed he had found a solution to the problem even though people like myself did not quite understand what he meant by the principle of 'Vowel Harmony' which occurred so often in his lectures and on which he based his suggestion of the final 'h'. The present writer has not yet been able to track down the records of sittings of the Ọnwụ Committee to synthesize the arguments for and against the various alternatives canvassed by the different parties. But somehow the S.P.I.L.C.'s commitment to the cannibalized Lepsius alphabet triumphed with only one major modification—it accepted the principle of eight vowels in the Igbo language as proposed by the new Africa orthography. It however extended the use of diacritic marks by deciding to create light vowels out of 'i' and 'u' by the use of subscript dots. This was in an attempt to throw out the two new symbols which the new Africa alphabet had introduced for these two sounds.[34] Some would see all this as the triumph of Protestant stubborness and conservatism.

But this view would not be entirely correct or fair. The Committee and the Society were concerned to minimize the number of radical changes to be introduced into the writing of the Language. The new symbols introduced by the new Africa orthography, as already said, required the manufacture of special typewriters for use in typing in Igbo language. This its opponents considered unduly expensive. Though it must be pointed out, that if the new script had been adopted for writing all African languages as originally suggested, the cost of such typewriters would have been greatly reduced. Also, argued the members of the S.P.I.L.C., the new characters of the Africa orthography made it impossible to send messages in the Igbo Language by teleprinter. In this regard, however, one may ask whether this can now be done using the Ọnwọ orthography which uses more diacritic marks than are found in the standard Latin alphabet used in teleprinters. Whatever the case, however, the Government accepted the Ọnwụ Orthography and imposed it on all and sundry. With this the old and the new Africa orthography disappeared from the scene. This shows what could have been achieved if in those early days there had been a government that felt strongly enough on the matter and that came out with a firm decision on the two vexed questions of literary dialect and orthography.

Attitudinal Impediments to the Growth of the Igbo Language:

In explaining the depressed state of Igbo Language, the tendency has been to concentrate on the apparently insuperable problems posed by the dialectal and orthographical questions discussed above. But it would appear to me that the failure to solve these two questions could also validly be regarded, to some extent at least, as symptoms of a more deep-rooted problem—the lack of any real interest in the language by our colonial masters who had helped to develop other neighbouring languages and worse still by the Igbo themselves. This lack of interest probably explains the absence of will in dealing with the two problems discussed above.

First the Europeans. The linguistic experts like Ward, Westermann and Green who made occasional excursions into this problem never tired of dinning it into the ears of Europeans and Africans alike that the Igbo language is particularly difficult to master. One or two examples will help to illustrate this matter. Writing in 1939, for instance, Mrs. Leith-Ross argued:

> the fact that it (Igbo) is a tone language, depending upon fine distinctions of sound for the meaning of its words and the grammatical construction of its sentences makes it so difficult for the average European.[35]

About three years before that, Professor Westermann in a review of Dr. Ward's *An Introduction to the Igbo Language* had asserted

> Ibo is one of the most difficult West African Languages, on account of its complicated dialectal variations, its richness in prefixes and suffixes and its intonation.[36]

Not satisfied with telling the Europeans that Igbo language was difficult to learn, Mrs. Leith-Ross assured them they had no 'special gift of ear'[37] to catch the complicated variations in the language. Add to this the fact that, as Miss Green correctly pointed out, 'few if any' of these Europeans had 'adequate linguistic training' before coming to the country, or 'enough time to work at the language after arriving' here[38] and we should be in a position to understand why these men simply lost hope about doing anything to promote the study of the Igbo language as their colleagues up north were doing to promote the study of Hausa. In 1941 Dr. Ward reported that the 'defeatist attitude towards Ibo as a difficult language'[39] had been for years widespread amongst the Europeans serving in Igbo land.

Even though according to the colonial service regulations it paid a political officer to master the language of the people amongst whom he worked, this extra incentive made little difference to the attitude of these men to Igbo language. In fact service east of the Niger was rather unpopular amongst the colonial servants partly because of the intractable political problems which the region presented and partly because of this belief that owing to the difficulties of mastering their languages, a political officer could never really come to enjoy the confidence of the peoples.

The educated Igbo failed their language even more than the European political service did. In fact it could be said that Igbo language is one of those aspects of Igbo life and culture which came to be almost completely overwhelmed by British imperialism. The Igbo resisted British political and economic domination but allowed their language to fall the abject victim of the English Language. The clearest demonstration of this fact is that while there is hardly any Igbo literature to talk of, the Igbo elite are in the vanguard of those who created what is now popularly known as African literature in English—that is works about Africa by Africans written in the English language.

I do not personally share the view of Dr. Obiajunwa Wali that there is no future for this brand of writing. For one thing, time has already proved him wrong. Many of the pioneers of this type of writing have already achieved world fame, some of them becoming legends in their life time. It has also won them immense material reward. It has become the subject of study in schools and colleges as a specific kind of literature. A few people are gaining entry into the coveted class of university dons by writing Masters and Doctorate thesis on it. But when all this has been said, one cannot ignore the fact that had all this writing, some of which are world class by any standard, been done in vernacular, especially had the ones by Igbo men been done in Igbo, that they would have gone a long way towards creating a viable literary language for the Igbo language Here one is reminded of what Boccaccio, Petrarch and Dante did for literary Italian, Chaucer and Shakespeare for English and Martin Luther for German. Igbo literary genius, unlike charity, did not begin at home.

The result is that the Igbo language has no literature. Yet as Professor Westermann has aptly observed: 'Script is but a form and a means, literature is the aim'.[40] Apart from *Ala Bingo* by D. N. Achara (1933), *Omenụkọ* by Peter Nwana (1933), *Ije Odumodu Jere* by L. B. Gam (1952) and *Elelia Na Ihe O Mere* by D. N. Achara (1952) and since the end of the Nigerian Civil War the novels by T. Ubesie there is really no Igbo literature to speak of, except translations of the Bible and its books, as well as religious tracts done by the missionaries. But these are hardly enough to give Igbo that buoyancy it needs as a living and growing language. The matter has often been presented as a vicious circle. Because of the uncertainty about the dialect and the script it was not possible to create a literature in the language, and because no great literature has emerged in the language the dialect and the script could not be standardized.

But this is probably an over-simplification of the problem. The plain truth seems to be that the overwhelming majority of the educated Igbo have never been interested in their language and most of them cannot even write or read their own dialect in any script without tears. This is by no means a recent development. A brief look at the earliest works on this matter makes this quite clear. Writing in 1939 Mrs. Leith-Ross observed:

> the adult (Igbo) frankly admits that it is easier for him to write in English than in Ibo, and were two passages put before him, one in

English and one in Ibo, he would unhesitatingly choose the English one, 'as being so much more easy to read'.[41]

The Igbo have had in the S.P.I.L.C., founded as long ago as 1949, an opportunity to dictate the pace of development of their language and culture, but they have left the few dedicated members of that Society to be reduced to the proverbial voice in the wilderness. The Society has led a heroic but rather unfulfilled existence having been denied the massive moral and material support it needs. And yet, as Mrs. Leith-Ross observed long ago:

> The ultimate future of the language must lie in the hands of the Ibo himself.[42]

The explanation for this Igbo attitude to their language is traceable to the lowly place assigned to education in the vernacular in the institutionalized Western school system introduced by our imperial masters. This matter is so vital to an understanding of crisis of the Igbo language that it must be investigated in some detail, for only by tracing the problem to its roots can we hope to tackle it effectively. To this end we shall discuss the state of the language in pre-colonial Igbo land and then the impact on it of colonialism. In what follows I contend that (i) Igbo language is part and parcel of Igbo culture and cannot survive in any meaningful sense if the culture which it gave and ought to give expression is allowed to wither and die (ii) the crisis of the Igbo language began with its divorcement from that culture in which it had its life and being, thanks to the imposition of the Western school system in which half-hearted education in the language was carried on separate from the indigenous culture (iii) to understand the present lowly place of Igbo language in our schools, we have to understand the place of the school in contemporary Igbo society (iv) in order to upgrade Igbo language, advance its study and make it the effective vehicle of our culture we have to revolutionize the philosophy which underpins our school system or ensure that education in Igbo language is as lucrative as education in English or science.

One thing is certain, and that is that in pre-colonial Igbo land the Igbo language was not a thing existing apart from the society and its culture. On the contrary it was an intrinsic part of that society and its culture. It is doubtful whether an Igbo man of those days would have thought or believed that anything, any idea or any concept, to which the language could not give expression existed or could exist. And because the language was the culture and the culture the language there was hardly any special system or institution or house set apart for teaching the young and strangers the language. At the same time since no effort was spared to ensure that every member of the group was properly acculturated, it also meant that instruction in the language was taken seriously. So effective was this system that it came to be said, in the case of children that they imbibed the language and the way of life of their people as they suckled at their mothers' breasts; and in the case of strangers that they acquired the speech of the land through drinking the water from its streams. As people grew up and helped their parents or older relations with the daily chores—hewed wood and drew water, cooked and ate, attended the farm and market, learnt village crafts, traded folk-tales or played in the moonlight—they learned the techniques, ethics, mysteries and values of each department of life along with the language appropriate to it. Among such great farmers as the Ezza of Abakaliki there runs a saying that the farm is the school for the young.

Yet it would be wrong to say that education in Igbo language and culture was entirely an informal affair. On the contrary training in each department of life was undertaken by the appropriate authority or authorities—one's mother or father or mates. Those seeking to enter a secret or title society were inducted into the secrets and language of the society by the older members. It was in this area that education in Igbo land came very close to the formal school system of the Western world, even to the extent of evolving sign writings for preserving and transmitting information. In such cases admission into the society involved careful instruction in the script used by the society as in the language in which its secrets and rituals were expressed. This was so with many of the secret societies in Igbo land, and till today the initiated talk of *ịkpa akwụkwọ mmanwụ* (literally reading the book of the masquerade, i.e. telling its secrets). In the Ngwa area, for instance, there is a secret writing called *uri ala* associated with the *Ọkọnkọ* secret society and which formed a substantial part of the material in which a novice who had reached the appropriate age and paid the prescribed fees was instructed. Among the Cross River peoples there was *Nsibidi* writing, said to have been invented by the Aro and which was highly developed and associated with *Ekpe* and other secret societies.

We need to say a little more about this sign writing which flourished for long, unknown to the outside world. This is necessary because it has often been claimed that the peoples of Southern Nigeria had no script. Surely they did not use the Roman or Chinese script. But some of them had a writing which enabled them to transmit the mysteries and techniques of certain aspects of their culture and language from one initiated member to another and from generation to generation.

The *Nsibidi* script was a closely guarded secret because it was used in recording the mysteries of various secret clubs. For this reason many early European visitors to the Cross River never came to know of its existence. The first European to gain that knowledge was Mr. T. D. Maxwell when he was acting District Commissioner in Calabar in 1904. 'By his ardent desire to understand native modes of thought', wrote Rev. J. K. Macgregor,

> he won to a large degree the good will of the people. Accordingly when he was asked by His Excellency the High Commissioner to superintend the arrangements for an exhibition of native goods, he was able to include in it twenty-four *Nsibidi* signs that he had received from one of the chief women of the Henshaw family. These were published by the command of the High Commissioner in the Civil List for the Protectorate in July 1905.[43]

In spite of Mr. Maxwell's discovery little effort was made to study this writing.

Then in April 1905 the Rev. J. K. Macgregor told a class of his school children that 'the civilization of the people in Nigeria was primitive because they had no writing' whereupon one child who resented this ignorant assumption told him they had a writing called *Nsibidi*. When he investigated the matter, he said, he discovered that the script 'originated amongst the great Ibo tribe' whose smiths could be met in every part of the Cross River, and that wherever a smith went he carried with him this secret writing. He also said he discovered that certain old women ran classes in which they instructed the recently initiated in the writing, reading and interpretation of *Nsibidi*. He also discovered that the writing was used for a wide variety of purposes including the recording of the proceedings of a court. 'I have in my possession', he said,

> a copy of the record of a court case from a town on the Enion (Enyong) Creek taken down in it, and every detail except the evidence,

is most graphically described—the parties in the case, the witnesses, the dilemma of the chief who tried it, his sending out messengers to call other chiefs to help him, the finding of the court and the joy of the successful litigants and of their friends are all told by the use of a few strokes.[44]

Probably only further research will reveal the connection between the *Nsibidi* of the Cross River Igbo, the *uri ala* of the Ngwa and the *akwụkwọ mmanwu* of some Northern Igbo groups. No doubt these secret writings and scripts were not as developed as the Roman, Arabic and Chinese scripts were, but they served the essential purpose of encouraging the education of the elite of the society in the language and higher culture of the land.

The important point is that induction into the secret or titled society was not just a training in how to read the secret script. It was also a process through which the aspirant gained further insight into and grasp of the intricacies of the language in which the secrets and values of the society were enshrined. Thus in traditional Igbo society training in the language was achieved through training in culture. And since in that society the journey from the womb of the mortal woman to the womb of the immortal earth goddess was one continuous education in the ways of the land, this meant that training in the tricky art of using language was a lifelong affair. This contrasts strongly with the contemporary levity which assumes that since Igbo is our mother tongue we do not require any special training in it.

The rigour and intensity of that training in the language would probably help to explain why the Igbo language acquired the strength it needed to survive the many threats posed to it by the language and culture of many neighbouring peoples, and even at times made inroads into the territories of these neighbouring languages. As already mentioned the Igbo were throughout history politically fragmented and did not evolve a state-system that incorporated any substantial section of the people. In addition the Igbo were not highly militarized. Their commonest and most favourite weapon was the matchet. Their arrow was not tipped with poison, while the gun probably arrived too late to radically change their type of warfare or strategy to any significant extent. Yet they were bordered to the south by the coastal city states, to the west by the Edo empire of Benin and to the north-west by the Igala kingdom centred at Idah. These were at times large and highly organized imperialistic states which had designs on Igbo land. It is probably a measure of the efficiency of the training in their language and culture which the Igbo received that they survived the threats of these hostile neighbours as a people with basically similar culture and institutions and speaking the same language—albeit with many dialectal variations.

But what is even more worthy of note, there is evidence that in spite of the political and military weakness of the Igbo, their language and usages penetrated the culture of these their aggressive neighbours. One or two examples can be given to illustrate this. The coastal states, for instance, were in such close contact with the Igbo that they came to face an 'Igbo peril'— the danger that their culture and language would be absorbed into the culture and language of the Igbo. In Bonny, where it would appear no special steps were taken to fight this threat, the people became bilingual—speaking both Ijọ and a dialect of Igbo with equal facility. Early in this century the Bonny dialect was to make some contributions to the formulation of the Igbo Esperanto—the Union Igbo. In Kalabari special efforts were made to ward off this Igbo peril by various means, especially through the special masquerade known as *Igbo* whose main function would appear to have been the preservation of the native Ijọ culture.[45] On the Northern side of Igbo land early European scholars found that Igbo language was spoken for many miles on the Igala side of the boundary.[46] Similar instances of the impact of the Igbo language and culture on the Edo and the Idoma can be found.

Thus without an institutionalized school system on the Western pattern Igbo society was able, like other societies, to educate its members in its language and culture. Then towards the end of the nineteenth century the Western school system was introduced into that society and with that the crisis of the Igbo language began. The question which this raises is why an institutionalized school system should constitute for Igbo language a source of weakness rather than of strength?

The answer to the question lies in the fact that it was not the Igbo who imported the Western school system, taking what they liked from the system and using it to attain goals and ideals arising from their own culture. On the contrary the school was imposed by the imperial power for the attainment of goals acceptable to it but unrelated to the cultural needs of the people. What was worse the two most powerful and best organized partners in the imperial establishment—the administration and the missions—were not agreed on the precise end the school was to serve beyond the vague idea that it was to be a light to lighten the benighted. This meant that while the two wrangled over the control of the school and the definition of its guiding philosophy, and while each sought to secure the ascendancy of its own point of view, nobody took serious thought of how to get the institution properly aligned to Igbo culture and values. The result was that while the school took root and in so doing stifled much of indigenous Igbo education, it was divorced from the culture of our peoples. And since what formal instruction in Igbo language there now was had to be done in the schools, the Igbo language of the schools was also divorced from the main stream of Igbo life and culture. With this divorcement the language started to atrophy. What are the facts?

As in many parts of Nigeria, Western Education through the institutionalized school was introduced into Igbo land by the christian missions. The detailed history of this can be read in the works of Professors J. F. Ade Ajayi, E. A. Ayandele and F. K. Ekechi, especially in the last work which is the latest and most detailed on the matter as far as Igbo land is concerned.[47] It is the concensus amongst scholars of the subject that the missionaries introduced and propagated the schools for evangelical reasons, rather than for purely educational or other social considerations.[48] The history of Bishop Shanahan's work in Igbo land shows that the missions would have equally happily used any other method that could have won them the converts they wanted faster than the schools did.[49] The schools were thus introduced not as a means of perfecting the process by which Igbo language and culture were transmitted from generation to generation, but as the most effective means of attracting our people out of what was considered their barbarous culture into the supposedly exciting new world of christianity as interpreted by Western civilization. This is very important in any effort to understand the low priority placed on Igbo language and culture in the schools.

But this was not all. Even more serious for the Igbo language was the fact that the two leading christian missions in Igbo land adopted differing attitudes to the teaching of the language. The Catholics who came late in the Igbo missionary field and who probably feared that Protestant England might place obstacles on their path, sought to off-set these supposed disadvantages through their educational policy. Discovering that the more novel the schools the more students/converts they attracted, the Catholic authorities introduced the teaching of English early into their schools. This is not to say that the Catholic missionaries did not recognize that ability to speak the Igbo language would be an advantage. On the contrary they did and paid early attention to acquiring a working knowledge of the language on their arrival. The crux of the matter was that they paid little or no attention to the teaching of Igbo in their schools.[50]

The authorities of the Church Missionary Society (C.M.S.) on their side, had always placed the emphasis on evangelizing every African group through their indigenous language. To this end they had early embarked on a systematic study of these languages (including Igbo) and on translating religious tracts into them. It also became their declared policy to emphasize the teaching of vernacular languages in their schools. Their policy statement on this matter in 1890 insisted that 'the teaching in these mission schools should be of the simplest kind—the chief aim of which being to teach the children to read in the vernacular, so that they may be able to study their bible when translated for them in the mother tongue'.[51] The reason for this C.M.S. attitude in the matter is still to be fully investigated. It has been suggested that they were anxious to prevent the boys they trained running off to take better paid appointments in the Government departments and commercial houses which they would surely do if made proficient in English. It has also been argued that since the missionaries who took over the affairs of the Niger Mission after the fall of Bishop Crowder were white supremacists, they wanted to deny the Africans competence in English in order to prevent them from ever thinking they were as good as whites.[52]

Whatever the reasons were, however, the important point for our purpose is that this policy failed because the Catholic approach proved more popular. Bishop Shanahan, the premier missionary of the Catholic Mission in Igbo land, went all out to bring home to the people the overwhelming advantages of knowledge of the English language and therefore, by implication, that it was a waste of time and resources to attend the Protestant schools only to learn to read and write the Igbo language. According to his biographer, when pleading with any Igbo village to accept a Catholic school he would argue:

> Why was the European D.O. in charge of tens of thousands of Ibos? Was it because he had more money or more wives or more influence?

No, the answer was that he was more educated. Why was the interpreter so contemptuous of local views and so insistent on heavy bribes before he would explain a case properly? Because he knew English which he had learnt at school, and because no local knew enough English to follow what he was saying. And look at the Court Clerk and Court Messengers, the most influential and the most feared men in the district. Why were they chosen for their jobs? Simply because they had been to school and understand English. Why, they all knew the Court Clerk could distort and recast every written word, while their titled men could not read a single line.[53]

This was a down-to-earth, if also a cynically materialistic, argument and it carried more weight than whatever the C.M.S. authorities could present as the advantages of reading the Holy Writ in Igbo. It is therefore no surprise that, according to the same author, to Shanahan's argument 'the old men in the audience (would show) their wisdom by shaking their heads at their stupidity in not being wiser men. A school was the only solution to their problems'.[54] And is it any surprise that at such a school no one demured at the fact that the Igbo language was not taught? The C.M.S. point of view was made more untenable by the attitude of the colonial administration which wanted clerks, accountants and other low grade workers who could read and write English. For a long time most of these had to be recruited from Sierra Leone and the Gold Coast, and this was denounced as expensive. Now it wanted these raised locally through the schools established by the missions. It even set up model schools where the emphasis was placed on English. Also it became its declared policy that any school which received a Government grant had to teach English.[55] It was not long before the C.M.S. missionaries noted that 'no up-to-date native gentleman would now think of using his own language to express himself'[56] and that English had become a status symbol, the master key that opened the door to respectable and lucrative appointments in the Government and mercantile houses. Soon too one of them confessed that 'the Romanists have a really good school (from some points of view), the chief attraction being that nothing is done in the vernacular and English is taught by an Irishman'.[57] Even though up till about 1913 the C.M.S. continued to resist the wholesale introduction of English in their schools, they were forced to abandon their earlier position and think of schools where the main language of instruction was English. They had to do this to keep their students from running off to Roman Catholic schools to learn English. As Archdeacon Dennis put it if 'they cannot get what they want with us, they will go to the Romanists'.[58] With this shift in policy the way was now clear for the English deluge!

Thus to some extent it could be argued that the crisis of the Igbo language is attributable to the virulence of the Catholic-Protestant conflict in Igbo land, a factor which was absent from the Yoruba mission field. There the C.M.S. were able to follow their chosen policy with inestimable advantage to the Yoruba language. In Northern Nigeria the policy of the Administration, which rigorously sought to limit the area of activity of the christian missions while encouraging traditional Koranic education and using Hausa as the second language of administration, redounded to the benefit of that language.

At the same time it must be conceded that the C.M.S. rendered remarkable services to the Igbo language through reducing it to writing, through their numerous evangelical tracts in the vernacular and, though this is disputable, through the 'manufacture' of the Union Igbo. And, as Dr. F. K. Ekechi has said:

> There is no question that as a result of the CMS insistence on the use of the vernacular, graduates from Anglican schools were far better grounded in the Igbo language than their counterparts from the Catholic schools. Even today Protestants read Igbo with greater ease than Roman Catholics.[59]

But be that as it may this was poor consolation for Igbo language. The Igbo taught in these schools was Igbo divorced from its cultural context—emasculated Igbo in fact. Add to this the fact of the artificial Union Igbo and we would be in a position to understand the decline of the language.

In addition to the above factor there was in the Igbo mission field another which helped to undermine the position of Igbo language and culture—this was a certain tendency to materialism, to judge institutions and professions by the criterion of whether in the shortest possible time and in the most direct manner they could bring material success as well as visible influence and respect. We are yet to achieve a detailed and satisfactory analysis of traditional Igbo culture and the connection between it and material success. But there can be no doubt that traditional Igbo culture appreciated the successful and influential man, if also it was antagonistic to the over-mighty man, the monarch or the tyrant. In any case it would appear that whatever amount of this materialistic trait there was in indigenous Igbo culture, came to find a very fertile field for growth in colonial society. Scholars have often wondered why the Igbo fell so abjectly for western education and the school, more or less abandoning their own culture in the process. Professor Ayandele thinks it was because the Igbo were conquered by force and that this conquest shattered their confidence in their culture. Some others have argued that this was because the Igbo have always loved that which could be shown to work and that the school worked like magic since all those who successfully went through it, including the despised *osu* and underprivileged slaves, became important and powerful, that is successful. There is the story of an Igbo elder who on his deathbed said when he came back to this life he would go to school in order to become a native court clerk and be feared by all around.

The propaganda of the missions, especially of the R.C.M. gave dangerous encouragement to this materialism, to this cult of success. In the quotation above on Shanahan's preaching we saw how he dwelt on the material advantages of reading and writing English. He ridiculed traditional values like polygamy and the title system because they could not help a man contend against the wiles of the court clerk and the interpreter, nor could they make a man important or respected in the emerging colonial society. By the same token ability to read and write Igbo was useless and unhelpful as the court records were kept in English.

Much more directly the missionaries attracted people to the school and church with material presents and the flaunting of material wealth. Thus according to Shanahan's biographer, when the egregious Father Luts found it difficult to persuade people to come to his church

> He thought out attractions. He gave a magic lantern show to the people.... They waxed enthusiastic. For a time afterwards they turned up for mass and doctrinal classes. He tried to hold them by decorating his little church, with Chinese lanterns, flags and bunting. He also gave a series of gramophones recitals after prayers. Naturally he did not fail to have popular appreciation.[60]

The Igbo would appear to have lapped up every word of this type of propaganda. With this beginning the church and school became largely a means to a material end. Education in particular became the quest for the magic scroll (certificate) which alone would enable a man to succeed in the new world which was unfolding. With this material-success-oriented psychology few came to give any thought to proficiency and competence in Igbo language since this would lead nobody anywhere. In fact any attempt to emphasize the teaching of Igbo came to be looked upon as a satanic waste of time, an imperialist plot to delay the prompt arrival of the Igbo nation. Schools which insisted on teaching Igbo were neglected.

This is still the prevalent attitude amongst the Igbo as the following anecdote clearly illustrates. At the end of the Nigerian civil war a number of scholars, not just Igbo scholars but also white scholars, decided to take a look at Igbo culture which the recent war had done so much to blast further. This led to the publication of a special issue of the *Conch Magazine* entitled *Igbo Traditional Life, Culture and Literature*.[61] This was probably the first time such a work was being done on the Igbo. The cultural renaissance which from the beginning had been an essential aspect of African nationalism had by and large passed Igbo land by. But it had produced most exciting results in the study and reinterpretation of the cultures of many other African peoples, for example of Edo and Yoruba cultures. One hoped that people would see the *Conch* special issue as reinforcing the argument for a similar treatment being extended to traditional Igbo culture. But on more than one occasion the present writer, who had 'perversely' contributed two articles to the publication, was accosted by two educated Igbo young men who wanted to know where this 'celebration' of what they contemptuously called 'Igbo Ukwu culture' would take anybody in this atomic age. The belief behind this attitude being, I suspect, that the nations which exploit atomic energy either do not have a culture or do not care about it!

Thus the main danger to the Igbo language is the belief that proficiency in it cannot bring one material success or visible influence and power or reveal to one the wonderful world of the atom. This belief, it hardly needs to be said, derives from the educational system which we have inherited from our colonial past and have continued to treasure and propagate. The solution to the problem is probably simple: either replace that system with another which will inculcate a balanced vision of life as it really is or *demonstrate* that the man proficient in Igbo language and versed in Igbo culture can also attain to as much material success, visible influence and power as the man who studies the

English language or probes the atom.

And finally we come to the point mentioned briefly above—the lack of inspired central direction or leadership in the matter. The colonial government did not and could not show enough interest in promoting the study of the language in view of the limited and selfish objectives of colonialism. It was not one of the aims of colonialism to preserve the cultural identity of subject peoples. In fact the opposite was the case. Hence there were powerful individuals and interests in colonial circles who felt that the Igbo language should be allowed to die a natural death as this would promote the spread of English. Or at least they felt the Igbo were better off with English than with their own vernacular language and frowned on efforts to encourage the study of Igbo language in schools.[62]

In spite of imposing a uniform orthography in 1961, the Eastern Nigeria Government which succeeded the colonial government cannot now be said to have provided a dynamic and inspired leadership in the matter of levelling the dialects, creating Igbo Literature and building up general interest in the language. Yet one would have expected such action in view of the cultural chauvinism of the nationalist movement. But this could not be. In the first place nationalism emphasized modernization through industrialization, science education and so on, and that immediately; a programme which placed a high premium on western education and western languages which held the key to the secrets of science. Also nationalism emphasized the subordination of the province to the nation. Here the rather romantic and starry-eyed pan-Africanist programmes of the N.C.N.C. Government which ruled Eastern Nigeria was a handicap to the flourishing of local cultural nationalism. What was more Eastern Nigeria was a multi-ethnic region and its government could not have shown pronounced interest in promoting the study of the Igbo language without conjuring up the ghost of some of the dilemmas it was trying to lay. The short-lived East Central State, which was made up entirely of Igbo-speakers, was seen by many as offering the best opportunity so far for attaining central and purposive direction in Igbo cultural life. Unfortunately its rulers, dominated by some thoroughgoing philistines, adopted an ostentatious anti-Igbo stance without being truly Nigerian. It remains to be seen whether the creation of two states out of that administration will work to promote the advancement of Igbo language and culture.

NOTES

1. D. Westermann, 'The Linguistic Situation and Vernacular Literature in British West Africa', *Africa*, Vol. 2, 1929.
2. R. C. Abraham, *Principles of Ibo* (Ibadan, 1967), see the last page of the Preface.
3. *Ibid.*
4. M. M. Green, 'The Present Linguistic Situation in Ibo Country', *Africa*, Vol. 9, 1936, p. 508.
5. M. N. Okonkwo, 'Report and Observations on the Sixth Meeting of the Nigerian Languages Working Party of the West African Examinations Council, held on Friday, 11.9.70', dated Enugu 8.9.70.
6. D. Westermann, 'The Linguistic Situation, etc.', *loc. cit.*, pp. 345–6.
7. V. C. Uchendu, *The Igbo of Southeast Nigeria* (Holt, Rinehart & Winston, 1966), p. 83.
8. I. C. Ward, *Ibo Dialects and the Development of a Common Language* (Cambridge, 1941), pp. 8–9.
9. Adams and Ward, 'The Arochukwu Dialect of Ibo', *Africa*, Vol. 2, 1929, p. 58.
10. D. Westermann, 'The Linguistic Situation, etc.', *loc. cit.*, pp. 339–40.
11. M. M. Green, 'The Present Linguistic Situation in Ibo Country', *loc. cit.* Apart from making this plea Miss Green put forth four criteria for demarcating dialects. According to her these were (i) Differences of verb formation, (ii) Differences of tone, (iii) Differences of vocabulary, (iv) Permutation of sounds, both vowel and consonants. On the basis of these criteria she, like others, distinguished between two main dialects—Onitsha and Owerri. 'Outside Owerri and Onitsha speech areas', she regretted, 'little material is available in published form and what is published is still quite incomplete and uncoordinated', pp. 509–18.
12. Adams and Ward, 'The Arochukwu Dialect of Ibo', *loc. cit.*, p. 58.
13. I. C. Ward, *Ibo Dialects*, etc., pp. 11–13.
14. M. M. Green, 'The Linguistic Situation, etc.', *loc. cit.*, pp. 509–18.
15. *Ibid.*, pp. 509–10.
16. I. C. Ward, *Ibo Dialects*, etc., see the Preface.
17. *Ibid.*, p. 11.
18. *Ibid.*, p. 10.
19. *Ibid.*, p. 10, M. M. Green, 'The Linguistic Situation in the Ibo Country', *loc. cit.*, pp. 509–18.
20. M. M. Green, 'The Linguistic Situation in the Ibo Country', *loc. cit.*, p. 510.
21. I. C. Ward, *Ibo Dialects*, etc., p. 12, footnote 1.
22. D. Westermann, 'The Linguistic Situation, etc.', *loc. cit.*, pp. 340–1.
23. M. M. Green, 'The Present Linguistic Situation in Ibo Country', *loc. cit.*, p. 508.
24. D. Westermann, 'The Linguistic Situation, etc.', *loc. cit.*, pp. 340–1.
25. C. Meinhof, 'Principles of Practical Orthography for African Languages', *Africa*, Vol. 1, 1928, p. 231.
26. *International African Institute Memorandum No. 1 Practical Orthography of African Languages* (O.U.P., 1930), pp. 1–6.
27. *Ibid.*, pp. 1–6.
28. *Ibid.*, pp. 1–6.
29. M. M. Green, 'The Present Linguistic Situation in Ibo Country', *loc. cit.*, p. 521.
30. M. M. Green, 'The Present Linguistic Situation, etc.', *loc. cit.*, pp. 518–19.
31. *Ibid.*, see also *International African Institute Memorandum*, No. 1.
32. I. C. Ward, *Ibo Dialects*, etc., pp. 2–6.
    Personal Letter from Mr. F. C. Ogbalu dated 3.8.71.

33. F. C. Ogbalu, School Certificate Igbo (Aba, n.d.), p. 6.
34. See the *Onwu Orthography*.
35. S. Leith-Ross, *African Women* (London, 1939), p. 57.
36. D. Westermann, 'Review of I. C. Wards *An Introduction to the Ibo Language in Africa*, Vol. 9, 1936, p. 501.
    See also M. M. Green, 'The Present Linguistic Situation in Ibo Country', *Africa*, Vol. 9, 1936, p. 508.
37. S. Leith-Ross, *African Women*, p. 57.
38. M. M. Green, 'The Present Linguistic Situation in the Ibo Country', *loc. cit.*, p. 508.
39. I. C. Ward, *Ibo Dialects*, etc., p. 1.
40. D. Westermann, 'The Linguistic Situation, etc.', *Africa*, Vol. 2, 1929, p. 349.
41. S. Leith-Ross, *African Women*, p. 58.
42. *Ibid.*, pp. 58-9.
43. J. K. Macgregor (Rev.), 'Some Notes on Nsibidi', *Journal of the Royal Anthropological Institute*, Vol. xxxix, 1909, p. 210.
44. *Ibid.*, p. 212.
45. R. Horton, 'Igbo: An Ordeal for Aristocrats', *Nigeria Magazine*, No. 90, September 1966, pp. 169-83.
46. M. N. Thomas, *Anthropological Report on Ibo-speaking Peoples of Nigeria*, Part IV (London, 1914), pp. 5-6.
47. J. F. A. Ajayi, *Christian Missions in Nigeria, 1841-1891: The Making of a New Elite* (Longmans, 1965).
    E. A. Ayandele, *The Missionary Impact on Modern Nigeria, 1841-1914: A Political and Social Analysis* (Longmans, 1966).
    F. K. Ekechi, *Missionary Enterprise and Rivalry in Igboland 1857-1914* (Cass, 1972).
48. In addition to the references in footnote 5, see A. E. Afigbo, 'The Background to the Southern Nigeria Education Code of 1903', *Journal of the Historical Society of Nigeria*, Vol. 4, No. 2, June 1968, pp. 197-225.
49. *Short Life of Bishop Shanahan* (Holy Ghost Fathers, Onitsha Diocese n.d.), pp. 32-5.
50. F. K. Ekechi, *op. cit.*, p. 176 ff.
    Short Life of Bishop Shanahan, p. 26.
51. F. K. Ekechi, *op. cit.*, pp. 179 80.
52. *Ibid.*, p. 179.
53. *Short Life of Bishop Shanahan*, pp. 50-1.
54. *Ibid.*, p. 51.
55. A. E. Afigbo, 'The Background to the Southern Nigeria Education Code of 1903', *loc. cit.*
56. F. K. Ekechi, *op. cit.*, quoted on p. 178.
57. *Ibid.*, quoted on p. 179.
58. *Ibid.*, quoted on p. 182.
59. *Ibid.*, p. 192.
60. *Short Life of Bishop Shanahan*, p. 16.
61. M. J. C. Echeruo and E. N. Obiechina (eds), *Igbo Traditional Life, Culture and Literature, Conch Magazine*, Vol. III, No. 2, September 1972.
62. S. Leith-Ross, *African Women*, p. 57.
    In reporting the existence of this school of thought Mrs. Leith-Ross wrote as follows: 'All the same one cannot agree with those who think that the Ibo language will disappear within fifty years and that English would have become the common tongue'.
    On this Miss Green also noted that 'the view has often been expressed that Ibo will and should be replaced by English'.
    See M. M. Green, 'The Present Linguistic Situation in Ibo Country', *Africa*, Vol. 9, 1936, pp. 508-09.

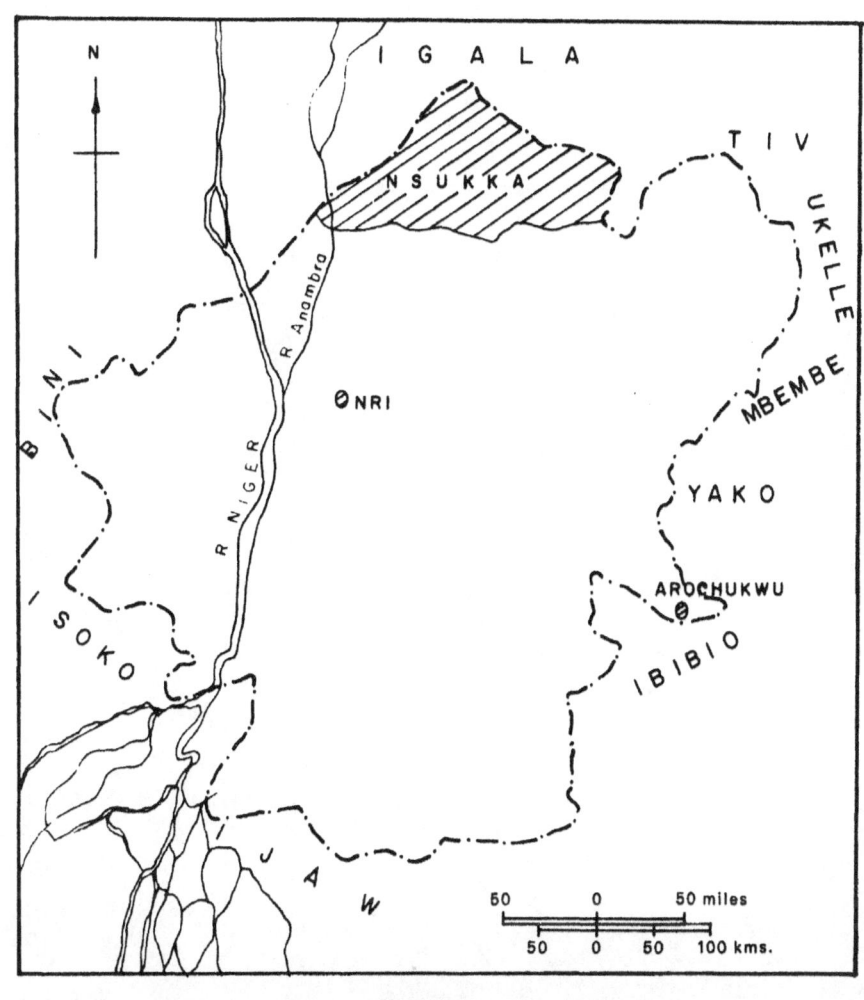

MAP OF <u>IGBO LAND</u> SHOWING :—
(I) NSUKKA AREA,
(II) THE HOLY CITY OF NRI,
(III) AROCHUKWU.

www.ingramcontent.com/pod-product-compliance
Lightning Source LLC
Chambersburg PA
CBHW021758220426
43662CB00006B/111